Charlotte Lennox

Charlotte Lennox

Correspondence and Miscellaneous Documents

Edited and
Introduced by
Norbert Schürer

Lewisburg
BUCKNELL UNIVERSITY PRESS

Published by Bucknell University Press
Copublished with Rowman & Littlefield
4501 Forbes Boulevard, Suite 200, Lanham, Maryland 20706
www.rowman.com

10 Thornbury Road, Plymouth PL6 7PP, United Kingdom

British Library Cataloguing in Publication Information Available

Library of Congress Cataloging-in-Publication Data
The hardback edition of this book was previously cataloged by the Library of Congress as
follows:

Lennox, Charlotte, ca. 1729–1804.
   Charlotte Lennox : correspondence and miscellaneous documents / [edited by] Norbert
Schürer.
      p. cm.
   1. Lennox, Charlotte, ca. 1729–1804—Correspondence.   2. Lennox, Charlotte, ca.
1729–1804—Sources.   3. Lennox, Charlotte, ca. 1729–1804—Criticism and
interpretation.   I. Schürer, Norbert.   II. Title.
   PR3541.L27Z485   2011
   823'.6—dc23
   2011034878

ISBN: 978-1-61148-390-1 (cloth : alk. paper)
ISBN: 978-1-61148-567-7 (pbk. : alk. paper)
ISBN: 978-1-61148-391-8 (electronic)

Contents

Miscellaneous Publications   307

Lists of Illustrations and Tables

ILLUSTRATIONS

TABLES

Acknowledgments

Scholarship about Charlotte Lennox would have taken a completely different and much more poorly informed course without the publication of "The Lennox Collection," so my first debt of gratitude goes to Duncan Isles and his groundbreaking work. Though I do not agree with every decision he made or every interpretation he offered, his collection was my constant and indispensable companion in the preparation of my own edition.

I am also extremely grateful for the assistance of librarians across the United States and the United Kingdom who assisted me in my research in person or by mail (and more recently e-mail). Libraries and institutions I visited or received information from include the Beinecke Library, Yale University; the Bodleian Library, Oxford University; the British Library, the Royal College of Surgeons, the Royal Literary Fund, the Royal Society of Antiquaries, and the Victoria and Albert Museum (all London); the Chawton House Library, Alton, Hampshire; the Clark Library, UCLA; the Chicago Historical Society; the Folger Library in Washington, D.C.; the Houghton Library, Harvard University; the Huntington Library, San Marino; the Morgan Library, New York; the John Rylands Library, Manchester; the Sheffield Archives; and the Library of George Washington Vanderbilt, Asheville, North Carolina. Where appropriate, I would like to thank the libraries and institutions for permission to use and replicate their material. Closer to home, my special thanks go to Alex Rambo, Kristie French, and Leslie Swigart at California State, Long Beach, who have helped me with difficult interlibrary loan searches, access to special collections, and purchases for our library.

Many teachers, colleagues, and friends have accompanied and supported this project. Two anonymous reviewers for Bucknell University Press (one later identify as O M Brack, Jr.) gave enormously helpful advice and made numerous corrections that helped me avoid embarrassing mistakes. Jennifer Thorn gave me leeway during my dissertation to pursue somewhat extraneous avenues of research. George Justice, Devoney Looser, Laura Runge, and Betty Schellenberg wrote letters of recommendation for various grants and fellowships that helped me complete this edition. Betty, who is working on some of the same letters for an edition of the correspondence of Samuel Richardson, read large parts of the manuscript and provided invaluable feedback. As a non-academic, Kate Chisholm offered a new perspective. Jennie Batchelor and Dave Motton (not to mention Leah) have made every (research) trip to the United Kingdom an academic success and a personal pleasure. Chris Mounsey provided beautiful lodgings, good food, excellent company, and wry commentary in London. Ruth Perry made helpful suggestions for the introduction of this book, and Isobel Grundy was consistently encouraging. Philip Smallwood gave insight into all matters Johnsonian, while Eve Tavor Bannet had an open ear for Lennox questions. Similarly, Paul Hunter and Cindy Wall have been supportive over many years. My chair Eileen Klink has cleared administrative and career paths for me, and my colleagues Tim Keirn and Clorinda Donato have contributed immeasurably to my intellectual development. Other friends and colleagues involved in small or large ways in the creating of this work (sometimes without their knowledge) include Emily Anderson, Ava Arndt, Barbara Benedict, Temma Berg, Judith Brückmann, Norma Clarke, Gillian Dow, Markman Ellis, Gerlinde Hollweg, Alessa Johns, Thoralf Kerner, Kathy King, Felicity Nussbaum, Nicole Pohl, Leslie Richardson, Jennifer Schaffner, Jörg Schendel, Jennifer Snead, Helen Thompson, and Debbie Welham. In spite (or because) of all these wonderful people, this project has taken entirely too long to complete. It will never be as perfect as I wish, and of course all imperfections are my own.

My book has accompanied me at Duke University, Wake Forest University, Xavier University of Louisiana, and now at California State University, Long Beach. It was supported by an ARCHIE grant at Wake Forest and several SCAC awards at CSULB. I was particularly honored by and grateful for an Editing and Translation Fellowship from the Women's Caucus of the American Society for Eighteenth-Century Studies. I would like to thank Greg Clingham at Bucknell University Press for taking on this project and the anonymous readers for their considerable and helpful feedback.

My entire academic career would have been unimaginable without the support of my parents, Gretel Schürer and Ernst Schürer. Finally, my largest thanks and undying gratitude are due to my friend, colleague, and wife Susan Carlile. I look forward to your biography of Lennox.

Editorial Practice

Each entry contains three main elements: the headnote, the paratextual material, and the text. The **headnote** consists of three elements.

Number:
In the "Correspondence" section, the items are numbered in chronological sequence. In contrast to the letters collected in Duncan Isles's "The Lennox Collection," this edition has assigned a date to every letter. The letters are ordered by their exact dates, with letters only dated by year or span of years inserted at the end of that year or at the end of the year *beginning* the span. For clarity's sake, the numbers for the material in the "Royal Literary Fund" and "Miscellaneous Documents" sections are preceded by A and B, respectively. Again, the documents are organized chronologically.

Correspondents:
In the "Correspondence" section, this line identifies the writer and recipient of each letter, where they are known. Writers or recipients who are not explicitly named in the address or salutation of the letter are presented in square brackets, and their identification is explained in a footnote. Short biographies of correspondents (with references to further sources) are provided in Appendix II. Unknown correspondents are identified as "Anon." In the "Royal Literary Fund Files" and "Miscellaneous Documents" sections, this line gives a title for the document. In the former section, I have provided titles; in the latter, the title is usually the title of the publication.

Date:
Each document is dated as closely as possible. In some cases, the documents include a month and day, but not a year; in others, no information at all. Where the exact date is unclear, the headnote offers either a year that can be ascertained

with some certainty ("[1759]"), alternatives ("November 8 or 15"), an approximation ("[late 1750]"), or a span ("[c. 1775–80]"). Additional uncertainty is indicated through "c." or "?."

In the "Correspondence" section, the **paratextual material** includes up to four entries. Where no information exists on a particular aspect, that entry is simply omitted.

MS:

This line gives the location of the manuscript of the item (where it still exists) as well as, in most cases, a call number.

Pages:

The following number indicates how many pages the letter has in manuscript.

Edition:

This line provides information on previous publications of the letter.

Address:

This replicates the address as it is given on the letter, where it still exists. Therefore, it attempts to capture the spatial relations of the words there. The address given here is *not* counted as a separate page within the numbering of the pages of a manuscript.

Each item in the "Royal Literary Fund" section contains two entries: a short summary of the item and a description of its physical format. In the "Miscellaneous Documents" section, only information on previous editions is presented.

The **text** of the letters is transcribed here to give the reader as good a representation of the original as possible without reproducing facsimiles each reader would have to decipher. This entails some of the following decisions:

Alignment:

The text is aligned as it is in the manuscript, so the date is often in the top right-hand corner (or the bottom left) and the complimentary close of the letter mostly in the lower right. In some cases, the salutation is not aligned with the text of the letter, and in a few cases—due to the shape of the paper—the alignment changes in the middle of a letter.

Lines:

The line breaks have been kept the way they are in the manuscript. A solid line indicates the end of a page, so the number of pages in the manuscript is recognizable on the printed page.

Spelling:

The spelling of the manuscript has been retained in all cases, including upper and lower case—which are frequently hard to discern. Unusual spellings are usually indicated by a following "[*sic*]."

Changes:

Changes are replicated as closely as possible to the way they are introduced in the manuscript, for example, with strike-outs or carets.

Lacunae:

Illegible words are indicated by square brackets and explained in a footnote. Words or letters missing due to tears in the paper are similarly offered in square brackets, always accompanied by a footnote indicating the position of the tear. Additions to the text are also included in square brackets and annotated in footnotes.

Superior Letters:

Superior letters have been left in their original position.

Abbreviations:

None of the abbreviations, symbols, or contractions in the text is expanded. If any of these are unusual, they are explained in a footnote.

Footnotes:

Footnote signs are the only intrusions into the text by the editor. Sources that are referred to more than once in the footnotes are identified by cue-titles and abbreviations.

Endorsements:

Endorsements and postmarks are not usually included, unless they raise specific questions about the letter.

Similar decisions have been made about items in the "Royal Literary Fund" section and for the manuscript items in the "Miscellaneous Documents" section.

Cue-Titles and Abbreviations

I.	Charlotte Lennox's Works
Berci	*The Memoirs of the Countess of Berci.* London: Millar, 1756.
Brumoy	*The Greek Theatre of Father Brumoy.* London: Millar, Vaillant, Baldwin, Crowder, Johnston, Dodsley, and Wilson and Durham, 1759.
Eliza	*The History of Eliza.* London: J. Dodsley, 1767.
Euphemia	*Euphemia.* London: Cadell and Evans, 1790. (Modern edition ed. Susan Kubica Howard; Peterborough: Broadview, 2008.)
FQ	*The Female Quixote.* London: Millar, 1752. (Modern editions ed. Margaret Dalziel; Oxford: Oxford University Press, 1970/1989 and ed. Amanda Gilroy and Wil Verhoeven; Harmondsworth: Penguin, 2007.)
Henrietta	*Henrietta.* London: Millar, 1758. (Modern edition ed. Ruth Perry and Susan Carlile; Lexington: The University Press of Kentucky, 2008.)
HS	*The Life of Harriot Stuart.* London: Payne and Bouquet, 1750. (Modern edition ed. Susan Kubica Howard; Madison: Fairleigh Dickinson University Press, 1995.)
Maintenon	*Memoirs for the History of Madame de Maintenon and of the Last Age.* London: Millar, Nourse, R. and J. Dodsley, Davis, and Reymer, 1757.
OCM	*Old City Manners: A Comedy.* London: Becket, 1775.

LM	*The Lady's Museum.* London: Newbery and Coote, 1760–61.
Philander	*Philander: A Dramatic Pastoral.* London: Millar, 1757.
Poems	*Poems on Several Occasions.* London: Paterson, 1747.
SI	*Shakespear [sic] Illustrated.* London: Millar, 1753–54.
The Sister	*The Sister: A Comedy.* London: J. Dodsley, 1769.
Sophia	*Sophia.* London: Fletcher, 1762. (Modern edition ed. Norbert Schürer; Peterborough: Broadview, 2008.)
Sully	*Memoirs of Maximilian de Bethune, Duke of Sully, Prime Minister to Henry the Great.* London: Millar, R. and J. Dodsley, and Shropshire, 1756.
Vallière	*Meditations and Penitential Prayers, Written by the Celebrated Dutchess de la Valliere, Mistress of Lewis the Fourteenth of France.* London: J. Dodsley, 1774.

II.	Other Works or Organizations
Abbott	Abbott, John. *John Hawkesworth: Eighteenth-Century Man of Letters.* Madison: University of Wisconsin Press, 1982.
AKL	*Allgemeines Künstlerlexikon.* Ed. Günter Meissner. Leipzig: Sauer, 1983-.
Berg, *Circle*	Berg, Temma. *The Lives and Letters of an Eighteenth-Century Circle of Acquaintance.* Aldershot: Ashgate, 2007.
Berg, "Letters"	Berg, Temma. "Charlotte Lennox and Lydia Clerke: Reflecting on Letters." *Eighteenth-Century Women* 2 (2002): 61–93.
BLJ	Boswell, James. *Boswell's Life of Johnson.* 6 vols. Ed. George Birkbeck Hill and L.P. Powell. Oxford: Clarendon Press, 1934.
Boaden	Boaden, James. *The Private Correspondence of David Garrick with the Most Celebrated Persons of His Time.* 2 vols. London: Colburn and Bentley, 1831–32.
Boyle	Boyle, Emily Charlotte, Countess of Cory and Orrery. *The Orrery Papers.* 2 vols. London: Duckworth, 1903.
Brack/Carlile	Brack, O M, Jr. and Susan Carlile. "Samuel Johnson's Contributions to Charlotte Lennox's *The Female Quixote.*" *Yale University Library Gazette* 77 (2003): 166–73.

Bracken/Silver   Bracken, James and Joel Silver (eds.). *The British Literary Book Trade, 1700–1820.* Detroit: Gale, 1995 (Dictionary of Literary Biography 154).

Browning   Browning, Reed. *The Duke of Newcastle.* New Haven and London: Yale University Press, 1975.

Burney   Burney, Frances. *The Early Journals and Letters of Fanny Burney.* 4 vols. Ed. Lars E. Troide and Stewart J. Cooke. Oxford: Clarendon Press, 1992–2003.

Carlile   Carlile, Susan. "Charlotte Lennox's Birth Date and Place." *Notes and Queries* n.s. 51.4 (December 2004): 390–92.

Claims   Williams, David. *Claims of Literature.* London: Miller, 1802.

Cochrane   Cochrane, James Aikman. *Dr. Johnson's Printer.* Cambridge: Harvard University Press, 1964.

Danzinger/Brady   Danzinger, Marlies K. and Frank Brady (eds.). *Boswell: The Great Biographer 1789–1795.* London: Heinemann, 1989.

Eaves/Kimpel   Eaves, T.C. Duncan and Ben Kimpel. *Samuel Richardson: A Biography.* Oxford: Clarendon Press, 1971.

Faulkner   Faulkner, Thomas. *History and Antiquities of Kensington.* London: Egerton etc., 1820.

Fleeman   Fleeman, John David. *A Bibliography of the Works of Samuel Johnson.* 2 vols. Prepared for publication by James McLaverty. Oxford: Clarendon Press, 2000.

Garrick   Garrick, David. *Letters.* 3 vols. Ed. David Little and George Kahrl. Cambridge: Belknap Press of Harvard University Press, 1963.

Gillespie/Hopkins   Gillespie, Stuart and David Hopkins (eds.). *The Oxford History of Translation.* Vol. 3: 1660–1790. Oxford: Oxford University Press, 2005.

Greenspan   Greenspan, Ezra. *George Palmer Putnam: Representative American Publisher.* University Park: The Pennsylvania State University Press, 2000.

Hawkins, *Anecdotes*   Hawkins, Lætitia-Matilda. *Anecdotes, Biographical Sketches and Memoirs.* London: Rivington, 1822.

Hawkins, *Life*   Hawkins, Sir John. *The Life of Johnson, LL.D.* Ed. O M Brack, Jr. Athens and London: The University of Georgia Press, 2009.

Hawkins, *Memoirs*	Hawkins, Lætitia-Matilda. *Memoirs, Anecdotes, Facts, and Opinions.* 2 vols. London: Longman, 1824.
Hazen	Hazen, Allen. *Samuel Johnson's Prefaces and Dedications.* New Haven: Yale University Press, 1937.
Highfill	Highfill, Philip H., Jr., Kalman A. Burnim, and Edward A. Langhans (eds.). *A Biographical Dictionary of Actors, Actresses, Musicians, Dancers, Managers & Other Stage Personnel in London, 1660–1800.* 16 vols. Carbondale and Edwardsville: Southern Illinois University Press, 1973–93.
Horwood	Horwood, Richard. *Map of the Cities of London and Westminster* (1794–99). 3rd ed. London: Horwood, 1813. Reproduced as *The A to Z of Regency London,* ed. Harry Margary in association with Guildhall Library, intro. Paul Laxton (London: London Topographical Society, 1985).
Ingamells	Ingamells, John and John Edgcumbe (eds.). *The Letters of Sir Joshua Reynolds.* New Haven: Published for the Paul Mellon Centre for Studies in British Art by Yale University Press, 2000.
Isles	= LC
Jones	Jones, Whitney R.D. *David Williams: The Anvil and the Hammer.* Tuscaloosa: University of Alabama Press, 1986.
Kramnick	Kramnick, Jonathan Brody. "Reading Shakespeare's Novels: Literary History and Cultural Politics in the Lennox-Johnson Debate." *Modern Language Quarterly* 55.4 (December 1994): 429–53.
Kynaston	Kynaston, Agnes. *The Life and Writings of Charlotte Lennox 1720–1804.* M.A. Diss., Birkbeck College, University of London, 1936.
LC	Isles, Duncan. "The Lennox Collection." *Harvard Library Bulletin* 18.4 (October 1970): 317–44; 19.1 (January 1971): 36–60; 19.2 (April 1971): 165–86; 19.4 (October 1971): 416–35.
Leigh	Leigh, Samuel. *Leigh's New Picture of London.* London: Leigh, 1818.
London Stage	Van Lennep, William, Emmett Langdon Avery, George Winchester Stone, and Charles Beecher Hogan (eds.). *The London Stage 1660–1800.* 5 pts. Carbondale and Edwardsville: Southern Illinois University Press, 1960–68.

McGarvie	McGarvie, Michael. *The Book of Marston Bigot: The Story of Marston House and the Earls of Cork and Orrery.* Buckingham: Barracuda Books, 1987.
Marks	Marks, P.J.M. *The British Library Guide to Bookbinding: History and Techniques.* London: The British Library, 1998.
Maxted	Maxted, Ian. *The London Book Trades 1775–1800.* London: Dawson, 1977.
McIntyre	McIntyre, Ian. *Joshua Reynolds.* London: Lane, 2003.
Namier/Brooke	Namier, Lewis and John Brooke. *The House of Commons 1754–1790.* 3 vols. London: Her Majesty's Stationery Office, 1964.
Nichols	Nichols, John. *Literary Anecdotes.* 9 vols. London: Nichols, 1812–15.
ODNB	*Oxford Dictionary of National Biography.* 60 vols. Ed. H.G.C. Matthew and Brian Harrison. Oxford: Oxford University Press, 2004.
OED	*Oxford English Dictionary*
Page	Page, Eugene. *George Colman the Elder.* New York: Columbia University Press, 1935.
Piozzi	Piozzi, Hester Lynch. *Thraliana: The Diary of Mrs. Hester Lynch Thrale (Later Mrs. Piozzi) 1776–1809.* 2 vols. 2nd ed. Ed. Katharine C. Balderston. Oxford: Clarendon Press, 1951.
Plomer	Plomer, Henry, G.H. Bushnell, and E.R. MacClintock Dix. *A Dictionary of the Printers and Booksellers Who Were at Work in England Scotland and Ireland from 1726 to 1775.* Oxford: Oxford University Press, 1932.
Private Papers	Scott, Geoffrey and Frederick Pottle (eds.). *Private Papers of James Boswell.* 18 vols. N.P.: Privately Printed, 1928–34.
Raven, *Business*	Raven, James. *The Business of Books: Booksellers and the English Book Trade.* New Haven and London: Yale University Press, 2007.
Raven, "Introduction"	Raven, James. "Historical Introduction: The Novel Comes of Age." *The English Novel 1770–1829: A Bibliographical Survey of Prose Fiction Published in the British Isles.* 2 vols. Ed. Peter Garside, James Raven, and Rainer Schöwerling. Oxford: Oxford University Press, 2000. I 15–121.

Redford   Redford, Bruce (ed.). *The Letters of Samuel Johnson.* 5 vols. Princeton: Princeton University Press, 1992–94.

Rhodes   Rhodes, Joshua. *Topographical Survey of the Parish of Kensington.* London: Bowles, [1766].

RLF   Royal Literary Fund

Rocque   Rocque, John. *Plan of the Cities of London and Westminster.* London: Pine and Tinney, 1746. Reproduced as *The A to Z of Georgian London,* ed. Harry Margary in association with Guildhall Library, intro. Ralph Hyde (London: London Topographical Society, 1982).

Rogers   Rogers, Pat. *The Samuel Johnson Encyclopedia.* Westport, CT: Greenwood Press, 1996.

Rose   Rose, Mark. *Authors and Owners: The Invention of Copyright.* Cambridge and London: Harvard University Press, 1993.

Schürer   Schürer, Norbert. "A New Novel by Charlotte Lennox." *Notes & Queries* n.s. 48.4 (December 2001): 419–22.

Small   Small, Miriam Rossiter. *Charlotte Ramsay Lennox: An Eighteenth Century Woman of Letters.* New Haven: Yale University Press, 1935; New York: Archon Books, 1969.

Stone/Kahrl   Stone, George Winchester, Jr. and George Kahrl. *David Garrick: A Critical Biography.* Carbondale: Southern Illinois University Press, 1979.

Waingrow   Waingrow, Marshall. *The Correspondence and Other Papers of James Boswell Relating to the Making of the* Life of Johnson. 2nd ed., corrected and enlarged. Edinburgh; New Haven and London: Edinburgh University Press; Yale University Press, 2001.

Wallis   Wallis, Peter John. *Book Subscription Lists: Extended Supplement to the Revised Guide.* Completed and edited by Ruth Wallis. Newcastle upon Tyne: Project for Historical Biobibliography, 1996.

Wendorf   Wendorf, Richard. *Sir Joshua Reynolds: The Painter in Society.* London: National Portrait Gallery, 1996.

Wheatley   Wheatley, Henry. *London: Past and Present.* 3 vols. London: Murray, 1891.

Introduction

Charlotte Lennox's career spans an extraordinarily long time, from the publication of her *Poems on Several Occasions* in 1747 to her death in 1804.
Her significance for eighteenth-century British literature shows in the suc-
cesses she achieved and in the company she kept. Around the middle of the
century, Lennox interacted with the literary behemoths Samuel Johnson,
Samuel Richardson, and Henry Fielding and published her critically and
commercially most successful novel, *The Female Quixote;* towards the end
of her life, she communicated with the entire Boswell family and published
her last novel, *Euphemia.* In between, Lennox brought out the first novel by
a major female author written specifically for serial publication—in her own
periodical; wrote the first full-length study of Shakespeare by a woman; had
two plays produced for the stage; and translated French works of literature,
history, and biography into English. On the one hand, her career is typical
for eighteenth-century female authors in the variety of her output and in
the decline in her reputation after her death. On the other hand, Lennox is
unusual in the size of her output, in the success she had with some of her
works, in her reliance on literature to make a living, in her involvement in
the literary marketplace, and in her abject poverty towards the end of her
life. These attributes make her an author well worth the increasing attention
she has been receiving in the past four decades. In addition, her achieve-
ments demand a closer examination of the person behind the works. This
investigation starts in this volume with a closer look at Lennox's career
through her correspondence, Royal Literary Fund files, and miscellaneous
publications.

A first part of Charlotte Lennox's correspondence, a package of 42 letters
to and from her, was published beginning in 1970 by Duncan Isles as "The

Lennox Collection." In the introduction to this seminal collection, Isles wrote that only one other letter of hers "is known to exist outside this collection."[1] Fortunately, Isles was wrong—beyond the letter he mentions in that instance (#75), he had already discovered two more himself by the time he published the last installment of "The Lennox Collection" in 1971 (#4 and #8). Since then, even more correspondence has surfaced in repositories such as the British Library, the Beinecke Rare Book and Manuscripts Library, Yale University, the Hyde Collection (now at the Houghton Library, Harvard University), and the Sheffield Archives, so now over 80 documents that are part of, or related to, Lennox's correspondence are known. In addition, other material pertaining to Lennox's career such as proposals for subscription editions of her works, her file at the RLF, and additional information relating to the publication of some of her works is now available. Finally, the publications of the 1780s in her own and her son's names show her presence in the literary marketplace and illuminate her relationship to her daughter, especially concerning her premature death. This material, as well as Lennox's entire existing correspondence, is collected and annotated here for the first time. The first section of the book collects letters to and from Lennox and a few other items like letters between other writers focusing entirely on her, her proposals for subscription publication, printers' ledgers, and receipts. These items are arranged chronologically, so the reader can follow the development of Lennox's career as it unfolds. There are some significant gaps in the correspondence—only two letters between 1761 and 1768 and only four in the entire 1780s have been found—but a coherent image can still be constructed.

From the letters and publications in this volume, a new picture of the author Charlotte Lennox emerges in at least three aspects. First, the letters document the publication history of *FQ* and show that far from a passive observer of the literary marketplace (as women supposedly were), Lennox was an active participant in the production and marketing of her novel. In addition, this material shows once and for all that Lennox herself—rather than Samuel Johnson—was the author of the penultimate chapter of *FQ*. Secondly, the correspondence of the 1770s, Lennox's various proposals for subscription publication, and her (or her son's) publications in the 1780s show her to be active in exploring old possibilities as well as new developments in the literary marketplace. While many authors, particularly women, were turning to publication for circulating libraries, Lennox turned back to publication by subscription. At the same time, she was aware of legal developments such as the 1774 ruling in *Donaldson v. Becket* and used them to advance her financial interests with her publishers. The publications of the 1780s in her and her son's names served the same purpose. Finally, the letters from the last decade of Lennox's life and her RLF file show an author in dire financial straits, desperately trying to find a way to survive. Once again, Lennox looked in several directions: While she solicited the Boswell family for their literary connections, she also applied successfully to the newly founded RLF for monetary assistance. These three aspects—her participation in the publication of *FQ,* her activities in the 1770s and 1780s, and her struggles in the last decade of her life—come together to illustrate how authors in general in the second half of the eighteenth century could participate in the literary marketplace by writing and promoting literature. At the same time, they document how this particular author succeeded for several decades in carving out a niche by exploiting a variety of avenues, but failed to provide for herself at the end of her life and died in penury.

THE FEMALE QUIXOTE

Charlotte Lennox (Ill. 1) was born in 1729 or 1730, probably in Gibraltar, as the son of James Ramsay, an officer in the British army.[2] Her childhood was unusually transient for an eighteenth-century individual: She moved from Gibraltar to England, from there to the New York colony, and then back to England around 1745. By that time, her father was dead, but the relative who was supposed to take care of her in England had either gone insane or died, leaving Lennox to her own devices. Apparently, she quickly acquired at least two aristocratic patrons—Lady Cecilia Isabella Finch (First Lady of the Bedchamber to their Royal Highnesses, the Princesses) and Mary, Countess of Rockingham (Isabella's sister and wife of Thomas Watson-Wentworth, first Marquess of Rockingham, and mother of Charles Wentworth, second Marquess of Rockingham). In addition, she entered the literary circle around Samuel Johnson and married Alexander Lennox, who as an employee of the printer William Strahan was already a well-connected member of the literary marketplace. At the same time (if not already previously in America), she had started writing poetry, and, in 1747, she published *Poems.* However, the work had no significant impact with critics or readers. Subsequently, Lennox turned to the still emerging genre of the novel and wrote *The Life of Harriot Stuart,* which was published in December 1750. This novel made an impression at least on some important literary figures, and Samuel Johnson organized a now notorious celebration of the book's release with the Ivy Lane Club. According to Sir John Hawkins, one of Johnson's first biographers,

> Mrs. Lenox,[3] a lady now well known in the literary world, had written a novel intitled, "The life of Harriot Stuart," which in the spring of 1751, was ready for publication. One evening at the club, Johnson proposed to us the celebrating the

Ill. 1. Portrait of Charlotte Lennox, engraving by Henry R. Cook after portrait by Sir Joshua Reynolds (1761) (author's collection)

birth of Mrs. Lenox's first literary child, as he called her book, by a whole night spent in festivity. [. . .] The place appointed was the Devil tavern, and there, about the hour of eight, Mrs. Lenox and her husband, and a lady of her acquaintance, now living, as also the club, and friends to the number of near twenty, assembled. Our supper was elegant, and Johnson had directed that a magnificent hot applepye should make a part of it, and this he would have stuck with bay-leaves, because, forsooth, Mrs. Lenox was an authoress, and had written verses; and further, he had prepared for her a crown of laurel, with which, but not till he had invoked the muses by some ceremonies of his own invention, he encircled her brows. The night passed, as must be imagined, in pleasant conversation, and harmless mirth, intermingled at different periods with the refreshments of coffee and tea. About five, Johnson's face shone with meridian splendour, though his drink had been only lemonade; but the far greater part of us had deserted the colours of Bacchus, and were with difficulty rallied to partake of a second refreshment of coffee, which was scarcely ended when the day began to dawn. This phenomenon began to put us in mind of our reckoning; but the waiters were all so overcome with sleep, that it was two hours before we could get a bill, and it was not till near eight that the creaking of the street-door gave the signal for our departure.[4]

Still, even *HS* and its reception hardly gave an indication of the extent of Lennox's literary abilities or brought her lasting fame. In contrast, her second novel, *FQ*, published in March 1752, immediately received extravagant praise from prominent literary figures such as Samuel Johnson and Henry Fielding, and Lennox has been known mostly as the author of *FQ* ever since. The novel stayed popular enough throughout and beyond the eighteenth century to be included as Vol. XII in James Harrison's *Novelist's Magazine* in 1793, to receive an edition from Charles Cooke in his series of classics in 1799, and to be published as Vols. XXIV and XXV in Anna Letitia Barbauld's *British Novelists* in 1810. Thus, it briefly entered the canon of English literature.[5] Lennox's novel subsequently lost popularity and critical status, and in 1843 John Mitford described it as "a work very little read in the present day."[6] This impression had not changed much 100 years later, when Allen Hazen wrote that Lennox's "works are read only by literary antiquarians."[7] However, since its republication in 1970, *FQ* has reentered the canon, and Lennox is known primarily as the author of this novel.

The same John Mitford who believed *FQ* was hardly being read was also responsible for one of the enduring myths about the book, namely that the penultimate chapter was written by Samuel Johnson. In the same article in the *Gentleman's Magazine* of August 1843, he wrote that "it appears to me [. . .] that the whole of the eleventh chapter of the ninth and concluding book of the 'Female Quixote' was written by Dr. Johnson [. . .] indeed I should have no scruple in admitting this chapter among the acknowledged works of Johnson."[8] In a later article of January 1844, Mitford summarized the evidence he believed supported his assertion:

> The proof of the [chapter] being the production of Johnson rests on its *internal* evidence; to which is to be added, that twice in the same book [. . .] Mrs. Lennox diverges from her subject to praise Dr. Johnson in the highest terms; that the heading of the Chapter is very significant of its not having been written by the author of the rest of the volume; that Dr. Johnson highly esteemed and praised the talents of Mrs. Lennox; and that this chapter is totally different both in style and subject from the rest of the work.[9]

Mitford's claim was upheld as recently as 2000 by the inclusion of the chapter in question in J.D. Fleeman's *A Bibliography of the Works of Samuel Johnson* as items 52.3LFQ/1–9.[10] In contrast, the first eleven items of correspondence collected here between Richardson, Johnson, and Lennox specifically concerning the publication of *FQ* (only six of which were known to Isles and the editors of the Oxford edition of *FQ*) prove beyond doubt that Lennox did indeed write the chapter herself. The first four deal mostly with the mechanics of the novel's publication and more specifically with Lennox's struggle to get her novel published in the first place. Her first book, the *Poems* of 1747, had been the first work of novice publisher Samuel Paterson as well. By 1751, Lennox had moved to the more well-known John Payne and Joseph Bouquet with her first novel, *HS*, but later had a falling out with these booksellers (#1). By the end of 1751, Lennox was trying to publish her next novel, *FQ*, with the prominent bookseller Andrew Millar (#20)—a move perhaps suggested by her friends Samuel Johnson, who was working with Millar on his *Dictionary*, or Samuel Richardson, who had printed the *Universal History* for Millar. However, in keeping with his usual practice, Millar had sent the manuscript to three independent readers, two of whom are named (though unidentified) in the present correspondence: Mr. Seymour and Mr. Gray. In November 1751, these readers condemned the manuscript of Lennox's novel to the extent that after talking with Gray she believed that "the many alterations he insists upon being made, and his exceptions to almost all the Characters, Incidents and language, make it necessary to write a new Book if I would please him" (#5).

Lennox's friends were also critical of the novel: Richardson wrote her a long note with comments and suggestions, most of which she willingly incorporated into her text (#3). For instance, she changed Sir George's claim to royalty in his fantastic romance autobiography, and she omitted Richardson's name at his request, at least in the first edition of the novel. But at the same time, both Johnson and Richardson appear to have supported the publication of *FQ*, and when they heard of Lennox's predicament with Millar they sprang into action. On November 21, 1751, Richardson saw Millar in the presence of Sarah Fielding and either Jane or Margaret Collier and expressed his strong approval of the novel (#4). Over the next month, Richardson and Johnson cooperated in their efforts to convince Millar to publish *FQ*, and as part of these efforts they asked their friend John Boyle, then Earl of Orrery,[11] to read the manuscript and to talk with Millar (#6). These transactions offer an interesting instance of literary patronage in action.[12] For one thing, they show two established members of the literary world—Johnson, a writer then most well-known for his poetry and essays, and Richardson, the author of the most popular novel of the previous decade—working together to promote the career of a young female author. This state of affairs reflects the difficulty of women entering publishing, but also the difficulty of any other author— with a volume of poetry and a novel already in print, though without much recognition—in asserting her own literary vision in the face of a powerful bookseller.[13] In response to Lennox's predicament, Richardson and Johnson provided not so much financial support—as a matter of fact, Johnson might have been borrowing money from Lennox's husband at this time (#18)—but rather assistance in getting the text accepted. That, in turn, allowed Lennox to make a financial profit, though definitely not nearly as much as the £1000 Millar paid Henry Fielding around the same time for the manuscript of *Amelia*—even in the 1770s, the standard remuneration for a novel was only around five guineas.[14] Nevertheless, this relatively unknown female author was able to take advantage of a network of well-known and well-connected male supporters to advance her literary career.

Even more interestingly, as Eric Walker has argued,[15] the publication history of *FQ* shows patronage working across class lines. Lennox's own class origin remains somewhat unclear: She came from a military family and had some connections in the gentry, but by 1750 was on her own and certainly not wealthy. Fortunately, she had friends in the literary elite instead: Richardson, Johnson, and Millar were all members of the burgeoning middle class, and they were all members of the literary and intellectual world that valued litera- ture in at least two senses: as a cultural artifact fulfilling a function in society and as an economic product providing a living for booksellers and authors. On the other side, Orrery, another patron of Lennox's, was a member of the high aristocracy and came from a family tracing back to the eleventh century, with recent family members being a privy counselor, a lord of the bedcham- ber, Members of Parliament, lord justices, and high treasurers.[16] It is impos- sible to know in retrospect what actually convinced Millar to publish *FQ*, but the conjunction of various class interests might very well have persuaded him that the novel was worthwhile and would have a readership large enough to make it a profitable venture. In any case, the combination of literary and aristocratic patronage begs several questions about the literary marketplace around the middle of the century. What aesthetic and economic functions did the literature of the time fulfill? Did it have a particular ideological purpose in terms of class? Were female authors, or unknown authors, excluded from publication in a way that might have created a disconnect between the literature available and what was desired by the public? There is no information to explain why Millar's readers disliked *FQ*—the "Characters, Incidents and language" (#5) Gray criticized cover pretty much every aspect of the novel (characterization, plot, and style). However, the entire situation raises the suspicion that the marketplace was controlled by booksellers more than by the demands of the public, at least in the sense that only certain kinds of literature were produced within the scope of what the public would read. After all, *FQ* went into a second edition almost immediately, so in spite of Millar's readers' reservations the reading public apparently enjoyed the novel enough to buy it in large numbers. The only specific reference in the letter is that Gray was unwilling to include "the History of Miss Groves" (#5), a story about an unmarried mother—so maybe literature violating decorum and promoting so-called loose morals was initially not acceptable to a publisher like Millar (or to the public).

Another difficulty with the publication of *FQ* was its placement in the London season of publishing, which around the middle of the eighteenth century extended from the fall until the late spring.[17] By February 1752, Lennox could be certain that her novel would be produced, but apparently Millar was having difficulties getting his printer to finish the book in time for the season. Since that printer was Richardson, who had supported the novel from the beginning, the reason for the difficulty in production remains unknown—perhaps he had taken on too many projects, or maybe he had problems obtaining enough paper, a frequent predicament in this period. Whatever the reason, Lennox was sure enough of the success of her novel that she already looked forward to a second edition, claiming that she needed it for financial reasons. In a letter to Johnson of February 3, 1752 (#8), she asked him to speak to Richardson to press forward with the printing, and her request was met, since the novel was ultimately published on March 12 or 13, 1752.

In addition to questions of patronage, propriety, and production, the letters here also resolve the vexed question of the authorship of the penultimate chapter of *FQ*.[18] Throughout the discussion of the publication of the novel, its conclusion had been an issue. On January 13, 1752, Richardson wrote to Lennox about the ending, and his letter implied that she was considering adding a third volume to the present two. Apparently, Lennox wanted to cure Arabella by means that "might flatter [Richardson's] vanity" (#7), but might also be construed by readers as a collaboration between Lennox and Richardson to promote the latter. Unfortunately, we do not know what constituted the proposed ending; perhaps it flattered Richardson by employing the Richardsonian Countess or a Richardson novel to bring about Arabella's change of heart. At the same time, Richardson counseled Lennox to consider long-term economic and critical implications: He advised her to think of this novel as the beginning of a long career and as a work that established her name, rather than as a piece of art that needed to be perfect in itself. Finally, Richardson suggested that Lennox consult Johnson, which she did, though mostly (at least in the existing correspondence) concerning Richardson's supposedly dragging his feet over the printing of the novel. Johnson actually supported Richardson's idea of waiting with the publication of the novel, claiming that "if you can stay till next year the prospect of [success] will be better" (#9). However, Lennox overruled her two advisors, convinced Millar, and had *FQ* published in the 1751/52 season.

Nevertheless, it is significant that the printed end of the novel, while mentioning Richardson, flatters Johnson instead, who is explicitly referred to and imitated in the figure of the divine. Some critics have taken this as an indication that Johnson actually wrote the conversion chapter himself, but the evidence shows the opposite. From Richardson's letter of January 13 (#7), it is clear that Lennox had not written the end of *FQ* by then, since the two are still discussing whether it should happen in the second or in a third volume. By February 4, however, Johnson wrote that the end "is [already] sent to Mr Millar" (#9), so it had been written and submitted to the publisher. It is highly unlikely that the decision to stick with two volumes, a request to Johnson to write the ending, the composition itself, and the dispatch to Millar could have occurred in about two weeks. Indeed, another letter adds to the evidence that suggests Johnson could not have written the penultimate chapter of *FQ*. On March 12, 1752, around the day of the publication of the novel, Lennox wrote to an unnamed correspondent and presented him with a copy of her new book (#10). This correspondent can be identified as Johnson from his response (#11) and from the provenance of the letter. In part, it asks the recipient "to read over the latter part of the second Voll. [*sic*] which you have not yet seen" (#10). The most convincing interpretation of this phrase is that Lennox was asking Johnson to peruse the one part of the novel he had not seen—because it had been under discussion until the last minute—that is, the ending. With this letter, the specter of Johnson's writing the penultimate chapter of *FQ*, and the idea that Lennox was not capable of bringing about the cure of her heroine on her own, can finally be banished.

AUTHORSHIP AND OWNERSHIP[19]

Still, there is no doubt that Johnson did contribute heavily to Lennox's career and writings. Hazen lists six dedications as well as some other material that Johnson wrote for Lennox: the dedications for *FQ, Shakespear* [*sic*] *Illustrated, Henrietta, Philander, The Greek Theatre of Father Brumoy*, and *The Memoirs of Maximilian de Bethune, Duke of Sully* as well as "the *Proposals* for publishing her Original Works [. . .] and two sections of her translation of Brumoy's *Greek Theatre*" (the "Dissertation Upon Greek Comedy" and the "General Conclusion").[20] Fleeman confirms these attributions and identifies another item Johnson composed for Lennox, the dedication to her translation of the *Memoirs for the History of Madame de Maintenon*.[21] But in addition to Johnson, others also helped Lennox: Oliver Goldsmith, for instance, supplied the epilogue to Lennox's drama *The Sister* (#44). John Boyle, now Earl of Cork and Orrery, perhaps because he had proven so helpful in securing the publication of *FQ* and of course because of his high class standing, was invited to contribute translations to Lennox's next endeavor, her *SI,* and he later provided "A Discourse Upon the Theatre of the Greeks," "A Discourse Upon the Original of Tragedy," and "A Discourse Upon the Parallel of Theatres" for Lennox's *Brumoy*. That volume involved a whole range of collaborators: Besides Johnson and Orrery, "James Grainger translated the 'Cyclops,' and John Borryeau contributed the prefatory notice thereto [. . .]; Gregory Sharpe translated and wrote notes on the 'Frogs,' and an unnamed 'young gentleman' wrote on the 'Birds' and 'Peace.'"[22] These examples, as well as numerous references in her correspondence, her reaction to the copyright decision of 1774, her use of subscription publication, and her promotion of her son's or her own work in the 1780s show that Lennox conceived of herself not so much as an independent author creating autonomous works of art, but as a laborer in the literary marketplace trying to make a living as easily and profitably as possible.

As early as the 1750s, Lennox abdicated artistic authority over her own works: She was quick to accept suggestions about ending *FQ* after two rather than three volumes from Johnson and Richardson, though in retrospect it seems those changes led to problems in the novel that critics have found fault with ever since. At the same time, Lennox insisted on a particular publication schedule, so she appears to have been more concerned with the economic than the aesthetic aspect of her literary creation. A similar dynamic is visible over the next two decades in Lennox's exchanges with David Garrick. Around 1759, Lennox had dramatized her own novel *Henrietta* as *The Sister* and had offered it to Garrick, who declined. However, in the letter rejecting the drama, Garrick wrote that he was "much flatter'd that the Author approves of the little hints I gave" (#36). In other words, Lennox had taken into account artistic suggestions made previously by Garrick and had adjusted her work accordingly. More obviously, Lennox addressed the same subject in her letter of October 25, 1768, when she wrote about the possibility of another play. In the body of that letter, she assured Garrick, "You may depend upon it that every alteration, and amendment which you judge necessary, will be readily, and thankfully admitted," and in a postscript she added that, "I have not yet written the concluding lines, but that can be done, when the piece has received your corrections" (#41). At this stage in her career, then—after a volume of poems, several novels, and many translations—Lennox still had no investment in what today might be termed the integrity or originality of her work. She did not consider herself as an author(ity) producing an unalterable work of art, but as a craftswoman shaping a text that could be formed according to the needs and desires of the parties involved—in this case, the director of the Drury Lane Theatre.[23] Lennox reiterated the same sentiment when she discussed a possible adaptation of Racine's drama *Bajazet* with Garrick several years later. On August 4, 1774, she wrote that, "Upon the whole, Sir, I submit [the play] to your judgment; give it a reading, and if you think it may be made fit for representation, I will be guided by your advice in every alteration to be made in it" (#51). This declaration is all the more interesting because it was made in a correspondence intended to become somewhat public: An accompanying letter explained that the present one, which included praises of the actress Mary Ann Yates, was supposed to be presented to Yates. So Lennox was willing to admit her lack of insistence on the particulars of her drama even to a third party. The last correspondence between Lennox and Garrick further elaborates the mercenary aspect of her writing. On August 20, 1775, Lennox wrote:

> I am not indifferent to theatrical reward; [. . .] but having once failed, when I had to a certain degree pleased myself, and several others, whose judgment I relied on more than my own, I am grown diffident, so diffident that, if I have any genius, I dare not trust it. (#57)

By "theatrical reward," Lennox means financial reward as well as simply the performance of her work. The failure she refers to is her play *The Sister,* which saw only one performance on February 18, 1769, but met with such a negative reception—apparently planned by individuals who objected to Lennox's stance on Shakespeare—that it was withdrawn immediately (#45). Lennox claimed that she was happy with her play before the performance and that she had relied on "several others," by whom she probably meant the proprietors of the theater, including George Colman, and Oliver Goldsmith, who had written the play's epilogue. Lennox registers her own opinion, but significantly relies on the judgment of others to assess her literary talent and the possibility of success in the marketplace. At the end of the present passage, she is ready to doubt that talent entirely: "if I have any genius, I dare not trust it." Once again, Lennox sees herself not as a literary artist, but as a professional writer trying to make a living by producing a play, led by the opinions of others.

Of course by 1775—the time of the last correspondence with Garrick—a change in the literary marketplace had occurred that can hardly be underestimated in its consequences[24] and that opened another avenue for Lennox to assert herself as a professional author. The London booksellers' hold on copyright—known as perpetual copyright—had been under fire for most of the eighteenth century, starting with the Statute of Anne in 1710. This statute, also called the Copyright Act, officially introduced the idea of limiting copyright to fourteen years (for publishers), but left the common-law status of copyright open. In 1769, Lord Mansfield's Court of King's Bench heard the case of *Millar v. Taylor,* which concerned Scottish printer Robert Taylor's publishing and selling a pirated edition of James Thomson's *The Seasons,* to which Millar held the copyright. In this case, the court "upheld the author's common-law right and the perpetuity of literary property,"[25] i.e., it argued that once an author had sold his or her copyright it was the bookseller's forever. This decision was not applied in Scotland, however, and Scottish printers continued to threaten the London market with cheap reprints. In the wake of the decision in *Millar v. Taylor,* London bookseller Thomas Becket succeeded in getting the Chancery in 1771 and 1772 to file a bill against Scottish printer Alexander Donaldson, who was also involved in producing *The Seasons.* A year later, Donaldson—encouraged by another decision, *Hinton v. Donaldson*—appealed Becket's injunction. Followed closely by the public and accompanied by a flurry of pamphlets, the King's Bench and then the House of Lords discussed the matter, breaking it down into three questions: "First, did the author have a common-law right to control the first publication of his work? Second, did the author's right, if it existed, survive publication? Third, if the right survived publication, was it taken away by the statute?"[26] While the court ruled in favor of authors in the first two questions and ambiguously in the third, the House of Lords, which had the final decision, was unequivocal: On February 22, 1774, they almost unanimously struck down perpetual copyright. In practice, that decision meant that an author could sell their copyright to a publisher, but that the copyright returned to the author (for private use, resale, or no use at all) after fourteen years if he or she was still alive.

Lennox soon reacted to this decision: On February 18, 1775, almost exactly a year after the ruling, she commented in a letter to William Hunter on the "late decision with regard to literary property" (#55). However, she did not express any concern about her works of literature being appropriated by unscrupulous booksellers and diminished as a work of art, and she did not talk about the public's right to reasonably priced editions of literature. Instead, Lennox was interested in the financial benefits she could reap for herself from the decision, which gave her "a right to reprint my original writings for the benefit of myself and my children" (#55). Several years later, Lennox was even willing to employ a lawyer to regain control over her writing, when she asked Samuel Johnson for an introduction to Arthur Murphy, who had worked on both *Millar v. Taylor* and *Donaldson v. Becket,* arguing against perpetual copyright in both cases. In this letter of June 17, 1777, Lennox was realistic enough to recognize that the true owner of her œuvre in eighteenth-century legal terms was her husband. Instead of referring to herself, she wrote that "Mr Lennox is [. . .] desirous of recovering his property out of the hands of the booksellers" (#64).[27] About a year later, Lennox once more referred to the copyright decision when she recounted how she confronted James Dodsley, who had just printed the fifth edition of the *Sully,* because "I apprehend they had no right to do this without my consent, it is more than fourteen years since that book was first published," and added that "they have reprinted it without consulting me although by the late decision concerning literary property the copy is mine" (#65). In this particular case, Lennox was successful with her complaint, either because of its own merit or because she employed the services of a lawyer—within one year, Dodsley and his colleagues had published not only their own fifth edition of *Sully,* but another "new" edition that was presumably based on Lennox's changes to her translation. In all of these instances, Lennox emerges as a writer not too concerned with the literary status of her work, but very much interested in the economic benefits of publishing. In this, she was probably not an untypical mid-eighteenth-century author: The concept of the artist as genius and the idea of an autonomous realm of art or literature were only just coming into being, so Lennox was defining herself in the more traditional terms that were available to her.[28]

At the same time, Lennox tried to exploit the possibilities of the literary marketplace not only by abdicating her authority as a writer or by applying legal decisions to her own situations, but also by using various modes of publication. Of course, like any mid-eighteenth-century author, she sold her copy to booksellers such as Andrew Millar or James Dodsley, who proceeded to publish her work. In that process, she made use of a wider range of patrons— literary and aristocratic—than many of her peers. On the one hand, she dedicated her works to Lady Isabella Finch (*Poems*), the Earl of Middlesex (*FQ*), Orrery (*SI*), and others, while requesting or receiving support from other aristocracy such as Lady Rockingham and the Duchess of Newcastle. She even tried to play both ends of the political spectrum, asking both Rockingham and the Earl of Bute for patronage (#42). On the other hand, she employed the literary and personal influence of Samuel Johnson and Samuel Richardson to secure the publication of *FQ* and to find employment as a translator. Lennox also attempted to write in the periodical format, which was frequently more profitable than individual novels, but her *Lady's Museum* finished after only eleven issues, when the main novel that kept readers coming back (later successfully released separately as *Sophia*) ended.[29]

In addition, Lennox tried to publish works by subscription to an extent previously unknown.[30] Three proposals for subscription editions of her works are collected for the first time in the present volume—*Poems* in 1752, *Original Works* in 1775, and *SI* in 1793—but there were at least two more attempts at this form of publication: The 1775 *Works* superseded a proposed subscription edition of *FQ* Lennox had been working on two years previously, and the 1793 *SI* was followed only a year or two later by the plan for a subscription edition of an opera, probably *Philander*. Contrary to the wide-spread perception that subscription publication was dying out at the end of the eighteenth century, it was actually just arriving at the height of its popularity. According to Peter John Wallis's *Book Subscription Lists: Extended Supplement to the Revised Guide*, the numbers of books published by subscription had stabilized between 1730 and 1770 at about 330 per decade, rose slightly between 1770 and 1790, and then jumped dramatically to 660 in the 1790s and 886 in the 1800s.[31] Thus, Lennox was perfectly timely with all three of her surviving proposals.

With her subscription editions, Lennox followed the general format of these publications. Many books offered this way were not new, just as none of Lennox's projects contained new material—except corrections and revisions, and a few new items for the *Original Works*. In the case of the surviving proposals, the format of the books was improved to make them more presentable: The *Poems* changed from an octavo to a quarto edition, and the *Original Works* were also quarto. Similarly, the original duodecimo of the 1753/54 *SI* was supposed to be enlarged to octavo, and—according to the proposal—was to be "elegantly printed" (#78). Nevertheless, for unknown reasons not a single one of Lennox's subscription editions ever materialized. The booksellers can probably not be blamed—they were all renowned publishers and had even frequently worked together successfully. The price of the subscriptions was not outrageous, so the public should not have had financial objections. In the absence of such obvious reasons, the suspicion must arise that perhaps readers were simply not interested in the particular writings of Charlotte Lennox offered at these specific times. Lennox's *Poems* had not met with huge success in the first place, and her main literary talent was not as a poet. Furthermore, the title was probably not very appealing—in the 1740s and 1750s alone, a total of at least 50 authors had collections with this title. The situation with *SI* in 1793 was even worse: Since the Garrick-led recuperation of Shakespeare in English letters, any negative opinions of that author would have been unwelcome, and Lennox's scathing criticism had not been forgotten, as the reactions to her drama *The Sister* demonstrate (#45). For her *Original Works*, the explanation of failure is less obvious, but in addition to residual negative sentiment because of the Shakespeare debates it can be speculated that since she had not published an original novel in over a decade, the mild success of *Old City Manners* was not enough to revive interest in the rest of her writing. In other words, the subscription proposals show an author aware of the various possibilities of publication that might improve her financial situation but not as attuned to, or lucky with, the reading desires of the public. In addition, Lennox's practices in securing subscriptions were apparently not entirely appropriate. According to one letter from Johnson, she pressured Frances Reynolds into using her connections at her brother's to solicit subscriptions, but Sir Joshua hid the applications. Here, Johnson tells her that "too much eagerness defeats itself" (#56) and advised her to have patience. Clearly, some subscriptions were sold (#80), but at least one correspondent complained that Lennox was trying to initiate another subscription edition before the previous one—for which she had sold subscriptions—had made it into print (#82). In other words, exploiting different avenues of publication was not enough to find success in the eighteenth-century literary marketplace: Authors also had to be able to assess the public's interest in particular works. In that aspect, Charlotte Lennox was not very successful.

In addition to deferring to colleagues like Johnson and Garrick, reacting to the copyright decision of 1774, and exploring various modes of publication, it appears Lennox entered the new market in periodical publication in the 1780s in her own name and in the name of her son George Louis Lennox. These publications (and some other material) are collected in the third section of this volume and illuminate the personal and professional struggles Lennox experienced.

First, the collection of papers discovered by Duncan Isles and now deposited at the Houghton Library contains an individual poem on Harriet[32] Holles Lennox and a series of six poems about Lennox. The former poem appears to be an epitaph on Lennox's daughter, who died at the young age of seventeen, leaving her mother devastated. Since this poem is written in Lennox's handwriting—and because of the subject matter—there is a good chance the poem is by her. Lennox clearly dealt with the experience of her daughter's death for a long time: Even twenty years later Lady Frances Chambers commented that Lennox had "lost in her daughter the only friend she had a claim upon" (#A13). Lennox might also be the author of the anonymous "On the Death of Miss Henrietta Hollis Lennox," a four-stanza reflection on Lennox's daughter first published in 1793 (#B15). The editor of the collection in which the poem appeared is unknown, and there are no other indications in the surrounding material about its authorship, but it does not seem unreasonable to suspect that Lennox wrote this poem.

The latter series of six poems from the Houghton Library consists mostly of praises of Lennox, comparing her to the poetess Sappho and to a Greek goddess and calling her a "happy genius" (#B2). However, there is also an interesting exchange (in anapestic meter) where one anonymous writer mentions Lennox's supposedly pitted face as a balance to her poetic prowess, which is answered by another author accusing the previous writer of being envious of Lennox. Even though these poems are written in Lennox's handwriting, the contents make it unlikely that they are by her. Three of the poems claim to be copied from magazines or newspapers, but neither Duncan Isles nor I have been able to find any sources. For the time being, then, the authorship of these poems remains a mystery. Still, this material can be taken as a gage of Lennox's reputation some time in the second half of the eighteenth century: sometimes criticized as an individual, but always praised as an excellent writer. It also shows that she was important enough in the literary marketplace that others wrote about her.

But more significantly in their contribution to our knowledge about Lennox's career, I have collected in #B below nine poems and two stories published in a wide variety of periodicals (*British Magazine, Edinburgh Weekly Magazine, New Novelist's Magazine, Whitehall Evening Post, Weekly Entertainer, Hibernian Magazine, Wit's Magazine*) between 1783 and 1786 attributed to Lennox's son George Louis (as well as one poem praising his abilities as a poet). Because of the boy's age and because of the material circumstances in which they were published, I suspect that these poems and stories were written by Lennox herself. Even if they were not, though, their existence in print still indicates an involvement in the literary marketplace that was previously unknown: If George Louis was ten years old, certainly his mother would have facilitated the publication.

The earlier poems are mostly pastoral and sentimental, written in iambs and dactyls, with characters like Sylvana and Calista, Strephon and Palemon. Almost all of these poems end tragically for the female protagonists with their lovers abandoning them, their fiancés falling in battle, or themselves dying. A small number of poems address more topical subjects, like the actress Mary

Ann Yates (#B3), the prime minister (#B11), and a lady with a son who has turned out poorly (#B12). Two poems that are particularly interesting are "Verses Written in the Character of an Unfortunate Young Lady" (#B8) and "Verses on a Beautiful Young Lady" (#B10). The lady in the former poem is unfortunate because she hears a church bell, which reminds her of "some poor departed soul." In the latter poem, the narrative persona sees the young lady "[o]n the dire bed of sickness laid" and by the end has to "number [her] with the dead." These poems appear to be autobiographical, since there is a striking connection to the situation George Louis must have experienced in 1783 with the sickness and death of his sister, Harriet Holles. Considering Lennox's probable involvement in publication, they offer a surprising amount of publicizing of her grief.

The short story "Annette," set in the rural France of Henri IV (1553–1610), is a fairly straightforward sentimental tale—with two twists that complicate the moral lesson. The young Eloisa is beautiful and vain; her sister Adelaide plain and virtuous. Having to decide between two noble suitors, Eloisa unsurprisingly marries the one with rank and money, but commits adultery with the other. Of course, she is discovered and ends up going into a cloister. In contrast, Adelaide is ready to suppress her passion because she is lower in status than her lover, but true love prevails and she marries into a noble family. "Annette" is strikingly similar to Lennox's novel *Sophia* in its constellation of characters, though there the more beautiful sister goes straight to being a mistress rather than taking the detour of marriage. However, two aspects of the short story are unique. First, the difference between the young women is a reflection of their parents. The eponymous mother Annette is similar to her daughter Eloisa, considering beauty a woman's most important asset in the marriage market and ignoring social convention to the extent of breaking one marriage contract for a more advantageous one. Since this is a position rejected by most eighteenth-century moralists, it is remarkable that Annette gives the story its title. Her husband Beauville is more traditional in that he values virtue over beauty, and the story has a conservative ending in that virtue wins over beauty. The second aspect of "Annette" that is interesting is that the story is set up like a fairy tale: The fairy Orinda lets each parent choose the main character trait for one daughter before her birth. Annette is set up as a sentimental character from the beginning, rescuing a stag (which turns out to be the fairy) from hunters and refusing to pick a reward for herself (she chooses to reward her unborn daughter instead)—but then makes a wrong choice by asking only for beauty for Eloisa. In contrast, commenting that different people find happiness in different ways, Beauville asks Orinda to give his second daughter virtue, which turns out to be the correct decision. Thus, "Annette" can be construed as a rejection of sentimentalism or at least as a validation of one form of sentimentalism over another. The female title character embraces a version of sentimentalism that leads to morally unacceptable results, while the only older male in the story makes all the right choices. However, the moral lesson remains unclear, at least between the two young women, because both can only behave according to the choices their parents have made for them. In other words, the blame for Eloisa's actions really lies with her mother, while Adelaide does not deserve praise for her virtue, for which Beauville is responsible.

The second (and much longer) short story attributed to George Louis Lennox is a similar, but much clearer sentimental tale. The young Evadne, daughter of Don Ferdinand, lives in seclusion in the countryside. On her only walk outside her home, she sees Lothario, the promiscuous Duke of Milan, and falls in love with him. Don Ferdinand realizes something is wrong with her, but cannot determine what it is. While she is alone in the countryside, Evadne falls from her horse and is rescued by Don Louis, who soon wants to marry her. When Don Ferdinand discovers the reason for Evadne's melancholy, he is all in favor of the match with Don Louis because of Lothario's reputation. However, before the marriage Evadne meets the mysterious Louisa, who it turns out was previously engaged to Don Louis. Evadne reunites the two lovers and escapes getting married herself. Subsequently, Lothario tries to use Don Louis to communicate with and seduce Evadne, but all attempts fail. In the end, Lothario repents of his licentiousness (becoming a reformed rake), proposes to Evadne, and the two marry.

Again, there are slight parallels to fiction by Lennox, most prominently in the figure of a young woman raised in seclusion in the country, who is like Arabella in *FQ*. There is even a reference to *Don Quixote* to emphasize the connection. Otherwise, though, the story is not very complex or challenging. Two points of friction, however, encourage a closer look. For one, the two female figures (Evadne and Louisa) are interesting in the way they are trapped in, and try to escape, their female roles. Evadne does love Lothario, but because she is aware of his reputation she resists her feelings to the extent of going to a convent. On the one hand, this is a capitulation to a patriarchal threat; on the other, she is escaping to the only female community available in the (fictional) eighteenth century. Similarly, Louisa has no recourse after she is abandoned by her fiancé but to stalk his new love-interest. Later, she is caught between the interests of friendship and marriage when her husband Don Louis asks her to convey Lothario's inappropriate messages to Evadne. Louisa refuses, but is implicated enough for Evadne to become angry at her. The two reconcile, but the friendship does not recover entirely. The other interesting point of frisson in the story is Don Louis's position. The last paragraph of "The Duke of Milan" says that Don Louis is "treated with cold

politeness" after Evadne and Lothario are married because of his previous
support of Lothario's intent to make Evadne his mistress. The conclusion of
the story opposes the flattery of the courtier with the firmness of the true subject who challenges his ruler, so it seems that Don Louis is being condemned.
However, without his intervention the marriage would never have happened,
so he cannot be criticized unambiguously. Similarly, there is no indication
that he has a choice about whether he wants to be a courtier, so again it is too
simple to blame him for being in a position he has not voluntarily selected.
In both stories, therefore, it seems that the author complicates the idea of
moral choice with the problem of the individual's situation and obligations
in society.

According to the original publications, Lennox's son George Louis Lennox
was the author of these poems and stories. If this was indeed the case, George
Louis must have been a remarkable prodigy, producing poetry at short notice
(after the installation of a new prime minister) and composing quite lengthy
tales ("The Duke of Milan" has almost 14,000 words) at the age of about
ten or eleven. If the author was really so young, it is perhaps not a surprise
that he would use plot constellations and character traits he knew from the
works of his mother. However, the literary quality of the poems and stories
is extraordinarily high for a ten-year-old, and if that ten-year-old was really
so talented it seems surprising that he never published literature again, especially if his family was in such financial straits. All this raises the suspicion
that the poems and stories were really written by Lennox herself.

At the very least, there are some indications that Lennox helped her son
hone his skills. In addition to the similar plots and characters, right after the
start of the series of poems the *British Magazine,* the *Edinburgh Weekly
Magazine,* and the *Whitehall Evening Post* printed "Memoirs" of Lennox
(see Tab. 1 below). Also, the entire series was interspersed with poems and
fiction that are by Lennox rather than her son. For instance, when the *Wit's
Magazine* printed George Louis's "The Fate of Sophia" in 1784 the poem
was immediately preceded by another one titled, "Extempore: On Reading a
Poem Written by a Lady of Quality" (1 [1784]: 75). This poem is only signed
"L——." but Lennox is the author: It first appeared in the first issue of her
periodical *LM* in 1760. Later, the *New Novelist's Magazine* printed "Annette"
and "The Duke of Milan" by George Louis, but also "The Tale of Geneura,"
which Lennox had previously included in *SI,* and "The History of the Count
de Comminge," which was excerpted from her *Memoirs of the Countess of
Berci.* Of course this does not prove that George Louis was not the author of
the works attributed to him, but it does hint at a different answer to the question of how such a young boy was able to write such accomplished literature:
His experienced mother had helped him. There are other connections between

the poems and Lennox—for instance the sad references to a deceased young woman in #B8 and #B10, which might refer to her daughter Harriet Holles, or the reference in #B3 to the actress Mary Ann Yates, who was a friend of Lennox's—that raise same the question. One possible explanation for this entire situation is that Lennox was promoting the publication of these poems and stories—whether they were entirely by George Louis, by mother and son together, or completely by Lennox—to put her own name in the limelight again. If this was her intention, she unfortunately did not succeed (beyond perhaps the publication of *Euphemia*), but spent the rest of her life neglected and in poverty.

CHARLOTTE LENNOX AT THE END OF HER LIFE

Lennox's lack of financial success—in spite of listening to more successful writers, paying careful attention to the implications of copyright decisions, exploring various form of publication, and promoting her son's (or her own) writing—became even more pronounced towards the end of her life. Since little correspondence from the 1780s survives, it is impossible to know what Lennox was doing in that decade beyond promoting the publication of poetry and stories under the name of her son George Louis—except perhaps *writing* those poems and stories. After about 1790, her literary production seems to have dried up entirely, while her health declined. Perhaps one of the reasons for her silence in the 1770s and 1780s was that she concentrated on raising her children Harriet Holles (who died in 1783/84) and George Louis—there are various references in the correspondence to their schooling, and in one case Harriet Holles even contributed to a letter to her godmother, Lady Lydia Clerke (#63).

However, in the early 1790s (after the publication of her last novel, *Euphemia,* in 1790), Lennox became active again in two ways: She applied to the Royal Literary Fund for financial assistance, and she engaged in correspondence with the Boswell family. The latter activity was a continuation of her use of literary patronage from the very beginning of her career as well as of her attempts at subscription publication. Apparently, Samuel Johnson had written at least the 1775 proposal for the *Original Works*; now, Lennox appealed directly to James Boswell to continue that tradition, asking him, "Will you Sir be in the place of dear Doctor Johnson to me on this occasion, and employ your elegant pen for half an hour, in drawing up my Proposals?" (#76). When Lennox wrote this letter in 1793, Boswell had recently become literary London's greatest celebrity: His *Life of Johnson* had been published in 1791. While early in her career Lennox had been patronized by the likes

Tab. 1.   Chronological List of Miscellaneous Publications Attributed to Charlotte Lennox and George Louis Lennox

Item	Title	Author	British Magazine and Review	Edinburgh Weekly Magazine	New Novelist's Magazine	Other Publications
B3	"Elegy [. . .] on Mrs. Yates"	GLL	June 1783	10/02/1783		Whitehall Evening Post, 07/15/1783
	"Memoirs" of Lennox	anon.	July 1783	10/09/1783		Whitehall Evening Post, 08/23/1783
B4	"Laura"	GLL	July 1783	09/25/1783		
B5	"Sylvana"	GLL	August 1783	10/29/1783		
B6	"On Miss Lenox"	GLL	August 1783	10/29/1783		
B7	"Verses, Occasioned by [...] Master George Louis Lenox"	anon.	September 1783	11/27/1783		
B8	"Verses Written in the Character of an Unfortunate Young Lady"	GLL	September 1783			Weekly Entertainer, 07/31/1786
B9	"Annette"	GLL	October 1783	12/18/1783	1786	Hibernian Magazine, December 1783; Gleaner, 1804

No.	Title		Date		Publication
B10	"Verses on a Beautiful Young Lady"	GLL	October 1783		*Weekly Entertainer,* 11/13/1786
B11	"Verses Addressed to the Prime-Minister"	GLL	November 1783	03/04/1784	
B12	"Verses, to a Young Married Lady"	GLL	December 1783		
B13	"The Fate of Sophia"	GLL		04/29/1784	*Wit's Magazine,* 1784
	"Extempore: On Reading a Poem Written by a Lady of Quality"	CL			*Wit's Magazine,* 1784
B14	"The Duke of Milan"	GLL		1786	*Weekly Entertainer,* 04/23/1787
	"The Tale of Geneura. From the Italian of Ariosto"	CL		1786	
	"The History of the Count de Comminge"	CL		1787	*Town and Country Magazine,* January 1781; *Hibernian Magazine,* February 1781

of Johnson, Richardson, and Fielding, now she solicited patronage from their successor. Boswell acceded to Lennox's request to the extent of writing the proposals for a subscription edition of *SI,* but the edition never came out.

At the same time, Lennox seems to have developed a stronger connection to the Boswell family than she ever did to the families of Johnson, Richardson, or Fielding—there are references to Boswell's children, and letters to both his oldest son, Alexander (Sandy), and to his oldest daughter, Veronica, survive. While the letter from Alexander is rather formal and concerns Lennox's enquiries into the state of her husband Alexander's attempts to win property in Scotland (#79), the letter to Veronica is more familiar, talking about her father's latest writings as well as social visits of other members of the Boswell family (#83). It can be speculated that Lennox, who was in her seventies in 1793/94, may have taken a maternal or grandmaternal role particularly with Boswell's daughters after their mother's death in 1789. But even more than that, Lennox appears to have developed relationships with women in a way that she did not earlier in her life, when according to Frances Burney, "Mrs. Thrale says that though her *Books* are generally approved, Nobody likes *her.*"[33] Later in life, Lennox corresponded with Mary Gwyn (although not in the friendliest of tones) and communicated with Frances Reynolds. At one point, Lennox used Reynolds's address, leading to speculation that the two lived together— but that seems unlikely since there is no corroborating evidence from either Frances or Joshua Reynolds. Nevertheless, this is another example of Lennox expanding an earlier relationship with a male (Joshua Reynolds) to include a female (his sister) and to advance her own agenda, here soliciting subscriptions. At this late point in her life, subscribers may not really have expected the production of books, but rather considered their subscriptions as a kind of charity for the indigent author.

This charity was more explicitly provided by the RLF. The RLF was founded in 1788 by the theologian and educator David Williams as a "Society, to support authors in distress; and to afford temporary relief to the widows and children of those who have any claim on public gratitude or humanity, from literary merit or industry."[34] In his debate clubs with friends like Benjamin Franklin and Adam Smith, Williams had floated a similar idea as early as 1773, but had found no support. He had approached politicians such as Charles Fox and Edmund Burke with just as little success. A newspaper advertisement in October 1786 asking for subscriptions *For the Friends of a Literary Fund* met no response.[35] At this time, a first version of the *Constitutions* was printed. Then, Williams's "luck changed in 1787 when classicist Floyer Sydenham died in a debtors' prison."[36] This event demonstrated how even prominent authors could become indigent and confirmed the need for a charity for writers. Early in 1788, a group of nine men got together—Alexander Blair, Thomas Dale, Hugh Downman, Alexander Johnson, James Martin, Robert Mitchell, J. F. Rigaud, Isaac Swainson, and Williams himself—and wrote an advertisement for a literary fund that ran in London newspapers starting on May 24, 1788. Simultaneously, a second version of the *Constitutions* was released, this one for a "Society to support men of genius and learning in distress."[37] This effort bore fruit—perhaps because now, as Cross argues, there had been a rapid expansion of the book trade (including the introduction of children's and pocket books), a rise of authorship as a profession, and a concomitant growing interest in authors.[38] Now, money arrived at the banker named in the advertisement, prominent individuals such as John Nichols and Captain Thomas Morris joined the project, and in 1790 the RLF gave out charity for the first time.

In that year, the RLF paid money to only one author. The following year, five individuals were relieved of distress (four authors and one widow), and in 1792, twelve. The first eleven applicants to the RLF had been

- Lieutenant Samuel Stanton, an officer who had written on dueling and the slave trade,
- Rev. Edward Harwood, a dissenting clergyman,
- Rev. William Tasker of Iddesley in Devon,
- John Louis De Lolme, a writer of political tracts,
- the widow of Rev. Philip Withers, who had written theological works,
- Alexander Bicknell, an author of sixteen histories, romances, and novels,
- Charles Allen, a private teacher of classics,
- the actor and dramatist Charles Macklin,
- Elizabeth Coxeter, the daughter of the editor and poet Thomas Coxeter,
- Charles Geneviève Louise Auguste André Timothée, Le Chevalier D'Eon, the notorious transvestite or transsexual, and
- Rev. Joseph Trapp, a German minister.

With the exception of Stanton, all of these applicants received financial assistance from the RLF. The twelfth applicant was Lennox, who was thus one of the first applicants in general, only the third woman, and the first woman to apply who was an author in her own right rather than the widow or daughter of a writer. The materials concerning Lennox contained in the RLF files are collected below in #A. Unfortunately, the exact circumstances of her application are unknown, but it was immediately approved: In May 1792, she was awarded ten guineas. A year later, Lennox applied to the RLF again with the only letter of hers surviving in the RLF file. This time, she specifically asked for money to send her son George Louis to the United States. Here, like other female authors who approached the RLF,[39] she presented herself as a distressed mother rather than as an accomplished author, requesting money to send her son to the American colonies. Once again, the RLF complied, and apparently George Louis made his passage to Norfolk and Baltimore in August 1793. After this, Lennox did not approach the RLF for almost a decade.

During this time, the RLF was developing rapidly. The first group of supporters included individuals from all parts of the political spectrum—radicals, reformers, Tories, and monarchists. Starting in 1792, the RLF published annual reports and held annual dinners with guests of honor like the Prince of Wales and the King of Belgium, "serving the dual function of attracting extra subscriptions and drawing public attention to its charitable work."[40] The fund grew, and in addition to subscriptions the society started collecting money for a permanent endowment. At this time, Williams still envisioned the society as ultimately encompassing a college, a library, and an archive. More and more members were called to be officers as vice-presidents, committee and council members, treasurers, and registrars. Aristocratic support was secured with the Marquess of Bute as the first president (1799–1801) and the Duke of Somerset as the second (1801–38). In 1801, the RLF asked Williams to write a history of the society, which was published in 1802 (including a list of subscribers) as *Claims of Literature: The Origins, Motives, Objects, and Transactions of the Society for the Establishment of a Literary Fund.* At this time, Williams came under fire for not raising enough money, for being too radical, and for not recruiting enough men of letters to support the organization, rather than receive assistance from it. Nevertheless, the RLF continued to grow, and in 1806 it moved into its new headquarters at 36 Gerrard Street in Soho. By then, Lennox had been dead for two years. However, the last two years of her life would have been much more difficult without the RLF. Apparently, William Beloe and Lady Frances Chambers—perhaps inspired by the late Bennet Langton—started lobbying for assistance for Lennox in January 1802, and the society immediately responded by giving her £10. Subsequently, she received a kind of regular pension which continued until her death in January 1804. During this time, she was frequently sick, apparently had no family or friends left, and seemed to suffer from memory loss—but at least the RLF remained a consistent source of income until her death.

This charitable support rounds out Lennox's career in two ways. First, it demonstrates that she still had some support and that she was thought to have a good reputation. Her case was brought forward by William Beloe, a well-known writer and antiquary, and by Lady Frances Chambers, a prominent member of the aristocracy. Beloe's backing indicates that Lennox was well-regarded in the literary community—indeed, in his memoirs he lists her in a company of "the most distinguished literary characters of the time" the first time he meets her.[41] In Lady Chambers, Lennox once again had upper-class patronage, this time from a woman well-connected in political and court circles through her husband, the judge Sir Robert Chambers. Like at the beginning of her career, Lennox could count on patronage from the literate middle class and from the aristocracy. This patronage could not have happened if her reputation had not been impeccable: Other female authors were rejected by the RLF for not being proper enough. Furthermore, Lennox was apparently able to get away with sending the RLF no formal acknowledgment for their financial assistance, even though regular assistance of the kind she received was rather rare and even though the RLF had specifically decided to demand acknowledgment from their beneficiaries. Of course, if Lennox was suffering from dementia or Alzheimer's disease, the RLF would have known this and would not have expected a response.

At the same time, the support from the RLF shows that for Lennox, writing as a profession and career had ultimately failed. The precondition for support from the RLF was that writers were demonstrably indigent, which was certainly the case for Lennox: One letter from her correspondence comments quite cruelly on her poor physical condition (#86), and the RLF file documents her continuing deterioration close to the time of her death. More successful writers in her situation would have saved money to supply their expenses in old age, but Lennox had not been able to do that. Many reasons can be cited for her ultimate financial failure. For instance, earlier she had pointed patrons to her husband rather than taking positions herself. Then, her health had never been very good. Her children had been born late in life, and—judging from the poetry collected below in #B—the loss of her daughter at a young age apparently incapacitated her emotionally as well. Since she lived such a long life herself, many of her connections in the literary marketplace and in the world of patronage simply died. The taste in literature had changed, and the kind of novels Lennox wrote in the 1750s and 1760s were not much in demand anymore. Perhaps she mis-speculated by relying on male friends and aristocratic patrons to stay solvent. In any case, she died in penury, supported only by the meager assistance of the RLF, and was buried at an unknown location.

CHARLOTTE LENNOX TODAY

After her death in 1804, Lennox stayed in the literary imagination for a while with republications of *FQ* around the turn of the century and occasional memoirs in periodicals like *The Lady's Monthly Museum*.[42] At that time, she was still included in most reference works of British literature. Subsequently, though, Lennox was mostly forgotten, and her works vanished into obscurity as women in general were written out of the canon and literary critics of eighteenth-century British literature like Ian Watt concentrated on the tradition of Defoe, Fielding, and Richardson. Lennox was only rediscovered when critics began to consider feminist concerns and recover women writers in the 1970s and 1980s. Yet, while *FQ* began to re-enter the canon of British literature with its re-publication in 1970, Lennox's other work remained shrouded in obscurity. In 1974, John Wain offered a parenthetical remark on Lennox's first novel *HS* in his biography of Johnson: "I have not read this book, nor met anyone who has, but it is said to be largely autobiographical, and certainly 'Harriot Stuart' is exactly the same kind of name as 'Charlotte Ramsay.'"[43] Fortunately, this kind of comment has become less and less common, and recently five of Lennox's novels—*HS, Henrietta, Sophia,* and *Euphemia,* along with a second edition of *FQ*—have been republished in modern critical editions.

While this recuperation of Lennox's work can only be welcomed, it leaves a serious lack in terms of understanding the author as a person and as a professional. This lack is addressed in the present collection of materials. Here, we see Charlotte Lennox as an individual who strove to establish herself in the literary marketplace not so much as an original genius, but as a producer of works to be consumed by the new reading public of the eighteenth century. Lennox emerges as a savvy operator who tried to hold on to the established format of subscription publication, exploit connections with patrons in the literary middle class as well as the gentry and aristocracy, and negotiate with booksellers over her (or rather, her husband's—and perhaps her son's) property. She kept abreast of legal developments and turned them to her advantage with some success, while she also approached the RLF, a new institution, for financial support. Because of these professional skills, because of her position as a female author, and of course because of her literary talent, we can appreciate and honor Charlotte Lennox by understanding the depth of her achievement in the terms presented in her correspondence.

NOTES

1. Isles 317.

2. See Carlile. To date, the most extensive account of Lennox's life remains 70 pages in Small. Carlile is working on a new biography.

3. In the eighteenth century, the author's name was sometimes spelled "Lennox" and sometimes "Lenox." The uncertainty can be seen in the Royal Literary Fund file, where in three cases "Lenox" was corrected to "Lennox" (#A16, #A17, #A19).

4. Hawkins, *Life* 172. On the evaluation of Hawkins's work, see O M Brack Jr., "Re-Assessing Sir John Hawkins's *The Life of Samuel Johnson, LL.D.*: Some Reflections," in *Reconsidering Biography: Contexts, Controversies, and Sir John Hawkins' "Life of Johnson,"* ed. Martine Watson Brownley (Lewisburg: Bucknell University Press, forthcoming).

5. On canon formation in the eighteenth century, see for instance Trevor Ross, *The Making of the English Literary Canon* (Montreal: McGill-Queen's University Press, 1998) and Jonathan Brody Kramnick, *Making the English Canon* (Cambridge: Cambridge University Press, 1998).

6. John Mitford, "Dr. Johnson's Literary Intercourse with Mrs. Lennox," *Gentleman's Magazine* n.s. 20.2 (August 1843): 132.

7. Hazen 89.

8. Mitford, "Dr. Johnson's Literary Intercourse" 132.

9. John Mitford, "Chapter by Dr. Johnson in 'The Female Quixote,'" *Gentleman's Magazine* n.s. 21.2 (January 1844): 41–48, here 41.

10. Fleeman I 323–33.

11. This individual is various referred to by contemporary scholars as Boyle or Orrery. I will refer to him as 'Orrery.'

12. On literary patronage, see Dustin Griffin *Literary Patronage in England, 1650–1800* (Cambridge: Cambridge University Press, 1996) and Michael Foss *The Age of Patronage. The Arts in England 1660–1750* (Ithaca: Cornell University Press, 1971).

13. On this topic, see Betty Schellenberg, *The Professionalization of Women Writers in Eighteenth-Century Britain* (Cambridge: Cambridge University Press, 2005).

14. See Raven, "Introduction" I 51–54.

15. See Eric Walker, "Charlotte Lennox and the Collier Sisters: Two New Johnson Letters," *Studies in Philology* 94.3 (Summer 1998): 320–32 and #2 below.

16. On the Orrerys, see McGarvie and Mildred Price, *The Literary Life and Position in the Eighteenth Century of John, Earl of Orrery* (Diss., Smith College, 1948).

17. Raven, *Business* 278.

18. On this issue, see for instance Leonard Orr, who writes that "it is generally agreed that Johnson either wrote or directed" the chapter ("Johnson and the Penultimate Chapter of Lennox's *The Female Quixote*," *Enlightenment Essays* 8 [1977]: 66) or Margaret Dalziel, who more cautiously suggests that "the attribution of the chapter to Johnson remains a plausible theory" (Charlotte Lennox, *The Female Quixote* [ed. Margaret Dalziel; Oxford: Oxford University Press, 1970]: 415).

19. This section title deliberately echoes the title of Mark Rose's excellent book, *Authors and Owners.* I rely mostly on Rose in my discussion of copyright below.

20. Hazen 90.

21. Fleeman I 709–12.

22. Fleeman II 1006–7. Fleeman writes that "Hamilton Boyle, 6th E. of Cork & Orrery [John Boyle's son] contributed the 'Preface' and was otherwise involved" (II 1006), but this seems highly unlikely considering Orrery's comments about the preface in #35, unless he is talking there about revising his *son's* work.

23. Of course, Lennox could also merely have been flattering Garrick.

24. However, some recent critics argue that the impact of the decision has been over-estimated: see Raven, *Business* 230–38 and Thomas Bonnell, *The Most Disreputable Trade: Publishing the Classics of English Poetry 1765–1810* (Oxford: Oxford University Press, 2008), 31–34.

25. Rose 78.

26. Rose 98.

27. See also #40, the memorandum between Alexander Lennox and James Dodsley about Lennox's *The History of Eliza*—the novel legally belonged to Alexander, not his wife.

28. The beginning of this shift in conceptions of authorship is frequently dated with Edward Young's *Conjectures on Original Composition* (London: Millar and Dodsley, 1759).

29. See my edition of *Sophia* (Peterborough, Ontario: Broadview, 2008).

30. On subscription publication, see the references in #14.

31. Cf. Wallis viii.

32. Lennox's daughter's name was sometimes spelled "Harriet," sometimes "Harriot."

33. Burney III/1 105.

34. *Constitutions of a Society, to Support Authors in Distress* (N.p.: n.p., [1786]), title page. The history of the RLF is traced in David Williams's own publications, *Claims* and *Incidents in My Own Life* (ed. Peter France; Brighton: University of Sussex Library, 1980). Two biographies of Williams—Jones and *David Williams: Founder of the Royal Literary Fund* by E.V. Lucas (London: Murray, 1920)—include information on the RLF as well. The best contemporary histories of the RLF are by Nigel Cross: "Literature and Charity: The Royal Literary Fund from David Williams to Charles Dickens" in his *The Common Writer: Life in Nineteenth-Century Grub Street* (Cambridge: Cambridge University Press, 1985), 8–37 and *The Royal Literary Fund 1790–1918* (London: World Microfilms Publications, 1984).

35. *Claims* 103.

36. Cross, *Royal Literary Fund* 10.

37. *Constitutions of a Society, to Support Men of Genius and Learning in Distress* (London: Nichols et al., 1788).

38. Cross, *Royal Literary Fund* 11.

39. See Jennie Batchelor, "The Claims of Literature: Women Applicants to the Royal Literary Fund, 1790–1810," *Women's Writing* 12.3 (2005): 505–21.

40. Cross, *Royal Literary Fund* 13.

41. William Beloe, *The Sexagenarian; or, The Recollections of a Literary Life* (2 vols.; London: Rivington, 1817), I 401.

42. Anon., "Memoir of Mrs. Lennox," *The Lady's Monthly Museum*, n.s. 14.6 (June 1813): 313–15. Reprinted in my edition of Lennox's *Sophia*, 213–16.

43. John Wain, *Samuel Johnson* (London: Macmillan, 1974), 160.

Correspondence

1

Samuel Johnson
to Charlotte Lennox

[LATE 1750[1]]

MS:	Houghton Library, Harvard University, MS Eng 1269 (3)
Pages:	1
Edition:	LC #1, Redford I 46–47
Address:	To Mrs Lenox
Text:	

Madam

I will speak to Mr Payne[2] and to Mr
Cave,[3] and hope to prevail with bothe the
one and the other to do as You would wish,
but cannot promise, what another man will
do. I shall endeavour at least to bring the
whole affair to succeed.[4] What you mention
I certainly told You,[5] but I did not tell it as
coming from Mr Payne, but as my opinion, and
I am inclined to believe, that they refused[6]
rather from some present want of Money[7]
than from any unwillingness to oblige You

> I am,
> Madam,
> Your most humble Servant
> Sam: Johnson

NOTES

1. On the dating of this letter, cf. n.4.

2. John Payne (d. 1787) worked in the book trade as well as the Bank of England for most of his life. He started at the Bank in 1744, became a chief clerk in 1769, deputy accountant-general in 1773, and was accountant-general from 1780 to 1785. As a publisher, Payne established himself in Paternoster Row around 1740 and later joined forces with Joseph Bouquet—with whom he published *HS* in December 1750. Payne corresponded with literary figures such as Thomas Birch (see #33) and wrote Christian literature himself. He became friends with Johnson as early as 1749, when he was elected member of the latter's Ivy Lane Club, which held the infamous celebration of *HS* in 1751. It is conceivable that this celebration was held in part because Payne was a member of the Ivy Lane Club. Starting in 1750, Payne published Johnson's *Rambler* (with Joseph Bouquet), a profitable enterprise for all involved. One of the most popular anecdotes about the *Rambler* is Payne offering Johnson two guineas per issue, considered a high remuneration at the time. Later, Payne and Bouquet were also part of the consortium that published Hawkesworth's *Adventurer*, to which Johnson contributed some essays. According to Lætitia-Matilda Hawkins (in a story she probably learned from her father Sir John, who was in touch with Payne until the 1780s), Payne fell out with Lennox some time after the publication of *HS* because of Lennox's bad temper. Lennox went to see him "to complain of some want of respect to her amorous story 'Harriot Stuart'" (*Anecdotes* 331), and, when she found out from his mother that Payne was not at home, "assailed the old lady with the eloquence which was intended for the son" (331–32). See also #24 n.1.

William Strahan's ledgers show that he printed *HS*: There is an entry for December 1750 under the title "Messrs Payne and Bouquet D^rs." that reads, "Harriot Stewart, 2 Vols, 20 ½ Sheets N°. 1000 @ £1:7: p Sheet £27 Sh13 P6" (Strahan Papers, British Library Add.Ms. 48800, f.86). There is a separate entry on the same page for half a year later listing "Titles to Harriot Stewart N°.1000, with 6 ½ Quires of Paper Sh10 P6," probably to use as advertisements (see Susan Kubica Howard, "Note on the Text," *The Life of Harriot Stuart*, by Charlotte Lennox, ed. Susan Kubica Howard [Madison: Fairleigh Dickinson University Press, 1995], 59). Similarly, another entry in Strahan's ledgers from July 1762, now under the title "Mr Andrew Millar D^r": "Titles to Harriot Stewart Sh7 P6" (Strahan Papers, British Library Add.Ms. 48800, f.120), is probably for advertisements.

3. Edward Cave (1691–1754) is best known as printer, bookseller, and founder of the *Gentleman's Magazine*, the first magazine. After working for various other periodicals from across the country, Cave published his first number in January 1730/31 under the pseudonym of Sylvanus Urban, Gent. By the end of the decade, his periodical was supposedly selling over 10,000 copies per issue. Johnson worked in various roles for the *Gentleman's Magazine* between 1738 and 1744: as contributor of poems, essays, biographies, translations, as well as the Parliamentary debates, as Cave's most reliable assistant, and for a while as editor. Starting in 1750, Cave participated in the publication of Johnson's *Rambler*, though his role is not quite

clear. According to Rogers, Cave was "[t]he most important figure behind the series on the publishing side" (321–22); according to Fleeman, he was the printer (I 195).

For a while between 1749 and 1751, Cave used the *Gentleman's Magazine* to promote Lennox. First, he published a poem titled "*To Mrs* CHARLOTTE LENNOX, upon seeing her POEMS, and PROPOSALS *for printing them*" in June 1749 (XIX 278), and then another called "*To Mrs* CHARLOTTE LENNOX. *On reading her Poems, printing by Subscription, in one Vol. 8vo, price 5 s*" signed by the unknown E.N. as well as "The ART of COQUETRY" and "AN ODE *On the Birth Day of Her Royal Highness the Princess of* Wales" by Lennox in November 1750 (XX 518–19; this was probably about the time of the writing of this letter). In December 1750, he included *HS* in his list of books and pamphlets in the category "*Poetry, Plays, and Entertainment*," describing it glowingly thus: "These volumes contain a series of love-affairs from 11 years of age, attended with a number of her adventures and misfortunes, which were borne with the patience, and are penn'd with the purity of a *Clarissa*. No part of the history is short enough to be detached, nor can it be abridged without great injury to the original" (XX 575). James Kuist's *The Nichols File of* The Gentleman's Magazine (Madison: The University of Wisconsin Press, 1982) does not identify an author for this review, but the favorable reference to *Clarissa* suggests that Johnson may have written or at least was somehow behind the review. In January 1751, however, Cave included a response to "The Art of Coquetry" called "*Advice to the* NOVICE *in* LOVE" (XXI 35). The resistance this poem shows to the first one might be an indication of a change in Cave's position towards Lennox parallel to Payne's falling out with her (see n.2).

4. As Isles argues (334 n.5), the "affair" to which Johnson refers is probably a new edition of Lennox's *Poems*. According to William Strahan's ledgers, Payne and Bouquet paid the printer 15 shillings for "1000 Proposals for Mrs Lennox, with Paper" (Strahan Papers, British Library Add.Ms. 48800, f.85) in October 1750, and since the only original work by Lennox at this time was her *Poems*, this was probably a proposal for subscription edition referred to in the poems of the *Gentleman's Magazine*. On the other hand, the letter was probably written *before* Bouquet's and Cave's change of heart as described in n.2 and n.3. (It also can hardly be taken to refer to the later 1752 proposal for a subscription edition of the *Poems*, where the publishers are Millar and Dodsley; see #14 below.) Therefore, the letter can be dated around or after the publication of the proposal, i.e., late 1750.

5. This perhaps refers to a lost previous letter of Lennox's to which Johnson is responding, or a remark in a previous conversation. It would seem to be a piece of information that Lennox is wrongly attributing to Payne.

6. It is unclear *what* Payne and Cave refused—perhaps another edition of the *Poems*, or of *HS*.

7. This would seem to suggest some sort of cash-flow problem on Payne and Cave's part—or that they simply did not want to work with Lennox.

2

Samuel Richardson
to [Samuel Johnson¹]

NOVEMBER 2, [1751²]

MS: Houghton Library, Harvard University, MS Eng 1269 (2)
Pages: 1
Edition: LC #2
Text:

Dear Sir,

I have not had Time to go through Mʳˢ. Lennox's
Piece: So far as I have read, I very much like it.³

Does the Lady want her Book?⁴ If she does not, I
should be glad to keep it a little longer.

I am concerned, that I was absent when You and She
did me the Favour of a Call in Salisbury Court.⁵ I
have been much indisposed, and likewise much busied,⁶
or I would have craved Leave to thank you for it in
Person. May I hope for a Visit from You and that
Lady? Or, shall I attend you?⁷

The Signification of your Pleasure, either Way, will
greatly oblige, Sir,

Your must humble Servant,

Sat. Nov. 2.   S. Richardson.

I should be glad of a Day's Notice.

You are extremely obliging in what you offer, about the
Paper you favoured with a Place—You will do with it,

what you please. The more it is Yours, the worthier it will be of a Place among Yours.[8] I am glad you are Re-printing the Ramblers.

NOTES

1. The recipient is made clear by Richardson's reference to the *Rambler*.

2. The year is identified through the references to *FQ* and confirmed by November 2 being a Saturday.

3. It can be surmised that at this date, Richardson had received and started to read a copy of the first book of *FQ*, but had not had a chance to finish it.

4. This would seem to refer to the draft of *FQ* Richardson had in his keeping on November 2.

5. Richardson had lived in this house on the west side of Salisbury Court since 1736 (Eaves/Kimpel 64). At the same time, he kept three other houses: two buildings behind Salisbury Court on Hanging-Sword Alley for his business and "a house on the edge of London, on North End Road in Fulham, as a kind of country retreat for himself and his family" (Eaves/Kimpel 495). Lennox and Johnson's visit to Richardson's residence *together* lends some support to Burney's claim about how Johnson introduced her to Richardson (see correspondent's biography).

6. At this time, Richardson was working hard on *Sir Charles Grandison*, in spite of the occasional dry spell. His most avid reader at the time, Catherine Talbot, started reading the manuscript in November 1751, saw the fifth volume of the manuscript in January 1752 and the tenth later the same month (Eaves/Kimpel 373). The health problems he refers to were his "nervous Complaints" that probably constituted a form of Parkinson's disease (Eaves/Kimpel 84), and which regularly attacked him in the spring and fall (Eaves/Kimpel 322)—i.e., the time of the writing of this letter.

7. Johnson's residence at the time was only a few blocks away in Gough Square (Rogers 164–65).

8. Isles's note (336 n.11): "This important postscript apparently refers to SR's contribution to the *Rambler*, namely, No. 97 (Tuesday 19 February 1751). Johnson revised the original *Rambler* papers extensively for the duodecimo collected ed. of 1752, and had obviously asked Richardson for permission to alter No. 97. Apart from re-arranging the paragraphs, the only major alteration in the reprint is the omission of a passage concerning young ladies who frequent public places and the 'young Fellows' who 'buzz around them as Flies about a Carcase.' See *The Rambler*, ed. W.J. Bate and A.B. Strauss (Yale Ed. of the Works of Samuel Johnson, Vols. III–V, New Haven and London, 1969), IV, 153–59." See also John Dussinger, "Samuel Richardson's Manuscript Draft of *The Rambler* No. 97 (19 February 1751)," *Notes and Queries* n.s. 57.1 (March 2010): 93–99.

3

Charlotte Lennox
to [Samuel Richardson[1]]

NOVEMBER 21, 1751

MS: Harvard Theatre Collection, Houghton Library, Harvard University, TS 934.5, III, 296 (TSM 394.39)

Pages: 2

Edition: [Small[2]]

Text:

Nov. 21_1751

Sir

      M[r] Johnson has inform'd me[3] of the generous concern you exprest [sic] for the severity of my Criticks,[4] and your inten tions to rescue my Book[5] from their censures and restore me to M[r] Millar's good opinion,[6] which in my present dependant [sic] situation it much concerns me to preserve.[7] I am not able to express how much I am affected with this instance of your goodness, but I beg you to beleive [sic] that I shall always preserve the most grateful remem brance of it–after the approbation you have been pleasd [sic] to hon our my performance with, I should be inexcusable if I sufferd [sic] any uneasiness from M[r] Gray[8] and his two Associates [sic] Contempt of it. I woud [sic] not appeal from your Judgment and M[r] John son's to that of any Person living,[9] and since your praise might flatter the ambition of any Author whatever surely I have reason to be perfectly happy in it, the censures of my three unmerci ful Criticks have given me no [pain[10]] further then [sic] my apprehen sions of their hurting my interests with M[r] Millar, and as he has neglected to call on me lately,[11] I have no reason to doubt of their influence. tis upon these occasions that inspite [*sic*] of the resignation and patience I indeavour [*sic*] to practice, that I cannot help lamenting the Condition to which fortune has

---

[re^{12}]duced me, and wholly unfit as I am to struggle with the morti [f]ications of a dependant State has yet made it necessary and unavoidable.^{13} I have taken the liberty to send the second Volume of my Book,^{14} and shall with the utmost an xiety expect your opinion of it. I must beg leave to acquaint you, that it being transcribed from my first Copy, it has yet [r]eceived no Corrections,^{15} and is therefore indeed unfit for your [p]erusal, but if with the allowance you will be pleasd to make [up]on that account, it should be so fortunate to meet with your approbation I shall go on with redoubled Spirit.^{16}

> I am with the greatest Respect
> Sir
> Your Must Obligd [*sic*] hum^l Sevt
> Charlotte Lennox

Novr the 21
Plow Court Fetter Lane^{17}
No 22

NOTES

1. The addressee can clearly be deduced from the content of the letter.

2. Small quotes the one sentence known at the time from this letter: "Mr. Johnson has informed me of the generous concern you exprest for the severity of my critics, and your good intentions to rescue my book from their censures, and restore me to Mr. Millar's good opinions" (12). It had been sold at auction at Sotheby's on November 27, 1889 as Lot 102, and this sentence was quoted in the catalog.

3. It is unclear whether Johnson "inform'd" Lennox—maybe in a personal conversation or perhaps in a lost letter.

4. These "Criticks" are probably the unidentified Mr. Gray and his two associates, perhaps including the equally unidentified Mr. Seymour mentioned in the following response to this letter (#4).

5. This reference is to *FQ*, which Lennox had partially written at this point.

6. It appears Millar's readers had rejected *FQ*, or at least expressed reservations about the novel. In this letter, Lennox asks Richardson to use his influence to change Millar's opinion; the next letter (#4) shows Richardson doing just that.

7. Lennox is "dependant" in the sense that she needs Millar to publish her novel.

8. Mr. Gray is one of Andrew Millar's three outside readers. His identity is unknown.

9. Lennox expresses a similar sentiment at several points in *FQ*—see #5.

10. This word is impossible to decipher. It seems to begin with a p or f, and ends with the letters "in." It probably is some synonym of pain, anger, worry, fright, etc.

11. Booksellers calling on their authors was not a common practice, but perhaps more frequent in the case of female authors, who were not as free to travel themselves.

12. Unfortunately, the left margin of the second page of this letter was trimmed while being mounted, so some of the first letters are difficult to make out.

13. This is the first in a long series of Lennox's laments about her financial position. Here, she seems to connect this situation to her gender: The "dependant State" probably means Lennox's dependence on her husband Alexander (and of course her bookseller Millar), and "the Condition to which fortune has [re]duced me" could be a reference to her status as a woman. Alexander Lennox seems to have a bad reputation among Lennox's friends, and there is little indication that he helped alleviate her financial situation.

14. This indicates that Richardson had at this point already seen the first volume of *FQ*, which included books I–IV.

15. This is one of only a few glimpses into the writing life of Lennox: It appears she wrote a first draft which was then copied by herself or others into a cleaner, but still uncorrected draft.

16. Lennox here specifically asks for encouragement in the writing process.

17. John Rocque's 1746 *Plan of the Cities of London and Westminster*, reproduced as *The A to Z of Georgian London* (ed. Harry Margary in association with Guildhall Library, intro. Ralph Hyde [London: London Topographical Society, 1982]) shows a Plow Yard off Fetter Lane (4Ac), while Richard Horwood's 1799 *Map of the Cities of London and Westminster*, reproduced as *The A to Z of Regency London* (ed. Harry Margary in association with Guildhall Library, intro. Paul Laxton [London: London Topographical Society, 1985]) shows a Plough Court (14Bb) in the same place. In other words, the place was considered a yard or a court at various times, and of course the spelling "plow" or "plough" was variable. Presumably on the basis of this letter, Highfil writes that, "As of November 1751 [Lennox] was living at No 22, Plow Court, Fetter Lane" (IX 237).

4

Samuel Richardson
to [Charlotte Lennox[1]]

[November 22, 1751[2]]

MS:	Houghton Library, Harvard University, MS Eng 1269 (17, 18)
Pages:	2
Edition:	LC #3
Text:	

Madam,

I had an Opportunity Yesterday to answer
M[r]. M.[3] of what I thought of your Piece.[4] I
gave it to him in the same sincere manner
that you heard me speak of it to Miss Collier
and Miss Fielding.[5]

M[rs]. Millar and her Sister[6] were present. He
spoke of you, Madam, very respectfully; and mentioned not one Word of any other Person's Opinion,[7]
or of having shown the MS. to any other Person.[8]

I gave him and the Ladies, a brief Detail;[9] and
hinted, how it was to be enter'd into, and consider'd.
It was before I had an Opportunity to read the Sequel.[10]
I was desirous of saying more upon the Subject, as he
had begun it; But we were broke in upon.[11]

I left them about Eight o'Clock, in order to
get home to read the Sequel,[12] as I thought you would
wish its speedy Return. M[r]. Seymour[13] had been
some time below with M[r]. M. And then came
up stairs [*sic*], to us.

If I hear any thing farther, that may be of
    I will acquaint you with it And if I
Service to you to know; ∧ or can do you Service with[14]
M[r]. M. I shall take great Pleasure in the
Opportunity of convincing you, that I am,
             Madam,
Friday Morn.   Your real Friend and humble Serv[t].
             S. Richardson.
I have ventured a few Lines, written as I read.
You will excuse the Liberty.
Excuse Haste.

As[15] you seem'd, Madam, to be apprehensive of Matter falling short for two
Vols. I have taken the Liberty by these Marks, in the beginning Pages [[[16] to
suppose New Paragraphs, which will, in the whole Work, greatly and properly
help you [sic]
    [[17] I am quite charm'd with the lovely Visionary's[18] Absurdity[19]
                                      to
(and the Perplexity which follows it, to Sir Charles, ∧ Glanville
and her self) on her supposing Sir Charles in Love with her.[20]
    But I think, that Sir Georges's [sic] Story, and of his Pretensions to
the Kingdom of Kent,[21] is carried too far. He ought not at least to
have made his Claim so recent—He might have made a Discovery of his Genealogy from the Saxons and the Heptarchy,[22] without
so immediately interesting his Father and Grandfather in it. It
is impossible, but she must know, that there had not been a Kingdom
of Kent for many Generations.[23] And it was too gross for Mr. Glanville
to bear, who had been sollicitous that Sir George should not play upon
Arabella.
    Omit, I beseech you, Madam, the middle Name in the first Line of
p. 238—Utterly unworthy of a Rank, or Mention, with the two others—[24]
    The story of the Highway-Men, and Arabella's Absurdity on their Appear-
ance, very pretty—[25]
You have very pretty Scenes before you, Madam, at Bath and London.[26]

NOTES

    1. Though the addressee is not specified, there can be no doubt due to the exten-
sive comments on *FQ*.
    2. This letter almost certainly constitutes an immediate response to Lennox's
previous letter (#3): Richardson has received, but not yet read, the second installment

of the novel. Since the letter is dated "Friday Morn." and November 22 was a Friday, the date is virtually certain. Isles dates the letter "8 or 15 November 1751" (336), but he is unaware of #3.

3. This is the publisher Andrew Millar.

4. The "Piece" is Lennox's *FQ*, or more precisely the first volume of the book. Here, Richardson describes how he is trying to convince Millar to purchase the copyright to that novel.

5. The two women mentioned here are Sarah Fielding (1710–68; ODNB XIX 511–13: Henry's sister and a successful novelist in her own right with works like *David Simple*) and one of the Collier sisters, Jane or Margaret. Henry Fielding was a friend of the family of Arthur Collier (1680–1732; ODNB XII 635–36), Jane and Margaret's father. Jane Collier (1715–55; ODNB XII 639–40) started living with Sarah Fielding some time in 1751. Jane wrote the satirical *Essay on the Art of Ingeniously Tormenting* (London: Millar, 1753) and co-authored *The Cry: A New Dramatic Fable* (3 vols.; London: Dodsley, 1754) with Sarah Fielding. When the Collier family fell into poverty, Margaret (1719–94; ODNB XII 655–56) lived in Henry Fielding's house as companion first to his daughter and then to his second wife. She accompanied Fielding on his final journey to Lisbon, and she also corresponded with Richardson. There is no way of telling for sure which "Miss Collier" was present on this occasion, though since Jane was living with Sarah Fielding it was probably her.

At this time (and throughout his life), Richardson frequently entertained a circle of friends and admirers, including these women. Lennox might have been a member of this group at least for a while. The reference to Sarah Fielding also suggests that her brother Henry might have known of *FQ* before its publication and long before he wrote his praising review of the novel.

6. From the Strahan ledgers, it is known that Andrew Millar married his wife Jane on May 4, 1730. The couple had three children, but all died as infants. Nothing is known about Jane Millar's sister (or sister-in-law).

7. This seems to be a response to Lennox's concern that Millar might listen to the opinion of critics such as Mr. Gray.

8. #5 below suggests that Millar did indeed at some point show the manuscript to other readers as well.

9. Here, Richardson might mean a summary of the action of *FQ* as drafted (and read by him) so far.

10. This "Sequel" could be any continuation of the novel beyond the first volume.

11. Why or by whom is unknown.

12. This suggests that Richardson received the draft of the "Sequel" mentioned in the previous letter (#3) between the day *before* the letter was written and the day of its writing, but had not read it yet.

13. Mr. Seymour is another of Millar's outside readers, though Richardson seems unaware of the fact in this letter.

14. "with" is written over another word, probably "in."

15. This sheet is written on horizontally, which explains the much longer lines. The first paragraph seems added after the rest of the text, since the last line butts into the "I" starting the next paragraph.

16. These brackets are in red ink. Unfortunately, the manuscript in which Richardson inserted them no longer survives.

17. This bracket is in black ink and may have been written with the previous paragraph.

18. This is a reference to *FQ*'s heroine Arabella.

19. The "y" is written over "ies."

20. For a while, Arabella believes that her fiancée's father Sir Charles is in love with her. Cf. *FQ* 161–70, 175, and 198–204.

21. In an attempt to seduce Arabella, the nobleman Sir George Bellmour makes up his so-called history in imitation of seventeenth-century French romances, which includes the claim that his family used to be rulers of Kent (*FQ* 209–50). If Lennox actually had Sir George claiming the Kingdom of Kent for himself in an earlier manuscript, she changed this passage in the final version, where "it is not much more than Eight hundred Years since my Ancestors, who were *Saxons*, swayed the Sceptre of *Kent*" (*FQ* 209)—hardly a "recent" claim.

22. This probably means to suggest that it would be credible to have Sir George trace his family tree back to the time of the Saxons (i.e., one of the mainland tribes that started coming to England in the middle of the fifth century) and of the Heptarchy (i.e., the division of England into seven kingdoms—the Saxon kingdoms Wessex, Sussex, and Essex, the Angle kingdoms East Anglia, Mercia, and Northumbria, and the Jute kingdom Kent—from the middle of the fifth century until Wessex became predominant at the beginning of the ninth), but not for his father and grandfather to be involved in the Kingdom of Kent.

23. Indeed, the Kingdom of Kent lost its power to Offa, King of Mercia in the middle of the eighth century and became a mere province of Wessex when it was conquered by Wessex's King Egbert in 825—even more than the 800 years previous to 1752 that Sir George claims.

24. The three names here are Edward Young, Richardson, and Johnson: Glanville criticizes Sir George for pretending to be able to "sit in Judgment upon the Production of a *Young*, a *Richardson*, or a *Johnson*" (*FQ* 253). In response to Richardson's request to have his own name removed, Lennox amended it to "R—" in the first edition of *FQ* (386) in what Isles calls "all-to-familiar Richardsonian mock-modesty" (338). From the fact that Richardson did not object to his name being mentioned in the penultimate chapter of *FQ* (377—in both editions), it can be speculated that he had not read that chapter at this point, and that perhaps it had not yet been written.

25. Arabella takes the highway robbers for "valiant Men" (*FQ* 258) who would rescue her from abduction in the coach she is riding.

26. In Bath, Arabella makes an impression on society with her outfits, enters into discussions with Selvin and Tinsel, and meets the Countess (*FQ* 262–331); in London, to Glanville's chagrin, she accosts a drunken lady masquerading as a man (*FQ* 332–40).

5

Charlotte Lennox
to [Samuel Richardson[1]]

[NOVEMBER 22, 1751[2]]

MS: The Morgan Library & Museum, MA 204
Pages: 2
Edition: LC #4
Text:

Sir

      Your Servant[3] was gone before I discoverd [sic] that
you had favourd [sic] me with a letter,[4] other ways he shoud [sic] ~~not~~ have
Carried back my thanks for the obligations you have laid on me
—I have seen M[r] Gray[5] this Morning; and understand he went
to M[r] Millar's last night with M[r] Seymour,[6] he told me, in regard to
my interest he[7] woud [sic] not declare his true opinion of my Book
but said in general, that it might be printed, that perhaps
it might sell,[8] but that he did not chuse [sic] to read any more of it,
            made
and added that there must be great alterations, ∧ in what he
had already seen, the many alterations he insists upon be
ing made, and his exceptions to almost all the Characters In
cidents and language, make it necessary to write a new Book if
I woud [sic] please him[9]—he assures me that the History of Miss
     in the first Vol.
Groves ∧ will not be printed, that M[r] Millar through his perswa
sions [sic][10] is resolved against it,[11] upon the whole I am Convinced the
strongest instances have been usd [sic] to prejudice M[r] Millar—
but since you Sir have been so good to engage on my Side

I think I may set these inhuman Criticks at defyance [*sic*]—.
I must beg leave to observe that what I have related, passd [*sic*] as I
understand after you was gone.[12] I am extreamly [*sic*] happy
in the approbation you have been pleasd [*sic*] to express of my
second Vol[13] and am perfectly Convinced of the justice of your
exceptions, I return you my thanks for them, and shall
not fail to make the alterations you point out to me—

You must excuse me Sir if I do not Comply with your injunction
Concerning the second Name[14]—in this particular I can never
be of your opinion, since my own is supported by the united
Voice of the World, which has agreed in giving your in
imitable performances a universal applause.

	I am with the greatest Esteem
	Sir
Friday 4 o clock	Your oblig'd and very hum[l] Serv[t]
	Charlotte Lennox

NOTES

1. There is some confusion about the addressee of this letter: An endorsement
on the manuscript reads "To D[r] Johnson." However, the comment in the text of the
letter on the "second Name" is a direct response to Richardson's request to delete the
"middle Name," i.e., his own, in #4, so the addressee must be Richardson.

2. Since this is probably a direct response to #4, it must have been written
around November 22. Since the end of the letter further specifies "Friday 4 o clock,"
November 22 and November 29 are possibilities. In addition, however, Lennox's
specification of the exact time of day, in contrast to Richardson's "Friday Morn" in
#4, suggests the letter was written the same day, November 22.

3. This servant could have been any one of Richardson's employees, about whom
very little is known.

4. Lennox is referring to the previous letter #4.

5. See #3.

6. See #4.

7. As Isles comments, "[t]he highly-ambiguous plethora of 'he's' throughout
this letter makes discrimination between the respective opinions of Gray and Millar
exceedingly difficult" (339 n.26). The interpretation that Gray is reporting his own
opinion, however, seems most likely.

8. In the context of the eighteenth-century literary marketplace, this is an
interesting comment: Gray (or Millar) concedes that the book might sell well, but

is still unwilling to publish (or even finish reading) it. In other words, their interest was not simply profit, but promoting what they considered good literature. Of course, here Gray implies that *FQ* is in the category of literature that "might sell" but is not actually worth reading entirely—perhaps a judgmental reference to the new and controversial genre of the novel.

9. Indeed Gray objects to every aspect of the book: "Characters" (characterization), "Incidents" (plot), and "language" (style). No wonder Lennox is disheartened.

10. The phrase "his perswasions" is ambiguous—it could mean that Millar is resolved against publishing *FQ* 1. because of his (own) beliefs or 2. because Mr. Gray (or Mr. Seymour) has convinced him.

11. In this passage, Lennox refers to a story that Miss Groves tells Arabella in *FQ*: Groves has entered an unwise liaison and has had two illegitimate children. It is unclear if Gray/Millar do not want to print the story because of its content—i.e., if they are unwilling to print what would have been considered immoral behavior—or whether the story was different in its manuscript form. In the end, the story was included after all (*FQ* 70–76). Isles suggests that the objections would have been political (339 n.27) because of the story's criticism of court society.

12. Lennox's use of the first- and third-person form of the verb "to be," instead of the second-person variant ("you was gone" instead of "you were gone"), is typical for her style and appears several times in *FQ*. Richardson uses this grammatical construction himself sometimes in his three novels.

13. Considering the following letter, the reference here must be to the parts Lennox had until then written *of* the second volume, i.e., not including the ending. Perhaps this was the second volume as she envisioned it, before Richardson advised her to abandon the proposed third volume.

14. See #4.

6

Samuel Johnson
to [Samuel Richardson[1]]

DECEMBER 10, 1751

MS:	Library of George Washington Vanderbilt, Biltmore Estate, Asheville, North Carolina
Pages:	1
Edition:	Eric Walker, "Charlotte Lennox and the Collier Sisters: Two New Johnson Letters," *Studies in Philology* 95.3 (Summer 1998): 320–32.[2]
Text:	

Dec. 10. 1751

Dear Sir,

I think it necessary to inform you how it happened that I seemed to give myself so little trouble about my Book[3] when I gave you so much.[4] I thought when I sent to you that you had the Paper.[5] Mr Payne[6] to whom the affair was entrusted[7] was disappointed by Mr Bloss,[8] but was I suppose unwilling to have me vexed,[9] and therefore never told me, he has himself had his share of the trouble, for he was with fourteen Stationers before he could be supplied.[10]

Lord Orrery[11] has read our Charlotte's Book and declares in its favour, though less ardently than we, he has spoken in its praise to Mr Millar.[12] It vexes me to think that scarcely any Man when he enters upon a Book gives himself up to the conduct of the authour [sic], but first images a way of his own, and then is angry that he is led from it.[13]

I am,
Dear Sir,
Your most humble Servant
Sam. Johnson
Decr. 10th. 1751

NOTES

1. This letter went on sale at Sotheby's in 1875, but the buyer was not revealed. The sales catalog left the addressee unidentified and reproduced (and amended) a portion of the text: "I thought it necessary to inform you how it happened that I seemed to give myself so little trouble about my Book when I gave you so much. [He speaks of Lord Orrery's favourable opinion of] our Charlotte's Book [and mentions other matters connected with literary subjects]" (qtd. from Redford I 55–56). Subsequently, George Birkbeck Hill in his edition of the *Letters of Samuel Johnson* (2 vols.; Oxford: Clarendon Press, 1892) reprinted that segment. Half a century later, Robert William Chapman in *The Letters of Samuel Johnson* (3 vols.; Oxford: Clarendon Pres, 1952) speculated that it might have been addressed to Orrery. A decade after that, still working from the fragment, T. C. Duncan Eaves in "Dr. Johnson's Letters to Richardson" (*PMLA* 75.4 [September 1960]: 377–81) argued for Richardson as a recipient. His argument is borne out by the full text of the letter.

2. Walker also provides a sophisticated reading of the letter in terms of class distinctions in the literary marketplace and in terms of the newly developing sympathetic mode of reading.

3. As this letter proves, Richardson printed at least part of the 1751–52 duodecimo edition of Johnson's *Rambler*.

4. The "trouble" to which Johnson refers here is "the daily trial of simply assembling materials—in this instance, paper—to get a book printed" (Walker 323).

5. I.e., the paper necessary to print the *Rambler* edition.

6. See #1.

7. Presumably the purchasing of paper.

8. John Bloss was a stationer based in Paternoster Row who seems to have collaborated with Johnson in the 1740s (Walker 324). He died on May 3, 1754.

9. Grammatically, the referent of this clause is Payne, but of course if Bloss was collaborating with Johnson it is strange Johnson would have been unaware of the paper shortage.

10. Walker suspects irony in Johnson's describing how no paper was available from *fourteen* stationers *at the same time* (324).

11. This is Orrery (see #13, #35, and correspondent's biography). Throughout this volume, I refer to him as 'Orrery.'

12. So Orrery read the manuscript of *FQ* and intervened directly with Andrew Millar to convince him to publish it, siding with Richardson and Johnson against

Millar's three critics (see #3, #4, and #5). However, it seems Orrery was less excited about the novel than his friends.

13. Johnson's "outburst against the failure of sympathy in reading" (Walker 325), i.e., readers' unwillingness to surrender control of the text to the author, has two possible targets: Orrery, who in the previous sentence has been described as not being fully appreciative of *FQ*, or Millar's readers (in the modern, academic sense) who disapproved of the novel (rather than—as Walker suggests—Millar himself, who might not even have read the novel).

7

Samuel Richardson
to Charlotte Lennox

JANUARY 13, 1752

MS: Houghton Library, Harvard University, MS Eng 1269 (19)
Pages: 1
Edition: LC #5
Text:

Dear Madam,

It is my humble Opinion, that you should finish your
Heroine's Cure in your Present Vols.[1] The method you propose,
tho' it might flatter my Vanity, yet will be thought a Contrivance
between the Author of Arabella,[2] and the Writer of Clarissa,[3] to do
Credit to the latter; and especially if the Contraste[4] [sic] ~~would~~ will[5] take up
much Room in the proposed 3d Volume. If it will not take up
much, it may be done, if you <u>will</u> do it, that way (which I
beg you to consider, and to consult Mr. Johnson before you resolve[6])
at the latter End of the Second Volume. You are a young Lady[7]
have therefore much time before you, and I am sure, will think
that a good Fame will be your Interest. Make therefore, your
present work as complete as you can, in two Volumes; and it
will give Consequence to your future Writings, and of course
to your Name as a Writer; And [sic] without a Complement I
think you set out upon an admirable Foundation.[8]

    Excuse Haste. I write while a Friend is with me.[9] And
have hardly time for Reperusal.[10]

I am, Madam,
Yours most sincerely
Jan.13.1752.   S. Richardson

NOTES

1. This letter indicates that, at this time, Lennox intended to add a third volume to *FQ*. In that volume, Arabella would have been cured differently than in the published version, or at least later, and with some sort of praise for Richardson. Isles calls Richardson's advice for Lennox to stick to two volumes "misguided though well-intentioned" and contends that Lennox's following it led to flaws "such as the quick scamper over the London section, the unconvincing termination of Arabella's friendship with the sensible and sympathetic Countess, and the unsatisfactory 'Cure' itself" (341 n.30).

2. I.e., Lennox.

3. I.e., Richardson.

4. It is unclear what this contrast would have been.

5. "will" is written on top of "would."

6. The following letter proves that Lennox did consult with Johnson, but at that point the consultation seems to have been more about the speed of publication than about the ending of the novel.

7. An "and" would make sense here, but is not in the manuscript.

8. Here, Richardson implies that Lennox should not be concerned so much with the perfection of *FQ* as with its long-term effect on her career: He believes that a two-volume *FQ*—which he still considers an "admirable" book—will increase her prominence ("Consequence") as a writer and set her up to succeed even more with later books. The phrase "your Name as a Writer" indicates that Richardson is thinking in terms of individual authorship and name recognition much more than Lennox at the time.

9. Richardson's "friends" at this time included men—Thomas Edwards, Giuseppe Baretti, William or John Duncombe (though in the present context probably not Johnson)—as well as women—Susanna Highmore, Hester Mulso (later Chapone), Elizabeth Carter, Mary Prescott, Catherine Talbot (cf. Eaves/Kimpel, chap. XIII, "Richardson and His Friends 1750–1754," 322–64).

10. It is unclear what Richardson thinks he should peruse a second time.

8

Charlotte Lennox
to [Samuel Johnson][1]

FEBRUARY 3, 1752

MS: Chicago Historical Society
Pages: 2
Text:

Sir

       Mr Millar being apprehensive the Book will not
be printed till it is too late to be publishd [*sic*][2] seems in that Case
[to[3]] think of keeping it till next Winter, my present perplexd [*sic*]
[sit]uation makes a second Impression (with the hopes of
which I had flatterd [*sic*] my self)[4] so necessary to my affairs[5]
that it will be an extream [*sic*] disappointment to me if I
have not the Chance of it this Winter, if it be possible
Sir to hurry the printing without any inconvenience to
your Self[6] I shoud [*sic*] look upon it as a particular favour
and since I have taken the liberty to explain my self so freely
I am perswaided [*sic*] the motive I have urgd [*sic*] will not want
weight with a Mind so generous and compassionate as
yours—Tho I am far from thinking writing my talent
[and] I am sure it is not my inclination,[7] yet since my ill-
[ness[8] o]ne has made it the only means of my Subsistence
[at] present[9] if you think me not wholly unworthy of
your recommendation I woud [*sic*] intreat your interest
with the Booksellers to procure me some employ
ment in the translating Way, as this woud [*sic*] be a great
deal easier then [*sic*] Composition, I am perswaided [*sic*] I

can make it as advantagious [*sic*] by industry and ha:
ving been already engagd [*sic*] in it[10] know what I am ca
pable of doing by proper application, yet Sir if
you will pardon me for mentioning a bolder wish, I
woud [*sic*] tell you your protection for M[r] Lennox woud [*sic*] make
me still happier then [*sic*] granted to my Self,[11] if you woud [*sic*]
be pleasd [*sic*] to recommend him to any little employment
your interest as I am informed [*sic*] with several great
People might easily procure it as you are yet

---

unacquainted with his Birth misfortunes, and dis
appointed expectations,[12] in which possibly you may [. . .]
something to engage your attention I will pur
sue this Subject in another Letter, if I may be per:
mitted to hope the application I have ventured to make
has not been disagreeable

I am
Sir
Your oblig'd hum[e] Serv[t]
Charlotte Lennox

Feb[ry] 3. 1752

NOTES

1. The recipient of this letter is somewhat uncertain. On the one hand, the reference to being able "to hurry the printing without any inconvenience to your Self" suggests it may be addressed to a printer, i.e., Richardson. Also, the passage about Alexander Lennox would seem to be more appropriate in the context of publishing: Alexander had been an employee of Strahan's, and perhaps Lennox was now asking Richardson to find him new work in the same industry. At the same time, "protection" could refer to any kind of employment, and perhaps this letter is asking Johnson to use his connections with the aristocracy to find a position for Alexander. In addition, the following letter #9 seems to be responding directly to this one, and it is signed by Johnson. For that reason, the conjecture that the addressee is Johnson is most probable.

2. The "publishing season ran from autumn until late Spring" (Raven, "Introduction" I 83), so *FQ* had to be printed soon to be available during the season.

3. There is a semi-circle-shaped tear in the paper here and below from the seal, but the words can be surmised with some certainty.

4. In the event, the first edition of *FQ* came out on March 13, 1752, the second a few months later on July 2 (after the season) with numerous, if minor, changes.

Lennox seems surprisingly confident that a second edition would be required quite soon—or the first edition had already been printed at the time of the writing of this letter.

5. This ("perlexd [sit]uation," "my affairs") is a reference to Lennox's straightened financial circumstances.

6. If the recipient of this letter is really Johnson, it is unclear what he could do to increase the speed of printing, or why that could or could not pose an inconvenience.

7. While heavily involved in the publication of her most successful novel, Lennox claims she is not talented as a writer. In addition, her phrase, "I am sure it is not my inclination," means that she does not *want* to be an author either. Of course, both statements could be merely stances of humility or propriety.

8. Throughout her life, Lennox apparently experienced a series of illnesses. This is the first reference to one of them.

9. This sentence can be construed as evidence for the claim, advanced by Raven in his "Introduction," that Lennox only "wrote to re-establish family fortunes" (I 50)—perhaps an inheritance could be a source of income at another time than "[at] present."

10. Isles speculates that this refers to the 1751 edition of *Sully* (433), supposedly translated by Lennox. However, there does not seem to be any evidence that Lennox was really involved in this edition, so it seems more probable she is referring to some other, unknown translation work. Isles believes that Lennox translated *The Age of Lewis XIV* between the publication of *FQ* (March 13) and July 11 (see #12), but it is also quite possible that Lennox had been working on Voltaire's text before February 3 and was referring to that book.

11. The word "protection" can take on a variety of meanings, from talking to members of the publishing world to hiring Alexander Lennox for a job to approaching members of the gentry or aristocracy to find a more or less work-related position for Lennox's husband, who seems to have been unemployed at this time. The following mention of "several great People" suggests the latter interpretation.

12. These "misfortunes" and "disappointed expectations" are unknown, unless Lennox means Alexander's belief that he was a member of the aristocratic Lennox family and had been wrongly deprived of his inheritance (see #42).

9

Samuel Johnson
to Charlotte Lennox

FEBRUARY 4, 1752

MS:	Houghton Library, Harvard University, MS Eng 1269 (4)
Pages:	2
Edition:	LC #6, Redford I 58–59
Address:	To Mrs Lennox
Text:	

Madam.

I am extremely sorry to hear that your Book suffers such
delays, and think you unkindly treated by Mr Richardson.[1] You
see how ill we judge of our own advantages, I wish Strahan[2]
had it even now,[3] for I am afraid you will be gr[eatly in[4]]
jured by so long delay.[5] What can be done? It is [already[6]]
sent to Mr Millar, and you cannot decently ma[ke any]
warm remonstrance. I wish I could help it. [But]
if you can stay till next year[7] the prospect of [success[8]]
will be better, and I will try to speak to [some]
others for employment in the mean time, bo[oks are]
not easy to be had.[9] I am much concerned [for you]

I am
Madam

Your most humble Servant
Sam: Johnson
Febr 4. 1752 1/2[10]

26

NOTES

1. I.e., Johnson thinks that Richardson has not been sufficiently timely in his printing of *FQ*.

2. William Strahan (1715-85; ODNB LII 1027–29) was one of eighteenth-century London's most important printers and booksellers. He established his firm in 1738, purchased many copyrights, and received the patent as the king's printer in 1770. Strahan was also a Member of Parliament from 1774 to 1784. He left extensive ledgers and diaries as well as correspondence with many important literary figures of his time. Strahan was friends with David Hume, Benjamin Franklin, and Johnson, and he was a member of the literary Essex Head Club. Isles gives a comprehensive list of items he printed in which Lennox was involved (342 n.35). See also Sandra Naiman, "William Strahan," in Bracken/Silver 270–77 and Cochrane.

3. Here, Johnson seems to be suggesting that Strahan—who had already printed Lennox's *Proposals* of 1750, *HS*, and an extra title page for *HS* (Isles 342 n.35)—would have been a better option as a printer than Richardson. Alternately, Strahan had "printed several works for Richardson when the latter was busy" (Eaves/Kimpel 161), so perhaps Johnson was suggesting that solution. Of course, Strahan would hardly have been able to give the kind of literary advice Richardson offered.

4. There is a long tear on the right side of this letter, so the final letters and words of the last eight lines are missing. The replacements here are only suggestions that a) complete the sentences in a grammatically correct way and b) fit what we know about Lennox at this time.

5. Johnson is uncertain about the publication of *FQ*. On the one hand, he argues that it will be disadvantageous to Lennox to have her novel published late in the spring season 1752, but later in the letter, he suggests that she move the release of her novel to the next season.

6. This conjecture for the missing text is open to discussion: Of course, it could be the exact opposite, something like "It is [not yet] sent to Mr Millar." It is equally unclear why Lennox "cannot decently ma[ke any] warm remonstrance" against Millar: either because it is too late to interfere in the printing, or because she has not sent in her manuscript on time.

7. By "next year," Johnson means the next publishing season, i.e., the fall of 1752.

8. This might also be a word indicating a specific *kind* of success, e.g., profit (cf. Isles 342 n.37).

9. This is a contrast to many claims that writing as a hack, i.e., doing compilations or translations, was work that was easy to come by.

10. In 1752, Great Britain switched from the Julian to the Gregorian calendar. In the Julian ("old style") calendar, the year began on March 25; in the Gregorian ("new style") on January 1. Most European countries had adopted the Gregorian calendar in the sixteenth century, so for three months the year had been different on the continent than the British Isles. Writers often acknowledged this discrepancy, especially in the

year of the switch in Britain, by writing dates such as "1751/2," indicating that the year on February 4 was 1751 on the continent and 1752 in Britain. The year 1752 was extraordinarily short: It started on March 26 and ended on December 31, and, in addition, eleven days were removed between September 2 and September 14 to make up for a lag between the Julian and the Gregorian calendars.

10

Charlotte Lennox
to [Samuel Johnson[1]]

MARCH 12, 1752

MS:	Beinecke Rare Book and Manuscript Library at Yale University, GEN MSS 237 (Herman W. Liebert Manuscript Collection), box 3, folder 85 (see Ill. 2)
Pages:	1
Edition:	Brack/Carlile
Text:	

Sir

Permit me to intreat your acceptance of the inclosd [*sic*]
Book[2] and of my sincere acknowledgements for your kindness during
the Writing of it. if you do me the favour to read over the latter
part of the second Voll. [*sic*] which you have not yet seen[3] you'll
find I have not cured my Heroine in the manner I proposd [*sic*]
being too much confind [*sic*] in Room[4] to do justice to the—
admirable Character I intended for her imitation,[5] and
was forced to content my self with shewing by a few Words
only my extream [*sic*] admiration of it.

I am with the highest esteem
Sir
Your most obligd [*sic*] hum^e Servt
Charlotte Lennox

March 12. 1752.

Ill. 2. Letter from Charlotte Lennox to [Samuel Johnson], March 12, 1752 (#10) (Beinecke Rare Book and Manuscript Library at Yale University, GEN MSS 237 [Herman W. Liebert Manuscript Collection], box 3, folder 85)

NOTES

1. The addressee can be deduced from the circumstances of the production of *FQ* and from surrounding letters. From the text, the addressee appears to be one of the individuals who were involved in the writing or production of *FQ*—Johnson, Richardson, Orrery, and Millar, as far as is known (I am excluding Strahan, Payne, and Millar's 'readers'). It is probably not Richardson, since Lennox writes in #3 above that she has "taken the liberty to send the second [vo]lume of my Book" to him; it is probably not Orrery since the letter to him is signed "Your Lordship's [...] Servant"; and it is probably not addressed to Millar, since there would be no reason to send him a copy of the book. It might also be conjectured that the letter was written to Johnson since she signs it "with the highest esteem" where she had signed to him previously "with the greatest esteem" (#5). In addition, since the following letter (#11) of the same day thanks Lennox for a present, it is not unreasonable to assume that this present would have been the volumes of *FQ* that Lennox refers to here.

2. Considering the date of the letter and the content as described, the book mentioned here must be *FQ*, which was published on or around March 13, 1752. The *General Advertiser* and the *Daily Advertiser* advertised the novel on March 12 as "Tomorrow will be publish'd," while the *London Evening Post* on that day wrote, "This Day is publish'd." On March 13, the advertisement in the *General Advertiser* read, "This Day is published."

3. If the addressee of this letter is indeed Johnson, the phrase "which you have not yet seen" serves as evidence that Johnson did *not* write the penultimate chapter of *FQ*.

4. Of course, this confinement (i.e., shortness) was due to Lennox following Richardson and Johnson's advice to keep the novel to two volumes. On curing Arabella "in the manner I proposd," see #7.

5. This sentence implies that Lennox originally intended *another* character, *not* the divine, to bring about Arabella's cure. The obvious candidate for that "Character" is the Countess, who appears and disappears abruptly in *FQ*.

11

Samuel Johnson
to Charlotte Lennox

MARCH 12, 1752

MS: Houghton Library, Harvard University, MS Eng 1269 (5)
Pages: 1
Edition: LC #7, Redford I 59–60
Text:

Madam

I am extremely obliged by your kind present,[1] and
wish it the Success which it deserves.[2]
Poor Tetty Johnson's Ilness [*sic*] will not suffer me to
think of going any whither, out of her call. She is
very ill, and I am very much dejected.[3]
Mr Millar has you in great esteem, and blames Mr R—.[4] He
says he hopes your book will eclipse Lord B—s Letters.[5]

> I am,
> Madam,
> Your most humble Servant
> Sam: Johnson
> March.12.1752.

NOTES

1. The "kind present" is almost certainly a gift copy of the newly released *FQ*. In
fact, this could be the copy to which Lennox refers in the previous letter (#10).
2. The reactions to *FQ* were mixed, perhaps in total slightly more positive. On the
reception of the novel, see Brian Hanley, "Henry Fielding, Samuel Johnson, Samuel

Richardson, and the Reception of Charlotte Lennox's *The Female Quixote* in the Popular Press" (*American Notes and Queries* 13.3 [Summer 2000]: 27–32). While Isles asserts that the review in the *Gentleman's Magazine* was *not* by Johnson (343 n.40), Hanley treats it as if it was.

3. Johnson's wife Elizabeth ("Tetty") died less than a week later, on March 17, 1752. Even though the spouses' relationship had not always been very intimate, Johnson reacted strongly to his wife's death: According to John Taylor, Johnson's letter speaking of Tetty's death was written "in the strongest manner he had ever read" (Boswell I 238), and John Hawkins reported in his *Life* that Johnson experienced a depression "of the blackest and deepest kind" and was "abandoned to sorrow, and incapable of consolation" (129 and 280).

4. R— is of course Richardson. So even after the printing of *FQ*, Millar was blaming Richardson for the delays.

5. The posthumous *Letters on the Study and Use of History* by Henry St. John, first Viscount Bolingbroke (1678–1751) were released exactly a week after *FQ*, on March 20, 1752. The *Letters* "produced a considerable reaction, because of Bolingbroke's attacks on Old Testament and Church history," with Lord Hyde, John Leland, and others launching attacks on the author (H.T. Dickinson, *Bolingbroke* [London: Constable, 1970], 297). Of course, critical attention does not necessarily correlate with commercial success—but it is remarkable that, "By 1755, two more editions [of the *Letters*], five translations, and at least thirteen responses (eleven of them hostile) had been published" (Simon Varey, *Henry St. John, Viscount Bolingbroke* [Boston: Twayne, 1984], 125 n.2). At that time, *FQ* had three editions (two in London, one in Dublin), one translation (into German in 1754), and a number of reviews—so it is difficult to assess who eclipsed whom.

12

Samuel Richardson
to Charlotte Lennox

APRIL 6, 1752

MS: Houghton Library, Harvard University, MS Eng 1269 (20)
Pages: 1
Edition: LC #8
Text:

Madam,

M[r]. Dodsley[1] has a small Thing to
translate from the French with
Dispatch.[2] You have asked me if
I knew of any thing of that kind.[3]
I know[4] not a better Writer, nor a
worthier Bookseller, to recommend
to each other, than Mrs. Lennox
and Mr. Dodsley. I am
always, Madam, if you'll excuse
this Bit of Paper, being in haste,[5]

                    Your most humble Serv[t]
6 April, 1752   S. Richardson

NOTES

1. This must be Robert Dodsley, who was at the prime of his influence in the 1750s (see #71 and correspondent's biography for his brother James).

2. According to Isles (basing his claim on Nichols VIII 435), the item Dodsley was offering Lennox for translation was Voltaire's *The Age of Lewis XIV*, which was published in July 1752 (344 n.45). However, there is nothing in that translation itself that confirms Isles's conjecture. In order to complete *Lewis XIV*, Lennox would have had to translate 728 pages in less than four months—not impossible, but probably more than a "small Thing." *The Correspondence of Robert Dodsley 1733–1764* (ed. James Tierney; Cambridge: Cambridge University Press, 1988) offers no clarification.

3. See #8.

4. This might also read "knew."

5. This may be an excuse—Richardson did also write quite lengthy epistles.

13

John Boyle, Earl of Orrery, to Charlotte Lennox

MAY 9, 1752

MS: Houghton Library, Harvard University, MS Eng 1269 (32)
Pages: 3
Edition: LC #9
Text:

It is with great pleasure, Madam, I shall un:
:dertake any part you will assign to me in your
intended work.[1] I heartily wish that ~~any~~ the[2] hints I
may chance to give, might prove of future be:
:nefit to you in any shape. You may depend
upon the zeal of my friendship.

You are entirely in the right, Madam, to
translate, and not to epitomize or imitate.[3] You
have cleared my doubts. Only I wish you to trans:
:late no part foreign to Shakespeares [*sic*] story,
unless the part be unavoidably connected.

I send you some papers relative to
MacBeth: as a specimen, that may determine

---

you, whether to order me to go on, or to stop
me & point out some new road.[4] I keep no
copies of my papers; They are entirely your own.
I have already forgot 'em. Burn them, alter them,
Do with them as you please.[5] They can be of no
use ever to me: if they are of any to you, my
wishes are answered.[6]

Remember, Madam, Friendship knows no
ceremony, no distance, no compliments. Treat me
accordingly. I have often wished to see the work
you are going to undertake.[7] I think it may
be a fine one, in such hands. If you approve

---

of what I now send, I shall transmit some
scraps concerning Harry the 8th.[8] I am obliged to go
into Hampshire for some days,[9] in all places,

Madam,
your obedient and faithfull [*sic*]
humble Servant

Marston house[10]   Orrery
May 9. 1752.

NOTES

1. This work is *SI*, which came out in May 1753 and had a dedication to Orrery probably written by Johnson (Fleeman I 400–402). Nothing in *SI* is directly attributed to Orrery, but he later contributed a preface and three essays to Lennox's *Brumoy* (Small 217–19) and at least one item, a note on *Macbeth*, to *LM* (Isles 37 n.51). The present letter suggests that Lennox worked on *SI* for at least a year, starting soon after the release of *FQ*.

2. The "the" is written over the "any."

3. This sentence probably refers to Lennox's theoretical approach towards translation in *SI*. Instead of adapting her French and Italian sources, she wants to offers straight-forward translations. On eighteenth-century theories of translation, see David Hopkins, "Dryden and his Contemporaries," Gillespie/Hopkins 55–66, and Louis Kelly, "The Eighteenth Century to Tytler," Gillespie/Hopkins 67–78.

4. Isles believes that this material "must have contained what became 'The *History of* Macbeth, *collected from* Holinshed's *Chronicles of* England, Scotland, *and* Ireland' in *SI*, I, 251–268" (37 n.51).

5. This passage is very similar to one Orrery wrote to Johnson two months later on July 12, 1752: "She [Lennox] may do with the papers as she thinks proper. I have no copy of them. If even some words in them may be of service to her I am happy. Do not let her pay them too great regards. They are not mine: they are hers, and she has a right to do with them as she pleases" (Boyle II 113).

6. If Orrery indeed contributed the item on *Macbeth* in *LM*, these comments must not be taken at face value—or Lennox wrote the note in *LM for* Orrery.

7. In a letter to Johnson, Orrery suggests his reason for not undertaking the work himself: "I would not walk into Mr. P. [Alexander Pope] and W.'s [William

Warburton's] province, who seemed to think Shakespear [*sic*] was the *Sanctum Sanctorum* where they only were sufficiently holy to enter" (Boyle II 113).

8. *Henry VIII*, co-authored by Shakespeare and John Fletcher. The section on *Henry VIII* in *SI* (III 171-230) is mostly a direct comparison of passages from the play with excerpts from Holinshed, and there is no indication what (if anything) might have come from Orrery.

9. Orrery wrote letters from Marston House before and after the present one on March 18, 1752 (Boyle II 107) and on July 8, 1752 (Boyle II 109), neither of which mention any travel. In several letters of July 1752, Orrery talks about a recent severe illness, so maybe the trip never took place.

10. Marston House was the Orrery family residence near Frome, Somersetshire (south of Bath). The manor was built between 1600 and 1640 and changed and expanded by subsequent generations of Orrerys. This Orrery added wings to the house, but mainly worked on the gardens (see McGarvie).

14

Proposal for Subscription
Edition of *Poems*

NOVEMBER 4, 1752

MS: Beinecke Rare Books and Manuscript Library, Yale University, Im L548 +752p;
Houghton Library, Harvard University, MS Hyde 10 (417)

Pages: 4

Text:

November 4, 1752.

PROPOSALS

For PRINTING by SUBSCRIPTION

P O E M S

ON

SEVERAL OCCASIONS[1]

BY THE

AUTHOR of the FEMALE QUIXOTE.[2]

[printer's ornament[3]]

SUBSCRIPTIONS are taken in by

Mr. MILLAR, in the Strand;[4] and Mr. DODSLEY, in Pall-mall.[5]

CONDITIONS.

I. The Work shall be printed in a neat Quarto Volume, on the same Paper and Letter with the Specimen annexed.[6]

II. The Work is ready for the Press, and will be delivered to the Subscribers towards the latter End of 1753.[7]

III. Those who are willing to encourage this Undertaking, by their
       Subscriptions, are desired to pay Half a Crown at the Time
       of Subscribing,[8] and another Half Crown on the Delivery[9] of
       the Book sewed in Blue Paper.[10]

R eceived of
    being the first Payment for[11]
of the above Book, which I promise to deliver agreeable to the Terms of
these Proposals.
       Charlotte Lennox[12]

[printer's ornament]

ON READING

HUTCHINSON on the PASSIONS.

T HOU who thro' Nature's various maze canst rove,
   And shew what springs the rapid passions move;
Teach us to combat anger, grief and fear,
Recall the sigh, and check the starting tear.
Why was thy soft philosophy addrest,
All to the vacant ear, and quiet breast
With ease may peaceful apathy be taught
To these who stagnate in a calm of thought:
Whose hearts by love or hate were ne'er possest,
Who ne'er were wretched, and who ne'er were blest:
Who one dull slumber through their lives maintain,
And only dream of pleasure and of pain;
Serenely stupid. So some gentle stream
Steals thro' the winding valleys still the same;
So silent down the muddy channel creeps;
While the soft zephyr on its bosom sleeps.

---

(2)

My fervent soul a nobler art requires,
Not to suppress, but regulate her fires:
Some better guides, who temperately wise
Allow to feel, yet teach us to despise.
To Reason's sway subject the Soul's domain,
And not subdue the passions, but restrain.[13]

[printer's ornament[14]]

NOTES

1. Lennox's *Poems* had originally been published by Samuel Paterson in 1747. Millar and Dodsley undertaking this subscription publication suggests that they had in the meantime acquired the copyright to Lennox's first text and that they believed the volume would be popular enough to make a profit for them.

2. This is the first time Lennox publicly identifies herself as the author of *FQ*–less than a year after the novel's initial publication.

3. This is the same printer's ornament that Strahan used for instance in John Lockman's *Occasional Verses* (London: For the Author, 1753), [3] and in Alexander Drummond's *Travels through Different Cities of Germany, Italy, Greece, and Several Parts of Asia* (London: For the Author, 1754), [1].

4. In 1752, Millar had his business opposite Catherine Street on the Strand.

5. In 1752, this would be Robert Dodsley, whose business was located at the Tully's Head in London's Pall Mall.

6. The 1747 publication was [iv] + 88 pages in octavo. An edition in quarto would have been targeted at a wealthier audience and might have been used for presentation. The "Specimen annexed" is the poem below.

7. Of course, since this was not a *new* work of literature, it was easy to say it was "ready for the Press" and promise it at a certain time. However, it appears the publication never happened. As far as I have been able to determine, there were not even advertisements for the subscription in the newspapers.

8. In subscription publication, readers paid a portion of the price of the book in advance and the balance on delivery. In return, they were often listed in subscription lists preceding the main body of the text. Since the subscriptions demonstrated a demand for the work, subscription publication was a way for authors to bring works to the public that publishers might otherwise have rejected. All parties benefited in different ways from subscription publication: Publishers were able to share publishing risk and costs with customers in advance (by collecting money), authors were able to demonstrate their social prestige (in subscription lists, which often included gentry and aristocracy and even nobility), and readers were able to show their commitment to literature publicly (in the subscription lists). Of course, the last two benefits only occurred when the edition materialized—and none of Lennox's many subscription projects ever came to fruition.

To my knowledge, there is no study of the relation between subscription proposals to actual editions. On various aspects of subscription publication, see for instance Thomas Lockwood, "Subscription-Hunters and Their Prey," *Studies in the Literary Imagination* 34.1 (Spring 2001): 121–35; Raven, "Introduction" I 54–56; Pat Rogers, "Book Subscriptions among the Augustans," *Times Library Supplement* (December 15, 1972): 1539-40; W. A. Speck, "Politicians, Peers, and Publication by Subscription 1700-50," in *Books and their Readers in Eighteenth-Century England* (ed. Isabel Rivers; Leicester: Leicester University Press, 1982), 47–68; Peter John Wallis, "Book Subscription Lists," *The Library* 5th series, 29.3 (September 1974): 255–86, and Wallis.

9. At a crown total (five shillings), the subscription edition was more than three times as expensive as the original, which cost only one shilling and six pence. Some of the price differential can be accounted for by the more expensive format (see n.6 above), but the large difference suggests that this volume—like many subscription editions—was probably intended mostly to support the author financially.

10. Unbound books (in sheets) were usually delivered in these blue wrappers to protect the text until the buyer could have them bound. Marks shows an example of this "plain blue wrapper" (33).

11. The lines are left open here to allow the insertion of the name of the subscriber and the number of subscriptions.

12. This is in a neat signature. The receipt is set off with a long line to be torn off.

13. This is Lennox's poem "On Reading Hutchison on the Passions" from her *Poems*. The version there reads quite differently (37–38):

On reading HUTCHISON on the PASSIONS.
THOU who thro' Nature's various Faults can rove,
And shew what Springs the eager Passions move;
Teach us to combat Anger, Grief and Fear,
Recal [sic] the Sigh, and stop the falling Tear.
Oh be thy soft Philosophy addrest,
To the untroubled Ear and tranquil Breast:
To these be all thy peaceful Notions taught,
Who idly rove amidst a Calm of Thought:
Whose Soul by Love or Hate were ne'er possest,
Who ne'er were wretched, and who ne'er were blest:
Whose fainter Wishes, Pleasures, Fears remain,
Dreams but of Bliss, and Shadows of a Pain;
Serenely stupid; so some shallow Stream
Flows thro' the winding Valleys still the same:
Whom no rude Wind can ever discompose,
Who fears no Winter Rain, or falling Snows;
But slowly down its flow'ry Borders creeps,
And the soft Zephyr on its Bosom sleeps.
Oh couldst thou teach the tortur'd Soul to know,
With Patience, each Extream [sic] of human Woe;
To bear with Ills, and unrepining prove
The Frowns of Fortune, and the Racks of Love:
Still should my Breast some quiet Moments share,
Still rise superior to each threatning [sic] Care:
Nor fear approaching Ills, or distant Woes,
But in *Philander*'s Absence find Repose.

14. This is the same printer's ornament that Strahan used for instance in Charles Labelye's *A Description of Westminster Bridge* (London: For the Author, 1751), 64 and twice in Christopher Smart's *Poems on Several Occasions* (London: For the Author, 1752), 165 and 192.

15

Samuel Johnson
to Charlotte Lennox

MARCH 6, 1753

MS: Houghton Library, Harvard University, MS Eng 1269 (6)
Pages: 1
Edition: LC #10, Redford I 66
Address: To Mrs Lennox
            over against the King's Bakers
            in Berry Street St James's[1]
Text:

Dear Madam,

I am very sorry for what happened, but cannot
find that I was the cause of it, for the effect had
been the same had he been out on any other occasion.[2]

The reason for which I said nothing to Mr Lenox [*sic*]
was no less than that I had nothing to say.[3] The
Marriage is not yet solemnised or not owned, and as
it would be improper for the young Gentleman to
ask a favour beforehand, it would be fit for me
to propose it. To ask it I have promised you, and
I will ask it in such a manner as I think most
likely to succeed, for I shall sincerely rejoice if [to do[4]]
you any good can be within the little power [of]

                      Madam
                      Your most humble servan[t]
March 6. 1753   Sam: Johnson

43

44

NOTES

1. Berry Street (Rocque 10Bb/Bury Street in Horwood 22Ca) is parallel to St. James's Street between that street and St. James's Square, close to St. James's Park and Green Park. I have not been able to identify the location or name of this King's baker.

2. It is unknown what Johnson is referring to here. The details that can be reconstructed from this letter are that the incident involves

- another male,
- a marriage, and
- a favor.

I suspect strongly that the favor was a dedication and that Lennox had asked, or was thinking about asking, some "Young Gentleman" to inquire about the possibility of a dedication (maybe of *SI*, which would suggest Lennox had not originally intended to dedicate it to Orrery). This dedication would have been to a person whose relative the "Young Gentleman" was about to marry. The "Young Gentleman" is probably the "he" whom Johnson visited for unrelated reasons and found absent ("out"). Apparently, Johnson had not mentioned the visit to Alexander Lennox. Johnson claims to have a closer connection to the potential dedicatee and promises to make the inquiry himself.

Orrery's eldest son Charles was married on May 4, 1753 "to Miss Hoare [Susannah Hoare, daughter of Henry Hoare] of Linc. Inn fields" (*Gentleman's Magazine* 23 [1753]: 248), but considering his support of her career Lennox could probably have approached Orrery herself about the dedication, so the incident remains unclear. In any case, if the "Young Gentleman" had been Charles Boyle, the marriage would have been irrelevant.

3. This comment, like #18 and #24, suggests contact between Johnson and Alexander Lennox independent of Lennox in this period.

4. The manuscript is torn here and below.

16

Samuel Johnson
to Charlotte Lennox

[c. April–May 1753[1]]

MS:	Houghton Library, Harvard University, MS Eng 1269 (7)
Pages:	1
Edition:	LC #11, Redford I 71
Address:	To Mrs Lenox
Text:	

Madam

I hope you take great care to observe the Doctor's prescriptions, and take your physick regularly, for I shall soon come to enquire.[2] I should be sorry to lose Criticism in her bloom.[3] Your remarks are I think all very judicious, clearly expressed, and incontrovertibly certain.[4] When Shakespeare is demolished your wings will be <u>full summed</u> and I will fly you at Milton; for you are a bird of Prey, but the Bird of Jupiter.[5]

> I am,
> Madam,
> Your most obedient Servant
> Sam Johnson.

NOTES

1. Because it refers to the upcoming publication of *SI*, which happened on May 18, 1753, Redford dates this letter as c. May 1753. Isles is a little more cautious, writing only 1753. Actually, since Johnson seems to have read *SI* and might very well have seen the sheets before their release, a time before May is quite likely.

2. Lennox was frequently sick (see #8) and at least in this case appears to have consulted a doctor. The end of the sentence indicates that visits between Johnson and Lennox were reciprocal.

3. This is a reference to the forthcoming *SI*.

4. As Isles points out, this is "SJ's only surviving critical assessment of *SI*" (38 n.56). With the "demolished" in the following sentence, Johnson is focusing on Lennox's criticism (in the sense of disapproving the object) of Shakespeare. I disagree somewhat with Isles's claim that we should read this letter as playful and *not* accept it "as a serious, objective judgment" (39 n.56)—I think the assessment is too positive to be entirely ironic or disingenuous.

5. "Full summed" is a technical term in falconry meaning "in full plumage, fully developed" (OED) and may be a reference to Milton's *Paradise Lost*, "but feathered soon and fledge/They summed their pens, and soaring the air sublime/With clang despised the ground" (VII 420–22), or *Paradise Regained*, where the Spirit is asked to "inspire,/As thou art wont, my prompted song else mute/And bear through highth or depth of nature's bounds/With prosperous wing full summed to tell of deeds/Above heroic, though in secret done" (I 11–15). Johnson believes that with *SI* Lennox's critical faculties are fully developed and that she is now able to attack and demolish Milton in the same way, i.e., with a translation and analysis of sources, a critical *Milton Illustrated*. However, Johnson compares her to an eagle ("Bird of Jupiter") rather than a hawk. The phrase "I will fly you" suggests that he may have been the initiating force behind *SI*.

17

David Garrick
to Charlotte Lennox

AUGUST 12, [1753[1]]

MS:	Houghton Library, Harvard University, MS Eng 1269 (21)
Pages:	2
Edition:	LC #12
Text:	

Londesburgh[2] in
Yorkshire
Aug[st] 12th

Madam,

Yesterday I receiv'd Yours, which
I find has been at Chiswick some
time, & by some Mistake was not sent to
me till y[e] last post[3]—I should
certainly have sent You y[e] letter according
to your desire, had I not destroy'd it;
The Remarks I had made were written
as I read y[r]. Book, & were perhaps
stronger Proofs of my Zeal for
Shakespear [sic], than of my Judgment.[4]
In the Whole, I imagin'd that you had
betray'd a greater desire of Exposing his
= Errors

than of <u>illustrating</u> his Beauties[5]—there appeared
to me (and indeed to many others[6]) a kind

47

of severe Levity & Ridicule, which
might with Justice have been exercis'd
upon Tom Durfey,[7] but (I think) is somewhat
unjustifiable, when us'd against so great
and so Excellent an Author[8]—let me
assure You of my best Wishes for Your
success in Every undertaking, & let me
desire You in [sic] behalf of my best
friend, & in ye words of an old saying,
that as <u>You are brave, be mercifull</u> [sic].[9]

I am
Madam
Y^r. very hum^le Servt
D: Garrick

NOTES

1. The year of this letter can be deduced from the references to the recently published *SI*.

2. This is the Elizabethan-style mansion Londesburgh Park near Market Weighton in East Riding, Yorkshire, that Garrick's friend Richard Boyle, Earl of Burlington and Cork (whose death in 1753 allowed his cousin John Boyle to unite the lines of Cork and Orrery; see correspondent's biography) had rebuilt in the 1730s. Garrick and his wife spent part of their summers there with Lord and Lady Burlington in 1750, 1751, and 1753. In 1753, they arrived from Chiswick House (see n.3 below) on July 16 and left for London around August 21 (Garrick I 194–200).

3. Chiswick House, built 1724–29, "is a testimony to the Earl of Burlington's taste for the Palladian style, and is a direct imitation of Palladio's Villa Rotonda near Vicenza in Italy. For the interior the Earl employed William Kent, thus introducing a rich contrast to the somewhat austere exterior which Burlington designed himself" (Alan Kendall, *David Garrick: A Biography* [New York: St. Martin's Press, 1985], 59). The Garricks visited Chiswick even more frequently than Londesburgh House, and in 1753 they had been there in June and until July 16. At the time of the writing of this letter, Garrick had been away from Chiswick for about four weeks, and apparently not all his mail had been forwarded.

4. In other words, Garrick had read *SI* as a Shakespeare enthusiast and had taken notes of criticism at the same time—and now claims to have destroyed those notes. Indeed, no notes fitting this description survive.

5. This is a piece of criticism (with a reference to the book's title) frequently leveled against *SI* until recently—see for instance Karl Young, "Samuel Johnson on Shakespeare: One Aspect," *University of Wisconsin Studies in Language and*

Literature 18 (1923): 146–226. In the past decades, critics have re-evaluated *SI*; see particularly Kramnick and Margaret Anne Doody's "Shakespeare's Novels: Charlotte Lennox Illustrated" (*Studies in the Novel* 19.3 [Fall 1987]: 296–310).

6. Isles gives a list of some such contemporaries who voiced criticism of *SI* as Thomas Birch, Claude Pierre Patu, Richardson, and the *Monthly Review* (40 n.61).

7. Thomas D'Urfey (1653–1723), satirist and dramatist whose 32 plays (mostly comic) and 500 songs were extremely popular at the beginning of the eighteenth century.

8. Garrick identifies an irreverent tone in *SI* that as a proponent of Shakespeare he was of course unwilling to tolerate. His position is further documented in a letter from Thomas Birch to Philip Yorke, 2nd Earl of Hardwicke of June 23, 1753: "Mrs. Lennox, the Author of the Female Quixote, has met with such ["such" superscribed] success in her Shakespeare Illustrated, that her Bookseller has engag'd her to add a third Volume. The Dedication to Lord Orrery is a very good one, but not her own performance, S. Johnson having lent her his Pen, as he had done to ["done to" superscribed] several other Writers. Her Observations on the use, which that Poet has made of the several Novel's & Stories, upon which his Plays are founded, [word here impossible to read] so many Freedoms upon him, as give great Offence to his Admirers, & Mr. Garrick has fix'd a Name upon her, which she highly resents, that of Mrs. Lauder" (British Library Add.Ms. 35398, f.121). "Mrs. Lauder" is a reference to William Lauder's *An Essay on Milton's Use and Imitation of the Moderns* (originally published London: s.n., 1741 and more recently by Lennox's own former publishers, London: Payne and Bouquet, 1750 [see #1]), an "unscrupulously dishonest attack on Milton as a plagiarist on the basis of forged evidence" (Isles 39 n.57). In other words, Garrick is suggesting that Lennox's attack on Shakespeare (as he saw it) was dishonest.

On the Lauder controversy, see a series of five articles by Michael Marcuse: "The Lauder Controversy and the Jacobite Cause," *Studies in Burke and His Time* 18.1 (Winter 1977): 27–47; "The Pre-Publication History of William Lauder's *Essay on Milton's Use and Imitation of the Moderns in His Paradise Lost*," *Papers of the Bibliographical Society of America* 72.1 (January-March 1978): 37–57; "Miltonklastes: The Lauder Affair Reconsidered," *Eighteenth-Century Life* 4.4 (June 1978): 86–91; "The *Gentleman's Magazine* and the Lauder/Milton Controversy," *Bulletin of Research in the Humanities* 81.2 (Summer 1978): 179–209; and "'The Scourge of Imposters, the Terror of Quacks': John Douglas and the Exposé of William Lauder," *Huntington Library Quarterly* 42.3 (Summer 1979): 231–61.

9. There does not seem to be any "old saying" surviving with these words, unless it is an adaptation of Othello's "I that am cruel am yet merciful" (V ii), which is not entirely unlikely given Garrick's Shakespearean background. Charles Somerset's rather obscure play *Crazy Jane* (London: Cumberland, 1829) has the line, "Since you are brave, be merciful as well" (II ii, 31), but of course that is long after Garrick is writing. To my knowledge, the earlier ballad versions of the Crazy Jane story do not contain the phrase.

18

Samuel Johnson
to Alexander Lennox

[c. 1753–56¹]

MS:	Houghton Library, Harvard University, MS Eng 1269 (2)
Pages:	1
Edition:	LC #43, Redford V 9
Address:	To Mr Lennox
	in Gerrard Street Soho²
Text:	

Sir

I beg the favour of you to lend
me another Guinea,³ if you can
by Frank.⁴ My compliments
to dear—⁵

> I am
> Sir
> Your most humble servan[t]
> Sam: Johnson

NOTES

1. The earliest date for this letter is defined by the address: The Lennoxes apparently moved to Gerrard Street some time after March 1753 (when Lennox uses a St. James's address, see #15), used the address at least twice (#23 and #27), and had moved to Kensington by April 1758 (see #30). At the other end, the letter must

have been written before Barber's absence from Johnson's household, which began late 1756 or early 1757 (see n.4 below).

2. Gerrard Street near Leicester Fields in Soho (Rocque 10Ca, Horwood 13Ac) has literary significance as the location of the Turk's Head tavern, where the Literary Club of Johnson and Reynolds met from 1764–83 (Wheatley II 106). Sir John Hawkins was one of the founding members and describes meetings and members in detail (*Life* 249–55). In addition, the founder of the RLF David Williams lived and died at #36, so there is a chance Lennox met him there (Wheatley II 107).

3. One guinea is, as Isles points out, rather "paltry a sum" (418 n.190). Isles argues that while Johnson was "frequently in financial trouble [. . .] an examination of SJ's finances at the time [. . .] indicates that if a more precise guess as to dating were required SJ's need for borrowing guineas was at its height in February and March 1756, during which time he was arrested for debt and helped by Samuel Richardson" (418 n.190). The formulation "another Guinea" suggests that this was not the first time Johnson was borrowing money from Alexander Lennox. Also, the mere fact of borrowing from the Lennoxes implies that at least in some of the 1750s, they were financially *better* off than Johnson.

4. This is Johnson's black servant Frank Barber (c.1742–1801). Born in Jamaica to a slave named Grace and originally called "Quashey," Barber came to England in 1750 with his owner Sir Richard Bathurst. Bathurst's son Richard gave Barber to Johnson in April 1752 to take care of him and freed him in his will of April 24, 1754 (James Clifford, *Young Sam Johnson* [New York: McGraw-Hill, 1955], 102). Barber ran away from Johnson in late 1756 or early 1757, probably because of a dispute, and first worked for an apothecary and later joined the Navy (Clifford 181). He returned to Johnson in October 1760 and stayed with him until the end of Johnson's life, starting his own family after marrying a white woman called Elizabeth Ball (Rogers 23). Barber was the main beneficiary of Johnson's will.

5. The obvious assumption here is that Johnson wants Alexander to give his compliments to his wife, but it is unclear why he does not write out her name.

19

Mary Jones
to Charlotte Lennox

DECEMBER 16, 1754

MS: Houghton Library, Harvard University, MS Eng 1269 (34)
Pages: 3
Edition: LC #13
Text:

Mad[m].

　　　　　I was favour'd wth. a Letter from you
about ten days ago,[1] w[ch]. equally surpris'd & pleas'd me,
& w[ch]. I shd have acknowledg'd immediately, but y[t]. my
Bro[r].[2] was then ill of a Fever, & is but just got abroad.[3]
I was surpris'd to find my self still more oblig'd, for hav=
:ing only shewn my Sense of an Obligation;[4] & pleas'd
wth. Sentiments y[t]. seem to flow so naturally & so gracefully,
& yet so much above y[e]. common Level. Few Creditors
think y[m] selves oblig'd by y[e]. bare Acknowledgm[t]. of a
Debt;[5] but M[rs]. Lennox, like other superior Beings, seems
to penetrate y[e]. Heart, & takes her Estimate from y[e]. In=
=tention, rather than y[e].[6] Act. By w[ch]. means she makes
me y[e] greatest Complim[t]. imaginable, & herself, deser=
:vedly, none of y[e]. least. Indeed, Madam, you soar so
much beyond me,[7] y[t]. even at first setting out, I despond,
finding my self unequal to y[r]. Wing;[8] & if I was to

to [sic] carry on y[e]. Metaphor of y[e]. Feather, shd at this
very Period drop my Quill. You have convinc'd me y[t].

52

tis possible to endure a Competitor (under certain Cir:
:cumstances) without Envy; but how is it possible ever
to rise again, after once sinking in Despair? This w^d.
require a Spirit equal to any Quixotism you've painted,
& none but y^e. ingenious Author of Shakespeare illustrated
c^d. set our Judgments right again, in so humiliating a
Situation.[9]

 For y^e. rest then, I will creep after you as
well as I'm able, in acknowledgm^t. of y^r. distance; con=
:fessing however at y^e. same time, y^t. from y^e. benignity
of y^r. Aspect, & y^e. Influence you heavenly Bodies natu=
=rally have over us sublunary ones, I hope to feel, I al:
:ready feel my self cherish'd wth. y^r. Rays, tho their
Light has (you own) been so long travelling down to me.
And now I'm got among y^e. celestial Signs, pray, where
is that Meteor, that <u>Rambler</u>, y^t. shew'd himself in
our Hemisphere last Summer,[10] & has never been heard of
since, except among y^e. Transactions of y^e. Literati?

If he is often at y^r. Elbow (a Situation he had y^e. Con:
:fidence to boast of to me) I shd be oblig'd to you if you'd
make my Complim^{ts}. to him.[11] He's so restless a Companion,
y^t. twas impossible to take my Observations of him, wth. any
Accuracy, in his Company; but now he's got Abroad, &
exhibits himself fairly to y^e. ~~public~~ Eye, I doubt not
of contemplating his Magnitude wth. y^e. greatest Satisfaction.[12]

 You enquire when I go to Town. I've been talking
of it these two Months, but have been prevented.[13] Whenever
I do go, twill be a high Gratification to me to have an
Opportunity of paying my Respects to M^{rs}. Lennox, & of
assuring her how much I honour her, as well as think
my self,

her greatly Oblig'd
& most Obed^t.
Humble serv^t.
M. Jones

Oxford. Decr. 16
 1754

NOTES

1. This letter no longer exists. As the following sentence explains, Jones was not expecting a letter, indicating that the connection between her and Lennox was not very close or even that they had never been introduced.

2. Oliver Jones, chanter of Christ Church Oxford, with whom Mary was living, probably as a kind of housekeeper.

3. I.e., healthy and out of the house.

4. It is unclear how Jones showed a sense of obligation.

5. This sentence suggests that Lennox owes some sort of debt to Jones, but it is unknown what that debt might have been.

6. This would indicate that Jones had promised some assistance, but not (yet) delivered.

7. Here, Jones suggests that Lennox's literary abilities are much more developed than her own. A similar sentiment is expressed below, where Jones writes about the "Influence you heavenly Bodies [Lennox] naturally have over us sublunary ones [Jones]."

8. This is reminiscent of Johnson's eagle metaphor around the same time (#16).

9. This passage is confusing. Possible, Lennox's letter had mentioned a "Competitor"—maybe to her *FQ* (referred to with "Quixotism"), maybe to her *SI*, maybe more generally—who in some way humiliated Lennox and whom Lennox endured. It is of course possible that Jones is this competitor. At the same time, Jones is calling Lennox *her* competition and learning the lesson of enduring a competitor *from* her.

10. Johnson, the literary "Meteor" and author of *The Rambler*, had visited Oxford in July and August 1754 (BLJ III 451).

11. This would indicate that Lennox was seeing Johnson regularly during this period. At the same time, the fact that Johnson boasted of being at Lennox's elbow constantly suggests that at this time Lennox was the one in the more powerful situation (and/or more famous and successful).

12. This phrase sounds rather ironic—see n.11 above.

13. Jones spent her entire life in Oxford, only visiting London ("Town") occasionally. It is unknown if she and Lennox ever met.

20

Charlotte Lennox
to [Andrew Millar[1]]

JULY 28, 1755

MS: Bodleian Library, University of Oxford, Ms.Montagu d.8,
               ff.124-26v.

Pages: 2

Text:

Sir

I hope you will not think it an unseason
-able importunity, if now that I have en
-tirly finishd my work,[2] I beg the favour
to see you to morrow or next day as it
shall suit your conveniency.[3] I was resolved, however pressing my exigencies[4]
might be, that I would not trouble you
as I have too often done with application
for money[5] before it was due,[6] and althoug[h]
I have now completed the work, I would
wait your leisure, were it not for a disa
-greeable circumstance that forces me to
solicit you to come sooner than you without
knowing my reasons probably intended.
M[r] Lennox has been obligd to keep the
house for this fortnight past. I want
to remove to some place of security, till I
can satisfy those persons he is most appre
-hensive of.[7] when they know he is out of

their reach, we can offer, and they will
accept easier terms, than they will now
hear of. but it is not in my power to go

---

till you are so good as to settle with me for Sully
—I am grieved to the soul about the [bree[8]]
I owe you, but what can I do so unhappily
circumstanced as I am. Do not imagine I
want to importune you, but let me say this once
that if you will allow me to pay you by the Work
I proposed,[9] which I am sure will be an advanta
-gious one to you, I will undertake it with more
chearfulness than ever I did any thing in my life
for however you may be prejudiced against me, yet
it is a most certain truth that I have ever look[ed]
upon you as one of the sincerest of my friends,[10] to
whom I have had the most obligations, and for
whom I shall ever have the truest esteem, and
regard, while I am

Charlotte Lennox

Monday July 28. 1755

PS
I have done great part of the trial.[11] I have foun[d]
it a most difficult piece of work on account of
the ignorance of the transcriber—I am very
anxious to have the book finishd, methinks the
Printers go on but slowly. the sooner it is pre
-sented to the Duke,[12] the better. excuse my writing to
you on Copy paper,[13] I had no other at hand.

NOTES

1. The addressee of this letter has not previously been identified. However, from similarities in content with the following letter (#21), particularly the references to a translation (here specified as *Sully*) and to Alexander Lennox's illness, it can be surmised that this letter is also to Millar.

2. This "work" is the three volumes of *Sully*, announced in the *London Evening Post* of October 18, 1755 for November 1 (though, in a common practice to keep it "new" longer, the book was dated 1756) and published by Andrew Millar. This

book was a translation of the French three-volume 1747 *Memoires de Maximillien de Bethune, Duc de Sully, Principal Ministre de Henry le Grand*, in turn adapted by Pierre Mathurin de L'Écluse des Loges (1715–83) from Sully's own text, which was originally published in 1638. In her English translation, Lennox followed the 1747 French edition closely, with the text proceeding chronologically (vol. I 1570–1599; vol. II 1599–1606; vol. III 1607–1611 [though the English edition only says 1610 in the margins until the end, the text marked 1611 in French is given here as well, only with 1610 in the margin], followed by a treatise on Henry IV's political projects, a supplement on Sully, and the index). The only real innovation the English edition offers is the trial of Ravaillac; see below n.11.

An earlier translation of Sully's memoirs was published in 1751, but the question of whether Lennox also translated that version will probably never find a satisfactory answer. This one-volume excerpt was titled *The Memoirs of the Duke of Sully; During his Residence at the English Court; to which he was sent Ambassador from Henry IV. of France, upon the Accession of King James the First* and published in London by Robert Dodsley and by George and Alexander Ewing in Dublin. It takes sections from the treatise on Henry IV's political projects at the end of the full text as well as passages on Sully's time in England, so that the pages from the 1756 edition that were previously translated here are (in that order) III 318-31; II 68–74; III 333–56; II 154–247 (with some bridging paragraphs and slight changes such as splitting paragraphs and deleting footnotes). The translations read fairly similar. For instance, where the 1751 (Dublin) edition has, "The Queen of *England*, upon Information of the King's being in *Calais*, imagined it a favourable Opportunity, to satisfy her Impatience to see and embrace her best Friend" (27), the 1756 reads, "The queen of England hearing the king was at Calais, thought it a favourable opportunity to satisfy her impatience of seeing and embracing her best friend" (II 68). While some words and phrases are repeated (favourable opportunity, her best friend), other items (upon Information of/hearing) and grammatical structures (to see and embrace/seeing and embracing) are changed—but the translations are too similar to be completely independent of each other. With the 1751 covering about 8.5% of the 1756 edition (ca. 125 page of the complete work's 1472, excluding Ravaillac's trial and the index), two conclusions are possible: 1) that Lennox had already done the 1751 translation and adapted it for the complete work, or 2) that Lennox, though not herself the translator, *used* the 1751 translation in preparing hers. The first version could be considered conjecturally supported by Lennox reference to having done translations before 1752, which could refer to the 1751 *Sully*. The shift between booksellers—with Dodsley as the sole proprietor of the 1751 edition and Millar as the primary publisher (with Dodsley as second) in 1756—does not send a clear message: Dodsley might have been willing to let Lennox use her earlier translation, if that is what it was, for this new and extended venture, but since he was involved in 1756 he might have been equally happy to let her use a previous edition to which he owned the copyright. Unless additional material surfaces from any of these sources, it will remain impossible to solve this mystery.

The long and prominent review of *Sully* in the *Monthly Review* (14 [June 1756]: 561–73; 15 [August 1756]: 97–106; 15 [September 1756]: 209–16), which in typical eighteenth-century fashion intersperses some commentary and summary between long quotes, adds no information on the question of the 1751 *Sully*. It does say "that the present translation is judiciously executed; that the language is easy, and proper for the subject, and such as may well become the fair hand to which the public is obliged for the *Female Quixote*, and *Shakespear illustrated*" (561). On Johnson's review in the *Literary Magazine*, see #24.

Sully continued to create headaches for Lennox—later in her career and after the 1774 copyright decision, she got into a legal fight with James Dodsley about the rights to reprint the book. On this affair, see #63, #64, and #66.

3. Judging from the following letter, Millar refused this request.

4. Lennox reference to her "exigencies" at this early point in her career is rather surprising. In the preceding three years, she had published her two most famous works—*FQ* and *SI*—she was under the patronage of Johnson and Richardson, and she received decent remuneration for other translation projects (see #26 n.4), so it is hard to explain why she would not have made a fair amount of money from these works.

5. This reference, too, is slightly puzzling, since it implies a long interaction. As a matter of fact, the only collaboration known between Lennox and Millar at this point was *FQ*, her 1752 *Proposals*, and *SI*—though of course there may have been several requests for money during these projects.

6. It appears Lennox was not paid in advance for her work—only famous writers were, and then only occasionally—but after its completion.

7. Alexander Lennox being "apprehensive" could be a mark of not wanting to repay his debtors (whoever they were) or an actual fear of being pursued by them. Since the Lennoxes want to move physically away from London, the latter is the more likely case. However, the following letter (#21) also suggests that Alexander may have been ill.

8. This word is clearly legible, but makes little sense. One would expect something like "book," "work," or "debt" (if Lennox had indeed received some sort of advance).

9. It remains unclear why Lennox would have had to pay money *to* Millar instead of receiving it from him—maybe she was still paying him for the 1752 *Proposals* or had received an advance. Equally uncertain is what "the Work I proposed" is. This could possibly be Lennox's next translation *Berci*, which was published on April 10, 1756, but that is pure speculation.

10. This is either insincere or a significant change of heart from the problems surrounding the acceptance and publication of *FQ*.

11. The trial Lennox refers to is probably the "Tryal of Ravaillac for the Murder of Henry the Great," which the subtitle of *Sully* promises. François Ravaillac, a Roman Catholic, murdered Henry IV of France as he was on his way to visit the sick Sully on May 14, 1610—for giving limited religious freedom to French Protestants. After the end of Sully's memoirs in the third volume, the text goes on to offer "The Tryal of Francis Ravaillac, for the Murder of King Henry IV. 1610" with the headnote

"Interrogatories exhibited to the accused of the murder of the late king, on the 17th of May, 1610. at the suit of the attorney-general, by Achilles de Harlay, first president; Nicolas Potier, president; John Courtin and Prosper Bavin, counsellors of our lord the king in his court of parliament, commissioners appointed by the said court for that purpose." The trial is then reported on pages 380–407. It seems these court proceedings—which were not part of the French edition of the memoirs—were transcribed by an anonymous author, about whose ignorance Lennox complains.

12. *Sully* is dedicated to the Duke of Newcastle. On the relationship between Lennox and the Newcastles, see Small, esp. 27–31, and #37 and #42.

13. Lennox probably means bastard or double copy paper, which might have been supplied by Millar. Bastard paper was in the middle range of papers: Of 36 types of paper taxed in 1713, 16 were taxed at a higher rate and 13 at a lower (Danby Pickering, *The Statues at Large* [Cambridge: Bathurst, 1764], 80-84). Since there were plenty of cheaper papers Lennox could have used (for instance Cartridge, Genoa Crown, Foolscap, or German), she apologizes for using bastard for her letter.

21

Charlotte Lennox
to Andrew Millar

AUGUST 1, [1755]

MS:	British Library, Department of Manuscripts, Evelyn Papers, UP 10
Pages:	2
Address:	To
	Mr Millar
Text:	

Sir,

I should imagine such a letter as mine
to you[1] deserved that you should condescend
to send me an answer with your own pen
and not the pen of your servant,[2] but let
me ask you Sir, for what reason do you
refuse to settle accounts with me till the book[3]
is printed off, have I not done my part
to it. is it not expressly said in the arti-
cles[4] that the ballance [*sic*] is to be paid when I have
finishd the work, and is not the work entirly [*sic*]
finishd. what more am I expected to do—
I have translated twenty sheets of Index[5]
which I had no business with, besides which
Mr Lennox has been employd six or eight
hours every day for near three months in
filling it up,[6] and a tedious difficult work
he found it—yet after all this generosity,

—I am denyd the balance, tho for the want
of it Mr Lennox who is not well has been

---

confind to the house near three weeks.[7] methinks
it is not a very kind return for the labour
he has been at. I beg the favour Sir
to hear from you immediately. I am not
well, and am very much vexd. I have
not, nor will not stir out while Mr Lennox
is obligd to stay at home, tho' my health
suffers greatly from such a confinement
     I am tird to death about the money
for the notes, in full expectation of seeing
you I appointed the man who translated
them[8] to call to morrow, after putting him off
several times before. he is to have five guineas
for the notes he has done, and he has well
earnd them. be so good Sir to reflect that
it is entirely owing to you that there has been
any altercation about this affair, for I only
made a reasonable and a just request, which
you thought proper to deny. consider the
disagreeable situation I am in at present
and then I am sure you will not delay to send

to Sir
your most humble Servt

August 1   C Lennox

NOTES

1. As explained in #20, n.1 above, the letter Lennox is referring to here is probably the previous one.

2. Instead of answering Lennox's letter himself, it appears Millar allowed a servant to write. This servant might have been Robin Lawless, whom Nichols describes as a "diligent and honest servant, who, for considerably more than half a century, had been so well known to, and much distinguished by, the notice and regard of many of the most eminent literary characters of his time, as one of the principal assistants to Mr. Andrew Millar" (III 387n).

3. Lennox is referring to *Sully*.

4. The "articles" of a (no longer surviving) contract presumably say that Lennox is to be paid on Millar's receipt of the translation—a common practice in the eighteenth century and the arrangement she mentions in the previous letter. The phrase "which I had no business with" implies that Lennox had probably not contracted to translate the index as well.

5. Lennox translated four books for Millar: *Sully*, *Berci* (1756), *Maintenon* (1757), and *Brumoy* (1759). Of these four works, only *Sully* contains an index, and at 124 (unnumbered) pages it almost fits Lennox's claim of twenty sheets.

6. This is one of only a few instances in which Alexander Lennox actually appears to be contributing actively towards Lennox's career.

7. More clearly than in the previous letter, Alexander Lennox is now supposedly staying at home for reasons of health. (Alternately, he might have become ill *because* of his isolation at home, as Lennox suggests for herself below.) The two weeks mentioned there plus the week between the two letters neatly add up.

8. It is well known that Lennox had assistance from other individuals, such as Johnson and Orrery, in translations. Here, it seems she additionally employed—for the price of "five guineas"—an unnamed man (who cannot have been known or important enough to Millar to mention him by name, or whose identity Lennox wanted to protect) who has helped her with the notes, presumably those included in the body of the text of *Sully* (or Lennox is using "notes" as a synonym for 'index').

22

Printing Ledger for *Sully* (1)

SEPTEMBER 5, 1755

MS:	British Library, Department of Manuscripts, Strahan Papers, Add.Ms. 48803A, f.14
Pages:	1
Text:	

1755
Sep.[5]

Partners in Sullys Memoirs[1]

Printing D°. 211 ½ Sheets N°. 500 @			
17 Sh p Sheet[2]	179	7	—
For 2000 Proposals for D°.[3]		15	—
Extra for 16 Sheets of Index[4] @ 7ᵛ	5	12	—
Conclusions in D°. throughout[5]	6	8	—
	192	2	—

1755 Octʳ. 18. From Mʳ Shropshire[6]	64: 0: 0
1756 June 2[7] From Mʳ. Dodsley	64: 0: 0
Settled with Mʳ Millar for	64: 0: 0
	192: 0: 0

NOTES

1. This entry is from the ledgers of the printer and bookseller William Strahan. It shows that 500 copies of *Sully* were printed in the first print run, and it confirms who the three publishers were (Shropshire, Millar, and [Robert and James] Dodsley). It appears Strahan did not own any of the copyright to *Sully* (in contrast to other books

in the ledgers), but was simply doing a printing job for three bookseller (functioning here as publishers) and collecting payment from them. The title page of *Sully* does not name Strahan, either because he did not own any share of the copyright or because he did not want to be seen as competing with his clients, i.e., with the booksellers who used him as a printer. On these ledgers, see Richard Arthur Austen-Leigh, "William Strahan and His Ledgers," *The Library* 3rd series 4 (March 1923): 261–78; Patricia Hernlund, "William Strahan's Ledgers: Standard Charges for Printing, 1738–85," *Studies in Bibliography* 20 (1967): 89–111; Patricia Hernlund, "William Strahan's Ledgers II: Charges for Papers, 1738–1785," *Studies in Bibliography* 22 (1969): 179–95; O M Brack, Jr., "The Ledgers of William Strahan," in *Editing Eighteenth-Century Texts*, ed. D.I.B. Smith (Toronto: University of Toronto Press, 1968), 59–77; and Cochrane.

2. As this line demonstrates, paper was the most expensive part of printing books in much of the eighteenth century.

3. Since *Sully* was not published by subscription, "Proposals" probably simply means advertisements. Printing advertisements was a common practice in the eighteenth century: For instance, the booksellers of Tobias Smollett's *Complete History of England* spent "£200 [...] for 'very large quantities of proposals" (O M Brack, Jr., "Tobias Smollett Puffs His Histories," in *Writers, Books, and Trade: An Eighteenth-Century Miscellany for William B. Todd*, ed. O M Brack, Jr. [New York: AMS Press, 1994], 267–88, here 267).

4. In the event, it appears the index was slightly longer: Lennox writes of "twenty Sheets of Index" (#21).

5. This might be the "Tryal of Ravaillac for the Murder of Henry the Great," which Lennox writes she was working on when the rest of the book was already at the printer's (see #20).

6. This is probably William Shropshire, who was active from the 1730s to the 1750s (Plomer 227). There is also a Walter Shropshire (Plomer 227, Maxted 204), but he did not become active until the 1760s. William Shropshire worked with Dodsley on several other publications, but *Sully* is his only collaboration with Millar. By the 1750s, it seems Shropshire was working mostly as a retailer rather than as a publisher—*The Inspector* of 1751 and *An Extract out of Pausanias* of 1758 are the only publications of the 1750s in which he took the lead.

7. These lines on Strahan's payment are interesting—only Shropshire seems to have paid in a timely fashion (*Sully* was published in late October or early November 1755), Dodsley much later, and Millar appears to have had some other kind of arrangement with Strahan.

23

John Hawkesworth
to Charlotte Lennox

APRIL 30, 1756

MS: Houghton Library, Harvard University, MS Eng 1269 (30)
Pages: 1
Edition: LC #14
Address: To
           Mrs. Lenox
           at Mr. Cooper's[1]
           in Gerrard Street
           Soho[2]

Text:

Madam

        I know not with what Apology to introduce my
request that you would accept the packet ~~that~~ which accompanies
this Letter.[3] I would indeed have sent it long agoe [*sic*] but hoped I should
be able to appoint a Time by the Messenger when I might have
brought M[rs] Hawkesworth[4] to wait upon you this has never yet been
in my power tho' almost continually in my thoughts. another
Vacation is coming on[5] of which I will not say any thing for
I have already made my promises cheap

                         I am
                         Mad[m]. with sincere Respect
S[t]. John's Gate[6]   Y[r] most obed[t] humble Serv[t]
30th. April 1756   J[no] [*sic*] Hawkesworth

NOTES

1. I have been unable to establish the identity of this person.

2. See #18.

3. As Isles writes, "The contents of the 'packet' are unknown. As Lennox had no known connection with [the *Gentleman's Magazine*] in this year, the 'packet' is probably of a personal rather than professional nature" (43 n.70). Apparently, the packet formed some sort of apology.

4. Hawkesworth married Mary Brown in 1744 after working as a writing teacher at her boarding school. She was apparently "a woman of sensitivity and intelligence" (Abbott 12). She survived her husband and unsuccessfully attempted to publish an edition of his works with Johnson (ibid., 192). It is unknown if Mrs. Hawkesworth ever met Lennox.

5. Since Hawkesworth did not really have vacations as the literary editor of the *Gentleman's Magazine*, this may refer to his wife's vacation from her boarding school.

6. St. John's Gate—the Northern end of St. John's Lane and entrance to St. John's Court (Rocque 4Bb, Horwood 4Cd)—was the official editorial address of the *Gentleman's Magazine* from 1731–81 (Wheatley II 314–15).

24

Samuel Johnson
to Charlotte Lennox

JULY 30, 1756

MS:	Houghton Library, Harvard University, MS Eng 1269 (8)
Pages:	4
Edition:	LC #15, Redford I 135–37
Text:	

Madam

The Letter which you sent me some time ago, was rather too full of wrath for the provocation.[1] I read both the reviews,[2] and though the Critical Reviewers, according to their plan, showed their superiority of knowledge with some ostentation, they mentioned you with great respect,[3] and the other Reviewers though less ceremonious, said nothing that can excite or justify much resentment.[4] They have both answred [*sic*] the original rather than the translation.[5] All that either has said is now forgotten except by those who have some particular motive to remember it, and therefore it will be best to leave Berci to his chance, without

---

a vain attempt to vindicate upon principles, what was not upon any principles of judgment undertaken.[6] The choice, if choice it might be termed, when you took the first book which was recommended to you, was unlucky.[7] Your Stile is commended

which is all the part, that I would wish you
to claim for by mentioning the alterations,[8] however
excellent, you become answerable for that which you
did not alter.[9]

I do not believe that either of the Reviews, intended you any hurt, it is certain that if they meant
to hurt you they will be disappointed,[10] and if you
were not too proud already, I would tell you, that
you are now got above their malice, and though you
cannot expect to be always equally succesful [sic], have such
a degree of reputation as will secure you from any neglect of readers or Stationers.[11]

When Mr Lennox brought me <u>Berci</u>[12] he said
<u>you desired me to say something about it</u>, which I

---

promised without hesitation, but I did not then
understand the request, nor imagined that he had
any thoughts of the pamplet [sic],[13] I conceived that you
wanted me to say something to Millar.[14] There is so little
room in the monthly book, that I believe no mention will ever be made in it but of originals, or books
of science or learning. This rule, however, I would
gladly break to do you either service or pleasure.[15]

If there be any episode or little story, more your favourite than the rest, than can be separated and
will fill about four or five columns, I will press its
insertion, and let it have its natural weight
with the publick.[16] But I do not think it worth
your while, our readers are few, and I know not
when they will be more.[17] to Sulli [sic] I am in
debt.[18] If you can point me out a passage that
can be refered [sic] to the present times, I will press for
a place in the Gentleman's Magazine, and write
an Introduction to it, if I can not get it in there

I will put it in the new book,[19] but their readers
are, I think, seven to one.[20]

I have seen Mrs Brookes, and Miss
Reid,[21] since I saw you, and I heard of you
at bothe [sic] houses, yet, what much surprised me
I heard no evil.[22]

I am,
Madam,
Your most obedient
and
most humble Servant
Sam: Johnson
July 30. 1756

NOTES

1. This previous letter is unfortunately lost. Johnson suggests that Lennox is overreacting to the situation, i.e., the mediocre reviews of *Berci*.

Lennox had a reputation for being somewhat aggressive and generally problematic as a person. On a literary level, Johnson complained of Lennox's "eagerness" in soliciting subscriptions (#55), and he criticized her manners in letters (#25). Perhaps for these reasons, she was never fully accepted as a member of the Bluestocking circle—though that may also have been due to her poverty relative to most of the Bluestockings.

Lætitia-Matilda Hawkins, the daughter of Johnson's first biographer Sir John Hawkins—who had reported on the celebration for *HS*—was Lennox's strongest detractor. She describes her first sighting of Lennox in court: "waiting at Hicks's-hall, till a trial came on before my father and the other justices;—a trial in which it must be confessed she had *some* concern; for it was an indictment preferred by her maid against her, for beating her! It came out that a battle had taken place between "the Female Quixotte," and her solitary domestic. How the legal question was decided, I have, I regret to say, forgotten:—it gave me an opportunity of seeing the illustrious lady, and at a safe distance" (331). The ironic "at a safe distance" suggests how traumatic this episode seems to have been for Hawkins, which she brings up twice more in her *Memoirs* (I 71 and II 13). On this matter, see Berg, *Circle* 133–34 and #60.

Hawkins also criticized Lennox for her deficient skills as a housewife and tutor. When Saunders Welch's daughters Mary and Anne became Lennox's pupils, Hawkins writes, Lennox proved to be "a lady of too eccentric a genius to render any service to a young person of less than moderate intellect" (*Memoirs* I 54). Hawkins claims that her household showed a "want of all order and method, all decorum of appearance, and regularity of proceeding" (*Memoirs* I 70–71) and suggests that these were "obliquities which to many would have been intolerable" (*Memoirs* I 70). Sometime in the 1780s or 1790s, an anonymous correspondent complained about Lennox's dirty fingernails and "horrid order" (#86), but by then her situation may have been a result of her increasing poverty. In any case, it is difficult to judge to what extent other women's comments may have been influenced by traditional ideas of decorum, personal animosities, jealousy because of Lennox's supposed beauty and success with men (as patrons, friends, or supporters), or even jealousy because of her literary success. On this subject, see also Norma Clarke, *Dr Johnson's Women* (London: Pimlico, 2000), 220–26 and Isles 175 n.149.

According to Hawkins, Lennox was also pushy in terms of her publications: When she had a disagreement with her second publisher, she went to confront him: "Payne was from home, and the person from whom she learnt this fact, being his aged mother, Charlotte, in that same genuine spirit which afterwards ripened into the Παιδισκημαχια or 'maid-fighting,' assailed the old lady with the eloquence which was intended for the son. The old crone, unused to the language of a lady who wrote books and translated 'les enfans perdus,' of an army, by 'the lost children,' as perhaps the old woman herself if she had got so far in learning might have done—cried out for quarter in the moving plea that she 'knew nothing, and was a plain old woman.' Charlotte, who might have urged the latter plea very fairly when I saw her, though she had waived every tittle [*sic*] of it at a time when her right would not have been disputed, indignantly turned away, repeating 'Plain enough! God knows!'" (*Anecdotes* 331–32; see also #1 n.2). Of course, Lennox was writing in an age in which decorum was especially important for women, so as a professional author she was in a double bind: be ignored by her publisher and keep her feminine reputation or impugn her reputation but perhaps make some headway with her publisher. Apparently, Lennox chose the latter approach, which did not endear her to many around her, especially women.

Perhaps for this reason, Frances Burney reported that "Mrs. Thrale says that though her *Books* are generally approved, Nobody likes *her*" (Burney III/1 105)— although no such sentiments are expressed in Thrale's own writing (see Piozzi, esp. I 99, I 328, and I 522).

2. The main literary review journals of the 1750s were Ralph Griffiths's *Monthly Review* (which began publication in 1749) and Tobias Smollett's *Critical Review* (which began in 1756). Both reviewed *Berci*.

3. The review in the *Critical Review* reads: "Since the ingenious lady who has favoured the world with this translation, was about to plunder the *French*, we could wish she had *taken* from them something of more importance. A woman of her reading surely could not be ignorant that this was an old romance newly vamped up; and the names of the personages changed from *Alcidion*, *Calista*, and others, which became it well enough, into *Count de Berci*, *the Chevalier D'Essars*, *the Countess de Berci*, &c. in which they cut as indifferent a figure as *Sancho* [Panza] in his government. It would however be doing injustice to the translator, if we did not observe that she has performed her part extremely well: the language is in general lively and spirited; and we are only sorry that it is expended upon a work, so antient and romantic. [Here follows a lengthy excerpt.] The chevalier *de Berci* is the *Drawcansir* [bully, boast] of the piece; we cannot think that such a character ever existed, nor indeed are the other characters copies from nature; notwithstanding which there is something entertaining in the manner of their being conducted. Though the dubbing of them with modern names spoils their appearance, and puts us in mind of the country 'squire who spoiled some venerable family pictures by employing a sign dauber to change their armour and helmets into short coats and tie periwigs. The original name of this romance was called

A Tragi-Comical History of Lysander *and* Calista: A translation of it was published in *London*, in the year 1635, in a thin folio, which it is not improbable may be found at some of the circulating libraries. And this we flatter ourselves will be deemed a reason very sufficient for our not saying any more upon *The Memoirs of the Countess* de Berci, which contains all the pomp of knight-errantry that is to be found in *Lysander and Calista*" (1 [May 1756]: 312–14). Johnson seems to think that the reviewer's demonstration of knowledge concerning the various versions of, or predecessors to, *Berci* constitutes "some ostentation" and is "ceremonious." The reviewer's comment that Lennox "has performed her part extremely well" could definitely be understood as a sign of "great respect." The review was written by Samuel Derrick (1724–69; ODNB XV 889), an Irish miscellaneous writer who produced criticism, poetry, translations, and later became Master of Ceremonies in Bath in 1763. He knew Johnson and was tutor to Boswell. Though Derrick was one of the four main contributors to the *Critical Review* in its first years, Smollett apparently did not have a very high opinion of him and mocked him in his novel *Humphry Clinker* (Derek Roper, "Smollett's 'Four Gentlemen': The First Contributors to the *Critical Review*," *Review of English Studies* n.s. 10.37 [February 1959]: 38–44).

4. In the *Monthly Review*, the review reads: "As we are unacquainted with the original of these Memoirs, we know not whether, from the words *taken from the French*, we should regard them as a mere translation; but be this as it may, the work bears a strong resemblance to the *romantic Romances* of the last century. The language, however, is very passable; and, it must be confessed, that the Lady to whom it owes its present appearance, is a much better writer than most of her cotemporary [*sic*] Novelists" (14 [June 1756]: 516–20). The rest of the review is a summary of the plot of *Berci*.

5. In other words, Johnson claims the criticism is not so much of Lennox's work as of the original French text's contents. This not entirely true, since the *Monthly Review*'s reviewer disavows any knowledge of the original. Instead, both reviews criticize *Berci* for being a throwback to the seventeenth-century French romance. On the other hand, Lennox had always shown great interest in French romances, as the entire plot of *FQ* demonstrates.

6. Johnson counsels Lennox against responding to the reviews since their claims are not based upon rational argument. Johnson never answered reviews himself because such responses did little good but could do harm instead. However, there is some rational basis to these reviews since the principle of both critics seems to be that the style and content of French romances are no longer appropriate.

7. This comment suggests that Lennox did *not* have much of a choice about which French work to translate after *Sully*.

8. As Isles lays out in detail (45 n.74), *Berci* was actually a combination of two French works: Vital d'Audiguier's *Histoire trage-comique de nostre temps, sous les noms de Lysandre et de Caliste* (1615, via Ignace-Vincent Guillot de la Chassagne's 1735 adaptation, *Le Chevalier des Essars, et la Comtesse de Berci*—which only the author in the *Critical Review* seems to be aware of) and Claudine Alexandrine Guérin de Tencin's *Memoires du Comte de Comminge* (1735). See also Fredrick W. Vogler,

"Vital d'Audiguier and Charlotte Lennox: Baroque Studies, Women's Studies, and Literary Resurrection," *Romance Notes* 36.3 (Spring 1996): 293–99.

9. This sentence is confusing—Isles inserts a comma after "claim." The gist of the second half of the sentence is that since Lennox has altered *part* of the translation, she was now also responsible for the parts she retained.

10. Johnson believes that the reviews were not written out of malice and claims that even if they were, they will not have much effect. Certainly the first part of the comment seems to be true, since the *Monthly Review* began a three-month-long highly positive review of *Sully* in the same issue as the more negative review of *Berci*.

11. Booksellers or publishers, not the Stationers' Company.

12. This is another instance of Alexander Lennox participating in his wife's literary affairs—see #15 and #18.

13. The "pamp[h]let," "monthly book," and "new book" are the *Literary Magazine*, which Johnson edited from May through August 1756. No review of *Berci* ever appeared there.

14. Andrew Millar was the publisher of *Berci*, so it is unclear what Johnson should have said to him, since Millar had already published the book.

15. "This rule" is indeed generally true, though the first issue of the *Literary Magazine* did include a review of *The General History of Polybius* (2 vols.; London: Dodlsey, 1756), translated by James Hampton (1721–78; ODNB XXIV 995–96). At least Johnson mentioned *Berci* among the "Books and Pamphlets [recently] Published" in the second issue of the journal (1.2 [May 15-June 15, 1756]: 99).

16. Book reviews in the eighteenth century often consisted of lengthy excerpts, or plot summaries, with a short commentary or assessment. This format would also have enabled Johnson to move the text from the review section to the front section of the *Literary Magazine*. While this did not happen for the *Literary Magazine*, Lennox did manage to reuse portions of *Berci*: The part from *Memoires du Comte de Comminge* was reprinted in Lennox's *LM* in 1760, in the *Hibernian Magazine* and the *Town and Country Magazine* in 1781, in the *New Novelist's Magazine* in 1787, and with names changed and a different ending under the title *The History of the Marquiss [sic] of Lussan and Isabella* in 1764 (Dublin: Hoey).

17. The *Literary Magazine* had just been launched in May 1756 and only lasted about two years, until July 1758.

18. This may be some specific debt, but more probably Johnson is simply praising *Sully* (in contrast to *Berci*).

19. "SJ's approach to *GM* was either unsuccessful or unattempted, as no extract from *Sully* appeared there. The *Literary Magazine* published an extremely flattering review, probably by SJ, in October 1756 (II, 281). This review did indeed stress the relevance of the memoirs to contemporary politics, and included an extract (not in itself a particularly good example of this relevance) from the work" (Isles 46 n.82). On the authorship of the review, see Boswell I 309 and Fleeman I 687 and 695–99. Johnson's review reads: "This translation has been already so well received by the public that we can add little to its reputation by the addition of our suffrage in its favour. But as the copies are about to be multiplied by a cheaper edition; it is not yet too late to remark,

that those memoirs contain an account of that time in which *France* first began to assume her superiority in *Europe*; that they exhibit a nation torn with factions, and plundered by tax-gatherers, rescued by a great king and an honest minister. There can be no age or people to which such a history may not be useful and pleasing, but it must more particularly invite the attention of those who like us are now labouring with the same distresses, and whose duty it is to endeavour at the same relief. But we live in an age where even profit is recommended in vain if it be not associated with pleasure, we therefore should scarcely solicit for this book the notice of the public, unless we could declare that it has the variety of romance with the truth of history; and that the style of the translation is easy, spritely, and elegant, equally remote from the turgid and the mean. It is difficult from a narrative well connected to detach a specimen. The following incident is selected only because it may be understood alone, and requires little room, not because it is otherwise preferable to other passages" (*Literary Magazine* 1.6 [September 15-October 15, 1756]: 280). The rest of the review is an excerpt from *Sully* narrating the taking of Fécamp by Captain de Bois-Rosé by intrigue, so—as Isles writes—the relevance to the political context Johnson describes is unclear.

20. Again, Johnson points out the relative insignificance of his *Literary Magazine*: The *Gentleman's Magazine*, he claims, has seven times more readers.

21. These two ladies remain unidentified.

22. This again refers to Lennox's poor reputation—she was considered aggressive and somewhat unfeminine. Alternately, Johnson believed that women could not say nice things about each other or was simply being ironic.

25

Samuel Johnson
to Charlotte Lennox

[c. 1757–79?[1]]

MS:	Houghton Library, Harvard University, MS Eng 1269 (13)
Pages:	1
Edition:	LC #44, Redford V 9-10
Text:	

Dear Madam

I am sorry you misunderstood me, I did not write for my
Books but for their names which you did not send me.[2]

I wish you would for once resolve to use any method
of transacting with your friends but that of letters. You will,
in whatever part of the World you may be placed, find man
kind extremely impatient of such letters as you are inclined to favour them with. You can send your letters, such
as the last but one, ~~any~~ only to two sorts of people, those whom
you cannot pain, and those whom you can, and surely
it is not elegible [sic] either to give mirth to your enemies or
to raise anger in your friends.[3] I have no[4] pleasure in
saying this, and am glad that I have delayed beyond the
time in which I might have been inclined to say more.[5]
I have no inclination to continue quarrels,[6] and therefore hope
y[ou wi]ll[7] again allow me, now I have vented my resent
m[ent] [,to be, ?]

> Dear Madam,
> [your] most obedient and most humble [servant]
> Sam: Johnson

NOTES

1. On the date of this letter, Isles writes, "Within the obvious limits of Lennox's initial friendship with Johnson (c. 1747–1750) and Johnson's death (December 1784), the period of writing cannot be satisfactorily conjectured. [...] The relative firmness of Johnson's handwriting, however, by contrast with [#67 and #68] removes the letter from the period of his so-called 'failing hand' [...] in the last years of his life" (Isles 419). Redford concurs with this assessment. However, the familiarity Johnson takes with Lennox, addressing her as "Dear Madam" and admonishing her on her style of interaction with her friends, suggests a somewhat ripened friendship. In addition, since no quarrel between Johnson and Lennox is known in the early years of their acquaintance, the earliest date for this letter might have been somewhere around 1757, when Johnson started criticizing Lennox's behavior (see #24). Johnson's writing started failing around 1779, so that would be the latest possible date.

2. The reference, apparently to books Johnson lent Lennox, is unclear. The previous letter with the request for "my Books" is lost.

3. Johnson's critique of Lennox's aggressiveness in her letters is similar to that voiced at the beginning of #24.

4. There seems to be a "t" "partially erased" (Redford V 10 n.3) after "no."

5. Johnson recognizes he is a hothead himself, which is the reason he has waited with his response to Lennox's lost letter.

6. The subject of the quarrel is unknown.

7. The manuscript is damaged on both sides here and below.

26

Publication Ledger for *Maintenon*

FEBRUARY 21, 1757

MS: British Library, Department of Manuscripts, Add.Ms. 38730, f.126 (see Ill. 3)

Pages: 1

Text:

1757

Feb: 21.[1]   Maintenon Memoirs. English. 5 Vol. 12°. N.1000[2]

Paid for a Sett [*sic*] in 15 Vols for the Translator[3] — —   1-13-3

—for the Translation 69 ½ Sheets at 1-5-0[4]   – – –   86-17-6

—for Paper for the Translator[5]   — — — —   0-16-6

—for Dictionaire de Trevoux 5V.[6]   ————————   4-4—

—M^r. Haberkorn[7] (27th. Decb^r. Last) for printing 40 ¼ Sheets @ 1-5-0 50-6-3

to pay Mr Hamilton[8] for printing   <u>29 ½</u> Sheets @ 1-5-0   36-17-6

                                         69 ¾

—M^r. Johnston[9] for 139 ½ Reams of paper at 12/9— ⎱ – –   88-18-7½

                       deliverd in June Cash ⎰

P^d for Advertisements in August Cash   — ————   1-8—

—for binding 1 Sett in Morocco,[10] hot pressed[11] – – – –   0-15—

—for —   1 more finely in Calf d° – – – – –   0- 7-6

—for —   <u>4</u> more in Calf gilt – – – – – –   1——

            <u>6</u> for the Translator[12]

To pay for Advertisements dp to Come[13]   ——   —— —   <u>10-2-6½</u>

                 1000 at 5/8, is   —   283-6-8

CV.[14]

1756 July 27.	By Cash of Dodsley[15] -7-7-0 — Aug 25. of Nourse[16] -7-7-0 } 29-8-0			
Au 23.	of Davies[17] 7-7-0. of Millar[18] 7-7-0		———	
Sept 9.	Another Call 5 Guineas each	–	— ———	21——
Oct 9.	Another Call 5 Guineas each	—	———	21——
Decb 11.	Another Call 5 Guineas each	—	———	21——

92-8-0

£ 190-18-8

Mr Millar's ¼ due is —   47:14:8
Nourse's   ¼ is —   47:14:8
Dodsley's ¼ is —   47:14:8
Davies —   47:14:8
190:18:8

Weds 21 Feb. 7 1757 of Mr Nourse Forty Seven
Pounds fourteen Shillings and eight pence
in full of his Share of the above
And. Millar[19]

NOTES

1. This date is difficult to make out, but seems to be the same as the one at the bottom of the sheet.

2. It is unknown whose ledger this sheet comes from, but—judging by Millar's signature below and by the fact that he is listed first in the imprint for *Maintenon*—it is reasonable to conclude that this was Millar's ledger.

3. This must be the 1755–56 Amsterdam edition of the *Memoires pour server à l'histoire de Madame de Maintenon*, which is the only one in fifteen volumes. This edition was advertised in the *Public Advertiser* 6722 (May 13, 1756): [1] as being on sale in the bookshop of Paul Vaillant (see Plomer 250).

4. This is one of only a few records concerning Lennox's payment for her literary work. With £86, she was being paid at the high end of the scale for her translation of *Maintenon*. Generally, translators in the eighteenth century had a reputation for being overworked and underpaid. For instance, Samuel Johnson was paid far less for his translation of Father Lobo's *Voyage to Abyssinia* than for his original poem *London*, even though the former was much longer (see Thomas Kaminski, *The Early Career of Samuel Johnson* [New York and Oxford: Oxford University Press, 1987], 73). Tobias Smollett went to the lengths of creating a fictional character in *Roderick Random* to express his own frustration with translation: After failing to get a drama produced on stage, Melopoyn is forced to earn money as a translator (see Alain René Le Sage, *The Devil upon Crutches*, tr. Tobias Smollett, ed. O. M. Brack, Jr., and Leslie Chilton [Athens and London: The University of Georgia Press, 2005], xv–xvi). However, more recently critics have begun to question this perception of translators as exploited and impoverished. See

Ill. 3. Publication Ledger for *Maintenon*, February 21, 1757 (#26) (© The British Library Board, Department of Manuscripts, Add.Ms. 38730, f.126)

for instance David Hopkins and Pat Rogers, "The Translator's Trade," Gillespie/Hopkins 81–95, esp. 81–84 and Raven, "Introduction" I 56–65, esp. I 63.

5. This provides an interesting glimpse into the process of translation work—at least in this instance, the booksellers supplied the translator (Lennox) with paper.

6. This is probably one of the editions of the *Dictionnaire universel françois et latin, vulgairement appellé Dictionnaire de Trévoux* from the 1730s (for instance Paris: Roullin, 1732 or Nancy: Antoine, 1734) that had five volumes.

7. John Haberkorn worked as a printer out of Gerrard Street, Soho, around 1755-65 (Plomer 112). It may or may not be a coincidence that Lennox was living in Gerrard Street at the same time (see #23 and #27).

8. Archibald Hamilton (Plomer 114) had only recently set up shop on his own; before that, he had been William Strahan's manager (Cochrane 121).

9. I have not been able to identify this Mr. Johnston. Plomer lists a dozen Johnsons or Johnstones (140–42), but none of them are described as stationers.

10. Morocco is a fine binding made from goatskin leather.

11. This phrase is difficult to read.

12. So Lennox was paid with books in addition to the £86 listed above. It remains unknown what happened to these six sets of *Maintenon*: Since they were probably bound in plain calf without gilt, they would look like any other copy, unless an inscription by Lennox was discovered.

13. This is probably a prediction for the cost of advertisements in the future ("to come"). *Maintenon* was advertised in the *Public Advertiser* almost every day between March 3 and March 21, 1757 and in other papers as well (e.g., *Daily Advertiser*, *Evening Advertiser*, and *London Chronicle*).

14. The transcription and meaning of this abbreviation remain unclear.

15. See correspondent's biography.

16. This is John Nourse (bap. 1705–80; ODNB XLI 219–20), who had his business at the Lamb without Temple Bar from around 1730 until his death. From 1762 until 1780, he was bookseller to the king. Nourse concentrated on scientific literature and on foreign books, so it is not surprising he participated in the translation of *Maintenon*.

17. Lockyer Davis (1717–91; ODNB XV 458) focused on buying and selling libraries and briefly worked with the RLF after its founding in 1789. He was member of the literary club that met at the Shakespeare tavern and was involved in Johnson's *Dictionary*, Shakespeare edition, and *Lives of the Poets*.

18. See #20 and #21 and correspondent's biography.

19. This is written in a different hand, presumably that of the signer Andrew Millar.

27

Samuel Johnson
to Charlotte Lennox

MARCH 10, [1757[1]]

MS: Houghton Library, Harvard University, MS Eng 1269 (9)
Pages: 1
Edition: LC #17, Redford I 150–51
Address: To Mrs Lenox
           at Mr Cooper's in Gerard Street
                   Soho[2]
Text:

March 10

Madam

      I saw last week at Mr Dodsly's[3] [sic] a Book, called Histoire des Conjurations par P. Tertre[4] which I told him was a good book, so far as could be judged by the title, for him to publish, and for you to translate.[5] He seemed not to dislike the proposal, but had not then all the volumes, I think he had only the Second.[6] Now you have ended Maintenon[7] you may perhaps think on it. I never saw it before, and saw little of it then but fancy it likely to succeed. Mr Dodsly will lend you his volume if you send for it.

I have no Ser-	I am, Madam
vant, and write	Your most humble Servant
therefore by post.[8]	Sam: Johnson

NOTES

1. This letter can be dated through the reference to *Maintenon*, which was published March 12, 1757.

2. On this address, see #18.

3. On Dodsley, see #71.

4. This is the *Histoire des conjurations, conspirations et revolutions célèbres, tant anciennes que modernes* (10 vols.; Paris: Duchesne, 1754–60) by François-Joachim Duport du Tertre (vols. 1–8) and Joseph-Louis-Ripault Desormeaux (vols. 9–10). Johnson is referring to Tertre as father (P. = père) because he was a Jesuit. No English translation of this work has ever been published.

5. Interestingly, Johnson is judging the book almost entirely by its cover (or title).

6. This comment suggests that eighteenth-century readers did not always read books in the order in which they were published. On this topic, see Jan Fergus, "Eighteenth-Century Readers in Provincial England: The Customers of Samuel Clay's Circulating Library and Bookshop in Warwick, 1770–1772," *Publications of the Bibliographical Society of America* 78.2 (1984): 180.

7. Lennox's translation of *Maintenon*.

8. Johnson's black manservant Francis Barber (see #18) ran away from him in October 1756 and worked for an apothecary in Cheapside for about two years. Therefore, Johnson writes by post instead of using Barber as his messenger.

28

Printing Ledger for *Sully* (2)

MARCH 1757

MS:	British Library, Department of Manuscripts, Strahan Papers, Add.Ms. 48803A, f.22
Pages:	1
Text:	

1757
March

Partners in Sully's Memoirs[1]

Printing D°. in 8vo.[2] 140 ½ Sheets N°. 1000		
@ £ 1: 2: 6 p sheet	158 1 3
Extra for 15 Sheets of Index of Do.	4 10 —
	162 11 3

pd Janry 19. 1758[3]

NOTES

1. On William Strahan and his ledgers, see #22.

2. While the first edition of *Sully* was three volumes in quarto, this second version was five volumes in octavo, i.e., a smaller format—though in a print run twice as large.

3. Again, it seems Strahan had to wait for an extended period of time for his payment.

29

David Garrick
to Charlotte Lennox

[FEBRUARY 8, 1758 OR FEBRUARY 23, 1757[1]]

MS: Houghton Library, Harvard University, MS Eng 1269 (22)
Pages: 3
Edition: LC #16
Address: To
             M[rs]. Lennox.

Text:

Madam,

  I have read over Your Pastoral
Opera[2] with great attention—
but it can't possibly be of
y[e]. least Service to You or y[e].
          y[t]. it sh[d].
Managers[3] ~~to~~ ^ appear upon our
Stage[4]—All y[e] Musical per:
:formances w[ch]. we have Exhibited
since y[e]. Chaplet & Lottery[5]
have not paid half y[e] Expences
of getting 'Em up—Nothing
can Support a Musical Drama
upon our Stage, but great Spirit
with
& Songs of a Comic Cast—We

---

are Engag'd to two performances

83

of this Kind y^e <u>British Enchanters</u>,
wch. is set by M^r. Arne,[6] & to
a Pastoral Drama (from ye Italian
I believe) but greatly Enliven'd
with Songs of Humor—
If we can possibly be Excus'd
from these or one of 'Em, we
certainly shall,[7] for not one
Musical Performance has
Answer'd to us but y^e <u>Chaplet</u>,
wch. was ye first, & written by
M^r. Mendes—I sh^d. have
answer'd y^r. Letter sooner
but my Business & Illness[8]

---

together have prevented
Me. I am
  Mad^m
  Your most obed^t
  hum^le Servt
    D: Garrick
PS.
 My objections to y^r. Opera
are, that there is a dramatic
Spirit & Interest wanting
thro ye whole—Not but there
are many detach'd beauties
wch. gave me great Pleasure.[9]
    Ashwednesday.[10]

NOTES

1. On this date, see n.10.

2. This must be Lennox's *Philander: A Dramatic Opera*. The play incorporated "sixteen songs, some of which were in turn adaptations or unacknowledged reprints from Lennox's own earlier publications" (Isles 47, n.85), so Garrick considered it a 'musical performance.'

3. Garrick and James Lacy had been co-managers of the Drury Lane Theatre since 1747, Garrick taking care of the creative side and Lacy of the business side (Garrick xxxiii).

4. Garrick implies two reasons for rejecting *Philander*: There would be, he suggests, no profit for the theater, and the play would reflect poorly on Lennox.

5. "Chaplet" refers to the after-piece *The Chaplet*, text by Moses Mendez and music by William Boyce, which was first performed on December 2, 1749. "Lottery" could mean Henry Fielding's ballad-opera *The Lottery*, which was performed eleven times between 1747 and 1751 at Drury Lane Theatre and another six times by 1756, or *Shepherd's Lottery* by Mendez and Boyce, which premiered in 1751 and was performed another twenty-three times by 1756.

6. This is probably Garrick's own *The Enchanter*, "a two-act miniature opera very much in the Italian style" (Ian McIntyre, *Garrick* [London: Lane/Penguin, 1999], 302) that premiered in the Christmas season 1760. As McIntyre bluntly puts it, "Arne and Garrick had never got on" (294n), and by 1760 Arne had transferred his allegiance to the Covent Garden theater, so the music for *The Enchanters* was composed in the end by John Christopher Smith, "who was one of Handel's pupils" (McIntyre 226).

7. The next pastoral drama produced at Drury Lane was *Arcadia, or, The Shepherd's Wedding*—libretto by Robert Lloyd and music by John Stanley—in the 1761–62 season. Since this was written in celebration of George III's marriage to Queen Charlotte on September 8, 1761, it seems unlikely that Garrick would be referring to it three or four years previously. Therefore, it appears Garrick was at least partially granted his wish: He produced his own piece, of course, but that was the only new musical show that premiered at Drury Lane between 1757 and 1763, when Garrick went to France.

8. This particular illness is not listed in Stone/Kahrl's wonderful (or sad) Appendix F, "Garrick's Health Record During His Professional Career" (672–73). However, if the sickness in question is the gravel (a disease where small crystals get passed with the urine) of February 1758, the letter might date from 1758 rather than 1757.

9. Other reviewers of *Philander* showed a similar ambivalence towards the play. The *Critical Review* wrote that its "sentiments are proper, soft and delicate: the versification is varied, spirited and correct; and the songs are well-turned, poetical and harmonious" but also warned that it had not been produced, and that that was "a criterion of merit with the generality of readers" (4 [November 1757]: 468). The *Monthly Review* called the play "altogether worthy the Authour of the Female Quixote" yet could only bring itself to describe it as "poetical, romantic, and pretty enough, upon the whole" (17 [December 1757]: 568). David Erskine Baker's *The Companion to the Play-House* (2 vols.; London: Becket, Dehondt, Henderson, and Davies, 1764) was more negative, calling *Philander*, "A Piece not intended, nor indeed of Merit sufficient for the Stage" (I n.p.).

10. From the discussion of *Philander*, Isles argues that this letter was written in 1757 (Isles 47, n.84). However, since Garrick speaks of having read *Philander*, which was announced in the *London Chronicle* on December 1–3, 1757 (unless he read a manuscript and Lennox later published it *because* he rejected it), and because of the illness of Garrick's documented in 1758, the later year seems a safer conjecture. The specific dates are deduced from Ash Wednesdays in these two years.

30

Gregory Sharpe
to Charlotte Lennox

APRIL 23, 1758

MS:	Houghton Library, Harvard University, MS Eng 1269 (35)
Pages:	1
Edition:	LC #18
Address:	To
	M[rs]. Lenox at
	M[rs]. Wilks's in
	Hubbards buildings[1]
	Kensington
Text:	

Madam,

   I receiv'd your kind invitation,[2] and
assure you nothing but the Gout, w[ch]. threatens
me, shall hinder me from paying my
respects to you on Tuesday; when I am
glad to find I have a better chance of
meeting M[r]. Scott[3] than at my house
or his own. My Compliments wait
on M[r] Lenox from,

Madam,
Y[r] most obed[t].
hum[le]. Serv[t].
G Sharpe

April 23. 1758.

NOTES

1. No maps of Kensington list a "Hubbards building." However, there is a document (#1088 in the *List of Deeds, Parochial Documents, Etc.* [London: Kensington Public Libraries, 1964–]) that mentions in 1779 "two customary messuages [structures] formerly built on site of orchard belonging to Bullingham House then late in tenure or occupation [. . .] of Thomas Hubbard and William Wilkes." (Bullingham House was on the bend of Vicarage Place and cannot be identified with certainty in Rhodes.) The document is not entirely clear, but it seems that Hubbard and Wilkes built their building around 1755. In the rate books of the time (the earliest from Kensington is from 1760), Hubbard consistently appears richer than Wilkes, so it is not surprising that the building would be called "Hubbards building"—though Lennox seems to be residing with Mrs. Wilkes. However, nothing else is known about these individuals apart from the fact that Thomas Hubbard died in 1770 and was survived by his son George.

2. Primarily, this is probably an invitation to visit Lennox. More generally, this would have been about the time Lennox was inviting Sharpe to contribute his translation of Aristophanes's *The Frogs* to her *Brumoy*.

3. Considering the close temporal proximity, it is likely that this "Mr. Scott" is related to the "Mrs. Scott" in #32. Isles speculates this couple could be George Lewis Scott (1708–80; ODNB XLIX 380) and his estranged wife, the novelist Sarah Scott (1723–95; ODNB XLIX 468–71). However, no connection between Lennox and the Scotts is known.

31

Charlotte Lennox
to John Boyle, Earl of Cork and Orrery

OCTOBER 29, 1758

MS: Folger Library, N.b.42, p.85
Pages: 3
Address:
Text:

My Lord

     When I saw the Book my Messenger
brought,[1] I concluded I had a feast for the whole Day,
and no luxurious Alderman ever sat down with
a keener appetite to a Lord Mayor's banquet,[2] than I did
to the rich repast you sent me. But alas I found
there was only a taste of those delicacies which
Your Lordship's [sic] knows so well how to supply, but
such a taste, as will leave me no relish for the
coarser fare I must feed on till you are pleased
to invite me again. I am rejoyced to see such
just, and such elegant praises given to M[r] John
-son[3]—and now will your Lordship forgive
me for the request I am going to make: As You
have taken notice of the french Novels,[4] if you think
the <u>female Quixote</u> and <u>Henrietta</u> not wholly

unworthy of your approbation, it would be of infinite
service to me to mention them tho in ever so slight
a manner.[5] To say the truth, I am not without some

little ambition, and the greatest might be gratified
by your praises, but in this case my interest is
concern'd,[6] if another edition of Henrietta is prin[ted][7]
the proffits [*sic*] of it will be all my own;[8] it has not
wanted for approbation among good judges, M[r]
Warburton,[9] M[r] Stone,[10] and many others of no less
note, have honoured it with their praises,[11] so
as to come to my knowledge;[12] I mention this, not
out of vanity, but because I would show Your
Lordship, that without the sanction of such
judgments in favour of <u>Henrietta</u> I would
not take the liberty to solicit Your Lordship
to say something of that book. If this request
be improper, I beg for my own sake my Lord,
that you will forget I ever made it. If I did
not know Your goodness to be excessive, I should

---

be surprised at the new instance you give me
of it, in offering to speak to Rivington about
Voltaire's new work, and to translate part
of it.[13] That clause[14] will I am sure have great
weight with him, therefore when it suits with
Your Lordship's conveniency, I should be glad
you would be pleased to send for him.[15] M[r] Lennox
will attend Your Lordship, to communicate some
hints about getting the french Copy in Sheets[16]
through M[r] Harte's[17] interest with Lord Chesterfield,
but this design need not hinder Rivington
from being spoke to, when ever Your Lordship
pleases. I am with the truest gratitude for
all your favours

My Lord

Sunday October 29
1758

Your Lordship's
Most obligd, and most
obedient Servant
Charlotte Lennox

NOTES

1. It is unclear what book Orrery sent Lennox. He was involved in the *Memoirs of the Life of Robert Cary, Baron of Leppington, and Earl of Monmouth* (London: Hughs and Dodsley, 1759) early the following year (the dedication is signed January 13, 1759), and there is a chance Lennox saw early copies of this work. As Orrery contributed only the preface to these *Memoirs* (iii–xxxiv), that could be considered "only a taste of those delicacies which Your Lordship's knows so well how to supply."

2. Every November 9 in the eighteenth century, the Lord Mayor of London held the Lord Mayor's Show, a parade to demonstrate his importance. The following Monday, he held the Lord Mayor's Banquet, which was frequently used by politicians to offer important policy speeches.

3. It appears Lennox may have seen an early draft of Orrery's preface to *Brumoy*. There, Orrery writes, "Mr. Johnson has shewn us the line of beauty" (I iii)—an instance of "elegant praises."

4. Orrery also writes, "They [the French] exceed us in criticisms, translations, agreeable letters, and entertaining novels. [...] Their novels are inimitable; they represent the times, the manners, the disposition of the whole nation; while we, to say the truth, are at once the constant detractors and imitators of our adversaries, and wandering from nature and probability, attempt only to represent persons who never existed even in imagination, faultless monsters, or aukward fine gentlemen. This appears to be the general distinction between the French novels and our own" (I iv–v).

5. Orrery apparently granted Lennox's request: The sentence following the one quoted in the previous footnote reads, "If particulars may claim an exception to this general remark, *The Female Quixote* and *Henrietta*, I hope may lay some claim to that distinction" (I v).

6. Here, Lennox seems to distinguish between critical "ambition" and financial "interest."

7. The end of the word is cut off in the margin, but the upswing of the letter "d" is still clearly visible.

8. Lennox seems to suggest that she would profit financially from a second edition of *Henrietta*. A second (and revised) edition did indeed come out in 1761, but there is no evidence that Lennox made more profit—as late as 1769, the copyright was being bought and sold by booksellers rather than herself (see #46).

9. This is William Warburton, the bishop of Gloucester, theologian, and literary figure (1698–1779; ODNB LVII 268–75). Warburton made his combative theological reputation with books about deism and miracles. On the literary side, he was friend and executor of Alexander Pope, friend of Richardson, and knew Fielding as well as Laurence Sterne. In addition, he was one of the eighteenth century's most important editors of Shakespeare. Warburton seems to have had an interest in Lennox: In addition to this untraced praise for Lennox, he apparently once wrote to Andrew Millar that "Nothing is more public than her writings, nothing more concealed than her person" (*British Magazine* 3 [July 1783]: 8). Unfortunately, that remark is untraced as well.

10. This "Mr. Stone" is almost certainly Andrew Stone (1703–73; ODNB LII 886–87), the Duke of Newcastle's secretary and later "companion and factotum" (Browning 63)—see also below #37. At the Duke's instigation, Stone became Member of Parliament for Hastings from 1741–61. There, Stone served "among the Duke's most trusted and influential advisers" (Namier/Brooke III 484). The praise Lennox mentions has not been traced.

11. For instance, the *Monthly Review* wrote: "We look upon this to be the best novel that has appeared since [Francis Coventry's] *Pompey the Little* [of 1751—even before Lennox's own *FQ*]. The incidents are probable and interesting; the characters duly varied and well supported; the dialogue and conversation-scenes, spirited and natural, both in genteel and low life; the satire generally just; and the moral exemplary and important" (18 [March 1758]: 273). The *Critical Review* concurred: "Mrs. Lennox has forfeited no part of her reputation by this publication; which we warmly recommend as one of the best and most pleasing novels that has appeared for some years. The story is simple, uniform and interesting; the stile [*sic*] equal, easy, and well kept up, sinking no where below the level of genteel life" (2 [February 1758]: 130).

12. This is a strange phrase, but clearly legible.

13. The reference here is unclear—neither of the Rivington brothers (ODNB XLVII 56–62) ever published any works by Voltaire. (According to ESTC, there is a copy of a "New Edition" of *Letters Concerning the English Nation* published in London 1760 by Rivington and others, but the same edition is in other libraries and ECCO without Rivington's name in the imprint.) Lennox would have worked with the conservative and successful John Rivington (1720–92) rather than his brother James (1724–1802), who was in trouble in the literary marketplace in 1758 for trying to undersell the London market with pirated copies and who emigrated to New York in 1760. Isles writes that Lennox wrote "possibly a translation of Voltaire's *Histoire de l'Empire de Russie sous Pierre le Grand*" (327) and that "a newspaper advertisement of a translation by Lennox of Voltaire's *Histoire de L'Empire de Russie sous Pierre le Grand*, to be published 'In a few Days,' appeared in the *Public Advertiser* for 1 and 2 August 1760." However, *The History of the Russian Empire under Peter the Great* (London: Nourse, Vaillant, Davis, and Reymers, [1763]) was not published until several years later and not by Rivington.

14. This word is difficult to decipher.

15. The phrase seems to demand, "I should be glad *if* you would be pleased to send from him," but there is clearly no "if" in the manuscript.

16. The "French Copy in Sheets" here might refer to Voltaire's text, to parts of *Brumoy*, or to the Guillaume Hyacinthe Bougeant's *Histoire*, discussed in the following letter (#32).

17. This name is not completely legible—it could be Harke or Harte—but the context establishes almost beyond a doubt that the individual in question is Walter Harte, tutor to Lord Chesterfield's illegitimate son Philip Stanhope (not to be confused with Lord Chesterfield's godson Philip Stanhope, later fifth Earl of Chesterfield) and later Lennox's correspondent (see #32).

32

Walter Harte
to Charlotte Lennox

January 13, [c. 1759[1]]

MS:	Houghton Library, Harvard University, MS Eng 1269 (45)
Pages:	1
Edition:	LC #42
Text:	

Windsor[2] Jan. 13.

Madam,

I shall always be sincerely glad to further, so far as lies in my
little Sphere, any work that you undertake.[3] I think in
this Historical age[4] Pare [sic] Bougeant's work[5] is no improper
Book, tho he often lies, like a true Frenchman, for y[e]. honour of his country. My book is either in Cornwall, or on
the ocean;[6] & it now vexes me that tis not in my power to send
it to you.[7] I have had thoughts of going from this place to
Bath,[8] to try what service those waters may do me; If I
come to town which will be partly upon your account, tis
likely I shall come ab[t]. the 28th. instant. Pray make my
best respects to M[rs]. Scot.[9] [sic]

Madam
Your most Sincere Friend
& Servant
W Harte

NOTES

1. The approximate date of this letter derives from Harte's biography and from the context. It was definitely written after 1751, when Harte had his positions in Windsor and Cornwall. At the other end, the letter must have been written before 1763, when Harte retired to Bath. The context of the letter suggests a time when Lennox was looking for a new project, which would not have been before 1759 but probably not in 1760, when she was working on *LM*, as well as a time that Harte considers a "Historical age," which might be 1759, when he published his *History of the Life of Gustavus Adolphus* (London: Printed for the Author).

2. Harte is writing from Windsor, where he was prebend since 1750.

3. Harte's "Sphere" may be the influence he has on Chesterfield. This letter is probably another instance of Lennox trying to secure patronage from the nobility. Alternately, Lennox is simply asking for a copy of Bougeant's *Histoire* (see n.5).

4. This was an "Historical age" indeed. In 1759 alone, the following books were published: *An Authentic and Complete History of Witches and Apparitions* (London: Woodgate and Brooks), *The History of the Rise, Progress, and Extinction of the Late Rebellion in Scotland* (Edinburgh: Gray), *The History of the Spanish Armada* (London: Dodsley), *A New History of the Old and New Testament* (London: Davis), *A New Universal History of Arts and Sciences* (London: Coote)—these all anonymous; Eleazar Albin's *A Natural History of English Song-Birds* (London: Ware), W.H. Dilworth's *The History of the Bucaniers of America* (London: Anderson), David Hume's *The History of England under the House of Tudor* (London: Millar), James Mackenzie's *The History of Health* (Dublin: Ewing), Benjamin Martin's *The Natural History of England* (London: Owen), John Newbery's *A New History of England* (London: Newbery), S. Nelson's *The History of Our Blessed Lord and Saviour Jesus Christ* (London: Coote), James Postlethwayt's *The History of the Public Revenue* (London: Knapton), James Ray's *A Compleat History of the Rebellion* (London: Brown), Henry Rimius's *The History of the Moravians* (London: Wilkie), William Robertson's *History of Scotland* (London: Millar), Temple Stanyan's *The Grecian History* (Dublin: Exshaw), and Nicolas Tindal's *The Continuation of Mr. Rapin's History of England* (London: Knapton etc.). This list does not even include translations from other languages, reissues of previously published histories, and novels titled as histories. Of course, 1759 was also the year Harte published his own *History of the Life of Gustavus Adolphus*.

5. Guillaume Hyacinthe Bougeant (1690–1743) was a Jesuit priest and author (see *The Catholic Encyclopedia*, 15 vols., ed. Charles Herbermann et al., [New York: Appleton, 1907], II 711). His comedies, which satirized the Jansenists, were fairly successful. His prose satirized the heroic romance. His *Philosophical Amusement upon the Language of Beasts and Birds* (London: Cooper 1739) went through several editions in English. Interestingly, one edition of his *Philosophical Letters upon Physiognomies* (London: Griffiths, Meyer, Payne, Bouquet, 1751) was published by Payne and Bouquet, with whom Lennox at one point was working on a subscription edition of her *Poems* (see #1). However, Bougeant was most noted for his history

of the Thirty Years' War, *Histoire des guerres et des négociations qui precedent le traité de Westphale, sous le règne de Louis XIII et le ministère du cardinal Richilieu et du cardinal Mazarin* (Paris: Mariette, 1727; later editions with slightly different titles in 1751 and 1757). The present letter suggests that Lennox was considering a translation of Bougeant's *Histoire*, which seems likely because the book fits into the pattern of Lennox's other translations in terms of genre and in terms of the period it covers. Also, since other works by Bougeant were available in English, there would have been a good chance for this translation to sell as well. In the context of this project, Lennox was probably requesting a copy of the French original from Harte. The project never came to fruition, though, since there is no translation of Bougeant's *Histoire* into English.

6. Harte was vicar of St. Austell and St. Blaizey in Cornwall on the English Channel. In the eighteenth century, goods from Cornwall were often transported on the ocean (see Isles 418 n.188).

7. If Lennox was considering a translation of Bougeant's work, she would obviously have needed the French original. Such originals were often supplied by friends or publishers—this seems to be an instance of the former.

8. Harte turned these "thoughts" into reality four years later in 1763, when he retired to Bath.

9. See above #30.

33

Charlotte Lennox
to Thomas Birch

MARCH 16, 1759

MS: British Library, Department of Manuscripts, Add.Ms.
             4312, f.135
Pages: 1
Edition: Small 25
Text:

Sir

       I beg leave to return to you my thanks
for your agreeable present,[1] and to assure you that I think
my self highly honoured by the favourable mention you are
pleased to make of me, and my little writings:[2] I wish you
may approve of my plan for a new work which I am—
advised to publish by subscription, I send you one of my
proposals[3] and shall be extremely obliged to you if you will
recommend my undertaking.

	I am
	Sir
March 16. 1759.	Your obliged, and very
	humble Servant
at Mr Austin's Engraver[4]	
in great George Street	
Hanover-Square	Charlotte Lennox

NOTES

1. What this present was is unknown—Small believes it might have been Birch's recently published *History of the Royal Society* (25). Alternately, Birch might have given Lennox his *Memoirs of the Reign of Queen Elizabeth* (1754), if the project she was working on was a history of that age (Isles 51 n.96; see also #34).

2. Where or to whom Birch mentioned Lennox—and in which "small writings"—unfortunately remains unknown as well. Small thinks Lennox might mean "one of the reviews of *Henrietta*, all of which were favorable" (25), but as far as I know Birch did not write any literary journalism. In the late 1750s, he was busy with a wide variety of projects (see Albert Gunther, *An Introduction to the Life of the Rev. Thomas Birch* [Halesworth: Halesworth Press, 1984], esp. 45–58 and 79–83), but none of those have any obvious relation to Lennox.

3. Small (25) speculates that the "new work" Lennox speaks of is *Brumoy*, which makes sense given the time frame. However, that work was not published by subscription, and no such proposal survives.

4. This is the long-lived engraver and painter William Austin, who is listed in various dictionaries of artists, booksellers, and engravers. Maxted has the following entry: "AUSTIN, William, engraver, printseller and drawing master, Knightsbridge, 1776; Brighton and London 1784; 41, St. James's Street 1785; 195, Piccadilly 1786; 197, Piccadilly 1787; 13, near Knightsbridge Chapel 1794. B. 1721, London; d. 11 May 1820, Brighton. Pupil of George Bickham but main attention devoted to teaching drawing th[r]ough published series of etchings and engravings including political satires. Ran Patriotick Print Rooms at St. James's Street 1785. Exhibited at Royal Academy 1776, 1785, 1786" (7). Austin copied works by such artists as Giovanni Paolo Pannini (*Ruins of Ancient Rome*), Andrea Locatelli (*A Specimen of Sketching Landscapes*), and Jan van Goyen (*Sea-Pieces*). His pieces at the Royal Academy were studies, a landscape, and "Southampton Castle." His political satires (he was a supporter of Charles Fox) included *French Spies Attacked by British Bees* (cf. AKL V 688–89).

More importantly in the present context, Ian Maxted's *The London Book Trades, 1735–1775* (Exeter Working Papers in British Book Trade History 3; Exeter: Maxted, 1984; 2) lists Austin as a printseller, drawing master, and importer of foreign prints at George Street, Hanover Square (Rocque 10Aa, Horwood 12Bc) in 1763. Still, the connection between Austin and Lennox apart from the address is unclear.

34

William Robertson
to Charlotte Lennox

APRIL 6, 1759

MS:	Houghton Library, Harvard University, MS Eng 1269 (36)
Pages:	4
Edition:	LC #19
Text:	

Madam,

   I had the pleasure, a few days ago,
of receiving from you ~~of~~ a[1] very obliging letter.[2] I am
extremely sensible of the indulgence of the publick,
in the favourable judgment, which it has passed
upon my book.[3] The approbation which you are so
good to bestow upon it, flatters me very much.
I should be very happy if it were in my power
to contribute any thing towards rendering your
<u>Age of Queen Elizabeth</u> as perfect, as the splendor
of the subject merits.[4] But my attention to the
reign of that Queen was confined ~~whol~~ almost[5] wholly
to those transactions which related to Scotland. As I am
scrupulously exact in referring to my authorities,

           you[6]

---

will easily find what printed books or Manuscripts
I have consulted.[7] My friend M[r]. Hume has taken
a larger view of Elizabeth's reign & character, & has
displayed, in my opinion, all that elegance of compo

97

sition, & depth of reflection, for which his writings
are remarkable. In this work, he quotes the Author's [sic]
he follows with great care, so that you will learn
from him what books it is proper to consult with
regard to English transactions.[8] Lord Royston has
a very large Collection of papers with regard to
that Reign, & all of them transcribed from the ori
ginals in a fair modern hand, which is a circum
stance of no small advantage; I suppose you will
find it no very difficult matter to get access to
these.[9] By the title which you give your work, I
imagine that you do not propose to confine yourself
wholly to historical transactions, but will treat at some
length, the taste, the authors, the manners &c of that age.[10]
This last is a curious subject. The influence of the

English

English nobles was still considerable in that age, & they
endeavoured to maintain ~~by~~ it[11] by continuing that profuse
hospitality which was of so much consequence in more
remote times. The country & not the town was the place
where they displayed their splendor. The condition of
citizens appears not to have been honourable. The stand
ard of fashion & taste was taken from the Spaniards &
Italians & not from the French. Hence the pomp of
dress & ceremony, the stately demeanour, & the spirit of
chivalry remarkable in those days. Of all these, & of
many other peculiarities in manner you'll find hints
not only in Shakespeare,[12] & other dramatic writers
of the time, but many facts with regard to this article
may be picked up in the numerous Collections of
Papers published concerning Elizabeth's reign. These
things I make no doubt have already occurred to
yourself in a better manner than I can point
them out. I mention them only to shew my willing

ness

---

ness to obey your commands. If in carrying on
your plan you find that I can be of the
least use, you have nothing more to do than

to lay your injunctions upon me I am with great regard[13]

Edinburgh 6th April 1759[14]

Madam,

Your most obedient & most humble Servant William Robertson

NOTES

1. The "a" is written over the "of."

2. This letter no longer exists. Judging from Robertson's following comments, Lennox must have complimented his *History of Scotland*, which had appeared on February 1.

3. This must be a reference to the first reviews of the *History of Scotland*. In the *Monthly Review* (20 [February 1759]: 163–78 and 20 [March 1759]: 193–207), the reviewer—probably David Hume—wrote that "we may safely recommend this work as the most compleat of all modern histories. [. . .] The Writer discovers a sufficient store of imagination to engage the Reader's attention, with a due proportion of judgment to check the exuberance of fancy: his descriptions are animated, and his reflections solid. His stile is copious, nervous, and correct; [there are] many conspicuous beauties in this work [. . .] we sincerely congratulate him on the agreeable discovery: and we heartily hope, that his success may prove equal to his wishes, and his deserts" (177–78). The *Critical Review* (7 [February 1759]: 89–103) offered, "If an historian chuses for his theme some particular and more confined period, it will then be expected, that he should descend into a more full detail of incidents and characters; that he should examine dubious facts with a more critical eye, and discuss them with more accuracy; and present us with a more minute inspection into the features of the human heart. This latter is the plan, on which the author now under consideration proceeds; and we must, in justice to him say, that he has acquitted himself with success. We have perused his work with pleasure, and can venture to recommend it to our readers, whether instruction or entertainment be the principal end for which they read. [. . .] But it is not this author's only praise to be an impartial and accurate historian. We must add, that he is an extremely agreeable writer: his narration is clear, animated, and interesting: his style such as becomes the dignity of history; nervous, regular, chaste, and uniformly supported" (90–91). This review was excerpted the same month in the *Scots Magazine* (21 [February 1759]: 77–81). In the *London Magazine*, David Hume anonymously published a letter quoting from the *History of Scotland* and confirming Robertson's interpretation of Queen Mary's position on Catholicism (28 [February 1759]: 79–80). In addition, the *Gentleman's Magazine* began printing excerpts from the *History* in April under the title, "*An Account of the Life of* MARY STUART, *Queen of* Scotland, *from Dr* Robertson's *excellent History*

of Scotland, *just published"* (29 [April 1759]: 151–54, here 151). The review in the *Annual Register* (2 [1759]: 489–94) was not published until later.

4. It appears that Lennox's project at this time was a history of the (first) Elizabethan age (see also #33). Since Lennox never published such a book, it is likely that she abandoned her plan later. However, this project would have been a departure from her previous historical writing, which consisted entirely of translations. Perhaps the success of writers such as Birch, Robertson, and Hume had inspired her.

5. The "almost" is written over the "whol."

6. Robertson does not repeat this catchword on the top of the next page, unlike the following two.

7. In the preface to his *History of Scotland* (London: Millar, 1759), Robertson discusses his sources: "Records [of the age of Mary and Elizabeth] have therefore been searched, original papers have been produced, and publick archives, as well as the repositories of private men, have been ransacked by the zeal and curiosity of different parties. The attention of Cecil to collect whatever related to that period, in which he acted so conspicuous a part, hath provided such an immense store of original papers for illustrating this part of the English and Scotch history, as are almost sufficient to satisfy the utmost avidity of an Antiquarian. Sir Robert Cotton (whose library is now the property of the public) made great and valuable additions to Cecil's collection; and from this magazine, Digges, the compilers of the Cabbala, Anderson, Keith, Haynes, Forbes, have drawn most of the papers with they have printed" (iv–v). These are books like James Anderson's *Collections Relating to the History of Mary, Queen of Scotland* (Edinburgh: Mosman and Brown, 1725–28), Robert Keith's *The History of the Affairs of Church and State in Scotland* (Edinburgh: Stewart and Symer, 1734), and Samuel Haynes and William Murdin's *A Collection of State Papers, Relating to Affairs in the Reigns of King Henry VIII., King Edward VI., Queen Mary, and Queen Elizabeth, from the Year 1542 to 1570* (London: Bowyer, 1740–59), all of which Robertson quotes by volume and page in his footnotes throughout the *History of Scotland*. Since the *Collection of State Papers* is a compilation by William Cecil, Baron Burghley (1520/21–98), this is certainly the Cecil to whom Robertson refers. The titles of these volumes show them to be the kind of "numerous Collections of Papers" Robertson mentions later in the letter.

8. Philosopher and historian David Hume (1711–76; ODNB XXVIII 740–58) had published his *History of England, under the House of Tudor*, 2 vols. (London: Millar, 1759) in March 1759—in other words, about a month before this letter. (Presumably, Robertson had immediately received a copy or read the work in manuscript—Hume had read his *History of Scotland* before its publication. See Ernest Campbell Mossner, *The Life of David Hume*, 2nd ed. [Oxford: Clarendon Press, 1980], 396–98.) Hume quotes some of the same sources as Robertson, such as Keith, but adds others, such as Peter Heylin's *English History, Containing a Succession of all the Kings of England* (London: Morphew, 1709) and *A Complete History of England* (London: Alymer, 1706) by White Kennett, John Hughes, and John Strype.

9. Lennox's connection to Philip Yorke (1720–90), who was created Lord Royston in 1754 and Earl of Hardwicke in 1764, was Royston's tutor and friend Thomas Birch

(see #33). Presumably, Birch could have gotten access to Royston's collection for Lennox. In his preface to his *History of Scotland*, Robertson thanks Royston himself, writing that "his Lordship was so good as to allow me the use of fourteen Volumes in Quarto, containing that part [. . .] which is connected with my subject" (vi). As Isles points out (52 n.100), Royston's collection of papers is now in the British Library.

10. Here, Robertson is perhaps distinguishing his own "historical" work from Lennox's more general and cultural approach.

11. The "it" is written over the "by."

12. Robertson is apparently not aware of *SI*.

13. No further correspondence between Robertson and Lennox is known.

14. Robertson had moved to Edinburgh in 1758.

35

John Boyle, Earl of Cork and Orrery, to Charlotte Lennox

[MAY 7, 1759[1]]

MS: Houghton Library, Harvard University, MS Eng 1269 (33)
Pages: 1
Edition: LC #20
Text:

Madam,

 I now can work for you, and I will. Whilst I was
in that dismal disagreeable house in Marlbro' Street, my
thoughts were locked up, and totally immersed in gloom and
melancholy.[2] new objects, my books, & a very convenient house
have released them,[3] and I begin to be again myself. I am
going over the Preface, correcting, and altering it.[4] I shall
enlarge it very much & I hope in a manner you will
like, but I must beg M[r] Lenox to bring me his transcript
that I may make it answer my own.[5] I could wish to
know exactly what plays that are in the <u>Theatre Grec</u>
have been imitated on our stage. I dare not ask you
to come to see me, least [sic] I offend your too great delicacy:[6] Orders
& attendance on workmen will I fear hinder me from
waiting upon you:[7] yet the Park is pleasant but y[r] pleasure
is always the wish of

Y[r] most humble Servant

Monday.   Corke[8]

NOTES

1. The letter is endorsed with this date, which was indeed a Monday, in a different hand on the reverse.

2. Orrery's second wife Mary, née Hamilton, had died in the house on Great Marlborough Street near Oxford Street (Rocque 10Ba/Horwood 12Cc) on May 24, 1758. Orrery signs his dedication of *Memoirs of the Life of Robert Cary* to his youngest son Edmund from Marlborough Street as well (see #31).

3. This may be the residence in Great George Street, Westminster, that John Duncombe mentions in *Letters from Italy in the Years 1754 and 1755* (London: White, 1773), xxxii. Great George Street was developed some time between the 1740s, when it was still George Yard (Rocque 11Ac) and the 1750s (Horwood 23Bc). See also Isles, 53 n.103.

4. Orrery wrote the preface for *Brumoy* (I i–xxviii). He also contributed to the first volume of that work "A Discourse upon the Theatre of the Greeks" (I i–xxi), "A Discourse upon the Original of Tragedy" (I xxii–lxxiv), and "A Discourse upon the Parallel of the Theatres" (I lxxv–cxx).

5. This comment offers an unusual glimpse into the production of *Brumoy*: Apparently, Orrery must have sent an earlier draft of the preface to the Lennoxes, which he is now asking Alexander Lennox to bring back to incorporate changes. (Presumably, that is the "transcript.") This is one of only a few references we have to Alexander being involved in the production of Lennox's works.

6. This raises again the question of whether Orrery and Lennox ever met in person (see #13). Apart from the class difference, it remains unclear why Lennox visiting Orrery would have been considered indelicate, unless she had not been officially introduced or was unchaperoned.

7. Orrery was probably overseeing work on the gardens at Marston House (see #32).

8. Orrery had inherited this title (Earl of Cork) in December 1753.

36

David Garrick
to Charlotte Lennox

MAY 29, [1759[1]]

MS: Houghton Library, Harvard University, MS Eng 1269 (23)
Pages: 1
Edition: LC #21
Address: To
            M[rs]. Lennox
            at
            Kensington
Text:

                    Tuesday
                    May 29th
Madam.

In my Multiplicity of Business at the
Close of our Acting Season,[2] I forgot to
Acknowledge the receipt of y[r]. Letter:[3]
 I always deliver my Sentiments w[th].
freedom, when I like, & with caution when
I dislike—<u>Henrietta</u>[4] pleas'd me
                    only
much, & wants, I think, ∧ some little
                    it.
alterations to compleat ∧ —I am much
flatter'd that the Author approves of
the little hints I gave.[5]

I am
Mad^m. Your most hum^{le}
Ser^{vt}
D Garrick

NOTES

1. There were two May 29th in this period that fell on Tuesdays: 1759 and 1764. However, Garrick was in France in May 1764, so the year of this letter must be 1759. This fits with the discussion of *Henrietta*, which—as a novel—had been published the previous year. See also Isles 54 n.105.

2. The season at Drury Lane ended on May 31 in 1759 (*London Stage* IV ii 732).

3. This letter no longer exists.

4. Here, Garrick is obviously not referring to the novel *Henrietta*, which had been published on January 28, 1758 and therefore could not receive any more alterations. Instead, Lennox was probably already working on a dramatized version of her novel, i.e., an early version of *The Sister* (see #41 below and Isles 54 n.107).

5. From this sentence, it would seem that Garrick had already seen and commented on a *previous* draft of the play based on *Henrietta* and that Lennox had incorporated his suggestions in a second draft before this letter. Alternately, they might have discussed the adaptation in person.

37

Charlotte Lennox
to the Duchess of Newcastle

OCTOBER 6, 1760

MS: British Library, Department of Manuscripts, Add.Ms.
                   33067, f.230
Pages: 2
Edition: Small 27–28
Text:

Madam

          As Your Grace has been
pleased to permit me to dedicate some of my works
to You,[1] I take the opportunity of a new Edition of my
Henrietta[2] to solicit that favour now. The first
edition was so hurried[3] Madam, that I had not
time to make an application to Your Grace, I
therefore sent it into the world without any—
dedication, for having in my own mind devoted it
to so illustrious a Patroness, any other name
would not satisfy my ambition.[4] The favourable
reception this performance has met with, both at
home,[5] and abroad, where it has been translated
several times,[6] gives me more confidence to
intreat that Your Grace will allow me to lay
it at your feet: it is a debt of gratitude Madam
which I am impatient to pay; I shall never forget

Your goodness Madam, nor the generosity with which

Your Grace relieved[7] my distress last Winter,[8] and
surely providence seem'd willing to give success to the
benevolent intention of Your Grace's present,
I have been in the Country almost ever since,[9]
and the air, together with proper exercise has
restored me to a very tollerable [*sic*] degree of health.

I have the comfort of hearing from M[r] Stone[10] that
Your Grace continues Your favourable—
intentions with regard to M[r] Lennox,[11] and this
hope supports me in my present Slavery to the
Booksellers,[12] whom I have the mortification to
see adding to their heaps by my labours, which
scarce produce me a scanty and precarious
subsistence.[13] If Your Grace will do me the—
honour to signify Your pleasure to me with regard
to the Dedication of <u>Henrietta</u>, a Message directed
for me at the Mineral Water Ware-house in
Bury Street St. James's,[14] will come safe to my hands.

	I am with the deepest respect
	Madam
London Bury Street	Your Grace's
October 6, 1760	Most grateful and devoted—
	Servant
	Charlotte Lennox.

NOTES

1. Lennox had not dedicated any previous works to the Duchess, but Sully was dedicated to her husband, the Duke.

2. *Henrietta* was originally released in February 1758. A second edition, with substantial revisions, was published in March 1761. See the new edition of *Henrietta*, ed. Ruth Perry and Susan Carlile (Lexington: The University Press of Kentucky, 2008).

3. There is no information on why the production of the first edition was done in any particular hurry.

4. Of course, the eponymous title character of the novel has the same first name as the Duchess. In 1765, Lennox named her daughter Harriet Holles—the Duchess's husband's family name—and named the Duchess her daughter's godmother. This was likely done in acknowledgement of favors granted and in hopes of further support. In at least one instance, Harriet signed her name as "Henrietta" (#63).

5. *Henrietta* received glowing reviews from both of the major journals of the period—see #31.

6. Indeed, *Henrietta* had been published in French twice in 1760, with the same title (*Henriette*) and in the same translation, but in two different places: London/Paris: Duchesne and Lausanne/Amsterdam: Chapuis/Rey.

7. The spelling might also read 'releived.'

8. There is no record of what this particular distress (financial or physical) in the winter of 1759/60 was, nor of what "present" Lennox received from the Duchess during that time.

9. At the time of the writing of this letter, though, Lennox is clearly back in London in Berry Street.

10. On Andrew Stone, see #31. Since he was the Duke's advisor and factotum, it is not surprising that Stone would have been relaying messages to Lennox from the Newcastles. There is a copy of *Brumoy* presented from Lennox to Stone at the Library of Congress.

11. The Duke of Newcastle supposedly "revelled in exercising patronage" (Browning 185). In that spirit, he apparently procured employment for Alexander Lennox in the Customs Office (Isles 59 n.121)—see also #A2 below.

12. Between 1755 and 1758, Lennox had translated at least four works from French: *Sully, Berci, Maintenon,* and *Brumoy.* This kind of work was considered arduous and poorly paid, explaining Lennox's reference to "Slavery." On the translation trade, see #26.

13. This was a common complaint of authors in the eighteenth century. For instance, Tobias Smollett wrote about having to "have Recourse to [. . .] beggarly Sollicitation" and complained about being "harrassed by duns" (*The Letters of Tobias Smollett,* ed. Lewis Knapp [Oxford: Clarendon Press, 1970], 17, 49).

14. This is Berry Street—see #15. I have not been able to find any information on a "Mineral Water Ware-house."

38

Saunders Welch
to Charlotte Lennox

JULY 7, 1761

MS: Houghton Library, Harvard University, MS Engl 1269 (38)
Pages: 1
Edition: LC #22
Address: To
               M[rs] Lenox
               the first House on the right Hand
               on Camberwell Green[1]
               with a Basket—[2]
Text:

Dear Mad[m].   Long Acre[3] 7 July 1761

    I am very well thank heaven—which
I think better placed in the front than in the rear;
as it settles the material point.[4]—Indeed the heat
of the day, the anxiety naturaly [sic] arising from the
                                 were
first riding a Horse of spirit whose dispositions ~~are~~
were [sic[5]] totaly [sic] unknown, added to the length of the
ride,[6] after three months disuse of that exercise,
made me quite Crop sick[7]—and to mend the
matter I eat an immoderate dinner—this I may
justly place to the account of a certain Lady,[8] but
to accuse her of a fault will gain no Credit[9] I shall
therefore bury my resentment at present, but there will
come a time I hope for reprisals.—But whatever my

resentments may be, that Lady will see that I scorn to make use of them <u>to save my Bacon</u>. Love respects and a thousand wishes for the health and prosperity of M^r & Mrs Lenox,[10] not forgetting the two Girls[11] &c

> I am Mad^m. most sincerely
> Your Friend & humble Servt
> Saunders Welch

NOTES

1. In the eighteenth century, Camberwell (Surrey) was a village to the South of London. Rocque shows a road to Camberwell (20Cb) and Horwood a Camberwell Toll Gate (35Ad). Today, Camberwell and Camberwell Green are part of Greater London and not nearly as bucolic.

2. It is unclear if "with a Basket" refers to a sign on the house in Camberwell or to a basket sent with the letter.

3. In the eighteenth century, Long Acre (near Covent Garden; Rocque 11A/Ba and Horwood 13B/Cc) "was a centre for cabinet-making and furniture design" (*The London Encyclopedia*, fully revised and updated edition, ed. Ben Weinreb and Christopher Hibbert [London: Papermac, 1993], 495), but apparently Welch lived there (or at least he was writing from there).

4. The first half of this sentence seems to refer to an earlier query by Lennox, no longer existing but answered in great detail below. The second half (after the hyphen) makes little sense to me. Perhaps, Welch wants to inform Lennox of his health at the beginning rather than the end of the letter; alternately, Welch might be saying that he would rather have heaven in front of him, i.e., be alive.

5. The end of the previous line originally had the word "are" stricken out and "were" superscribed. Then, the word is repeated here. See also Isles 55 n.109 on the deterioration of the paper at this spot.

6. From Long Acre to Camberwell Green—which required crossing the Thames via Westminster Bridge, completed in 1750, since Blackfriars Bridge was not completed until 1769—would have been a ride of five or six miles.

7. "Disordered in stomach, *esp.* as a result of excess in eating and drinking" (OED IV 45).

8. This is probably Lennox (see Isles 56 n.111), and "Lady" is meant playfully.

9. Isles believes that this is a reference to Lennox's "oversensitivity to criticism" (56 n.111).

10. This suggests that Lennox and her husband were still living together in 1761.

11. The reference is to Welch's daughters Mary and Anne, who also send their respects. See correspondent's biography and #24.

39

Sir William Musgrave
to Charlotte Lennox

JUNE 5, 1765

MS:	Houghton Library, Harvard University, MS Eng 1269 (38)
Pages:	1
Edition:	LC #23
Address:	To
	Mrs Char: Lennox
Text:	

S^r. W^m. Musgrave makes his Compliments
to M^rs. Lennox & is much obliged to her for
the very agreable [*sic*] present of her Writings[1]
which he accepts & values for their Intrinsic
Merit—He is sorry she sho^d. think any
acknowledgments necessary for the little Dis=
=tinctions which he may have had it in his
power to shew Mr Lennox & which are
entirely due to the very good Character he
has heard of him.[2]

Cleveland Court[3]
5. June 1765.—

NOTES

1. It is unclear which "Writings" these are, since those works of Lennox's
Musgrave is known to have owned were not published until later. See correspondent's
biography and Isles 57 n.114.

2. This is the only known *positive* reference to Alexander Lennox's character. The "little Distinction" was probably some recognition at Alexander's workplace in the Customs Office.

3. Cleveland Court, St. James's Place (Rocque 10Bb, Horwood 22Ca) was Musgrave's residence at least until 1768 (Wheatley I 422).

40

Memorandum between James Dodsley and Alexander Lennox

OCTOBER 25, 1766

MS: Folger Library, PN 2598 G3 F5 copy 4 Ex Ill. V.7, no. 48
                   (after p.376)

Pages: 1

Text:

Memorandum   Oct. 25. 1766.

    That it is this day agreed between
M[r] Lennox & M[r] Dodsley, that they shall
be joint & equal Sharers in the Copyright[1]
and in the Expenses & Profits of publishing[2]
& selling the first Edition, and all future
Editions, of the History of Eliza;[3] and that only
one Thousand Copies of the said Book shall
be printed in the first Edition;[4] and also th[at][5]
whenever the said M[r] Dodsley shall fi[nd]
it necessary to print a Second Edition of [the]
said Book,[6] that then he shall pay [to]
the said M[r] Lennox the sum of Twenty
Guineas, as a consideration for his
half share of the Copyright of the
said History of Eliza.

                 A. Lennox[7]
                 Ja Dodsley[8]

NOTES

1. This business arrangement—the author (or her husband) maintaining 50% of the copyright—was fairly unusual in the eighteenth century; usually, the bookseller (or publisher) owned the entire copyright. Of course, as the memorandum goes on to point out, owning half of the copyright also meant that the Lennoxes had to invest in the production of *Eliza*.

2. This word is difficult to read.

3. This memorandum is one of the documents that establishes Lennox's authorship of *Eliza*; see Schürer.

4. This is a normal print run for a book in the eighteenth century (even slightly on the large side), so the Lennoxes and Dodsley thought of *Eliza* as a typical novel.

5. Part of the manuscript page is torn off here and in the following lines.

6. No second edition ever appeared, though there was a pirated edition (Dublin: Faulkner, 1767).

7. In *Nobody's Story*, Catherine Gallagher speaks of Lennox's "lack of full ownership of herself and her words" (200). Alexander Lennox's signature here dramatically reinforces that statement: Legally, *he* rather than his wife owned her literary works. Later in Charlotte Lennox's life, when she was living separate from her husband, she dealt directly with Dodsley (see #49, #71, #74, and #75).

8. According to an endorsement on the page, this letter is written in James Dodsley's hand.

41

Charlotte Lennox
to [David Garrick]

OCTOBER 25, 1768

MS: British Library, Department of Manuscripts, Add.Ms.
                 29300, f.45
Pages: 2
Edition: Boaden I 319
Address: M[rs] Lennox
                 Ltr to David Garrick[1]
                 Purchased at Mess[rs].[2] Sotheby's
                 10 May 1875
Text:

Sir,

      The success which has lately attended
Writers for the Stage, and some of them too, of my
own Sex,[3] has encouraged me to write a comedy,[4] which
I beg you will read with your usual candor [*sic*], and
that indulgence you have always shown for
my writings. You will find that I have pursued
a hint you gave me some years ago,[5] which
has furnishd [*sic*] me with one of the most interesting
incidents in the whole piece; You may depend
upon it that every alteration, and amendment
which you judge necessary, will be readily, and
thankfully admitted.[6] I am so fully persuaded
of your justice, and benevolence, that I do not
think you will reject my play unless you find

it wholly destitute of merit,[7] and by accepting
  confer a great obligation upon me, and
it you will ∧ put it in the power of my friends to
serve me, in a way in which they have often
wishd [sic] to serve me, and often recommended to me.
  But whatever be your determination[8] Sir, I

earnestly entreat you to acquaint me with it
soon; suspense is a most uneasy state of
mind, and on this occasion, delay will be
productive of great inconveniences. I am

                              Sir
                              Your Obligd humble
                              Servant
I have not yet written
the concluding lines, but   Charlotte Lennox
that can be done, when the
piece has received your corrections.
Somerset-House[9] October 25. 1768.

NOTES

1. This endorsement is written in a different hand and in pencil.
2. This word is difficult to make out.
3. The last successful plays by women were *The Double Mistake* by Elizabeth Griffith (1727?–93), which was performed 15 times in 1766/67 at Covent Garden, and Frances Sheridan's (1724–66) *The Discovery*, which saw a good run of 17 performances at Drury Lane in the 1763/64 season. Otherwise, female authors were not always successful: Elizabeth Griffith's *The Platonic Wife* "lasted only long enough to give the author a sixth night" (*London Stage* IV ii 1070) in 1765, and Jane Pope's afterpiece *The Young Couple*, based on Sheridan's *Discovery*, saw only a single performance on April 21, 1767. The most successful writers for the stage in the five or six years previous to 1768 had been

- George Colman (see #43),
- Arthur Murphy (1727–1805) with *No One's Enemy But His Own* in the 1763/64 and *The School for Guardians* in 1766/67 at Covent Garden as well as *Zenobia* in 1767/68 at Drury Lane, and
- Isaac Bickerstaff (1733–1808) with the first English comic opera *Love in a Village* (music by Thomas Arne) in the 1762/63 season, *The Maid of the Mill*—the

"hit of the season" (*London Stage* IV ii 1071) in 1764/65—*Love in the City* in 1766/67, and *Lionel and Clarissa* in 1767/68, all at Covent Garden.

4. This is Lennox's comedy *The Sister*, based on her novel *Henrietta*. It seems to be a revised version of the manuscript she had offered to Garrick several years previously; see #36.

5. Probably a reference to recommendations Garrick had made back in 1758 (see #36).

6. Lennox seems very little invested in the authority or integrity of her text—she is happy to change anything Garrick might suggest, and she has not even bothered writing an ending yet.

7. This might be a veiled reference to #36, where Garrick had admitted in the postscript that there were *some* good points to the manuscript play.

8. In the end, Garrick rejected the play, and Lennox produced it with George Colman instead. On the performance history of *The Sister*, see #45.

9. This is Old Somerset House, the Tudor palace built from 1547 to 1550 for Lord Protector Somerset. In the early seventeenth century, the house witnessed masques organized by Ben Jonson (who had an apartment there) and Inigo Jones (who died there in 1652), and Oliver Cromwell lay in state there in 1658. In 1676, Old Somerset House was supposedly the first building in England to have parquet flooring. Both Charles I's wife Henrietta Maria and Charles II's wife Catherine of Braganza lived there for a time, but in the eighteenth century the building went into decline. After her marriage to King George III in 1761, Queen Charlotte had a choice between Somerset House and Buckingham House as residence, but chose the latter. In 1771, seven apartments of the house were put at the disposal of the newly-founded Royal Academy, and the academy's schools, library, and administration moved there. The old building was demolished in late 1775 or early 1776 to make way for the new Somerset House, which was built starting in 1776 according to plans by William Chambers. On the history of the house, see Leonard Maurice Bates's *Somerset House: Four Hundred Years of History* (London: Frederick Muller, 1967). In the years before being torn down, Old Somerset House served as a residence for artists and writers.

42

James Murray
to Charlotte Lennox

FEBRUARY 8, 1769

MS: Houghton Library, Harvard University, MS Eng 1269 (39)
Pages: 3
Edition: LC #24
Text:

Madam

   I beg pardon for not answering
your letter sooner,[1] but I was very much
Indispos'd when I had the pleasure to
receive it, & was confined for a week
after, I very much applaud the goodness
of your Scheme,[2] in providing for your
little Girle [sic],[3] & I heartily wish it m[a]y
answer your most sanguine expec=
=tations, but I must acknowledge my=
=self the worst judge in the world of
the propriety of your Intentions,[4] with
respect to the Great Personage you
mean to dedicate your performance
           know   thing
to,[5] I neither ∧ whither its a uswell[6]
                         it
or the proper method of doing ∧ or if
done, wthither [sic] it will be attended with
any advantage to your self, & unless

118

there is a probability of the latter
I should think, its [sic] not worth the trouble
of solliciting [sic] such fine Ladys[7] to
accomplish your purpose, but of
this you are best judge, [sic] Lady Gower[8]

_____

I never care to prevail upon to embarque[9]
in an[y] Solicitations & My Wife has no
Interest,[10] for the same reason that the
protection of a Noble Lord was
                              viz:
withdrawn from you ʌ on account
of Mr Lennox having got a Place
from the late Duke of Newcastle[11]
so all I can say is, that when your
performance is to [be] Acted, I shall
with pleasure attend it, with as—
many of my acquaintances as I can
prevail upon to go & I most sincerely
wish it may meet with the most
favourable Reception[12] & I am

                    Madam
                    Your Most Obt. Servt.
Stanhope Street[13]   Jas. Murray.
Feb: 8th 1769

_____

pray excuse this Scroll. but I am obliged
to go out in five minutes & much hurried

NOTES

1. This letter has not survived.

2. This looks more like 'Schime.'

3. The "Scheme" is probably a subscription edition of *The Sister* (see #45 and Isles 57 n.117). However, it is unclear how that would have provided for Lennox's "little Girle," Harriet Holles (see #37, #58, #59, and #62).

4. This phrase suggests that Lennox had asked Murray for advice about a possible dedication of *The Sister*.

5. The published edition of *The Sister*, which was *not* a subscription edition, carried no dedication. It is unknown to whom Lennox wanted to dedicate the edition, but it seems to have been a member of the Bute faction (see below n.8).

6. usual

7. The "fine Ladys" are probably Lady Gower and her sister Catherine, Murray's wife. Lennox seems to be asking that Murray in turn ask these two to approach an unnamed dedicatee.

8. Susanna Leveson-Gower, née Lady Susan Stewart (1742/3-1805; ODNB XXIII 139–41), was the wife of Granville Levenson-Gower, second Earl Gower (1721–1803). In 1761, she became woman of the bedchamber to George III's sister Princess Augusta. Lady Gower spent her time at court looking for jobs and preferments for friends and clients. Nevertheless, she was socially quite active and well liked. The Gowers were members of the anti-Newcastle faction of the Duke of Bedford, who was the Earl's brother-in-law, and of the Earl of Bute. In other words, Lady Gower was in the opposite faction from her brother-in-law Murray, which explains why he had no interest in asking Lady Gower to approach a possible patron for Lennox. For her part, Lennox had probably recently changed affiliation from Earl of Bute (who was on the Gowers's side) and may not have been aware of the political conflict.

9. This word is difficult to make out.

10. I.e., Murray's wife has no influence with the person whom Lennox wants to approach for a dedication.

11. According to the memoir "Mrs. Lenox" in the *British Magazine* 3 (July 1783): 8–11, the Duke of Newcastle ("late" because he died in 1768) had offered Lennox a pension, which she "declined, in favour of her husband; for whom she solicited a place, which the duke promised to procure him the first opportunity" (9). It is not known who the "Noble Lord" is whose protection Lennox apparently lost on this occasion.

The implication of this entire passage is that Lennox, a member of the Newcastle/Rockingham faction, is trying to approach a member of the Bute faction for permission to dedicate a work. Neither of the two intermediaries Murray mentions can help Lennox: Lady Gower because she is part of the Bute faction (unlike Lennox) and Murray's wife because she is part of the Newcastle/Rockingham faction (unlike the potential dedicatee). For a much extended discussion of the political situation here, cf. Isles 58–60 n.120–21.

12. It is unknown whether Murray actually attended the premiere of *The Sister*. In any case, it certainly did not meet with a "favourable Reception" (see #45).

13. Stanhope Street, Clare Street, Clare Market (Rocque 11B/Ca, Horwood 13Dc) is parallel to Drury Lane between Covent Garden and Somerset House.

43

George Colman
to Charlotte Lennox

[*ANTE* FEBRUARY 12, 1769[1]]

MS:	Houghton Library, Harvard University, MS Eng 1269 (25)
Pages:	1
Edition:	LC #25
Address:	To
	M[rs]. Lennox
	Somerset House
Text:	

M[r]. Colman presents his Compliments
to M[rs]. Lennox, & returns her many
thanks for the very acceptable
present she has made him.[2]

The M.S. is in the hands of the
transcriber of the parts.[3] It shall be
sent for if M[rs]. Lennox desires it:
but M[r]. C.[4] thinks it would be a
pity to interrupt him, especially
as the alterations will be so slight,
& the parts can be easily corrected
afterwards.[5]

Great Queen St[rt].[6]
Monday Morn[g].

NOTES

1. This letter was clearly written before the following one and long enough before the premiere of *The Sister* on February 18 for the actors to rehearse the play from their separate parts. Plays were usually rehearsed less than four weeks. For instance, *The Clandestine Marriage*, a collaboration between Colman and Garrick that went into rehearsal in January 1766 and premiered at least six weeks later on February 20, had already experienced "several postponements" (Page 114), so the rehearsal time should have been much shorter.

2. The present is unknown—perhaps a thank-you for agreeing to produce her play.

3. The "M.S." is that of *The Sister*. The identity of the transcriber is unknown.

4. I.e., Colman

5. This comment suggests that Lennox had tried to make (slight) changes to her play even before it went into production.

6. No addresses are known for Colman in London, though at some point he apparently lived in Soho Square (Wheatley III 266). In close proximity to both Covent Garden Theatre and Drury Lane Theatre, Great Queen Street (near Lincoln's Inn Fields, Rocque 3Bc/Horwood 13C/Db) would have been a perfect residence for Colman.

44

George Colman
to Charlotte Lennox

[February 12, 1769[1]]

MS:	Houghton Library, Harvard University, MS Eng 1269 (26)
Pages:	1
Edition:	LC #26
Address:	To
	M[rs]. Lennox
	Somerset House
Text:	

Madam,

I have according to my promise
scratched out some lines wch[2] I think will
do for a Prologue, but I am sorry to tell
You that D[r]. Goldsmith has disappointed
us, & written no Epilogue.[3] I wish he
had not promised, because having
relied on him, we are now quite
unprovided. I am at present too dull
and too busy to supply You, & must beg
You to find something of that nature
by Wednesday Evening at furthest, as we
must otherwise unavoidably defer
the Comedy for want of it,[4] & Wednesday
is the latest time we can give the
performer to prepare against the
Saturday following.

I am, Madam;
Y^r. most obed^t. serv^t.
G. Colman

NOTES

1. This letter was written the Sunday before the premiere (and only performance) of *The Sister* on February 18, so Colman is giving Lennox four days to come up with an epilogue.

2. There is a line or tilde above the c.

3. In the week between this letter and the premiere, Oliver Goldsmith apparently did oblige, since *The Sister* was performed with both the prologue by Colman (spoken by Isabella Mattocks, née Hallam [1746–1826]; see Highfill X 147–54) and the epilogue by Goldsmith (spoken by Mary Bulkley, née Wilford [1748–92]; see Highfill II 393–98). Since Goldsmith was in Oxford from Tuesday, February 14, he had either already started the epilogue this Sunday or wrote it *very* quickly. Goldsmith's early biographer James Prior calls his contribution to Lennox's piece "an excellent epilogue, the best perhaps he has written" (*The Life of Oliver Goldsmith*, 2 vols. [London: Murray, 1837], II 197). It is unclear how Lennox and Goldsmith were acquainted or why he contributed the epilogue to *The Sister*—the only other known connections between the two writers are Goldsmith's review of *Maintenon* (Isles 166 n.128) and the fact that both were friends of Johnson's. In addition, they might have known each other through the Horneck family (see #82). Apart from writing epilogues to his own plays *The Good Natur'd Man* and *She Stoops to Conquer*, the only other similar piece Goldsmith wrote was a prologue to Joseph Craddock's tragedy *Zobeide* in 1771. In all cases, the plays were performed at Covent Garden, so the connection was probably between Goldsmith and Colman rather than Goldsmith and Lennox—though then it is strange that Colman puts the burden of finding a new epilogue on Lennox.

According to *Lloyd's Evening Post*, the prologue and epilogue to *The Sister* "were both received with uncommon applause from the very considerable share of merit they possessed" (1814 [February 17–20, 1769]: 178). Both were quickly reprinted in the newspapers—for instance in *St. James's Chronicle* 1245 (February 18–21, 1769): 4, *Lloyd's Evening Post* 1815 (February 20–22, 1769): 186, *The London Chronicle* 1902 (February 21–23, 1769): 180, *Whitehall Evening Post* 3574 (February 21–23, 1769): 2, and the *Gazetteer and New Daily Advertiser* 12473 (February 22, 1769): [4]—and both were included in the published version of the play.

4. Apparently, Colman considered a play incomplete without an epilogue, and indeed practically every eighteenth-century play ended with an epilogue. It is unclear if he expected Lennox to find another author or write an epilogue herself.

45

George Colman
to Charlotte Lennox

FEBRUARY 20, 1769

MS: Houghton Library, Harvard University, MS Eng 1269 (27)
Pages: 3
Edition: LC #27
Text:

Madam,

        I am not ashamed to own
that your Letter has brought tears into
my eyes, and I do assure you that none
of the many trials I have experienced in
the direction of the Theatre have
given me more real uneasiness than
the present event.[1] From this time
I abjure all prognostication in stage-matters:
for I thought I had never read a play that
was more certain of comanding[2] [sic] a patient
hearing;[3] and yet I have even since
my return from Richmond[4] been
informed that more mischief was
meditated against it, had it been
represented this evening, which I took
it for granted it would be, when I
left town yesterday.[5] If there be any

---

real foundation for these reports—and their

125

being so general seems to speak the truth
of them—your resolution[6] has been as prudent
as it is spirited, and perhaps has in it more
real dignity than would have appeared in
your hastily withdrawing the play on
Saturday,[7] which might have been ascribed
to a sudden movement of spleen and
resentment.—Some deficiencies there
always are in performers at a first represen=
=tation;[8] but I still think, notwithstanding
my deference to M^{rs}. Powell's[9] sentiments,
that if the play had been continued, it would
not have been ill sustained by the Actors,
whom I shall inform of your candid con=
=struction of their efforts in your Service.[10]
I am heartily glad you intend to publish
the piece,[11] & the manner in which You propose
to give it to the world, is at once noble
& delicate.[12] It is my sincere opinion, that
however your interest may have suffered,
your reputation will ultimately receive

---

no wound: for when the Publick come to
compare The Sister with some other plays
which they have followed & admired, I think
they will wonder at your ill success.[13] If I can
any way be of Service to You, it will give me
the greatest pleasure; for it is impossible
for you to be more thoroughly satisfied
with my proceedings than I have been with
your own.[14] I propose myself the pleasure
of waiting on You very soon. In the mean
time M^{rs}. Colman[15] joins me in congratula=
=tions on the recovery of your dear little
girl,[16] as well as all other good wishes,
with wch[17] I remain,

Madam,
Your very faithfull
Great Queen St^{r}.[18]   & obed^{t}. Servant
Feb. 20. 1769.   G. Colman

NOTES

1. The "present event" was the successful disturbance of *The Sister* during its premiere on February 18, on which the London newspapers reported in detail. *Lloyd's Evening Post* described the evening: "It [the play] met with a good deal of opposition from part of the audience, who, indeed, appeared to come prejudiced against the performance, as they began their attack upon it even in the first Act" (24.1814 [February 17–20, 1769]: 178). The *Whitehall Evening Post* went on: "part of the audience shewed great marks of disapprobation, which interrupted the piece for some time; it went on, notwithstanding much opposition, until the beginning of the fifth Act, when the noise was so great that the actors were unable to proceed in their parts. After some time Mr. Powell [William Powell, one of Colman's lead actors, who played Courtney in *The Sister*; Highfil XII 130–39] addressed the house, hoping they would be so kind as to give the play a patient hearing, at the same time assuring them, that if it was found unworthy of their encouragement, it should be performed no more; this produced an intermission of the disturbance until the conclusion of the Comedy, when it seemed to be in general condemned" (3753 [February 18–21, 1769]: 3). Subsequently, *The Public Advertiser* confirmed: "The new Comedy of the Sister, acted at the Theatre Royal in Covent Garden on Saturday, was given out, according to the Usage of the Theatre, for a second Representation, but the Author was no soon [*sic*] apprized that it did not meet with general Approbation, than she determined to withdraw it" (10706 [February 20, 1769]: 2). The *London Chronicle* was more lackadaisical in its description, offering merely that the play "met with a good deal of opposition from part of the audience" (225.1901 [February 18–21]: 173).

At the same time, at least two papers strongly condemned the audience's behavior. In the column on "Theatrical Intelligence," the *St. James's Chronicle* wrote: "On Saturday last was *half*-acted at this Theatre, a new Comedy called *The Sister*, written by the truely [*sic*] ingenious Author of the Female Quixote, and partly founded on another of her Productions, called Henrietta. In an Age so favourable to Sentimental Comedy, and Novels in Dialogue, we cannot help thinking the Censure passed on the fair Author rather severe. As far as we were capable of judging from so interrupted an Exhibition, the Piece is neither deficient in Interest, Sentiment, or Diction" (1245 [February 18–21, 1769]: 4). The *Gazetteer*'s critique was even stronger: "I cannot help condemning the ill-nature of a part of the audience, who, to gratify a bad disposition, considered not the anxiety they occasioned to one who may have spent many tedious days in producing for them a few hours rational entertainment; nor the quiet of another who has devoted herself to their service, who has given general satisfaction, and whose delicacy has been found much superior to the generality of those of her profession, as well as on her first appearance on the present occasion; nor regarded how much they disturbed the entertainment of the far greater part of the audience; but doubt not it will be more indulgently received at future representations" (12471 [February 20, 1769]: 4). This last claim was unfortunately unwarranted: The play never saw a second performance. However, in the following days all of the newspapers quoted above (with the exception of the

Public Advertiser) printed the prologue and epilogue to Lennox's play. Apparently, Lennox wrote a letter about the incident to Colman between February 18 and 20, probably withdrawing the play.

The reason for the disturbance is not entirely clear. One explanation, suggested by Goldsmith, was that the hissing was organized by individuals still upset with Lennox's critique of Shakespeare in *SI* (Ralph Wardle, *Oliver Goldsmith* [Lawrence: University of Kansas Press, 1957], 189)—who approached Goldsmith to join in the condemnation of the play. This explanation was later reported by Bennet Langton (see #85) and by James Boswell (see #73). However, if this is true, it certainly seems strange that the individuals would approach the author of the epilogue to the play to join their cause. Another explanation, offered by Hester Thrale, was that the disturbance was organized by the playwright Richard Cumberland, though the reason is not clear (Piozzi I 135 and BLJ IV 10). In either case, the condemnation—a form of literary protest not uncommon at the time—was successful enough that Lennox withdrew the play entirely. She had the consolation of the *St. James's Chronicle* writing, "We shall, however, defer a further Examination of [the play's] Merits, till it appears in Print, in which Form we hope the Author will again submit it to the Public" (4). Unfortunately, though, the withdrawal meant that Lennox did not have the benefit of a third performance, which would have at least earned her some money with *The Sister*.

2. There is a line or tilde above the m.

3. Indeed, one of the things Colman's partners accused him of in their law suit was bad judgment of plays (Page 172, 178). *The Sister*, probably in an earlier form, had apparently been rejected by Garrick (see #36 and #41), so in this case the accusation might have been true.

4. Colman had recently built a villa in Richmond; it was completed in 1766 (Page 128–29).

5. This comment indicates that in spite of the disturbance at the premiere, Colman wanted to go ahead with further performances.

6. I.e., the resolution to withdraw the play.

7. I.e., during or immediately after the performance.

8. Isles suggests that the *St. James's Chronicle*'s comment that *The Sister* was "*half*-acted" indicates that the acting was bad (168 n.130), but I tend to believe that the word refers to the interrupted performance.

9. This is probably the wife of William Powell (see above n.1), Elizabeth née Branson or Branston. From the context, it seems that Mrs. Powell believed the acting in *The Sister* had been and would stay bad. However, it appears Mrs. Powell had no acting background, so it is unclear why Colman and Lennox would have listened to her opinion.

10. This implies that Lennox had not blamed the actors for the disturbance of the play, but had commended their efforts.

11. *The Sister* was published on March 3 by James Dodsley. It was apparently popular enough to warrant a second edition by March 19.

12. #42, written before the debacle at the premiere of *The Sister*, suggests that Lennox was planning to publish the play by subscription.

13. The *Gentleman's Magazine* agrees with this assessment in their review of the published version of *The Sister*. After writing somewhat equivocally that the play's "dialogue is natural, lively and elegant, the incidents are uncommon, yet within the pale of dramatic probability, and the sentiments are just and refined; it wants an intermixture of light scenes, such as a familiar acquaintance with the stage might have furnished, without the abilities of Mrs Lenox, and which, if her abilities had been still greater, could not, perhaps, have been furnished without a familiar acquaintance with the stage," the review concludes, "The audience expressed their disapprobation of it with so much clamour and appearance of prejudice, that she would not suffer an attempt to exhibit it a second time. She has published it without either remonstrance or complaint, and those who read it in the closet will probably wonder at its treatment on the stage, especially considering the merit and the sex of the writer" (39 [April 1769]: 199–200). In a five-page review, the *Monthly Review* similarly referred to the disturbance—"it was exhibited only one night at the theatre in Covent-garden; the audience expressed great disapprobation, and would not suffer it to be given out for another exhibition"—and commented, "This disapprobation does not appear to be justified on a perusal of the piece" (40 [March 1769]: 245–49, here 245). At the same time, the reviewer allows some criticism: "In character and humour this play is certainly deficient; the principal parties are mere passions personified; we have love, honour, generosity, and resentment, without the striking peculiarities in their expression, which constitute character, and distinguish one man of honour, and one lover, from others" (246). These two reviews were quite possibly both written by John Hawkesworth (Abbott 94–96).

The *Critical Memoirs* began their review cautiously: "That this performance has been in the theatrical stile, *damn'd* on the stage, does by no means influence our judgment with regard to its merit" (1 [March 10, 1769]: 326–28, here 326). The following assessment, though, is rather devastating: "On the most impartial perusal however, we cannot help acquitting the audience; we wish we could do the same by the manager, who shewed so little judgment as to misemploy his company in making so gross a trial on the patience of the publick" (ibid.). The review goes on to suggest that Lennox should have taken out insurance on her play in order to have *something* to show for it. At the same time, the *Critical Memoirs* did find some merit in *The Sister* and wrote in a later issue in a short notice, "The Criticks seem all to have adopted *our* sentiments respecting this unsuccessful, though not undeserving piece" (1 [April 10, 1769]: 522).

14. In spite of this mutual congratulation, there seems to have been no further collaboration between Colman and Lennox. She produced her next play, *OCM*, with Garrick instead (see #52).

15. Mrs. Colman was the notorious Sarah Ford. Ford, an actress probably born in Jamaica, was seduced by another actor before she met Colman. The two had at least two children together (Harriet, who played infant roles on stage, and George the Younger) before they got married sometime in June or July 1767. Sarah

Colman died suddenly in 1771. The relationship must have been quite strong, since Colman more or less chose Sarah over a large inheritance (Page 75–77, 141–42, 147–48, 191–92).

16. This must be a reference to Lennox's daughter Harriet Holles previously being ill; unfortunately, nothing else is known about her health at this time.

17. There is a line or tilde above the c.

18. See #43.

46

Assignment for the Copyright of *Henrietta*

SEPTEMBER 20, 1769

MS: British Library, Department of Manuscripts, Add.Ms.
                38730, f.126
Pages: 1
Text:

London Septr. 20th. 1769--Received from M^r.
Thomas Lowndes[1] Bookseller in London two pounds
five shillings and sixpence for one third share of M^rs.
Lennox's Henrietta, bought by us at M^r. Miller's [*sic*]
sale June 13th. 1769,[2] M^r. Lowndes obliging himself
that, as far as his interest goes, this book shall
be reprinted by us, when the present edition is
sold off;[3] and that if it is sold to any other
person it shall be on the same conditions

Willm. & John Richardson[4]

Salisbury Court[5]
Septr. 20th. 1769.

NOTES

1. Thomas Lowndes (1719–84) was a publisher and circulating library proprietor who made most of his considerable fortune with the series "The English Theatre" and with the annual *London Directory*. He also published novels, most notably Frances Burney's *Evelina*. See my "Four Catalogues of the Lowndes Circulating Library, 1755–66," *Papers of the Bibliographical Society of America* 101.3 (September 2007): 329–57, esp. 332–35.

2. Andrew Millar had died on June 8, 1768, and his copyrights were sold at auction a little over a year later.

3. In their new edition of *Henrietta*, Ruth Perry and Susan Carlile claim that Lowndes "printed a new issue right away" (viii), but it remains unclear whether the remainders of *Henrietta* ever sold out, and it seems unlikely that a new edition was printed.

In March 1769—half a year *before* the assignment under consideration here—Lowndes advertised in the papers several times for "*This day is published*, [. . .] The Second Edition, of HENRIETTA" as "Printed for A. Millar, and sold by T. Lowndes" (for instance *Lloyd's Evening Post* 1819 [March 1, 1769]: 220, *Public Advertiser* 10717 [March 4, 1769]: [4], and *London Chronicle* 1908 [March 7, 1769]: 232). Unfortunately, no copy of this version survives, but the language suggests that Lowndes had purchased Millar's stock after his death and was trying to sell the remainder of *Henrietta*. (The phrase "This day is published" did not always mean what it said in the eighteenth century, but rather that a bookseller was trying to sell an old edition as new.) The timing was no coincidence: Lowndes ran his advertisements while *The Sister* was on the public's mind. The ad ends, "☞ The new Comedy of the Sister, is founded on this celebrated Novel," and Dodsley was advertising for *The Sister* at exactly the same time and in the same papers (though never on the same day, as far as I am able to tell).

About a year later, Lowndes ran another advertisement for *Henrietta*, this one saying "*This day was published* [. . .] HENRIETTA [. . .] Printed for T. Lowndes, at his Circulating Library, in Fleet-street" (*London Evening Post* 6613 [March 27, 1770]: [2]). Once again, no copy survives, so there is no way of telling whether this version was actually a new printing or simply Millar's old stock with a new title page. In April and June, Lowndes ran more advertisements in which, in a list of works available at his shop, he mentioned *Henrietta* as "a new edition" (for instance *General Evening Post* 5693 [April 7, 1770]: [3], *London Evening Post* 6623 [April 19, 1770]: [3], *Gazetteer and Daily Advertiser* 12874 [June 5, 1770]: [4], and *Public Advertiser* 11079 [June 16, 1770]: [4]). This could mean an actual new printing or a typical eighteenth-century attempt to sell an old edition as new.

This information suggests that Lowndes bought the remainder of Millar's stock and tried to sell it long before the Richardsons (see below n.4) bought the copyright to *Henrietta*. It would seem the sale of "the present edition," i.e., Millar's remaining stock, was in Lowndes's hands, and he would only have to deal with the Richardsons if that stock sold. At least two scenarios are imaginable for the edition advertised in 1770: It could have been the remainder of Millar's stock with a new title page, and it could have been an actual new edition printed by the Richardsons for Lowndes, with the three sharing the copyright. Unfortunately, without evidence from surviving editions, it is impossible to clarify the situation.

4. William Richardson (1701–88) was Samuel Richardson's nephew and worked in his uncle's business before taking it over around 1768 (Plomer 212–13). It is unclear what relation William Richardson had with John or even which John Richardson this was—Plomer lists one John and one J. (210), and Maxted names three

Johns (187). In *The First John Murray and the Late Eighteenth-Century London Book Trade* (London: Oxford University Press, 1998), William Zachs mentions them simply as "the London printers, William and John Richardson" (19). The fact that the Richardsons bought the copyright to a book that had not even sold its first print run suggests that they considered Lennox's novel worth the financial risk.

5. Plomer lists William Richardson as located at Castle Yard, Holborn (212). Salisbury Court is to the south of Fleet Street near Fleet Ditch (Rocque 12Ba/ Horwood 14Cc).

47

Charlotte Lennox
to Sir Joshua Reynolds

MAY 20, 1773

MS: Houghton Library, Harvard University, MS Hyde 10 (415)
Pages: 1
Edition: Small 44–45
Address: To Sir Joshua Reynolds
           Leicester Square[1]
Text:

Sir,

So many years have interven'd since
I had the pleasure of your acquaintance,[2] that I
know not whether there is not some impropriety
in asking a favour of you—but I depend greatly
upon that benevolence in your character, which
I had formerly an opportunity[3] of observing
                    you
and which if report be true ʌ still possess in
a very high degree. It is in your power to
assist me in a little affair in which my interest
is concernd[4]—if you will give me a quarter
of an hour, I will explain the nature of my
request to you, and if you will likewise let
me know in a line by the penny post,[5] what
day, and what hour it will be convenient
for you to see me you will greatly oblige

Sir
Your very humble Servant
Charlotte Lennox

My compliments
to Miss Reynolds[6]

Great Tower Hill
the corner of Muscovey Court[8]
May 20 1773

NB.[7] The favour above
requested, was to give
Mrs. Lennox Designs for
copper plates to adorn
an new Edition, with
great Improvements,
of The Female Quixote[9]
Endorsement in hand
of Thomas Percy, Bp.[10]

NOTES

1. Reynolds rented the house at 47 Leicester Fields (Rocque 10Ca/b; also known as Leicester Square, Horwood 13Aa) starting in 1760 and died there in 1792 (McIntyre 119–22 and 526–28).

2. Lennox sat for a portrait by Reynolds in January 1761, over a decade before this letter (Charles Robert Leslie, continued and concluded by Tom Taylor, *Life and Times of Sir Joshua Reynolds*, 2 vols. [London: Murray, 1865], I 200), explaining Lennox's (at least rhetorical) reluctance to approach him again. A diary note at the earlier time says, "Mrs. Lennox send to Mr. Selwin" (Algernon Graves and William Vine Cronin, *A History of the Works of Sir Joshua Reynolds*, 4 vols. [London: Graves, 1899], IV 1480), indicating perhaps that George Selwyn (1719–91, a politician who never once spoke as a Member of Parliament and a compulsive gambler who was portrayed by Reynolds several times) had commissioned the portrait or maybe that Reynolds "was interceding with Selwin for aid for Mrs. Lennox" (Small 33). The portrait was never finished, and there is no evidence that Lennox and Reynolds were in touch at all between 1761 and 1773. However, Kynaston comments that "apparently this portrait was altered as late as 1773. This is the opinion of the authorities at the National Portrait Gallery who base their assumption principally on the style of the hairdressing" (22), so Reynolds might have continued working on his own.

Two engravings based on Reynolds's image survive: one by Francesco Bartolozzi (see #48) for *Shakespeare Illustrated* by Sylvester and Edward Harding (London: Harding, 1793—this work is entirely different from Lennox's *SI*) and another by Henry R. Cook (active 1804–49 in London and Paris, mainly portraits, some copies of Old Masters, see AKL XXI 45), accompanying a "Memoir of Mrs. Lennox" in *The Lady's Monthly Museum*, (n.s. 14.6 [June 1813]: 313–15).

3. The fourth letter could be an o, an e, or an u.

4. Lennox uses an apostrophe above ("interven'd"), but not here.

5. The Penny Post was the postal system, set up in 1680, by which letters were delivered within London for the price of one penny, usually on the day they were sent.

6. Frances Reynolds (1729–1807), painter and author. Frances lived with her brother Joshua as his housekeeper between 1753 and the late 1770s at Leicester Fields and Reynolds's previous house (McIntyre 78, 87–88, 328–29)—see #56. Always in the shadow of her brother, Frances mostly produced miniatures—and a portrait of Johnson—and wrote *An Enquiry Concerning the Principles of Taste* (1785), which was published anonymously and only later identified as hers. She corresponded with several of the Bluestockings, including Elizabeth Montagu and Hannah More. Frances left Joshua's household around 1779 to live on her own. Wendorf writes that "[a]fter her brother's death in 1792 [February 23], she received an inheritance of £2500 for life [. . .] and promptly purchased a large house on Queen Square" (74). It seems that Lennox might have even lived in this house for a while—see #74.

7. According to the endorsement below, this *nota bene* was written by Thomas Percy (see below n.10). That endorsement itself is written in a third hand.

8. Muscovey Court off Trinity Square, Great Tower Hill Street (Rocque 14Aa, Horwood 16Ad) was named either because the office of the Muscovite ambassador was there or because of the proximity of the Czar of Muscovy pub (Henry Harben, *A Dictionary of London* [London: Jenkins, 1918], 426). This is probably where Lennox lived after Somerset House was torn down (see #41) until about 1775. Later (see #48), the address is given more specifically as No. 6 Great Tower Hill.

9. No other edition of *FQ* was published with Lennox's (known) cooperation in her lifetime. As Isles points out (169 n.134), Reynolds was not actually designing "copper plates," i.e., illustrations, but the frontispiece portrait of Lennox. There is also a chance that Percy was entirely wrong in his analysis of the situation and that Lennox was already preparing for the subscription edition of her works she proposed in 1775 (#54).

10. This is the writer and cleric Thomas Percy (1729–1811; ODNB XLIII 747–50). Percy became dean of Carlisle in 1778 and bishop of Dromore (Church of Ireland) in 1782. He is better known today for his *Reliquies of Ancient English Poetry* (London: Dodsley, 1765), which—though full of mistakes in terms of representing actual "Ancient English Poetry"—was a landmark publication that changed the course of British poetry. A member of the Club since 1768 (see Bertram H. Davis, *Thomas Percy* [Boston: Twayne, 1981], 20), Percy moved in the political, literary, and artistic circles of Johnson, Boswell, Burke, Hume, Garrick, Goldsmith, Elizabeth Montagu, and Reynolds.

48

John Hawkesworth
to Charlotte Lennox

OCTOBER 16, 1773

MS: Houghton Library, Harvard University, MS Eng 1269 (31)
Pages: 1
Edition: LC #28
Address: To
               M^rs. Lennox.
               at N°.6. Great Tower Hill[1]
               London

Text:

Bromley Kent 16th. Octr. 1773[2]

My Dear Madam

       Though it has not been in my power to wait upon you, I have
not neglected the little affairs in which you employed me.[3] Mr Henry[4] sent me the
                    that he
enclosed letter the same Night Ɨ ʌ returned from Worcester,[5] and I am very sorry the Contents
are not more favourable to our wishes.[6] Sir Joshua I could not see till this Morning
when I called upon him as I was coming out of Town;[7] he says that he hopes his Absence
from London when you wrote will apologize for his not having Answered your Letter;[8]
that he came to Town but last Sunday, and that he this Morning saw Bartolozzi[9]
about your affair, from whom he learnt that Cipriani[10] was in the Country; that—
Bartolozzi fears that the Cuts for the Female Quixotte are not in their way, as the figures
must be dressed in Coats and waistcoats, and other parts of the modern Dresses of both
sexes, whereas they have been used to design in the higher Stile, with more of the Naked,
and a slighter Drapery that is loose and flowing;[11] Bartolozzi however has written
Cipriani upon the Subject, an Answer is expected in a few days, and I will venture

to say that you will meet with every Instance of polite Attention in Sir Joshua which a Ł liberal Mind, and a Love of Genius can produce.[12] I know not what to recommend as a new Undertaking,[13] but I will not dismiss the Subject from my Thoughts, and will do myself the pleasure to receive your further Commands the next time I am in London,

I am with great Regard
D[r] Mad[m] your faithfull & obed[t] humble serv[t]
Jn[o] Hawkesworth

NOTES

1. See #47.

2. The Hawkesworths kept a home in Bromley, where Mary had her boarding school, throughout their life. They probably retired there around June 1773 (Abbott 13). However, John was apparently moving back and forth from London, since he died in London only a month after writing this letter on "November 17, 1773, at the home of his friend Dr. William Grant in Lime Street" (Abbott 190). Less than a week later, he was laid to rest in Bromley (Abbott 191).

3. As the previous letter (#47) clarifies, the "little affairs" seem to be organizing images (frontispiece and illustrations) for an edition of *FQ*.

4. David Henry (1709–92) was the brother-in-law of Edward Cave, the founder of the *Gentleman's Magazine*. In 1754, Henry became joint publisher of the *GM* with Ralph Cave, Edward's nephew, and after Ralph's death in 1766 Henry became the sole publisher. Henry also published James Cook's travels, contributed to the *GM*, and wrote "popular guidebooks to the Tower of London, St. Paul's Cathedral, and Westminster Abbey" (ODNB XXVI 518).

5. Henry would have been in Worcester because he "had a financial interest in the successful porcelain factory established in Worcester in 1751" (ODNB XXVI 518).

6. The "enclosed letter" does not survive. Since the content of that letter was "not [...] favourable," it probably consisted of some kind of rejection of participation in the project described in the previous letter (#47).

7. Probably on his way from London to Bromley.

8. This is probably #47.

9. Francesco Bartolozzi (1728–1815; ODNB IV 188–90) was one of the most important engravers working in London at the time. Born in Florence, Bartolozzi studied in Venice and in Rome with Piranesi. In 1764, he came to London and spent the next quarter of a century there. He engraved images from paintings by such artists as Reynolds (such as Lennox's portrait, see #47), Henry William Bunbury (see #82), and Angelica Kauffman—in a special technique he developed called stipple—and exhibited at the Royal Academy. His main collaborator in London was Cipriani, with whom he produced almost 350 prints. In 1801, Bartolozzi moved to Lisbon, where he spent the rest of his life.

10. Giovanni Battista Cipriani (1727–85; ODNB XI 715–16) was an Italian-born painter who came to England in 1755, where he married an English woman and spent the rest of his life. In portraits, landscapes, and interiors, Cipriani painted in the neoclassical style. He designed the diploma of the Royal Academy, which—like many of his works—was engraved by Bartolozzi. Cipriani also worked with theatres: In 1771, for instance, he assisted in the production of *The Fairy Prince* by George Colman the Elder. He was also a prominent teacher and exerted influence beyond the grave through his *Rudiments of Drawing*, which were published posthumously by Bartolozzi and supplied the source for many book illustrations.

11. This passage suggests that Cipriani had started work on illustrations for the subscription edition of *FQ*, but had gotten the style entirely wrong since it was a departure from his usual work. Bartolozzi's job would have been to make engravings from the paintings. Any correspondence the two might have exchanged about the project no longer exists.

12. The "Attention" would have been in the form of painting a portrait.

13. Isles writes, "There is no known connection between [Hawkesworth] and Lennox's next published work (*Vallière*, c. December 1774)" (179 n136). Since Hawkesworth died less than a month after writing this letter, he obviously could not have been involved. In any case, his contribution may have been to steer Lennox from a subscription publication of *FQ* to an edition of her collected works (see #53), perhaps in the context of recent copyright decisions (see #55).

49

Receipt (Charlotte Lennox from [James¹] Dodsley)

JANUARY 10, 1774

MS: Houghton Library, Harvard University, MS Hyde 10 (418)
Pages: 1
Text:

Rec'd Jan. 10. 1774. of Mr Dodsley
Ten pounds² in part for the Copy Money³
to be paid to me by him for the
Meditations & Prayers of the Dutˢ dela
Valiere⁴   Charlotte Lennox

NOTES

1. Since Robert had died in 1764 and since *Vallière* was "Printed by J. Dodsley," this is James.

2 Unfortunately, since it is not specified what part of the payment for Lennox's translation of Vallière this is, it remains impossible to reconstruct how much Lennox was paid for her work.

3. At this point, Lennox seems in control of the copyright to her translation rather than deferring to her husband (cf. #38).

4. *Vallière* was published in May 1774 (rather than "c. December 1774," as Isles writes [327]); either way, Lennox received her payment several months in advance. *Vallière* was advertised for instance in the *General Evening Post* 6325 (May 3, 1774): [3]; the *Public Advertiser* 13015 (May 5, 1774): [1]; the *London Evening Post* 2813 [actually 8132] (May 10, 1774): [2]; and the *Gazetteer* 14108 (May 14, 1774): [4]. All of these advertisements say "This day was [or were] published." That is clearly problematic in the contemporary sense of a specific publication date, but makes perfect sense in the eighteenth-century meaning of 'now publicly available.'

50

David Garrick
to Charlotte Lennox

July 22, [1774¹]

MS:	Houghton Library, Harvard University, MS Eng 1269 (24)
Pages:	2
Edition:	LC #29
Text:	

Madam.

    I have been ill & came
but Yesterday to Town,[2] or
I should have answer'd y[r].
Letter Sooner[3]—I am Engag'd
to more new Performances
than I can possibly perform
this next Season,[4] some of
them will be deferr'd to y[e].
Season after[5]—therefore it
will be impossible for Me,
should I approve of y[r]. Play,
to act it next Winter—

_____

If you can depend upon y[e].
Secresy of S[r]. Tho[s]. Robinson,[6]
I will insure You that of

of [*sic*] Madam
Y^r. most obed^t
Servt

<u>July y^e. 22^d.</u>   D Garrick

NOTES

1. The year of this letter is a conjecture. Since the project to which Garrick refers is either Lennox's later abandoned *Bajazet* or her *OCM*, the period of the letter must be around 1774 or 1775. Garrick was ill in May, June, and July of 1774 and in March, April, and May of 1775 (Stone/Kahrl 673), so either year is possible. The exact dates of Garrick's movements in the summers of both of these years are not known, but in 1775 he was in London as early as June 29 (cf. Garrick III 1017), so 1774 seems more likely. In addition, since Garrick appears to be speaking about a manuscript or play he has *not yet* read, placing this letter chronologically *before* the following two.

In a letter to Elizabeth Griffith of June 3, 1775, Garrick referred to a script he had not read: "Mrs Lenox who was so unfortunate at Covent Garden Theatre, put into my hand last Year an alterd play, which upon my honour, I have not yet had leisure to consider as I ought" (III 1010). Little and Kahrl identify this play as *OCM* in their footnotes, but it could also be the adaptation of Racine's *Bajazet*.

2. On Garrick's illness and movements, see previous note.

3. The letter to which Garrick is responding unfortunately no longer exists.

4. Indeed, Garrick staged an amazing eleven new plays at Drury Lane in the 1774/75 season, in spite of continuous health problems.

5. It is unclear which of the seven plays that premiered in the 1775/76 season—Garrick's last season—were held over from the previous year.

6. Palladian architect and man of fashion Sir Thomas Robinson (1700?–77), known as "Long Sir Thomas" (Warwick Wroth, *The Pleasure Gardens of the Eighteenth Century* [London: Macmillan, 1896], 40n) for his size, came from a wealthy family, spent his fortune, and became rich again as Governor of Barbados 1742–47. He rebuilt his family home at Rokeby and later had to sell it for lack of money. On his return to London in 1747, he built a house next to Ranelagh Gardens, where he was the principal shareholder and manager—and was known as "its Maypole and Garland of Delights" (Wroth 200). His association with Garrick dated back to at least 1753, and in 1775 Garrick called him "Sr Knight of Ranelagh" (Garrick III 1030). Both were regular visitors at Chiswick House (see #17), Robinson being "a frequent unwanted guest at Lord Burlington's villa" (Charles Saumarez Smith, *The Building of Castle Howard* [London: Faber and Faber, 1990], 180). However, the connection with Lennox is unclear, as is what his secrecy (and in what matter) would achieve. The letter certainly seems to suggest that Lennox and Robinson knew each other.

For the most extensive treatment of Robinson, see Michael McCarthy's "Sir Thomas Robinson: An Original English Palladian," *Architectura* 10.1 (1980): 38–57.

51

Charlotte Lennox
to David Garrick

AUGUST 4, 1774 (1)

MS: Folger Library, Y.c.1665
Edition: Boaden I 647–48
Text:

August 4th, 1774.[1]

Sir,

    I need not tell you, who are so good a critick
in the french [sic] drama,[2] that Racine's Bajazet[3] is
allowd [sic] by all good judges to be one of the best of
his tragedies,[4] my own humble opinion coin-
ciding with this general one, I resolved to translate
it, and by hazarding a few alterations adapt
it to the taste of an english [sic] audience.[5] The princi
pal female character in this play, if acted by
Mrs Yates,[6] would alone I think ensure its success—The haughty, the impassion'd, the beauty-
ful Roxana, seems drawn expressly for such
an actress. she [sic] is in her look, and acting the
very image of the poet's thought, and I had her
in my eye in every line that I translated of this
part. The alterations I propose to make will be
in the fifth act, which is not busy enough for
our taste[7]—I think it might be turn'd entirly [sic]
new, and by one of those sudden revolutions
common enough in the turkish [sic] government,[8]

Bajazet instead of being murdered, might be

placed upon the throne, as for Roxana if the
general plan of the play makes it necessary
that she should die, her death might be rendered more affecting[9] some circumstances of terror
and pity, which are not found in the original.

Upon the whole, Sir, I submit it to your
judgment, give it a reading, and if you think
it may be made fit for representation I will
be guided by your advice in every alteration
to be made in it[10]

I am Sir
Your very humble servt

August 4 1774   Charlotte Lennox[11]

NOTES

1. On the copy of this letter from Boaden pasted into the Forster Collection at the National Art Library at F.48.F.32, Vol. XXVIII, no. 112, there is a hand-written "not" or "mot" written above the date. The meaning of this note is unclear—perhaps that the autograph for this letter is not included in this volume of the Forster Collection (but then there is no such note above the letter of October 25, 1768 [#41], which also does *not* have the autograph manuscript in the Collection), or maybe that the date is incorrect (but there is no evidence given for this).

2. Garrick would of course have been familiar with the works of writers such as Racine, Corneille, and Crébillon. In addition, many of his own plays had French sources: *The Lying Valet* (1741) in Noel Le Breton Sieur de Hauteroche's *Le Souper mal apprêté*; *Miss In Her Teens* (1747) in Florent Carton Dancourt's *La Parisienne*; *The Guardian* (1759) in Barthélemi-Christophe Fagan's *La Pupille*; *Neck or Nothing* (1766) in Alain René Le Sage's *Crispin rival de son maître*; *The Irish Widow* (1772) in Molière's *Le Mariage Forcé*. Garrick's *Zara* of 1766 was an adaptation of Voltaire's play. Furthermore, Garrick had recently spent several months in France on his Grand Tour between 1763 and 1765, where "[i]nevitably the conversation progressed to a comparison of French and English drama" (Stone/Kahrl 298). However, unfortunately for Lennox, he reportedly observed at one point "that Racine, so beautiful and enchanting to read, cannot be acted because he *says everything*, and leaves the actor nothing to do" (qtd. in Stone/Kahrl 210).

3. *Bajazet* (1672) by Jean Racine (1639-99) is set in Turkey. The main characters are Bajazet, the sultan's brother, who is loved by Roxane, the sultan's favorite, but himself loves Atalide, and the grand vizier Acomat. Acomat wants to overthrow the

sultan and therefore allows a relationship between Bajazet and Roxane—feigned on the former's part, true for the latter—to move forward. When Roxane finds out about the mutual love between Atalide and Bajazet, a bloodbath ensues in Act V: Roxane has Bajazet killed, Atalide commits suicide, and the sultan orders Roxane to be executed.

4. Not everyone agreed with this assessment: David Erskine Baker in *The Companion to the Play-House* (2 vols.; London: Becket, Dehondt, Henderson, and Davies, 1764) wrote that this was "A Piece which of itself is esteemed the very worst of that Author's Writings" (I n.p., under "The Sultaness").

5. Racine's play had previously been translated in 1717 by Charles Johnson (1679–1748) as *The Sultaness: A Tragedy* (London: Wilkins et al.). The drama had been put on at Drury Lane, and the text was popular enough to see two editions the same year.

6. Mary Ann Yates (1728–87) started her acting career inauspiciously, being criticized for her voice in Dublin and being hired as a mute in London. However, under Garrick's tutelage at Drury Lane, where she performed from 1753 to 1767, she developed into one of the three leading tragic actresses of her generation (with Susannah Maria Cibber and Hannah Pritchard). She was married to the actor Richard Yates. When Garrick was no longer willing to pay her high salary, she switched to Covent Garden until Garrick decided to rehire her in 1774. Lennox's letter is written in the middle of these negotiations (see #52 below).

Yates stayed at Drury Lane another five seasons before once again moving to Covent Garden and retiring in 1783. For a longer biography, see Highfill XVI 322–38. Cf. also #A9 below.

7. Perhaps Lennox means that the various deaths don't actually happen on stage but are only present as reports or orders.

8. Here Lennox exhibits a bit of Orientalism concerning the instability of Muslim governments.

9. The text here seems to demand a word like "by" (which Boaden inserts), but there is nothing in the manuscript.

10. This sentence is highly reminiscent of Lennox's earlier interaction with Garrick in 1768, where she writes, "You may depend upon it that every alteration, and amendment which you judge necessary, will be readily, and thankfully admitted" (#41).

11. On the recto of the second page of this letter, there is a short biography of Lennox in an unknown hand:

Charlotte Lenox (or, as she spells her name) Lennox, was born in America, her father, a field officer, being Lieutenant Governor of New York. At the age of fifteen Charlotte was sent to England, to be placed under the care of a wealthy aunt; but on her arrival in this country, she found her aunt a lunatic, and such she remained. How the young girl was supported, or by whom protected, is not said; for I find no mention of her till 1752, when she was thirty three years of age, and published the novels of "The Female Quixote," and "Harriet [*sic*] Stuart." In 1753 she published "Shakspeare Illustrated," a work which was neither to Shakspeare's credit, nor her own. In 1756 she published "Memoirs of the Countess de Berci, taken from the French," and translated "Sully's Memoirs," 3 vols, quarto. In 1758 she published "Philander, a Dramatic Pastoral," and "Henrietta," a novel; in 1760 a translation of "Father Brumoy's Greek Theatre," in which she was assisted by the Earl of Cork and Orrery, and Dr. Johnson; in 1762 "Sophia," a novel; in 1769 "The Sisters," a comedy; in 1773 "Old City Manners," a comedy; and in 1790 "Euphemia" a novel.

A woman who could obtain the notice and esteem of Dr. Johnson and Lord Cork and Orrery, of Garrick and Mrs. Yates, must be a person of no common talents. I have read her Henrietta and her Euphemia; the one fifty, the other forty years ago—distances of time long enough to forget them; but I know that the general impression they have left is highly in their favour.

Charlotte Lennox died miserably poor, in 1804, at the age of eighty four. She left a son, and it is probable that she married, and became a widow, during the time that I find no public notice of her.

How melancholy that this lovely face should become the victim of age and poverty!

52

Charlotte Lennox
to David Garrick

AUGUST 4, 1774 (2)

MS:	National Art Library, Victoria and Albert Museum, Forster Collection MS no. 213 (Garrick Correspondence, vol. 28, no. 38), Pressmark F.48.F.32. Reproduced with the kind permission of the Trustees of the Victoria and Albert Museum.
Pages:	2
Edition:	Boaden I 647
Text:	

Aug. 4. 1774

Sir,

enclosed is the letter we agreed I should
write,[1] but in sending it you I must beg leave
to declare, (for the sake of my own reputation for
candor, which I do not think I have yet forfeited[2]) that what relates to M[rs] Yates, tho' wrote
expressly for her perusal, are my real sentiments.
—M[r] Colman[3] can tell you, that I spoke in the
same manner to him, and at a time, when it
was heresy to say she was equal to her great
theatric rival M[rs] Barry;[4] I was a bold, and
daring schismatic, and always mentaind [sic] she
was superiour [sic] to her—This indeed following
the rules of politeness, would not be fit to say
to you, if M[rs] Barry held the same rank in

147

your house which she did last winter, but as
things are, I conceive I am at liberty to speak
my sentiments—You will perceive that this
article of flattery is a nice point with me—
I own it—I would not for any consideration
fall under the suspicion of it—it is true, that
when I praise it is with warmth, with a kind

---

of enthusiasm—such is my natural temper,
but I mean what I say, and it is well worth a
life of habitual sincerity, to purchase the pleasure
of being believed when one gives vent to the
effusions of one's heart,[5] as at present when
I tell you that your disinterested, kind, and
noble manner of proceeding with [sic][6] proves you
to be as good a Man, as you are a great Actor
and I think no flight of flattery can go
beyond that plain and simple truth.

> I am Sir
> Your much obligd [sic] humble
> Servant

August 4 1774   Charlotte Lennox

NOTES

1. This opening explains that both letters dated August 4, 1774 (#51 and #52) were sent to Garrick by the same post. This second one suggests that the first one was written specifically for the eyes of Mary Ann Yates, whom at the time Garrick was trying to recruit away from Covent Garden for Drury Lane. The need for this second letter is not quite clear: Lennox would not really have had to insist to Garrick that she *really* prefered Yates over Barry. However, perhaps this letter was *also* intended for Yates, to confirm the first one.

In the end, Lennox's adaptation of *Bajazet* was never produced and presumably never finished. Neither Mary Ann Yates nor Anne Barry ever performed in any of Lennox's plays.

2. This might be a veiled reference to the questionable reputation Lennox seems to have had, explaining her harshness as honesty rather than as bad will.

3. See correspondent's biography on Colman. Lennox might have expressed the opinion mentioned here in 1769 when she was working with Colman on *The Sister* and when Yates was still at Covent Garden (though not part of the cast of *The Sister*), but it is not recorded in any other letters.

4. This is the actress Anne Barry (1734–1801), who with her husband Spranger Barry (1717?–77) started their acting careers (separately) in Dublin before joining the Drury Lane Theatre in 1767 at a combined salary of £1300. Spranger Barry, it seems, saw Lennox as an actress much earlier—see correspondent's biography for Garrick. At Drury Lane, both Barrys became stars, but Anne in particular "gave Garrick considerable difficulty in settling on plays and performance dates because of her temperament and her many illnesses, both real and feigned" (Highfill I 342). The Barrys were issued a specific contract in 1771 (Garrick II 735–37), but relations with Garrick never got much better. In spite of extended contract negotiations "[a]fter the season of 1773–74 Mrs. Barry and her husband left Drury Lane for Covent Garden" (Garrick III 929), allowing Garrick to re-engage Mary Ann Yates. Therefore, previous to the summer of 1774, Lennox would have been out of line criticizing Anne Barry, while in August 1775 praise of Mrs. Yates was in order. After Spranger Barry's death, Anne remarried and continued her acting career as Mrs. Crawford all over Great Britain until 1798. For a longer biography, see Highfill I 339–51.

At the time of Lennox's letter, the critic William Hawkins compared Barry and Yates in his *Miscellanies in Prose and Verse* (London: Printed for the Author, 1775): "This great actress [Yates], in the present theatrical hemisphere shines a perfect constellation, (*i.e*) in the haughty and passionate parts of tragedy; here she surpasses all her female co-temporaries, and ascends to the topmost seat of perfection; particularly in her favourite character Mandane in Cyrus, and the like. Hence we find excellence but barely answering her deserts, from her noble presence, majestic gait, piercing eyes and voice, with manner and action so suitably great, that she seldom fails of transporting the most rustic or refined admiration; but where tender passions, stiffled [*sic*] pangs, or soft feelings are to be expressed, Mrs. *Yates* is quite at a loss: Here we must indisputably call forth her rival Mrs. Barry, who appears in the former's deficiencies like Melpomene herself, and with such tender expression and graceful action, as must excite every feeling auditor, and strike criticism dumb: thus we are to view Mrs. Yates amazingly great in scenes of rage and disdain, and as cordially admire Mrs. Barry in grief and despair: though I shall not presume to draw any farther competition of those two ladies [*sic*] excellencies, for fear I should exceed the bounds of simple truth, and render it too profuse for a work of this kind" (21–23).

5. Of course, the following praise of Garrick is hardly without self-interest: This is the period when Lennox was trying to get him to produce a play of hers.

6. Here, Boaden inserts the words "Sir Joshua Reynolds's nephew's play." This is a reference to Reynolds's nephew Joseph Palmer, whose play *Zaphira* Reynolds had submitted to Garrick in the summer of 1774 (Garrick III 954–55). Since Garrick had rejected Palmer's play, Lennox can only be referring to the apparently polite way in which Garrick phrased his rejection.

53

Sir Joshua Reynolds
to Charlotte Lennox

JANUARY 18, 1775

MS: Houghton Library, Harvard University, MS Eng 1269 (28)
Pages: 1
Edition: LC #30, Ingamells #44
Text:

Leicesterfields[1] Jan 18th 1775

Madam

                 I am very glad to find
you have changed your design of publishing
~~the~~ an[2] edition of the Female Quixote alone,
to that of publishing a complete edition
of your works.[3] I am ready to contribute
the ornamental part which lyes [sic] within
my province whenever you are at leasure [sic]
to sit. I am with the greatest respect

> Your most humble
> and obedient Servant
> Joshua Reynolds

NOTES

1. See #47 above.
2. The "an" is written on top of the "the."

150

3. This is proposal #54, which promises to come "with a Frontispiece, painted by Sir *Joshua Reynolds*." It is unclear if Reynolds was supposed to finish his earlier portrait, started in 1761, or paint a new one. Apparently Lennox had abandoned her idea of a new edition of *FQ* (see #47) in favor of collected works. As Isles points out (172 n.141), the proposal was *not* for a "complete edition," since Lennox's poetry (as well as her journalism and translations) were missing.

54

Proposal for Subscription Edition of *Original Works*

FEBRUARY 14, 1775

MS: Beinecke Rare Books and Manuscript Library, Yale University, GEN MSS 89 (Boswell Collection), series V, box 62, folder 1303 (P77)

Pages: 2

Text:

FEBRUARY 14, 1775.

P R O P O S A L S[1]

For PRINTING by SUBSCRIPTION,

DEDICATED TO THE QUEEN,[2]

A NEW and ELEGANT EDITION, Enlarged and Corrected,[3]

OF

THE ORIGINAL[4]

W O R K S

OF

Mrs. CHARLOTTE LENNOX

CONSISTING OF

The FEMALE QUIXOTE;	⁝	ELIZA;[5]
SHAKESPEAR Illustrated;	⁝	The SISTER, a Comedy;
HENRIETTA;	⁝	PHILANDER, a Dramatic
SOPHIA;	⁝	Pastoral;

And OTHER PIECES, never before printed.[6]

CONDITIONS.

I. THAT the Work shall be printed in Three Volumes,[7] Quarto, on a fine Paper and new Type; with a Frontispiece, painted by Sir *Joshua Reynolds*, and engraved by one of the best Masters.[8]

II. THAT the Price to Subscribers will be Two Guineas; one to be paid at the Time of Subscribing, and the other on the Delivery of the Book in Sheets.[9]

III. THE Work will be ready for Delivery to Subscribers in *October* 1776.

*₊*Most of the Pieces, as they appeared singly [*sic*], have been[10] read with Approbation, perhaps above their Merit, but of no great Advantage to the Writer.[11] She hopes, therefore, that she shall not be considered as too indulgent to Vanity,

or

---

or too studious of Interest, if, from the Labour which has hitherto been chiefly gainful to others, she endeavours to obtain at last some Profit for herself and her Children.[12] She cannot decently enforce her Claim by the Praise of her own Performances; nor can she suppose, that, by the most artful and laboured Address, any additional Notice could be procured to a Publication, of which HER MAJESTY has condescended to be the PATRONESS.[13]

SUBSCRIPTIONS will be taken in, and RECEIPTS delivered,[14] by Mr. DODSLEY,[15] in *Pall-Mall*; Mr. BECKET, in *The Adelphi*; Mr. WHITE, in *Fleet-street*; Mr. WILKIE, in *St. Paul's Church-yard*; Messrs. DILLY, in *The Poultry*; Mr. PRINCE, at *Oxford*; Mr. WOODYER, at *Cambridge*; Mr. FREDERICK, at *Bath*; Mr. SPRANGE, at *Tunbridge*; Mr. BALFOUR, in *Edinburgh*; and Mr. FAULKNER, in *Dublin*.

No[16]

RECEIVED, *the*   *Day of*   177[17]

of[18]   One Guinea,

being the First Subscription[19] *for the above-mentioned* WORKS; *which I promise to deliver, when printed, agreeably to these Proposals.*

NOTES

1. This proposal was almost certainly written by Johnson: In his diary, there is an entry for January 2, 1775 that reads, "Wrote Charlotte's Proposal" (*Diaries, Prayers, and Annals*; ed. E. L. McAdam [New Haven: Yale University Press, 1958, vol. 1 of The Yale Edition of the Works of Samuel Johnson, general editor Walter Jackson

Bate], 224). See also Fleeman II 1240. Apparently the proposal was not published until March: The *London Chronicle* 2845 (March 2–4, 1775) writes, "This Day were published Proposals for printing by Subscription a new and elegant Edition of the Original Works of Mrs. Charlotte Lennox" (212).

2. No evidence survives that Queen Charlotte (1744–1818; ODNB XI 179–84) agreed to accept this dedication, but it is difficult to imagine that Lennox and Johnson would have dared to print this proposal without some kind of arrangement. See also Lennox's claim in #55.

3. It is unclear from *what* this edition is "Enlarged and Corrected." At quarto, the format was once again larger than the earlier editions of Lennox's own works (as opposed to her translations), and presumably Lennox would have corrected typos from earlier publications, but it is unlikely she would have actually revised her earlier writings.

4. Here, Lennox (or Johnson) is using the word "original" in at least two senses: in the sense of a work of literature conceived without any particular source (works like *FQ*, i.e., new novels), and in the sense of new combinations of older material, i.e., works like *SI* that are compilations and translations of older literature supplemented by the author's comments.

5. The reference to *Eliza* here, in a proposal sanctioned by Lennox, is a strong indication that that novel was indeed written by her (cf. Schürer).

6. Unfortunately, these previously unprinted pieces remain unknown.

7. The proposal does not offer information on which pieces were to be included in which volumes. The titles mentioned are four novels (of varying length), two plays (both short), and *SI*, so a possible distribution could have been two novels each and *SI* with the two plays in the third.

8. See #53 on this portrait. The engraver mentioned is almost certainly Bartolozzi.

9. At least four aspects of this proposal suggest that it was targeted for a luxury audience. In contrast to the previous proposal (#14), this one is not to be delivered bound, so subscribers would have had to pay for (custom-)binding as well, which meant that the publishers expected the edition to be purchased by a wealthier audience. Similarly, this edition is more expensive than the 1752 subscription: The earlier edition costs five shillings (one crown) for one volume, this one a relatively high total of 42 shillings (two guineas), so fourteen shillings per volume. The price in guineas also indicates an appeal from the publishers to a higher class of readers: The guinea was considered a payment for a gentleman, while pounds were used in trade. Finally, the quarto format confirms the wealthier target audience.

10. Above this line, a hand-written note is inserted that ends, "was written by Dr. Samuel Johnson." Unfortunately, the first three words are struck through by a hand-drawn square covering the entire sheet above this line, making them illegible.

11. Here, Lennox is appealing to her readers (through Johnson's words in the proposal) to recognize (or at least believe) that prior to 1775, the main beneficiaries of publishing were the booksellers, while this particular edition—either because it is by subscription, or because it is after the 1774 copyright decision—would bring *her* profit.

12. By 1775, Lennox's children Harriet Holles (*1765) and George Louis (*1771) had both been born. Lennox makes a similar claim in her letter to Hunter (#55).

13. In a fairly conventional note of humility, Lennox locates literary authority in the person of the Queen—her own opinion, she claims, pales in comparison.

14. This appears to be the only enterprise where this particular combination of booksellers came together. However, most of them had cooperated previously. Dodsley and Becket frequently worked together, though usually with James Robson, Isaac Taylor, William Richardson (see #46), and Leonard Urquhart. In 1780, the two published the *Select Odes of Pindar and Horace*, translated by William Tasker, with Prince and a Sprange from Tunbridge Wells and others. In 1774, Dodsley and Becket worked with the Dillys and others on John Walker's *A General Idea of a Pronouncing Dictionary of the English Language*. White and Wilkie frequently cooperated in the 1770s and 1780s, and in 1775 published Samuel Hayes's short *Duelling: A Poem* with Dodsley and Prince. Wilkie also brought out William Hayward Roberts's *Poems* with Frederick and Woodyer (and others) in 1776.

15. The individual booksellers are:
- James Dodsley (see correspondent's biography)
- Thomas Becket (fl.1760–1815) had his business at the Tully's Head on the Strand at the east corner of the Adelphi—the housing complex where Garrick lived—near Surrey Street from 1760 to 1778. He went bankrupt in 1779, but reemerged in 1783 with premises on Pall Mall (Plomer 20–21, Maxted 17).
- Benjamin White (the elder, †1794) traded from the Boyle's Head on Fleet Street from 1749 and then from the Horace's Head on Fleet Street from 1767 to 1792 (Plomer 261, Maxted 244).
- John Wilkie (†1785) had his premises at 71, Bible, St. Paul's Churchyard from 1757 until his death (Plomer 264, Maxted 247).
- Edward (1732–79) and Charles (1739–1807) Dilly's place of business was the Rose and Crown at 22 Poultry from 1755. The Dilly brothers concentrated on theological literature, but also published Catherine Macaulay. They were friends with Johnson and James Boswell (Plomer 74–75, Maxted 66–67). See also Daniel W. Hollis III, "Edward and Charles Dilly," in Bracken/Silver 97–102.
- Daniel Prince (†1796) had his business at the corner of New College Lane in Oxford. By the time of his death, he was one of the oldest booksellers in England (Plomer 204).
- John Woodyer, bookseller and publisher in Cambridge at No. 1 Trinity Street since 1759, went bankrupt in 1782 (Plomer 271).
- William Frederick (†1776) worked from No 18 The Grove in Bath. He was an agent for the London lottery in 1757 and was elected a member of the Bath Corporation in 1766. Plomer calls him one of "the chief men in the book-trade in the West of England during the latter half of the eighteenth century" (97).
- This bookseller is the Jasper Sprange of Tunbridge Wells mentioned in Raven, *Business* 241. There was also a Sprange who flourished in Tunbridge

Wells as a printer starting 1794, mostly with auction and sales catalogues, but it seems unlikely that the two would be the same person.

- John Balfour (†1795) worked with William Smellie throughout the 1770s until the partners split in 1778. His name does not usually appear on its own before 1780 (Plomer 281).

- George Faulkner (1703?–75) worked as a printer in Dublin from 1724 to 1775 and was known as "Swift's printer." Other authors of his included George Berkeley, Orrery, and Sir George Lyttelton as well as several Irish writers. Next to William Bowyer, Benjamin Motte, and Richardson, Dodsley was one of the members of the London book trade with whom Faulkner worked regularly. Cf. Plomer 384 and Mary Pollard, *A Dictionary of Members of the Dublin Book Trade 1550–1800* (London: Bibliographical Society, 2000), 198–206.

16. In contrast to the previous proposal (#14), these receipt slips are numbered.

17. While above Lennox writes that the edition will be finished by October 1776, the digits "177" leave the possibility of three more years open. However, the number could also simply be chosen to accommodate 1775 and 1776. The open spaces are intended to include a date and month.

18. The open space here is intended for the name of the subscriber.

19. It is unclear why Lennox refers to the "*First*" subscription—the implication is that she is considering a second or more calls for contributions.

55

Charlotte Lennox
to Dr. William Hunter

FEBRUARY 18, [1775[1]]

MS:	Royal College of Surgeons of England, Hunter-Baillie Papers, Vol. 1B, f.56, Ref. MS0014/2
Pages:	1
Edition:	*The Correspondence of Dr William Hunter, 1740–1783*, 2 vols. (ed. C. Helen Brock; London: Pickering & Chatto, 2008), II 189–91.[2]
Text:	

Sir

   The late decision with regard to—
literary property[3] having given me a right
to reprint my original writings[4] for
the benefit of myself and my children,
I have been advised by my friends to
publish proposals for a Subscription.
   Her Majesty has been so gracious as
to patronise this undertaking,[5] and
thence as You may easily imagine, I
derive my best hopes of success. I have
taken the liberty to enclose some of my
proposals,[6] and if any favourable
opportunity offers to mention them
among your acquaintance,[7] I shall
be much oblig'd to you, if you will—

remember me.   I am with great esteem
                                Sir
Feb[ry] 18
Great Tower Hill[8]   Your very humble Servt
                                Charlotte Lennox
Dr Hunter

NOTES

1. This letter is dated by its internal references to the "late decision with regard to literary property," which happened in 1774 (see below n.2), and to the proposal Lennox mentions (#54), which is dated February 14, 1775—only four days before the letter.

2. There are several divergent transcriptions in Brock's edition. Most importantly, she misreads Lennox's address as "Great Suiver Hill."

3. The landmark 1774 copyright decision by the House of Lords in the case of *Donaldson v. Becket* had ended perpetual copyright (which meant that the booksellers only had to pay authors once when they originally bought their copy) and set a limit of fourteen years (after which the copyright now reverted to the author). The decision is often celebrated as a victory for authors in that they could now make a living more easily, and it is frequently claimed that as a result literature became cheaper, but the story was probably not that straightforward. Still, it was clearly a significant step in the direction of intellectual property rights. On the changes in copyright and their ramifications in a legal and cultural context, see Rose, Raven, *Business* (esp. 230–38), and John Feather, *A History of British Publishing* (London: Croom Helm, 1988).

According to the 1774 decision, the copyright to anything published before 1760—which included the popular *Sully*—returned to Lennox. Like many other authors at the time, she soon started asserting her rights against the booksellers (see #63, #64, and #66).

4. The use of the word "original" is interesting here in the light of Lennox's later career, which included only one original novel. In contemporaneous terminology, it implied books which she authored herself rather than simply translated. By 1778, though, Lennox had become embroiled in a dispute with James Dodsley over a translation, which today is not always considered "original" (see #54 and #64), so she was applying the 1774 copyright decision to a translation as well.

5. Hunter was the queen's personal physician.

6. There are no proposals in Hunter's papers. For the proposal, see #54.

7. There is no evidence that Hunter did this. None of the letters addressed *to* him in the following months, nor any surviving letters of *his* from that period, make any reference to Lennox.

8. See #47.

56

Samuel Johnson[1]
to Charlotte Lennox

MAY 2, 1775

MS:	Houghton Library, Harvard University, MS Eng 1269 (10)
Pages:	3
Edition:	LC #31, Redford II 201–2
Text:	

Madam

In soliciting Subscriptions,[2] as perhaps in many
other cases, too much eagerness defeats itself.[3] We must
leave our friends to their own motives and their own
opportunities. Your Subscription can hardly fail of success,[4]
but you must wait its progress. By telling your friends
how much you expect from them you discourage them,
for they finding themselves unequal to your expectation, will rather do nothing and be quiet, than do
their utmost, and yet not please.[5] You complain of
Miss Reynolds[6] who probably knows not three people
whom She can properly solicite [sic]. Sir Joshua has made

it a rule to act on these occasions only as a Gentleman.[7]
When Miss Reynolds used to lay my proposals in the
way of Sitters,[8] he always hid them, and un-
doubtedly did right.

You tell me of a numerous acquaintance, and
of the vain and the gay, who will be proud of standing in the same list with the Queen.[9] Among those

whom I know how many are there to whom I should be
welcome if I asked them for a Guinea?[10] With the
Vain and the Gay I cannot be supposed to have much
conversation, nor indeed with any who will enquire
the opinion of the court on the matter.

Do not think that I advise you to desist or to
despair. I think you will certainly succeed to a
moderate, and probably, to an eminent degree.[11] Your
powers are acknowledged, and your character must be
respected, if it be not that by some ~~indecencies~~ peculiarities[12] with

respect to religion, of which I have heard complaints.[13]

pretty triffler [*sic*] upon occasion[14]

As to your being a [illegible word stricken through] that concerns
only your intimates, and cannot operate upon the Subscriptions. Your manners as far as the publick needs to
know, are very elegant and ladylike.[15]

I therefore venture to tell you again, that in
my opinion you will have no reason to fear, but you
must be a little patient. The work must be done principally by the great Ladies.[16]

I had not written this, but that Mr Lenox, who if not a good solicitor, is a special tea-
zer, had not told me that he could not go without it.[17]

I am

Once more, I think
you will succeed. Send
your proposals to every
hand without expressing
large expectations.

Madam
Your most obedient Servant
Sam: Johnson
May 2. 1775

NOTES

1. The authorship of this letter is confirmed by an endorsement reading "Doctor
Johnson may be published" in Lennox's hand. The endorsement suggests that either
Lennox or someone else, perhaps Boswell, was considering publishing it. The changes
made to the text of the letter could have been amendments for that publication. Isles

speculates "that CL at one time formed, and subsequently abandoned, a plan to write her own memoir of SJ" (173 n.143).

2. These subscriptions would be to her *Original Works* (#54).

3. Johnson seems to be berating Lennox for pursuing subscriptions too aggressively. From the following sentences it appears mutual friends of Lennox and Johnson complained to the latter about her pressure.

4. This bit of optimism on Johnson's part is interesting—and wrong, as the failure of the edition shows.

5. Subscription publication allowed various individuals to contribute different amounts of money by subscribing to any number of copies.

6. Lennox appears disappointed with Frances for not soliciting enough subscriptions for her collected works (see #47).

7. That apparently means not to promote subscriptions, especially to Reynolds's paying customers.

8. Interestingly, Johnson used Frances the same way as Lennox, namely to solicit subscriptions. He is implicitly criticized for this practice by Joshua, who might have been annoyed to have his clients disturbed. Since Joshua moved to London in 1752, Johnson is presumably referring to his *Proposals for Printing the Dramatick Works of William Shakespeare* of 1756. In either case, Joshua does not seem to approve of this method of soliciting subscriptions.

9. The *Original Works* were to be dedicated to the Queen (#54), and probably she would have been one of the subscribers.

10. Of course, back in the mid-1750s, Johnson had borrowed several guineas from Alexander Lennox—cf. #18.

11. This is somewhat more equivocal than the beginning of the letter, where Johnson writes that the edition "can hardly fail of success."

12. This word might have been changed to make the publication of the letter less injurious to Lennox's reputation (see n.1 above). Isles seems certain that this change and the one below (see n.14) are in Lennox's hand (Isles 173 n.143), but they look more like Johnson's hand to me.

13. Nothing is known about Lennox's religious proclivities except what is implied by the letter she received from Thomas Winstanley (#72).

14. This phrase is superscribed (see n.12). Again, the emendation might have changed a harsher comment into "pretty triffler," one of Lennox's favorite terms—she used "trifler" in her early poetry and in *LM* as her authorial persona.

15. The implication is that Lennox's manners in private are less than elegant and ladylike—see #24—though it is also interesting that Johnson is talking about Lennox's public reputation rather than her private behavior. Significantly, the support Lennox received from *men* throughout her career conjures up the somewhat misogynist suggestion that perhaps these observations—all by *women*—might have been due to other circumstances, such as Lennox's alleged beauty, her relative success as an author, or Johnson's preference of her over other female writers. Still, it is striking that in the course of over 20 years of correspondence, Johnson criticizes Lennox on various occasions for a number of character flaws.

16. In light of the possibility that Lennox had particular difficulties with the female sex, this remark would probably not exactly have pleased Lennox.

17. The word "solicitor" here means not a legal official, but a person who solicits subscriptions. The description of Alexander Lennox suggests that, as Isles writes, his "defective rhetoric is more than compensated for by his skill in making a nuisance of himself" (176 n.150). The sentence as a whole indicates that Alexander must have *asked* Johnson to intervene with his wife and explain the basics of soliciting subscriptions.

57

Charlotte Lennox
to David Garrick

AUGUST 20, 1775

MS:	Folger Library, Y.c.1666
Edition:	Boaden II 77–78
Address:	To David Garrick Esqr[1]
Text:	

Sir,

When your letter was left for me
I was confind [sic] to my bed by a fever[2]—I am
now better, and hope to be able to attend
your summons to the Adelphi[3]—indeed
you wrong me if you suppose I did not
take pains[4]—it is true I depended upon
your assistance—you permitted me to do
so, and I well know how easy it is for
you to make that piece as pleasing as
any we have had for a long time—I am
not indifferent to theatrical rewards; could
I obtain them, they would assist me to
bring up my little boy, and my girl,[5] but
having once faild [sic], when I had to a certain
degree pleasd [sic] my self, and several others
whose judgment I relied on more than
my own,[6] I am grown diffident, so diffident
that if I have any genius, I dare not
trust it: a little success would embolden

me—and this success I hope to owe to
you—and I shall be always ready to
acknowledge to others, with the same
sincerity that I do now to you—that
if from this piece I should have any share
either of reputation or profit, it will be
entirly [*sic*] your gift[7]

—I am Sir
Your Much obligd [*sic*] Servant
August 20. 1775   Charlotte Lennox.

NOTES

1. On the recto of the letter (the same side as the address), there is an endorsement in an unknown hand that reads,
    Mrs Lennox
    about the
    Plays
2. From the context of the previous correspondence with Garrick (#50, #51, and #52) and the content of this letter, it can be conjectured that, in the meantime, Lennox had submitted a manuscript, probably of *OCM*, and received a response where Garrick criticized her for sloppy work. That response no longer exists, but Lennox must have changed her play enough to make Garrick feel confident enough actually to produce it. *OCM* opened on November 9, 1775 to great critical praise.
3. Since March 1772, the Garricks had been living at No. 5 Royal Terrace in a housing development called "The Adelphi." The Adelphi, built by the Adams brothers Robert and James, old friends of Garrick's, was still under construction when the Garricks moved in. They stayed there until Garrick's death in 1779.
4. So Lennox contests Garrick's claim that she did not put enough effort into her play.
5. In 1775, Harriet Holles was about ten years old, George Louis about four.
6. Lennox is referring to her disastrous experience with her first play, *The Sister*, in 1769—see #45. Even though Colman and Lennox had thought the play worthy of performance—i.e., it "pleased myself, and several others"—it flopped on its opening night.
7. There is no particular reason to doubt the sincerity of this statement—Lennox did indeed always acknowledge the assistance of others, such as Johnson with dedications and Orrery with translation.

58

Mary Stuart, Countess of Bute, to Charlotte Lennox

NOVEMBER 14, 1775

MS:	Houghton Library, Harvard University, MS Eng 1269 (40)
Pages:	1
Edition:	LC #32
Address:	To
	Mrs Charlotte Lennox
	Great Tower Hill[1]
Text:	

Lady Butes comp[ts]. to M[rs] Lenox & congratulates her
on the success of her Play;[2] Lady Bute wou'd be
Glad to be of any service to her, but is averse
to seeing her name in print,[3] Hopes M[rs] Lennox
will send her a copy of her Play when it comes
out.[4]
Luton Park[5] Nov: 14th / 1775

NOTES

1. See #47.
2. This is Lennox's play *OCM*, which was performed seven times between November 9, 1775, and January 8, 1776, at Drury Lane. The second and third performances were November 11 and November 13 (see *London Stage* IV 1928–31, 1933, and 1943), so by the time Lady Bute was writing this letter Lennox had had

the benefit of the third performance, which qualified as "success"—certainly by the standards of Lennox's previous dramatic venture *The Sister* (see #45).

3. Probably, Lennox was asking for permission to dedicate the printed version of *OCM* to Lady Bute. Considering the pro-Newcastle/Rockingham politics of Lennox's previous dedicatees (see #42), her application was not likely to find approval, and indeed Lady Bute's tone is fairly terse and cool. "[S]eeing her name in print" may also be an allusion to the letters of her mother Lady Mary Wortley Montagu, which had been published starting 1763 to Lady Bute's great displeasure (Isles 177 n.155).

4. *OCM* came out on November 27 with no dedication. It is not known if Lennox sent Lady Bute a copy of the play.

5. This was "Luton Hoo, a Bedfordshire estate which comprised the mansion, sometimes known simply as The Hoo, together with over 4,000 acres, traversed by the River Lea" (Peter Brown, "Bute in Retirement," *Lord Bute: Essays in Re-Interpretation*, ed. Karl Schweizer [Leicester: Leicester University Press, 1988], 241–73, here 242).

59

Charlotte Lennox
to Samuel Johnson

[1776[1]]

MS:	John Rylands University Library of Manchester, English MS.537
Pages:	1
Edition:	J. D. Wright, "Some Unpublished Letters to and from Dr Johnson," *Bulletin of the John Rylands Library* 16 (1932): 32-76, here 57; Small 53
Text:	

Mary-bon[2] Monday

Dear Sir

M[r] Lennox thinks
a hundred and fifty Copies will be
sufficient,[3] we are both greatly
obligd [*sic*] to you for so kindly undertaking to manage this little
affair—permit me only to hint
          as
that ∧ it is of great consequence
to me to have the book presented
to Her Majesty,[4] before I am quite
forgot,[5] the sooner you begin to
treat with Mr. Strahan the better.[6]

I am Sir
Your grateful humble

                        Servt
                    Charlotte Lennox
Doctor Johnson
N[r] eight Bolt Court[7]
Fleet Street[8]

NOTES

1. As Small argues (and I agree), the letter refers "to the first volume of the proposed edition" of Lennox's *Original Works* (see #54). Small tentatively dates the letter 1778, but also writes that "I see no reason for putting the letter in a specific year" (53). Isles goes along with the conclusion that the letter is about the *Original Works*, but calls 1778 "conjecturally misdated" (176 n.151), presumably because the proposals for the edition had been printed in 1775. In the end, the letter can only be placed chronologically by the addresses: Lennox lived in Marybon no earlier than 1775 and no later than 1782; Johnson moved to Bolt Court in March 1776. The letter suggests that Lennox wants to get the volume out as quickly as possible ("before I am quite forgot"), so I believe the date must have been close to the publication of the proposal in February 1775.

2. Marybon (or Marylebone) is the church St. Mary Le Bone on the northwestern outskirts of eighteenth-century London. In #64, Lennox clarifies that she lives at "No.7 Nottingham Street near Marybon Church." On Rocque's 1746 map, the Mary Le Bone area is still clearly outside the city (1Ac), connected to it only through one road, and with the church burial grounds to the west and the Marylebone Gardens to the east. By the time of Horwood's 1792 map (1Dd), the gardens are gone, the entire area has been settled, and the street on which the church lies has been renamed High Street.

Gordon Mackenzie's *Marylebone: Great City North of Oxford Street* (London: Macmillan, 1972) describes the development of the village in detail. Early in the eighteenth century, John Holles, Duke of Newcastle, had bought the Marylebone estate, which may or may not be a coincidence considering Lennox's connections with the Newcastles. Newcastle passed the estate on to his daughter Lady Henrietta Harley and her husband, the book collector Edward Harley, second Earl of Oxford and Mortimer. In the 1770s, Marybon was a fashionable and literary area: Richard Sheridan and Elizabeth Linley were married in its church (the inside of which William Hogarth used for one of the plates in *The Rake's Progress*); elaborate parties were staged in the Marylebone Gardens (Johnson created a disturbance during a party in 1774) before they were closed in 1778; and such worthies as Sarah Siddons and Elizabeth Montagu lived there. Unfortunately, Mackenzie does not discuss the development of Nottingham Street in particular.

Lennox seems to have frequented Marylebone before living there. Ezra Stiles (1727–95), theologian and president of Yale, reports on a visit with Catherine Macaulay in his diary on June 30, 1772: "After Tea we all walked an hour or two into Maryrybone [*sic*] Gardens. In our walk we met with the celebrated Mrs. *Lenox*, Authoress of the *Female Quixote*, and several other Novelle performances. Mrs. Macaulay stopped and spoke with her" (*The Literary Diary of Ezra Stiles*, ed. Franklin Bowditch Dexter [3 vols.; New York: Scribner, 1901], I 320).

3. Apparently, Lennox and her husband agreed that an initial print run of 150 for the first volume of the *Original Works* would be sufficient.

4. The *Original Works* were dedicated to Queen Charlotte (see #54), so probably Lennox wanted to give her a presentation copy. Small transcribes the phrase as "His Majesty," but the manuscript clearly says "Her."

5. Here, Lennox maybe reveals her greatest fear—not so much being in poverty, even though that was constantly on her mind, as no longer being remembered as a writer.

6. Lennox is asking Johnson to negotiate with William Strahan (see #3), which suggests that her work on the *Original Works* had progressed at least to the point of involving a printer.

7. Johnson moved to No. 8 Bolt Court, north of the corner of Fleet Street, in March 1776 (Rogers 42).

8. See #46.

60

Charlotte Lennox
to [Alexander Lennox[1]] (draft)

[c. 1776–78[2]]

MS:	Houghton Library, Harvard University, MS Eng 1269 (15)
Pages:	4
Edition:	LC #48
Text:	

I have talkd [sic] with M[r] Johnson,[3] and
other persons of good sense and experi
ence, upon the expediency of sending Har
-riet to Boulogne[4] for her education[5]—
and they are all of opinion, which they
supported with very good reasons, that
a Boarding school here, will be equally
advantageous [sic], equally cheap, and is liable
to fewer inconveniencies than a Convent.
Their reasons have convinced me, and that
is the cause that they will never convince
you[6]—therefore I submit to your despotick will, with this condition only, that
I go with her, and see her settled[7]—this
point I never will give up—the next
thing to be considered, is what necessaries
must be provided—I will give you a
list of what cloaths [sic] and Linnen are
usually sent even to the cheapest schools
- Half a dozen frocks.
she has two already

170

a dozen pr of stockings
<u>she has four pr but they are old</u>
half a dozen night caps
<u>she has one</u>
four under petticoats
<u>of this article she has none but rags</u>
Morning gowns
<u>of these she has four which I think is enough</u>
Three quilted caps with lace border
<u>of these she has none</u>

---

a dozen shifts
<u>of these she has five new ones, three</u>
<u>not made up—and the others are rags</u>
a handsome Skirt, to wear on Sundays
All the skirts she has had, for more
than two years past, have been made out
of my gowns—she has two of these
now, but more than half worn out
and only fit to wear in common[8]

there [*sic*] are other little articles, but what
I have set down is the principal I
beleive [*sic*]—when these things are bought,
the cheapest, and the readiest way, will
be to give them out to be made—at the
rate Nanny works, they will be a year
doing at home,[9] and for what M[rs]
Hubbard[10] does, she is paid three times
the value—besides she could not get them
down[11] in any reasonable time—

I cannot help mentioning to you
what Lady Clerke[12] once proposd [*sic*] to me
and which on many accounts seems
highly advantagious [*sic*] to Harriet.
there is a school about four miles
distant from Gosport,[13] the terms
reasonable, the masters and teachers,
Lady Clerke assured me very good
and the Governess a sensible prudent

---

woman—here Lady Clerke beggd [sic] me
to place Harriet, assuring me she woud
in every respect supply the place of a
mother, to her—that she woud [sic] see her
every week or fortnight, take her
home to her Mama's house during
every vacation,[14] and write me regular
accounts of her health, her improvements
and her behaviour—you may—
affect to treat what I am now going
to tell you with ridicule—but for all
that, it is a fact—Lady Clerke has
already mentioned Harriet in her
will[15]—she is fond of her—and from the
natural sensibility of her heart that
fondness will be increasd [sic] by the child's
being confided to her care—without
building castles in the air, many—
advantages for Harriet may be expectd [sic]
Lady Clerke's situation considered[16]—
at least she will be in fortune's way,
and in Lady Clerke, she will have a
wise, and virtuous monitress, who
will not only endeavour to inspire her
with the love of virtue by precepts, but
shew how lovely, and desirable it is
by her own example—Lady Clerke
promised me to be in Town last month,[17]
if she comes, she will be glad to take
Harriet down with her, and will be at

---

all the trouble of settleing [sic] Harriet at
the school—pray think on what I have
written on this subject, and let me
know your determination.[18]

NOTES

1. It would appear that this is a draft for a letter to Alexander Lennox since Lennox
is discussing the education of their daughter Harriet. The need to write a letter suggests

that the couple were not living together at this time—perhaps because Lennox was living in Marybon and her husband near the Customs Office in London (see #63).

2. The approximate date of this letter derives first from Harriet's year of birth, 1765—she would have been sent to boarding school between the ages of ten and fifteen. Secondly, Lennox was most intimate with Lady Clerke in 1776 and 1777 (see #61 and #63), so the letter was probably written around those years.

3. I.e., Samuel Johnson.

4. There is a good chance this would have been the school of the Ursuline order in Boulogne-sur-Mer. The Ursulines had been founded in 1535 specifically with the mission of female education. They had boarding schools in their convents all over France, which explains the references to those two terms in the present letter. Furthermore, many English parents sent their children to the school in Boulogne, which was fairly close, right across the Channel and south of Calais. The Ursulines had a school in Boulogne from 1624 to 1792. See John McNarris, *Church and Society in Eighteenth Century France*, 2 vols. (Oxford: Clarendon Press, 1998) and Mère Marie de Chantal Guedré, *Histoire de l'Ordre des Ursulines en France*, 3 vols. (Paris: Éditions Saint-Paul, 1958–63).

5. Women's education was a much-discussed topic in eighteenth-century England; see for instance Kathryn Sutherland, "Writings on Education and Conduct: Arguments for Female Improvement," *Women and Literature in Britain 1700–1800*, ed. Vivien Jones (Cambridge: Cambridge University Press, 2000), 25–45. In more practical terms, education outside the home (at a boarding school), while not entirely unusual, was also not common. Lennox's wanting to send Harriet away to school might be interpreted as an indication of her aspirations for her daughter—or as a realization that as a working mother (and probably living singly) she could not educate her daughter herself.

6. This testy comment—as well as the following reference to Alexander's "despotick will"—suggest that he and Lennox were not on good terms.

7. There is no evidence that Harriet or Lennox ever went to France. If they did not, it seems that Lennox got her way with respect to Harriet's education after all.

8. This list is a clear indication of Lennox's poverty at this time. Harriet has only about half of the shifts she needs, a third of frocks and stockings, one out of six nightcaps, and none of the petticoats and quilted caps. Lennox's specific mention of the recycling of her own clothes for Harriet is also a sign of their indigence.

9. If Lennox had a nanny for Harriet, that would indicate that she was not entirely poor at the time of this letter. Then again, the comment on that nanny does not exhibit a high opinion of her. This may also be Ann Brown, the person Lennox and her daughter supposedly assaulted in 1778 (London Metropolitan Archives MJ/SR 3358)—see #24. "Nanny" could also be a nickname for "Ann."

10. This person is possibly related to the Hubbards mentioned in #30. While the document cited there mentions no women, the fact that Thomas Hubbard had a son strongly suggests that he was married.

11. "Done" would make equal or more sense here, but the manuscript clearly reads "down."

12. On Lady Lydia Clerke, see correspondent's biography and #61 and #63.

13. On Gosport, see #63. I have not been able to identify the school outside of Gosport.

14. It is unclear if this means to Lady Clerke's mother or to Harriet's mother, i.e., Lennox.

15. This will no longer exists. In any case, Harriet died at a young age, long before Lady Clerke.

16. This suggests either that the present letter was written before Sir John's death on October 11, 1776, or that Lady Clerke's situation was still considered good even after his death. According to Berg, *Circle*, Lady Clerke "received a substantial sum from a Nabob" (126) after her husband's death (see also Berg, *Circle* 38).

17. I.e., Lady Clerke promised one month earlier that she would be in London in the near future. This might refer to the interaction described in #63.

18. The phrase here suggests that Lennox would have submitted to her husband's decision, but it remains unknown whether Harriet ever went to boarding school, either in Boulogne or near Gosport.

61

Charlotte Lennox
to Lady Lydia Clerke

AUGUST 30, [1776[1]]

MS: Royal Society of Antiquaries, Cely-Trevelian Bequest
                    MS 444/19

Pages: 3

Edition: Berg, "Letters" 69–70; Berg, *Circle* 123–24

Address: To Lady Clerke
                    Buxton

Text:

Oh my dearest Lady Clerke what a letter[2] have
you wrote me! how shall I comfort you, how
shall I comfort my self—I feel I have philosophy only for my own misfortunes—Yours
depresses me quite—believe me I neither feign
nor exaggerate—I am overwhelmed with
Your affliction—I can think of nothing but
You, and ever since I have received Your
letter I have not been able to speak a civil
Word to any body[3]—peevish quarrelsome,
and out of humour with my self and every
thing about me—good god! what a
reverse—You have known nothing—
hitherto but prosperity—how severely
must you feel this stroke—I have been
a wretch since I was thirteen years old[4]
when I lost my father—adversity is habi[-]
tual to me—but You—oh my dear friend

my heart bleeds for you—what an
affecting picture do you draw of your present
situation—wandering alone[5]—wishing
to seclude your self for ever among the
rocks that surround you—but my
dear friend you shall not while I have
life, live in a cottage alone[6]—I will
accompany you in any retirement, I
will join my pittance to yours,[7] and your
dear society would perhaps awake some
sparks of genius again[8] and enable me
to enlarge our little income by my pen[9]
—such is the wish of friendship—oh
that M^r L[10] would allow me some thing
yearly that I might put this scheme[11] in

---

execution—that abominable Lord
Rochford[12]—what can he say for himself
—is he not bound[13] to finish his own
Work[14]—why did he encumber you with
a title?[15] why draw you in to impoverish
yourself to fit out your husband for this
fatal expedition[16]—I could stab him
—alas! my dear Lady Clerke amidst
so many solid causes for affliction, I am
likewise tormenting my self about one
which indeed compared with the rest is—
trifling and yet I feel it sensibly—You
tell me you are going to your old lodgings
because you suppose I have not a spare
bed as I did not mention it—good God!
My dear friend, how could you serve
me so—I have been utterly ignorant
of your motions,[17] I thought you would
have told me when you left Leverpool.[18]
I knew not that you were at Buxton[19]
I was in doubt whether you intended
to come to town[20] or not—I have dispatched
my horse[21] to Panton street[22] with directions
to find out if you have absolutely engagd [sic]
the lodgings, and if you have not, to tell

them that it was a mistake[23]—and that
you are to be with me—I have likewise
ordered her[24] to await your arrival on
Friday and to attend you here—could
I have hoped that this letter would have
reached you at Buxton before you left
I should have sent it to the post—but
I have but this moment got your letter

───────────

this is Monday evening, and you are
to set on Wednesday, and sense[25] tells
me you would not get my letter in time
—M[r] Lennox this moment tells me
that if I send my letter now, you will
get it before you leave Buxton, I have
not a moment to lose—I will send it
away—remember my dear Lady Clerke
you must come directly here—I shall
die with grief if you go to a lodging
for heaven's sake spare me this morti[-]
fication—adieu my dearest friend
I must not add another word for
fear of delay. Yours ever & entire[ly,]

C L[ennox][26]

[Gre[27]]at Tower hill
[Au]gust 30

NOTES

1. This letter is extremely difficult to date. The elements that contribute to the dating are:
   (1) The letter is (probably) dated "August 30," and the text at one point reads, "this is Monday evening."
   (2) Lydia Clerke has experienced some misfortune, perhaps involving a male relative.
   (3) John Clerke is involved in some "fatal expedition."
   (4) The letter is apparently written after the end of Lord Rochford's term in office (see n.12 below).

According to (1), the letter was written on a Monday, August 30. In the general vicinity of Lennox's other letter to Lady Clerke (#63 of June 13, 1777), August 30 fell on a Monday (according to the University of Notre Dame's perpetual calendar,

178

http://archives1.archives.nd.edu/perpetua.htm) in 1773, 1779, and 1784. The present letter was certainly written before #63 (because of the change address Lennox refers to there), but 1773 seems very early. Also, perhaps August is a misreading in the first place or Lennox is imprecise about her dating.

The misfortune in (2) could be Sir John Clerke's death on October 11, 1776, but then the letter would have to have been written in 1777 at the earliest (the first August 30 after his death), so *after* #63, which seems impossible. The misfortune could also be some debt Sir John incurred (which would explain the poverty referred to in the letter) or his departure to India in 1772 (which would have left Lady Clerke without her husband and his resources).

The "fatal expedition" (3) could similarly be the trip to India—which Sir John describes in two letters to Rochford of May 4, 1772 (India Office Library, London: Home Office Papers Misc. Series 109 [9], f.155) and November 26, 1772 (India Office Library, London: Home Office Papers Misc. Series 107 [10], ff.373–75)—or a particular assignment there, such as the "more disagreeable visit" to the Sultan of Zooloo he was intending to undertake in 1775 (India Office Library, London: Home Office Papers Misc. Series 122 [2], ff.7–8).

Finally, the reference to the end of Rochford's term (4) seems to date the letter after 1775, when he ended his tenure as Secretary of State for the Southern Department.

In other words, the date could be 1773 (the most recent Monday, August 30; after Sir John had incurred some debt or had left for India—but then Rochford was still in office) or 1776 (after Rochford's departure from office in October 1775; but before #63—but then Monday, August 30 would have to be a misinterpretation). Berg chooses 1776 without any elaboration; I tend to agree with her, though I am not entirely certain.

2. Lady Clerke's letter to Lennox does not survive. It is unclear to what "misfortunes" Lennox refers, though Berg deduces from the mention of "prosperity" that "John [Clerke] has suffered a devastating financial mishap" (*Circle* 126).

3. Since Lennox refers to the loss of her father, Lady Clerke's "affliction" may be the loss of a close male relative. Clerke's husband died on October 11, 1776; it is unknown when her father passed away.

4. This reference confirms what Lennox says about her biography in other places. Assuming she was born around 1729/30, it indicates that her father died in 1742/43. See Carlile and Berg, *Circle* 122.

5. Lady Clerke is "wandering alone" because her husband is in the East Indies.

6. It is unclear whether Lady Clerke is *already* living "in a cottage alone" or whether Lennox wants to save her from this fate in the future.

7. Clerke's poverty might suggest that her husband is already dead. Even during his lifetime, though, "John Clerke had a long history of extravagance" (Berg, "Letters" 63), and his deployment to the East Indies may have been a scheme to become solvent again.

8. Lennox's only publications in the 1770s were *Valliere* in 1774 and her drama *OCM* in 1775. However, the former was a translation and the latter an adaptation, so neither can really be seen as productions of Lennox's "genius."

9. This is an instance of Lennox thinking of writing as a source of income rather than an outpouring of genius.

10. Presumably, Alexander Lennox. This remark seems to confirm that Lennox and her husband were living apart at the time, and indicates that she was receiving no regular financial support from him. However, at the end of the letter Lennox seems to be speaking directly with her spouse.

11. The scheme of living together in a little cottage.

12. This is William Henry Nassau van Zuylestein, fourth Earl of Rochford (1717–81; ODNB XL 260–63). Rochford became member of the privy council in 1755, was named ambassador to Spain in 1763 and to France in 1766. In 1768, Rochford was appointed Secretary of State for the northern department. He was moved to the southern department 1770–75, where he was responsible (among other things) for the oversight of the East India Company. Rochford resigned because of the problems with the American colonies in 1775 and received several pensions and grants in the following years. He became a knight of the garter in 1778. Several letters between Clerke and Rochford exist, and "we know that John [. . .] expected much from his friendship with Rochford" (Berg, "Letters" 64).

13. Berg reads this word as "trustd" (*Circle* 123).

14. Rochford retired in November 1775, so after that time he could not have finished any work he started earlier. Berg mentions that Rochford "failed to come through with promised insurance money for lost ships" (*Circle* 38).

15. Berg transcribes this as "and" (*Circle* 123). It is unclear what connection Lord Rochford might have had with Lady Clerke's title—perhaps he suggested her husband for knighthood in 1772 (as Berg believes, *Circle* 37).

16. If "fatal" is to be taken literally, the expedition would be Sir John's trip to the East Indies where he died—and the letter should be dated after 1776. Once again, Lord Rochford's connection to the matter remains unclear.

17. Lennox seems to be complaining that Lady Clerke has not kept her apprised of her movements, i.e., not been sufficiently in touch.

18. Liverpool. It remains unclear why Lady Clerke had been there.

19. This is probably the spa town Buxton in Derbyshire, which is more or less on the way from Liverpool to London. No other letter in *Circle* is addressed to or from Buxton.

20. To London.

21. If she could afford her own horse, Lennox cannot have been too destitute at this point. Berg transcribes the word as "Nurse" (*Circle* 123).

22. Panton Street is between Haymarket and Whitcomb Street (Rocque 10Cb, Horwood 13Ad).

23. The sequence of events seems to be as follows: Lennox knows that Lady Clerke left Liverpool earlier, but is unaware—previous to the receipt of the named (unknown) letter—that she has stopped at Buxton. That letter tells her that Lady Clerke is intending to stay at her old lodgings in Panton Street (in London), but Lennox would prefer if she stayed with her. Therefore, she sends a horse there to find out how solid Lady Clerke's booking is. Lennox also first doubts that her present letter will reach Lady

Clerke at Buxton, but then learns from her husband (who seems to be living or at least staying with her at this moment) that it might make it there in time after all. The letter is written on Monday, and Lennox hopes it will reach Lady Clerke in Buxton on Wednesday, who is expected in London on Friday.

24. Perhaps a messenger or maid sent with the horse to Panton Street—or the nurse.

25. Again, Berg transcribes this word as "nurse" (*Circle* 123).

26. Both lower corners of the letter are torn off.

27. The corner of the sheet is torn off, but the address can be ascertained from surrounding correspondence, and for the date the word August is most likely, since the postmark reads "AV/30" (Berg, "Letters" 69)—but see also n.1.

62

Sir Joshua Reynolds
to Charlotte Lennox

OCTOBER 9, 1776

MS: Houghton Library, Harvard University, MS Eng 1269 (29)
Pages: 1
Edition: LC #33, Ingamells #57
Text:

Leicesterfields[1] Oct. 9th 1776

Madam

    I did not answer your
Letter, waiting till I should be able
to fix a time for your sitting,[2] If
next Monday will be convenient
I shall be then at leasure [sic], I will
expect you in half an hour after one
o'clock unless I hear to the contrary[3]

    I am with greatest respect
    your most humble
    and obedient servant
    Joshua Reynolds

NOTES

1. See #47.

2. In the twenty-one months between Reynolds's last known correspondence with Lennox (#47) and this letter, Lennox apparently sent at least one letter.

3. It is unknown whether Reynolds was trying to touch up his 1761 portrait (see #47 and #53) or paint a new one and if this sitting ever took place. Of course, October 1776 was already the month in which subscribers had been promised the delivery of Lennox's *Collected Works* (see #54).

63

Charlotte Lennox
to Lady Lydia Clerke

JUNE 16, 1777

MS:	Royal Society of Antiquaries, Cely-Trevelian Bequest MS 444/19
Pages:	4
Edition:	Berg, "Letters" 71–73; Berg, *Circle* 124–26
Address:	[Lady] Clerke
	at Mrs Hammond's[1]
	Gosport[2]
Text:	

Marybon[3] June 16, 1777

My Dear Lady Clerke,

Mrs Thornton[4] indulgd [*sic*] me
with the perusal of a letter[5] from you on a late
melancholly [*sic*] event[6]—I say indulgd [*sic*] me, for although my eyes streamd [*sic*] at every line, I would
not have exchanged the sweetly painful emotions I felt, for the broadest mirth of unfeeling
prosperity—Never did such natural and
affecting eloquence flow from your pen be[-]
fore! it is your heart that speaks, and you
speak to the heart so powerfully, that I wept
as much at the third reading of your letter
as I did at the first—I freely confess to you
that I have this letter now in my possession
I forced it from M[rs] Thornton in order to

convert some of the infidels of the other sex,
who mentain [*sic*] that no woman was ever
generous enough to forgive certain offences
in a husband[7]—That unaffected display of
the most tender, the most generous senti[-]
ments that ever warmd [*sic*] a human breast,
does you so much honour, that they ought
not to be conceald [*sic*], and form the noblest
apology for the mistakes of the dear Object
of your regrets, since no one can doubt for
a moment, that he who could inspire so
pure and constant a passion in such a
breast[8] as yours, must have possessd [*sic*]
many, and great Virtues—and let it be
your consolation that he did possess them
and that he will now reap the full benefit
of them—for he is gone where falshood,
envy, and malice can neither aggravate
his failings, nor rob his merits of their
just reward[9]—You say your health is

impaird [*sic*], I fear it will be more so my dear
friend, if you continue to give way to
grief—amiable as that grief is, you ought
to suppress it, when its effects are likely to be
so fatal—patience under inevitable—
evils, is not more an act of duty, than
necessity —"We are all (says a certain
Philosopher) born with a heavy clog[10] to
which we are chaind [*sic*], but he who takes it
up, and carries it, feels less inconvenience
than he who drags it along."[11] I hope this
letter will find you on your return from
Wales,[12] in better health, disposd [*sic*] to admit
comfort,[13] and to enjoy tranquility, which
while you were continually fluctuating
between hope, and fear,[14] was not to be expec
-ted—I ought to make you an apology
for not letting you know of my removal
from Tower hill[15]—I can not palliate, nor
disguise the truth, therefore I will honestly

own, that not having received any answer
to two or three letters which I wrote to you,
—I thought I owd [*sic*] so much respect to my
self, as to be silent for the future—I am
here at Marybon where I have the greatest
part of a pretty house, in a very pleasant
situation—Your Harriet[16] is with me, and
one maid makes all my equipage.
—my dear little boy is always with me
from Saturday till Sunday evening, when
he returns to the Academy of which—
young as he is,[17] he is the ornament, and
delight—As I have a spare bed chamber
Mr Lennox is here, as often as his business

---

will permit—he has an apartment near
the Custom house, and for the present supplies
my expences[18]—but how long he will be able
to do it I cannot tell, for the American
War has greatly reduced his income,[19] while
it has left him the same habits of expence
—My sufferings were so great during the
last twelve month that I resided at Tower
—hill, that I was reduced to a most deplor
                    this
-able state of health, and ∧ added at least ten
years to my looks, as every one who saw
me could easily perceive—I thank you
my dearest Lady Clerke for your subscription[20]
and for what you mention concerning
Marmontel's book[21]—my necessities will
I fear oblige me to take up my pen again,
—but I doubt much whether I can bear
any sort of study, my nerves are so much
affected by the continual agitation of
my mind for so long a time: besides I
am likely to be engaged in a War with [the[22]]
booksellers—who have ventured in [defi-]
ance of an Act of Parliament[23] to prin[t a]
new edition of Sully's Memoirs, whi[ch is]
now my sole property—Doct[or Johnson]

has been with me on this occa[sion and]
pointed out to me what measur[es I need]
to pursue[24]—I believe I shall not find it difficult to find Lawyers who will serve me
with out fees—but Lord Camden[25] is the
person who could do me most good, and
him, I am affraid [sic] I hav[e[26]]
Garrick who brought [. . .]
to visit me at Tower hill, [. . .]
very much disposd [sic] to be [. . .]
I have disobligd [sic] Garrick [. . .]

---

the comedy of Old City manners to him, as he
hopd [sic], and even in an artful way requested
I would—he has been my enemy ever since
and doubtless will prevent Lord Camden with
whom he is very intimate from being
of any use to me. Harriet begs I will leave
room for her to write a few lines to you whom she
truly dotes on—my best compliments wait on
Your Mama—I am my Dear Lady Clerke ever

Yours affectionately
direct for me at N.º 7   C. Lennox
Nottingham Street, near Marybon Church[27]

My Dear Lady Clerke,[28]
my ma[ma . . .[29]]
to say I love you, but no to [. . .]
that would require a whole [. . .]
leave space enough for me [. . .]
faithful
Henrietta-Holles Lennox[30]

NOTES

1. Hammond was Lady Clerke's maiden name, so this is probably a close relative. Lady Clerke's mother Lydia (Isgar) Hammond was born in 1700, so she would have been quite old in 1777 (Berg, *Circle* 252), but the reference to "Mama" at the end of the letter suggests this was indeed her.

2. Gosport is a harbor town and naval station to the south and slightly east of London, right next to Portsmouth. As a navy officer, Lady Clerke's husband Sir John

would have been stationed there. The most recent history of Gosport is *The Story of Gosport* by Leonard White (rev. ed.; Shirley, Southampton: Ensign, 1989).

3. See #59.

4. This is Sylvia Thornton, née Brathwaite (1730s?–93), who was a close friend of Lady Clerke's (Berg, *Circle* 203–16). She remembered Lennox in her will, leaving her "'my grey Cabinet, my Black Cloak not trimmed, my White Dimity Cloak, and five guineas'" (215). Sylvia was married to Bonnell Thornton (1724–68), a member of the circle around Johnson and co-author, with George Colman, of *The Connoiseur* (see correspondent's biography) and *Poems by the Most Eminent Ladies of Great Britain and Ireland* (1755). While the first edition of this two-volume collection did not include any poems by Lennox, the second volume of a later (1785?) edition started with Lennox's "The Art of Coquetry."

5. Apparently, Sylvia Thornton had shared a letter from Lady Clerke with Lennox, who read it several times.

6. The "late melancholy event" was almost certainly John Clerke's death on October 11, 1776.

7. According to Berg, "with Susannah Dobson's epistolary innuendos in mind it seems likely that the transgression was sexual" (*Circle* 126).

8. Berg transcribes this word as "heart" (*Circle* 124).

9. Since this is one of only a few references to religion in these letters, it is unclear if Lennox is sincere or merely invoking a commonplace to comfort her friend.

10. Berg transcribes this as "log" ("Letters" 75 and *Circle* 124), but see n.11 below.

11. This is an adaptation from *Seneca's Morals* by Roger L'Estrange, which came out in many editions in the course of the eighteenth century. In the most recent edition before 1777 (London: Ballard et al., 1775), the quote reads: "While we are in the Flesh, every Man has his Chain and his Clog, and it is looser and lighter to one Man than another; only he is more at Ease that takes it up, and carries it, than he that drags it" (107). In her novel *Sophia*, Lennox quotes from Seneca/L'Estrange several times.

12. Nothing else is known about Lady Clerke's trip to Wales.

13. Berg transcribes this word as "company" (*Circle* 124).

14. Presumably about the well-being of her husband or the state of her financial affairs.

15. Sometime between August 1776 and this letter (June 1777), Lennox had moved from Tower Hill to Nottingham Street in Marybon—see #59.

16. This is Lennox's daughter Harriet—see #60.

17. Born in 1771, George Louis would have been about six years old.

18. This passage paints an interesting picture of the Lennox marriage. On the one hand, the two had separate residences because of Alexander's work. On the other hand, he had a separate bedroom when he visited Marybon, which he seems to have done frequently. At the same time, he is financially supporting his wife.

19. Obviously, the American War of Independence had a significant impact on international trade and hence on customs.

20. Probably a subscription to Lennox's *Original Works* (#54), which were long supposed to have appeared—so Lady Clerke's subscription was really more a form of charity.

21. This is clearly a reference to Jean-François Marmontel (1723–99), the French author and encyclopedist. Probably, Lady Clerke was suggesting that Lennox undertake a translation, which she does not sound thrilled about. The book is probably the romance *Les Incas* (1777), which came out later that same year in an English translation (London: J. Nourse, P. Elmsley, E. Lyde, and G. Kearsley). This edition does not name the translator, but since Lennox had not worked with any of these booksellers recently (and only with John Nourse 20 years earlier on *Maintenon*, see #25 and #26), it is unlikely it was her.

22. Two large pieces are torn out of the letter here and at the corner. The words of the first part of damage can be reconstructed with some certainty.

23. This is the copyright decision of 1774—see n.25 below.

24. On this affair and Johnson's involvement, see #64, #65, and #66.

25. This is Charles Pratt, Baron and later Earl of Camden (1714–94; ODNB XLV 211–15), chief justice of the Court of Common Pleas (1761–66) and Lord Chancellor (1766–70). Camden was instrumental in the decision of 1774 that abolished perpetual copyright (see Rose, esp. 98–109).

26. The words missing here can only be guessed with some conjecture. Berg has, "I am afraid I hav[e lost him]. Garrick who brought [Lord Camden] to visit me at Tower hill, [is now] very much disposed to be [angry with me]. I have disobliged Garrick [by not giving] the comedy of Old City Manners to him" (*Circle* 125). This is confusing, though, since *OCM* was performed at Garrick's Drury Lane theater and since Lennox thanked him in an acknowledgement in the printed version of the play.

27. See #59.

28. This note is written on the back of Lennox's letter.

29. Once again, it is difficult to guess the remaining words of Harriet's note. Berg offers "my ma[ma tells me] to say I love you but not to [say how much] that would require a whole [page and not] leave space enough for me [to sign myself]" (*Circle* 125–26).

30. Interestingly, Harriet uses the first name of her godmother Henrietta Holles, Duchess of Newcastle here—see #37.

64

Charlotte Lennox
to Samuel Johnson

JUNE 17, [1777[1]]

MS:	Houghton Library, Harvard University, MS Hyde 10 (414)
Pages:	2
Edition:	Small 50
Address:	Doctor Johnson
	Bolt Court Fleet Street[2]
Text:	

Sir

You cannot imagine what—
pleasure it gave me to hear you say[3]
You would come and eat apple dump-
lings of my making—You may be
sure I will hold you to Your promise,
—but alas! apples will not be ripe
this long time,[4] and I am impatient
for Your company—suppose You
were to try my hand at a goosberry [sic]
tart—if I might venture to say it with
-out being thought vain, I could tell
You that my tarts have been admir'd.
—indeed You will make me very happy
by nameing [sic] a day for another visit
to my cottage,[5] and I will take care You
shall not be tried with the noise of
my little boy,[6] who I am sensible

190

was very troublesome when You
was here. Mr Lennox is so desirous
of recovering his property out of the
hands of the booksellers,[7] that he gives
me leave to take any measures that

---

shall be judgd [*sic*] proper[8]—it will be—
necessary to have the advice of some
gentleman of the law, I am not known
to Mr Murphy,[9] but if You will be so good
to mention my affairs to him, and let
me know where he lives, I will call
upon him—The person who leaves
this at Your house, will call again
for an answer, which if You please
may be left with Your servant[10] for
him—dear Sir if You write me a
line[11]—tell me in one word if there are
any hopes of a reprieve for poor D^r
Dodd[12]—I was sadly shockd [*sic*] when I
heard of the determination of the
Council—

I am Sir Your Obligd [*sic*]
humble Servant
Charlotte Lennox
Marybon June 17. (1777)[13]
N° 7. Nottingham Street near Marybon—
—Church

NOTES

1. Though the year of the letter is not specified, Lennox's question about a reprieve for the soon-to-be-executed Dodd (see n.12 below) places it squarely in 1777.
2. See #59.
3. Either in a letter or in personal conversation.
4. Apples actually ripen between late summer and late autumn, depending on their variety, so Lennox's "long time" might be no more than a month or two. The gooseberry, in contrast, is in season for most of the late spring and summer.
5. This word implies that in 1777 No. 7 Nottingham Street was a small house—see also #63, where Lennox writes that she has "the greatest part of a pretty house."

6. In 1777, George Louis would have been about six years old.

7. Alexander Lennox is not so much concerned about his wife's writing as about *his* property—see #38.

8. From the following sentence, it is clear that these measures include taking legal action.

9. Arthur Murphy (1727–1805; ODNB XXXIX 832–33) was an Irish lawyer as well as a writer and actor who met Johnson around 1754. He edited the *Gray's Inn Journal* from 1752 to 1774 and was called to the bar in 1762, from which he retired in 1788. Murphy was friends with various literary figures of his time and wrote lives of Fielding (1762), Johnson (1792), and Garrick (1801—see Rogers 271). He was also involved in the case (*Donaldson v. Becket*) that ended perpetual copyright, which precipitated Lennox's activity against Dodsley et al.

10. This is presumably Johnson's servant Frank Barber; see #18.

11. The following letter indicates that Johnson did not respond to this missive.

12. There is a footnote on the manuscript here, indicated with an "x," and on the right (off the letter) there is a sentence in a different hand, "x Dr. Dodd was executed for forgery 27. June 1777."

Clergyman William Dodd (1729–77; ODNB XVI 400–402), nicknamed "The Macaroni Parson," was born in Lincolnshire and came to London around 1750. There, he preached the "inaugural sermon at the opening of the Magdalen House, a home for reformed prostitutes" (Rogers 121) and published the popular *Beauties of Shakespeare* (1752). Through his success as a preacher and writer, Dodd entered high society and soon started living beyond his means. In financial straits, Dodd forged a bond for £4200 in the name of his former student Philip Stanhope, fifth Earl of Chesterfield. The forgery was exposed, and Dodd was put on trial and sentenced to death on May 16, 1777. During and after the trial, Johnson wrote various pieces in support of Dodd. Although it appears King George III was willing to grant clemency in response to many calls for mercy, his advisors convinced him to let the sentence stand in a Privy Council meeting on June 13—probably what Lennox calls "the determination of the Council." Three recent works on Dodd are O M Brack, Jr.'s keepsake for the Samuel Johnson Society of Southern California, *The Macaroni Parson and the Concentrated Mind: Samuel Johnson's Writings for the Reverend William Dodd* (Tucson, AZ: Chax Press, 2004), Gerald Hawson's *The Macaroni Parson: The Life of the Unfortunate Dr Dodd* (London: Hutchison, 1973), and Edwin Willoughby's *The Unfortunate Dr Dodd: The Tragedy of an Incurable Optimist* (London/New York: n.p., 1958).

13. The year, in parenthesis, is added in pencil in a different (third) hand.

65

Charlotte Lennox
to Samuel Johnson

MAY 29, [1778[1]]

MS: John Rylands University Library of Manchester, English
            MS.537
Pages: 1
Edition: J. D. Wright, "Some Unpublished Letters to and from Dr
            Johnson," *Bulletin of the John Rylands Library* 16 (1932):
            32–76, here 56–57; Small 51–52
Text:

Mary bon[2] May 29.

Sir

    Although I have no answer to my last
letter,[3] yet I venture to write again about my
little affairs,[4] and beg you will let me know
when I may call upon you—I saw Mr Dodsley
yesterday, and he told me they had printed another
edition of Sully's Memoirs[5]—I apprehend they
had no right to do this without my consent,[6]
it is more than fourteen years since that
book was first publishd [sic];[7] and about a year
ago, I offerd [sic] to give them my corrected copy
for a reasonable consideration, which
Dodsley in the name of the partners
refusd [sic][8]—and now they have reprinted it
without consulting me although by the
late decision concerning literary property

the copy is mine—I am advisd [*sic*] to publish
it for myself in numbers,[9] and if the partners
expect to sell another edition, I have some
reason to hope that I may have success by
publishing it in this manner, as the purchase
will be so much easier—but I must be
speedy, for Dodsley owned the book was
almost ready[10]—it will be necessary I
suppose to draw up a little address to the
publick explaining my reasons for publishing Sully my self, and in this manner
—this favour I earnestly entreat of you
—as likewise that you will appoint a
day for my calling upon you—if the
bearer is so fortunate as to find you at home
he will bring me your answer, but if that
should not happen I send my direction
again lest my former letter should be lost

> I am Sir
> Your most hum[e] Servt
> C. Lennox

No 7 Notingham [*sic*] Street,
near the Church Marybon
To Doctor Johnson
Bolt Court Fleet Street[11]

NOTES

1. This letter can be placed in 1778 because of the new edition of *Sully* that Lennox mentions (see below n.5)

2. See #59.

3. It is unclear if Lennox is referring to #64 or some more recent letter.

4. The "little affairs" are Lennox asserting her copyright against her publishers.

5. This is the 1778 edition of the *Sully* "Printed for J[ohn]. Rivington and Sons, J[ames]. Dodsley, S[tanley]. Crowder, G[eorge]. Robinson, T[homas]. Cadell, and T[homas]. Evans," also called "The Fifth Edition." The book had remained vastly popular after its original publication in late 1755, seeing new editions every few years between 1755 and 1778: The Dodsleys, Millar, and Shropshire brought out a second (1757), third (1761), and fourth (1763) edition (cf. Small 251–53).

6. Of course, the legal rights (and profits) of the official publishers had also been challenged by the many pirated editions of *Sully*. For one, Alexander Donaldson published two editions in Edinburgh in 1760 and 1770 (the latter, not listed by Small, cheekily and precisely advertising itself as "Sold at his shops, the corner of Arundel Street, Strand, London, and at Edinburgh"). For another, there were three editions in 1773 in Edinburgh. The two five-volume 1773 Edinburgh editions Small mentions— one (with a dedication) with four volumes printed for John Robertson and the fifth for Alexander Kincaid and William Creech; the other (without a dedication) entirely for Kincaid and Creech—are indeed probably the same, with individual booksellers simply adding their own title pages. A fourth bookseller might have also been involved: There is a 1773 Edinburgh edition "Printed and sold by Gavin Alston."

Even when two editions were available after 1778 (see n.5 above and n.8 below), the pirates did not relent: An edition not listed in Small came out in Dublin in 1781. Calling itself a 5th edition, this publication was "Printed by R[obert]. Marchbank, for Messrs. W[illiam]. Watson, [William] Sleater, [George] Burnet, [William] Colles, [Richard] Moncriefe, [Caleb] Jenkin, [Thomas] Walker, [John or Edward] Beatty, [Laurence Larkin] Flin, [John?] Exshaw, [William] Halhead, [William] Gilbert, [Thomas] White, [John] Burton, [Thomas] Byrne, and [Michael] Parker"—quite the assembly of Irish booksellers.

7. Since *Sully* had originally been published (technically) in 1756, the rights returned to Lennox after the 1774 decision. See #55.

8. It seems Dodsley relented, perhaps after interventions from Johnson and/or Arthur Murphy (see #64): The fifth edition of *Sully* was swiftly followed by "A New Edition," also by Dodsley, Millar, and Shropshire, that points out it is "Translated from the French, by the Author of the Female Quixote." From this, Small concludes that "we may assume that [the publishers] were persuaded to take Mrs. Lennox's 'corrected copy for a reasonable consideration' and bring it out as a new edition" (52–53). Thus, Lennox did earn some money after all.

9. The source of this advice is unknown, but publication "in numbers" or serially was indeed the most profitable form of publishing.

10. At this point, Lennox conceives of her serial publication of *Sully* as competition to the official fifth edition.

11. See #59.

66

Samuel Johnson
to Charlotte Lennox

November 9, 1778

MS: Houghton Library, Harvard University, MS Eng 1269 (11)
Pages: 1
Edition: LC #34, Bedford III 138
Text:

Mrs. Desmoulings[1] will show you Mr Murphy's
letter,[2] and will tell you why it will be best for us
to go to his Chambers. I shall be ready to wait on
you. Do not be frighted, I believe there is no danger[3]

> I am,
> Madam,
> Your most humble Servant,
> Sam: Johnson
> Nov. 9. 1778

NOTES

1. This is Elizabeth Desmoulins (1716–86), daughter of Johnson's godfather Samuel
Swynfen and Johnson's houseguest (or employee—"SJ had paid her half a guinea a week
for her household duties" [Rogers 112]) from 1778 until Johnson's death. Johnson's servant Frank Barber (see #18) studied with her husband, who was a writing master.
2. It seems that Johnson had been conferring with Arthur Murphy (see #64) and
had developed a plan of action against Dodsley with him. No correspondence between

Johnson and Murphy survives, and it is unclear why Murphy wants them to come to his chambers—perhaps something to do with the "danger" mentioned below.

3. It is unclear who would have been in what kind of danger here—perhaps Lennox and, by association, Johnson were in danger of offending the booksellers, or Lennox was scared about the financial burden of using a lawyer like Murphy.

67

Samuel Johnson
to Charlotte Lennox

[c. 1779–84?[1]]

MS:	Houghton Library, Harvard University, MS Eng 1269 (14)
Pages:	1
Edition:	LC #45, Redford V 10–11
Address:	To Mrs Lennox

Text:

Dear Madam

When friends fall out the first thing to be considered is how to fall in again,[2] and he is best that
makes the first advances, I have designed to come to
you ever since half an hour after you ran from me
but I knew not whither.[3] I did not when I began intend
to say more [than[4]] the first sentence, nor when I left off, to
have a final quarrel. Pray, my dear, think no more
of it, but come to me or let me know when I can come
to you, for the thought of driving you away will
be very painful to,

Dearest Partlet,[5]

I have not read your
Letter nor will read it,   Your most obedient &c
till I know whether it is
peevish or no, for if it be   Sam: Johnson
you shall have it again.[6]   Thursday night

197

NOTES

1. Both Isles and Redford date this letter through Johnson's failing handwriting. While Isles offers c.1780–84, Redford more widely suggests c.1779–84.

2. The reason for the falling out between the two is not known, but might be another example of Lennox's supposedly temperamental personality. Nevertheless, Johnson does not consider it a serious breach of the friendship and initiates a reconciliation.

3. This might mean that Johnson does not know Lennox's address or—more likely—that he is not sure where she went.

4. This word is not in the manuscript, but necessary for the sentence to make sense.

5. In his *Dictionary*, Johnson defines "Partlet" as "A name given to a hen; the original signification being a ruff or band, or covering for the neck" (n.p.). The *OED* defines it as a "word used as the proper name of any hen, often *Dame Partlet*; also applied, like 'hen,' to a woman." The earliest reference is to Chaucer in the Nun's Priest's Tale. As Isles points out, Shakespeare uses the name in *The Winter's Tale* to describe a domineering woman (in a quotation Johnson gives in the *Dictionary*) and in the first part of *Henry IV* in "a mood of affectionate exasperation" (420 n.194). That mood would seem to apply here.

6. The letter referred to here no longer exists. However, it is interesting to note that Johnson considers Lennox's peevishness not to be limited to her personality, but also part of her writing style (see #24 and #25).

68

Samuel Johnson
to [Charlotte Lennox]

JANUARY 25, [c. 1782¹]

MS: Houghton Library, Harvard University, MS Eng 1269 (12)
Pages: 1
Edition: LC #35, Redford V 11–12
Address: Westminster²
Text:

Madam

   That mistake may not gather strength
by time,³ I make this haste to assure you, that
between hurry and sickness joined with other
causes of confusion, I did not Yesterday
morning know either your Face or your Voice,⁴
and that the answer which I happened to give
you was intended for another, very unlike
you, so that you must not be angry with,

Madam,
Your humble Servant

Jan. 25.   Sam: Johnson

NOTES

   1. Bedford cautiously assigns this letter no specific year, arguing it could be any
year between 1779 and 1784. In contrast, Isles hones in on 1782 and 1784 (between
Lennox's move to Westminster around 1779 and Johnson's death in 1784), when

Johnson was ill in January, and gives preference to 1782 (178 n.162). Actually, I am not sure what evidence Isles has for his claim that "the 'Westminster' address indicates—on the basis of what has so far been learned about Lennox's various changes of residence—that the year of writing can be no earlier than 1779" (ibid.)— she uses Kensington addresses in 1782 (#69) and 1784 (#71). No explicit connection between Lennox and Westminster I am aware of exists before 1793, but obviously that is too late for a letter from Johnson. Still, I accept Isles's conjecture.

2. This appears to be the last line of an address—the rest of the sheet is torn off.

3. Once again, Johnson and Lennox seem to have fallen out—this time due to a misunderstanding on Johnson's part because of his illness.

4. Throughout his life, Johnson suffered from poor eye-sight, perhaps as a result of infant scrofula. By about 1765, he was also almost deaf, maybe because of a tubercular disease (Rogers 177)—though he still seems to have minded noise; see #64.

69

Charlotte Lennox
to [Walker King¹]

MAY 7, 1782

MS:	Sheffield City Council, Libraries Archives and Information: Sheffield Archives, WWM/R108/28
Pages:	1
Text:	

Sir

        I have been prevented by
illness from returning you my sincere thanks
           which
for the very polite and humane manner in ∧ —
you have communicated to me my Lord—
Rockingham's pleasure²—I am truly sensible
of His Lordship's great goodness in receiving
my petition so favorably.³ My health is so
impaird [*sic*] that a journey to Bristol is—
prescrib'd [*sic*] for me,⁴ but in my present circum
stances, a journey to Bristol is as little in
my power, as a journey to the Moon—but
I look forward with hope, and rely securely
on Your kind promise to remind His Lordship
of me
  ∧ —I must entreat you to excuse this scrawl,
I have had a violent inflammation in my
eyes,⁵ which has left them so weak, that
I shape my letters merely by guess.–When I am

to be favoured with a line from you Sir, please
to enclose it to William Armitage Esqr[6]—
Parson's Yard,[7] Kensington.—I am truly

> Sir
> Your oblig'd, and very humble
> Servant

May 7 1782   Charlotte Lennox

NOTES

1. While the *Location Register of English Literary Manuscripts and Letters: Eighteenth and Nineteenth Centuries* (2 vols.; ed. David C. Sutton [London: The British Library, 1995], II 573) asserts that this letters is addressed to Lord Rockingham, the text makes it clear that it is actually written to someone close to Rockingham, but not himself. Since the title of the manuscript collection R108, where this letter is found, is "Miscellaneous correspondence and petitions, some addressed to the Marquis [Lord Rockingham] and some to Walker King, asking for various forms of official patronage," the addressee (and topic) seems clear.

2. Probably, King wrote a letter to Lennox communicating Rockingham's sentiments.

3. This would likely have been a petition for patronage. However, in spite of the favorable reception—perhaps because of Rockingham's death less than two months after this letter—no payments are recorded.

4. Lennox is probably referring to Bristol Hot Well, a hot spring near Bristol. This is the spring visited by the Bramble party in Tobias Smollett's *Humphry Clinker*; see *The Expedition of Humphry Clinker*, ed. O M Brack, Jr., introduction and notes by Thomas Preston (Athens and London: The University of Georgia Press, 1990), xlii–xliii. Whether or not Lennox traveled there is unknown.

5. Here, Lennox for once specifies what her health problems are. However, her hand-writing in this letter is not really that different from other letters.

6. Unidentified. There was a Robert Armitage (1736–87) in the circle around Sylvia Thornton (see #63)—he was Sylia's brother-in-law and Thomas Winstanley's (see #70 and #72) stepson—but the only son of Robert Armitage I am aware of was called Whaley (Berg, *Circle* 249), and I do not know whether they lived in Kensington.

7. According to Faulkner, "Parson's Yard, now called Holland Street, on the west of Church Street, is said to have been the site of a monastery, but this tradition is unsupported by any records" (296). Parson's Yard can also be seen as #19 in Rhodes.

70

Vicesimus Knox
to Thomas Winstanley

February 19, 1784

MS: Houghton Library, Harvard University, MS Eng 1269 (16)
Pages: 3
Edition: LC #36
Address: The Rev:[d] M[r] Winstanley
                Petty France[1]
                Westminster
Text:

Rev[d]. Sir

                         I beg leave to return my best
Acknowledgements for your very friendly Letter.[2] My
father, ~~after~~[3] concerning whom you are so kind as to enquire,
died, after a very painful and lingering Illness,
four years ago.[4] I remember the Connection which,
for a short Time, subsisted between you and him,[5]
and have frequently had the Pleasure of hearing
you at S[t] Dunstan's,[6] the Church, which, ~~I~~
(at that time a Schoolboy, and unknown to
you,) I used to frequent. I consider the Favour
of your Letter[7] as a Testimony of your Remembrance
of my Father, and it is, on that Account, particularly agreeable to me.
    The Lady who, I apprehend, is the Mother
of the young Gentleman,[8] for whom the Terms
of the School are desired, is well known to me

204

as an eminent literary Character;[9] and, if I
am not mistaken, I have heard of the young

Gentleman's Talents for English Poetry.[10]
It would be a Pleasure to me to be able to
promote the Improvement of so promising a
Scholar.[11] My School is at present very full.[12]
and If the young Gentleman has been used
to any particular Indulgences, such as being
a Parlour Boarder or a private Pupil,[13] I am
afraid my School, where all share alike &
where the Way of living &c is that of the old
fashioned Schools,[14] may not be in every
Respect agreeable. The following is an
Account of the Terms.—I have written
them on the other Side, for the Convenience
of tearing them off separately.

I am, Rev[d] Sir,
Tunbridge School[15]   with Respect, yr obliged
Feb:19, 1784   hble Serv[t]
                          V. Knox

Board &c and classical Instruction twenty five
Guineas per Ann: Entrance Fee D°. three
Guineas.

£

Music, if required, 1.1.0 Entrance &c D° per Quarter
Dancing 15[s] D°. D°.
Drawing 12[s].. [sic] 6 D°. D°.
French 15[s] D°. D°.
Fencing 1.1.0 D°. D°.
Writing and Arithmetic 10[s].6 per Quarter
The Vacations are at Midsummer and Chris[tmas]
one Month each.
N.B. One Guinea per Ann is charged at Christmas
towards the Payment of Assistants
Extra Washing is paid for.
The Accounts are sent in at Midsummer
and Christmas.
The Boys sleep two in a Bed, without any
Exception.

NOTES

1. Petty France, the extension of Tothill Street and Broadway in Westminster (Rocque 18Ba), had been renamed York Street (Horwood 22Dc) sometime between Rocque (1746) and Horwood (1792).

2. I have found no record of this letter.

3. This word is almost completely erased.

4. Apparently, Knox and Winstanley had not been in touch for at least four years since the death of Vicesimus Knox the elder (also his son's predecessor as headmaster of Tonbridge School) in 1780.

5. The connection is probably St. Dunstan's, where Winstanley was rector and Vicesimus Knox the elder "for some time aided Dr. John Jortin as morning preacher" before he became headmaster of Tonbridge School in 1782 (Septimus Rivington, *The History of Tonbridge School* [London, Oxford, and Cambridge: Rivingtons, 1869], 124). David Churchill Somervell, *A History of Tonbridge School* (London: Faber and Faber, 1947), calls Knox the "curate" of St. Dunstan's (36).

6. See correspondent's biography.

7. This letter from Winstanley to Knox no longer survives.

8. Lennox and her son, George Louis, who was about thirteen years old in 1784.

9. As Isles implies, this does not mean that Knox actually *considered* Lennox "an eminent literary Character"—he neither mentions her in his *Elegant Extracts* nor lists her among examples of good literature by women (180–81 n.166).

10. The *British Magazine* and the *Edinburgh Weekly Magazine* began publishing George Louis Lennox's poetry and prose in 1783—see below #B3–14.

11. George Louis Lennox is not listed as a pupil of Tonbridge School at any time, so it seems he never attended in spite of Knox's interest here. On the Lennoxes educating their children (and their financial difficulties doing so), see also #60.

12. As Isles points out (181 n.167), this did not remain the case much longer—the school began losing pupils after Knox's outspoken support of the French Revolution.

13. A "Parlour Boarder" was a student at a boarding school who had a special status above the other students by virtue of living with the headmaster's family, having access to the parlor, or some similar arrangement. Being a private pupil meant that the student had one-on-one instruction.

14. On Knox's educational philosophy and on the subjects mentioned below see his *Liberal Education*. This book came out in one volume in 1781 (London: Dilly) and went through eleven editions by 1795 (2 vols.; London: Dilly).

15. Tonbridge (or Tunbridge) School was (and still is) a boarding school in Tonbridge (Kent) founded in 1553 and supported by the Worshipful Company of Skinners. See Rivington and Somervell.

71

Charlotte Lennox
to [James] Dodsley

May 10, 1784

MS: Beinecke Rare Book and Manuscript Library, Yale Uni-
               versity, MSS Vault Hilles (Frederick W. Hilles Manuscript
               Collection), box 14
Pages: 1
Edition: Small 55
Address: To
               M[r] Dodsley, Bookseller
               Pall-Mall[1]
Text:

Kensington May 10. 84

Sir
             If you are willing to
treat with me for a work of the novel
kind, which I sketchd [sic] out some years
ago,[2] and which I have since been
employd [sic] upon at different times—
let me know what day, and at
what hour you will be at home,—
and I will call upon you[3]—I am
at present at Kensington, where I
propose to stay all the Summer,
but as I frequently go to town,
it will be no inconvenience to
me to call at your house—pray
let me have your answer immediately.

—direct for me at M[r] Annis's[4]
on the Terrace Kensington.[5]
—I am Sir

        Your humble Serv[t]
        Charlotte Lennox

NOTES

1. James Dodsley had his business premises at the Tully's Head in Pall Mall from 1757 to 1797 (Maxted 68, Raven, *Business* 187–88). The fact that Lennox inquires after his "home" and "house" suggests he may have *lived* somewhere else.

2. Small speculates that the work Lennox mentions here is her novel *Euphemia* (56). However, that book was eventually published not by Dodsley, but by Thomas Cadell and James Evans, even though Dodsley was still working in 1790.

3. In contrast to three decades previously (#3), Lennox no longer expects booksellers to call on *her*.

4. This Mr. Annis is probably "Mr. Annis, carpenter," mentioned in #708 of the *List of Deeds, Parochial Documents, Etc.* (London: Kensington Public Libraries, 1964–). This Mr. Annis lived "on the highway to Brentford [i.e. High St. Kensington]" [*sic*] in 1784, and "the Terrace" was part of High Street Kensington (see *Diagrams of the Parish of Saint Mary Abbotts, Kensington* [Brompton: Peers, 1847], 94). Faulkner describes Kensington Terrace as "a neat row of houses" (321). Nothing else is known about Annis or why Lennox might have used his address.

5. While the previous letter #69 from 1782 shows Lennox living in Kensington, the addresses are different—now she is directing to the Mr. Annis on the Terrace. In combination with Lennox's remark that she is "at present at Kensington, where I propose to stay all the Summer," this new address suggests that she found various seasonal lodgings in Kensington.

72

Thomas Winstanley
to Charlotte Lennox

AUGUST 30, 1787

MS: Houghton Library, Harvard University, MS Eng 1269 (41)
Pages: 2
Edition: LC #37
Text:

Aug[t]. 30th.—87

My dear Madam

           Previous to your receiving the Sacra:
ment,[1] which I hope M[rs]. Thornton and her son Robert[2]
will join with you in very soon,[3] I think I could
not offer to your serious perusal[4] anything more
suitable to the purpose, than the following reflections
   Depend on it, you are upon good ground—only
suffer not yourself to be perplexed about the <u>Why</u>
and the <u>Wherefore</u>, of divine things. Be content
that 'It is written';—though it surpasses your un
derstanding to account for it.[5]
                  Yours ever &c
                  T. Winstanley
        The Sacrament[6]
   I do not go there—to <u>give</u>—but—to <u>receive</u>;—not
to tell my Lord, how good <u>I</u> am,—but to think, how
good <u>he</u> is.—I have a great many sins and wants
to tell him of—more, than would take up the
whole day:—and when I have told him all I know

of myself, it is but a very little of what he knows
of me.—I go as a <u>sinner</u> to the Saviour. To whom
else should I go, with my blind eyes, foul leprosy,

---

hard heart, rebellious spirit?
They tell me, I must have I know not how
many graces and <u>qualifications</u>, to go to the
Sacrament with.—But I can no <u>stay</u> for them;
my wants are urgent;—I am a dying man.[7]—My
Lord says, with his known kindness,—Come, "Do this
in remembrance of me."[8]—<u>His</u> invitation is qua:
lification enough.—I long to feed on him, to thank

put

God for him, to take him into my heart.—I go to ~~him~~
myself under his wings, and fly to him for refuge

is

from that monster sin, which ready to devour me.
   "Do this in remembrance of me."—Remember
who I am; and <u>what</u> thou art.—Remember me, as thy
<u>Saviour</u>. Remember me, as thy <u>Master</u>.—Remember
<u>my love</u>. Remember <u>thy obligations</u>.—Remember
me, as <u>bearing</u> thy sin. Remember me, as <u>hating</u>
thy sin.—Remember me, and <u>fear</u> not.—Remem:
ber me and sinn [*sic*] not.—Remember me;—to live
<u>by</u> me, <u>for</u> me, <u>with</u> me.

NOTES

   1. As the reflections below show, the sacrament in question is communion.
Lennox may have not been receiving communion because of unspecified religious
"peculiarities" (#56).
   2. On Sylvia Brathwaite Thornton, see #63. Her son Robert John Thornton
(1768?–1837) studied at Cambridge and at Guy's Hospital medical school and pursued a career as a physician (Berg, *Circle* 213–14, 256).
   Between 1799 and 1807, Robert John Thornton published *The Philosophy of
Botany, Being Botanical, and Philosophical Extracts Including, a New Illustration
of the Sexual System of Linnæus* (2 vols.; London: Bensley). This work includes
an engraving titled "Flora, Æsculapius, Ceres, with Cupid, Honouring the Bust of
Linnæus" (n.p.). On the pedestal of the bust, Cupid is inscribing a poem attributed in
a footnote on the following page to Lennox:

All *animated* Nature owns my sway,
Earth, sea, and air, my potent laws obey,
And thou, divine LINNÆUS, trac'd my reign
O'er trees, and shrubs, and FLORA's beauteous train,
Proved them obedient to my soft control,
And gaily breathe an aromatic soul.

The footnote continues, "This lady was invited by the late illustrious Dr. Samuel Johnson, to meet all his literary acquaintances. After dinner, the Doctor gave, 'To the Muses,' and as one of them, he publickly crowned this celebrated authoress with *bays*." Robert John's father Bonnell Thornton would have been one of Johnson's "literary acquaintances." It remains unknown how Robert John came into possession of the lines quoted here supposedly by Lennox, though when he was working on the *New Illustration* in the late 1790s Lennox was still alive.

3. It is unclear whether Sylia and Robert Thornton were (also) guilty of some religious indiscretion.

4. This might be a reference to a prior (and lost) letter from Lennox to Winstanley.

5. This insistence on the insignificance of doubt (or suffering) and on scriptural authority—coupled with a dismissal of human rational faculties—does not sound like a very helpful response (especially considering that Lennox's daughter Harriet had probably died recently). Berg calls Winstanley's attitude towards her in this letter "admonitory, almost accusatory" (*Circle* 48).

6. This prayer is taken from *Posthumous Works of the Rev. Thomas Adam, Late Rector of Wintringham* (3 vols.; York: Ward, 1786). There, the passage reads: "I do not go to the Lord's table to give, but to receive; not to tell Christ how good I am, but to think how good he is. I have a great many sins and wants to tell him of, more than would take up the whole day; and when I have told him all that I know of myself, it is not the half, but a very little of what he knows of me. I bring myself, that is sin, to him, believing that he will be all to me, and do all for me that is in his heart; and I know it is a very compassionate one. I go as a sinner to the Saviour. To whom else should I go, with my blind eyes, foul leprosy, hard heart, and rebellious will? You tell me I must have I know not how many graces and qualifications to go to sacrament with; but I cannot stay for them: My wants are urgent; I am a dying man. My Lord with his own kindness, says, "come; do this; remember me." His invitation is qualification enough; and I long to feed on him, to take him into my heart. I will go to behold him crucified, and his blood poured out for me, in spite of all my sins and fears, and though all the saints on earth stood up with one mouth to forbid me. I go to put myself under Christ's wings, and fly to him for refuge from the monster sin, ready to devour me. [. . .] 'Do this in remembrance of me;'—remember who I am, and what thou art; remember me as thy Saviour; remember me as thy master; remember my love; remember thy obligations; remember me as bearing thy sin; remember me as hating thy sin; remember me and fear not; remember me and sin not; remember me, to live for me, by me, with me" (I 241–42).

Thomas Adam (1701–84; ODNB I 212–13) served at his church in Wintringham, Lincolnshire, for over fifty years. He was an evangelical who exerted most of his influence as a spiritual guide rather than through preaching or conversion. It is unknown whether there was any personal connection between Adam and Winstanley. Winstanley's plagiarism here (quoting Adam without acknowledgement) would not have been considered problematic in the eighteenth century—Winstanley might have committed Adam's prayer to a commonplace book and copied it for Lennox from there.

7. This might be a reference to Winstanley's failing health (he died two years after writing this letter), or it could be a reference to humanity's mortality.

8. During the Last Supper, Jesus says, "this do in remembrance of me" (Luke 22: 19, King James Version).

73

Charlotte Lennox
to James Boswell

JANUARY 3, 1792

MS:	Beinecke Rare Books and Manuscript Library, Yale University, GEN MSS 89 (Boswell Collection), series I, box 26, folder 614 (C1725)
Pages:	1
Edition:	Waingrow 357
Address:	Mrs. Charlotte Lennox
	James Boswell Esq.
	Great Portland Street[1]
Text:	

Sir

    At the same time that I hear
from every mouth the highest praises of your life of
Doctor Johnson,[2] I hear likewise of the honourable—
mention you make of me in that elegant performance
—what I could not hope for from my own—
writings you have bestowd [sic] upon me, and
by recording your illustrious friend's favourable
Judgment of me,[3] have given me a share in that
immortality which your own pen confers on
yourself.

        I am with great respect
        Sir

> Your obligd [*sic*] and very
> humble Servant
> Charlotte Lennox

My compliments
to the Ladies of your family
whom I had the pleasure
to see at Mrs Reynolds's.[4]
Jan'y 3d 1792

NOTES

1. This is the house in Great Portland Street where Boswell moved on January 19, 1791 (cf. Danzinger/Brady xix) and where he lived until he died there.

2. This is of course a reference to Boswell's recent *Life of Johnson*. Actually, reviews were mixed, but the book sold extremely well after its release on May 16, 1791: "Of a total of 1,750 sets printed, 800 were sold in one or two weeks, 1,200 by the end of August, 1,400 by December" (Danzinger/Brady 142), shortly before Lennox wrote this letter.

3. Lennox here certainly refers to Johnson's comparison between various learned women in 1784 as reported in the *Life of Johnson*. Boswell writes: "On the evening of Saturday, May 15, he was in fine spirits, at our Essex-Head Club. He told us, 'I dined yesterday at Mrs. Garrick's, with Mrs. Carter, Miss Hannah More, and Miss Fanny Burney. Three such women are not to be found: I know not where I could find a fourth, except Mrs. Lennox, who is superiour to them all" (BLJ IV 275).

4. As there is a gap in Boswell's journal between April 11, 1791 and August 16, 1792 (cf. Danzinger/Brady 140), because no papers remain from Boswell's daughters, and since letters make no mention, it is impossible to reconstruct the exact date of this visit by Veronica, Euphemia, and/or Elizabeth Boswell to Frances Reynolds. (Boswell's wife Margaret had died in 1789, so she cannot be one of the "Ladies.") From the following letter (#74), it seems possible that Lennox was living with Reynolds at the time.

74

Charlotte Lennox
to James Dodsley

JANUARY 30, 1793

MS:	Houghton Library, Harvard University, MS Hyde 10 (413)
Pages:	1
Address:	Mr Dodsley
	Pall Mall[1]
Text:	

Sir

       Having never settled accounts for the
second edition of the Sister which you publishd [*sic*],[2] I calld [*sic*]
upon you with a hope that something might be due to
me from that quarter—being realy [*sic*] at present in
distress[3]—The victim of a disinterestedness from which
the most ungrateful of men has derived great advantages,[4] I am reduced to an income of forty pounds a
year,[5] and out of that obligd [*sic*] to assist my son[6]—his
selfish father having prevented a provision for him
which a powerful friend I have in the Ministry[7]
intended with his concurrence[8] (which was necessary)
to bestow. Under my present difficulties, I have
recourse to your candor, and humanity, that however
small my claims may be, since by the loss of the copies
       now
they cannot ∧ be ascertaind [*sic*],[9] you will assist me with
a trifling sum in my present necessities.[10] I have
some pretentions to the favour of the Booksellers, and

I have heard of some generous actions of theirs towards authors.[11] Your character, and your opulence,[12] and the nature of my request encourage me to make this application, and to hope for its success.—Some time hence, my circumstances will in all probability be much altered for the better,[13] but I am now in real distress. —Your answer left for me at Mrs Reynolds in Queen Square West^{r}[14] will come safe to my hands.

I am
Sir
Your very humble Servt

Jan.^{ry} 30 1793   Charlotte Lennox

NOTES

1. See #71.

2. In 1769, Dodsley had printed two editions of Lennox's comedy *The Sister* in quick succession. After the play was performed at Covent Garden on February 18, the first edition was announced in the *London Chronicle* of March 4; the second was advertised in the same paper less than two weeks later, on March 15.

3. Lennox's distress seems to have been particularly acute in 1793, when she appealed to Dodsley, Richard Johnson (#81), and probably Alexander Boswell (#79) for financial assistance and launched another subscription edition of one of her works. This was also the year Sylvia Thornton left her "my pale Grey Cabinet, my black Cloak not Trimmed and my White Dimity Cloak and five Guineas" (National Archives PROB 11/1234; see also Berg, *Circle* 215).

4. This would seem to be a reference to Alexander Lennox's profiting financially from his wife's work.

5. This is the only surviving specific information on how wealthy or poor Lennox really was. With an income of £40 per annum, Lennox made more than a beadle (£20 p.a.) or a housekeeper (£28 p.a.) and about the same as a cook (£40 p.a.), but less than most hairdressers (£40–80 p.a. in London in 1797) or mantuamakers (£60 p.a. in London in 1797; cf. Kirstin Olsen, *Daily Life in 18th-Century England* [Westport, CT: Greenwood Press, 1999], 140–45). However, it is completely unclear where this money was coming from—from her husband, from her own income, or from some outside source.

6. See #81 below.

7. This friend, or the position he or she intended to bestow on George Louis Lennox, remain unidentified.

8. This word is difficult to make out.

9. So Lennox is aware of the fire that destroyed part of Dodsley's stock—see #75.

10. Lennox is shifting between an outright demand for money she is *due* because of the second edition of *The Sister* and an appeal to *charity* for a small sum of money.

11. Relations between booksellers and their authors in the eighteenth century were notoriously difficult. On the one hand, some critics such as Harry Ransom claim that relations were generally good—he gives Dodsley as an example of a bookseller being particularly fair towards his authors—and that it is only "[f]rom the author's point of view [that] the writing profession is often portrayed as either enslaved by economic tyranny or courageously rebellious against it" ("The Rewards of Authorship in the Eighteenth Century," *Texas University Studies in English* 18 [1938]: 47–66, here 64). On the other hand, more recent research by Raven suggests that while the average of *surviving* payments for novels between 1770 and 1799 is £80, a fee of only five guineas (or a little over £5) might have been more typical ("Introduction" I 50–54).

12. By the 1790s, James Dodsley was quite rich: When he died in 1797, he left behind a fortune of £70,000 (James Tierney, "R. Dodsley, R. and J. Dodsley, J. Dodsley," in Bracken/Silver 102–122, here 121). Even though he tried to be discrete about his wealth—apparently, he tried to keep the public from knowing he owned a carriage (Raven, *Business* 219)—Lennox was clearly aware of it.

13. Lennox might have been expecting a windfall from the subscription edition of *SI*.

14. This address is Queen's Square (or Queen Square) in Westminster, directly south of St. James (Rocque 10Cc, Horwood 22Dc). Wendorf writes of Frances Reynolds that "[a]fter her brother's death in 1792 [February 23], she received an inheritance of £2500 for life [. . .] and promptly purchased a large house on Queen Square" (74), so this is probably the house to which Lennox is referring. Isles implies that this address "reveals that [Lennox] was living with Frances Reynolds" (183 n.172), but really all the letter shows is that Lennox was using Reynolds's *address*. A week later (#66), Lennox was using a different address in Westminster.

75

[James Dodsley[1]]
to Charlotte Lennox

FEBRUARY 2, 1793

MS: Houghton Library, Harvard University, MS Hyde 10 (191)
Pages: 1
Text:

I conceive that if the remaining
Copies[2] had not been burnt in the
Fire which consumed a Warehouse
of mine to a great amount,[3] you
could nevertheless have had no
claim on me on this account.[4]

        as you represent yourself[5] in
But ∧ distress, difficulties, and
         these
necessities, ∧ have always a claim
upon humanity. I am sorry this
should be your situation, and
therefore have inclosed a Note,[6]
and shall be glad if it prove accept-
-able.
Mrs. Lennox
        Feb.2.93

NOTES

1. The reference to the warehouse fire (see below n.3) proves that this letter is from James Dodsley. Also, it suggests strongly that this letter is a response to the previous letter (#74).

2. I.e., the remaining copies of the second edition of *The Sister* (see #74).

3. Dodsley is referring here to the fire of June 7, 1787, in which he lost £2,500 of stock. Nichols describes this scene: Dodsley "kept no public shop, but continued to be a large wholesale dealer in books, of his own copy-right. Of these a part, to the amount of several thousand pounds, was burnt by an accidental fire in a warehouse which he had not prevailed on himself to insure; but the loss of which he was philosopher enough to bear without the least apparent emotion; and, in the presence of the writer of this article, who dined with him before the fire was well extinguished, sold, to a gentleman in the company, the chance of the fragments of wastepaper that might be saved, for a single hundred pounds" (VI 438–39).

4. In other words, Dodsley rejects any legal claim Lennox might make—but goes on to offer his charity.

5. Dodsley's addition of the words "as you represent yourself" might be completely innocuous, but could also be construed as registering doubt as to Lennox's claim to poverty.

6. Unfortunately, the note does not survive, so the extent of Dodsley's charity—who was otherwise known for his generosity as well, see #74—is not known.

76

Charlotte Lennox
to James Boswell

February 5, 1793

MS: Beinecke Rare Books and Manuscript Library, Yale University, GEN MSS 89 (Boswell Collection), series I, box 26, folder 614 (C1726)

Pages: 1

Address: James Boswell Esq.
             Great Portland Street[1]

Text:

M[rs] Charlotte Lennox 1793.
asking me to write Proposals for a
new Edition of her Shakspeare illustrated
which I accordingly did.[2]

Sir

                                I have a request to
make you which I hope you will have the goodness to
comply with; My situation makes it necessary for me
to appear again in print[3]—I am invited to publish a
new Edition of my <u>Shakespeare Illustrated</u>.[4] and am
promisd [sic] such countenance, and support in this design
as to hope for considerable advantages by it—
   Will you Sir be in the place of dear Doctor Johnson
to me on this occasion,[5] and employ your elegant—
Pen for half an hour, in drawing up my Proposals?[6]
I will wait on you any morning you please to—

219

appoint to settle this little business; a line directed for
me at N° 17. in Dartmouth Street West.[7] will come—
safe to my hands—excuse me if I beg to have your
answer soon—I am with compliments to the young
Ladies[8]

Sir
Your most obedient humble
Servant

Feb[ry] 5th 1793   Charlotte Lennox

NOTES

1. See #73.

2. This endorsement is written in Boswell's hand on the side of the sheet with the address.

3. Once again, Lennox refers to her financial straits.

4. If anyone actually "invited" Lennox to publish a new edition of *SI* (originally published forty decades earlier in 1753/54) or promised support, it would probably have been the publishers who underwrote the proposal: Thomas Cadell, Charles Dilly, Thomas Hookham, and Thomas Becket (see #78). The edition of *SI* never appeared.

5. According to Hazen, Johnson had written dedications for several of Lennox's works: *FQ* (94–98), *SI* (104–10), *Sully* (110–16), *Philander* (102–4), *Brumoy* (91–94), and the second edition of *Henrietta* (98–102). In his Johnson bibliography, Fleeman gives the same list—*FQ* (I 325), *SI* (I 401), *Sully* (I 698), *Philander* (I 723), *Brumoy* (II 1007), and *Henrietta* (II 1022)—and tentatively adds *Maintenon* (I 711). Of course, Johnson has also written the proposal for Lennox's 1775 *Original Works* (#54). Now, she asks Johnson's friend and biographer Boswell to continue that tradition.

6. As Boswell's comment on the address side of this letter as well as the following item show, he did indeed fulfill Lennox's request.

7. Lennox probably lived at this address—No. 17 Dartmouth Street in Westminster, which can be seen on the maps of both Rocque (10Cc to 18Ca) and Horwood (23Ac)—since if she was asking correspondents to write to intermediaries who would pass on the letter, she usually specified this.

8. Lennox refers to Veronica, Euphemia, and Elizabeth Boswell here.

77

James Boswell
to Charlotte Lennox

FEBRUARY 17, [1793[1]]

MS:	Houghton Library, Harvard University, MS Eng 1269 (42)
Pages:	1
Edition:	LC #38
Address:	M^{rs}. Lenox
	Dartmouth Street[2]
Text:	

M^r. Boswell's compliments to M^{rs}. Lennox
& sends her a Sketch of the Proposals,[3] which
she will please to consider and suggest
any alterations or additions which may
occur to her, and send them to him by the
penny post.[4]
Great Portland Street[5] N° 47.
17 feb^{ry}.[6]

NOTES

1. This letter is dated in relation to the previous one (#76), to which it clearly responds.
2. See #76.
3. The "Proposals" to which Boswell refers is Lennox's proposal for a subscription edition of *SI* (#78). This letter confirms that Boswell did indeed write the proposal, as she had requested (#76). The note subsequently solicits comments, but it remains unknown if Lennox made any suggestions. Boswell's draft unfortunately does not survive.

4. See #47.

5. See #73.

6. In #76 of February 5, Lennox had requested "to have your answer soon." The present letter could be the first response to Lennox's request (confirming that Boswell was willing to write the proposals by the enclosed draft) or a later response (after an earlier [lost] one merely confirming that he was willing to write the proposals).

78

Proposal for Subscription Edition of *SI*

March–April 1793[1]

MS:	Beinecke Rare Books and Manuscript Library, Yale University, GEN MSS 89 (Boswell Collection), series V, box 65, folder 1348 (P151) (see Ill. 4)
	Houghton Library, Harvard University, MS Eng 1269 (48)
Pages:	1
Edition:	LC #47
Text:	

P R O P O S A L S[2]

FOR PUBLISHING

A NEW AND IMPROVED EDITION[3]

OF

SHAKSPEARE[4] ILLUSTRATED.

BY

CHARLOTTE LENNOX.

Dedicated by permission to Her Royal Highness[5] The Duchess of York[6]

AT a very early period of the Author's life this Work was written,[7] and published with all the vivacity and confidence of youth: Elated by discovering that she had traced from whence the immortal dramatic Poet of our nation had borrowed many of his plots, and fond of displaying her critical sagacity in shewing that he made use of the old translations of CYNTHIO, BANDELLO and ARIOSTO's Tales and Novels,[8] and not of the originals, of which she gives a new translation in this Work, she was thought by some to have treated

SHAKSPEARE with less reverence than might have been wished.[9] Nevertheless the Public was pleased to see so much merit in the performance, that it was received with very general favour,[10] and was honoured by such marks of attention, as not to acknowledge would argue rather arrogance than modesty. The learned Professor GOTSCHED of LEIPSIC translated her remarks into the German language,[11] and the illustrious Dr. JOHNSON adopted some of them in his edition of SHAKSPEARE.[12] He presented her book to the University of Oxford,[13] depositing it in the Bodleian library; and quoted it as one of the authorities in his Dictionary.[14]

Now, when the fame of SHAKSPEARE has had considerable accessions by the labours of various commentators,[15] and when, by a wide diffusion of good taste, his works justly enjoy a popularity so extensive, that the world is ready to afford the most liberal patronage to correct, elegant, and splendid editions of them, she is willing to flatter herself that her friends are not mistaken in thinking that her book, entitled, SHAKSPEARE ILLUSTRATED, may now advantageously be produced in a more respectable form, and with the improvements which, at a mature age, she trusts she can give it: She therefore proposes to publish it on the following

CONDITIONS

I. THE Work to be elegantly printed in Two Volumes octavo;[16] the price to Subscribers to be Twelve Shillings in boards.[17]

II: The Work to be out to the press as soon as there is a sufficient number of Subscribers;[18] and it is to be hoped it will be ready for delivery in January 1794.[19]

SUBSCRIPTIONS[20] *received at* Mr. CADELL'S, *in the Strand*; Mr. DILLY'S *in the Poultry*;
Mr. HOOKHAM'S, *in Bond Street; and* Mr. BECKETT'S, in Pall-mall.

These proposals were drawn up by
the late James Boswell Esq[r].[21]

NOTES

1. The proposals are dated from the correspondence surrounding their composition, particularly #76, #77, and #80. In February 1793, Lennox and Boswell were discussing the exact wording of the text; by May 1793, Lennox was thanking an anonymous subscriber—so it is reasonable to conjecture that the *Proposals* had been published in between. I have not found any advertisements for these proposals in the newspapers of 1793.

2. There is convincing evidence to prove that these proposals were written by James Boswell. In #76 above, Lennox asks Boswell to take Johnson's place in writing this kind of material for her (see #54), and he agrees, writing on the letter,

P R O P O S A L S

FOR PUBLISHING

A NEW AND IMPROVED EDITION

OF

SHAKSPEARE ILLUSTRATED.

BY

CHARLOTTE LENNOX.

Dedicated by permission to her Royal Highness the Dutchess of York

AT a very early period of the Author's life this Work was written, and publifhed with all the vivacity and confidence of youth: Elated by difcovering that fhe had traced from whence the immortal dramatic Poet of our nation had borrowed many of his plots, and fond of difplaying her critical fagacity in fhewing that he made ufe of the old tranfla-tions of CYNTHIO, BANDELLO, and ARIOSTO's Tales and Novels, and not of the originals, of which fhe gives a new tranflation in this Work, fhe was thought by fome to have treated SHAKSPEARE with lefs reverence than might have been wifhed. Neverthelefs the Public was pleafed to fee fo much merit in the performance, that it was received with very general favour, and was honoured by fuch marks of attention, as not to acknowledge would argue rather arrogance than modefty. The learned Profeffor GOTSCHED of LEIPSIC tranflated her remarks into the German language, and the illuftrious Dr. JOHNSON adopted fome of them in his edition of SHAKSPEARE. He prefented her book to the Univerfity of Oxford, depofiting it in the Bodleian library; and quoted it as one of the authorities in his Dictionary.

Now, when the fame of SHAKSPEARE has had confiderable acceffions by the labours of various commentators, and when, by a wide diffufion of good tafte, his works juftly enjoy a popularity fo extenfive, that the world is ready to afford the moft liberal patronage to correct, elegant, and fplendid editions of them, fhe is willing to flatter herfelf that her friends are not miftaken in thinking that her book, entitled, SHAKSPEARE ILLUSTRATED, may now advantageoufly be produced in a more refpectable form, and with the improvements which, at a mature age, fhe trufts fhe can give it: She therefore propofes to publifh it on the following

CONDITIONS.

I. THE Work to be elegantly printed in Two Volumes octavo; the price to Subfcribers to be Twelve Shillings in boards.

II. The Work to be put to the prefs as foon as there is a fufficient number of Subfcrib-ers; and it is to be hoped it will be ready for delivery in January 1794.

SUBSCRIPTIONS *received at* Mr. CADELL's, *in the Strand ;* Mr. DILLY's, *in the Poultry ;* Mr. HOOKHAM's, *in Bond Street ; and* Mr. BECKETT's, *in Pall-mall.*

"Mrs Charlotte Lennox 1793 asking me to write Proposals for a new edition of her Shakspeare illustrated which I accordingly did." Then, there is Lennox's handwritten annotation at the end of the sheet (on both the Harvard and the Yale copies), "These proposals were drawn up by the late James Boswell Esqr."

3. Once again, it is unknown how exactly Lennox intended to improve her 40-year-old book.

4. Throughout her career, Lennox varied her spelling of the Bard's name. The 1753/54 edition was titled *Shakespear* [*sic*] *Illustrated*, while this one reads *Shakspeare Illustrated*.

5. This sentence—in one neat line in the Yale copy; in two scribbled lines of text above and below the separation line in the Harvard copy ("Dedicated by permission to Her Royal Highness/The Dutchess of York")—are an annotation written in Lennox's hand. As Isles argues, "It therefore appears, first, that the permission of the Duchess was not obtained until after the Proposals had been printed (so that each copy had to be hand-endorsed before publication), and, second, that the copy under discussion was Lennox's own reference copy, not intended for circulation to the public" (421–22 n.199). The second part of that claim might be applied more specifically to argue that the *Harvard* copy (with scribbled writing) was Lennox's personal copy.

6. Princess Frederica Charlotte Ulrica Catherina (1767–1820) was the eldest daughter of Frederick Wilhelm II, King of Prussia. She married Frederick Augustus, Duke of York and Albany (1763–1827)—the son of King George III and younger brother of the future King George IV—in 1791. The two spent most of their lives apart, Frederick involved in politics and wars and Frederica at their country estate of Oatlands Pary, Weybridge, Surrey. The couple had no children, and there were some rumors about indiscretions on both sides, but no more than typical of a noble couple.

At Oatlands, the Duchess of York seemed mostly interested in her animals, but at least three artists were known to have been in her service: Henry Bernard Chalon, William Marshall Craig, and Henry Daniel Thielcke. She permitted a number of dedications in a variety of publications, from illustrations of scenes from Shakespeare by Henry William Bunbury (see #82) promoted by the printseller Thomas Macklin to the medical text *Practical Observations Towards the Prevention and Cure of Chronic Diseases Peculiar to Women* by John Leake (London: Evans, Murray, and Egerton, 1792) to Serafino Buonaiuti's cantata *Lamentation of Marie Antoinette* (London: Sivrac, 1794).

7. Lennox was probably 24 when *SI* was published.

8. These three are
- Giovanni Baptista Giraldi, known as Cinthio (1504–73), whose works provided the plots for *Measure for Measure* and *Othello*,
- Matteo Bandello (1485–1561), whose writings inspired (parts of) *Othello* and *Much Ado About Nothing, Twelfth Night,* and
- Ludovico Ariosto (1474–1533), who contributed to *Much Ado About Nothing* as well as (perhaps) to *As You Like It, Othello,* and *A Midsummer Night's Dream* (see Stuart Gillespie, *Shakespeare's Books: A Dictionary of Shakespeare's Sources* [New York and London: Continuum, 2004]).

9. This is Lennox's (or Boswell's) response to the reactions she received for *SI*. It seems sentiment took a long time to quiet down—even in 1769, her play *The Sister* was hissed down probably because of *SI* (see #45).

10. Actually, only the review in the *Gentleman's Magazine* was positive—the *Monthly Review* was rather critical (cf. Small 198–99). Of course, this proposal is not an objective rendering of responses to *SI*, but an attempt to drum up subscriptions for a new edition.

11. This is a reference to the highly positive German review in *Das Neueste aus der anmuthigen Gelehrsamkeit* [The Latest from Graceful Erudition] 5.7 (Heumond 1755): 501–10 by Johann Christoph Gottsched (1700–66), one of the most important German drama critics of the eighteenth century. Gottsched starts his review, "It seems the English are starting to look at the stage according to critical rules. After they allowed their wit all kinds of excesses for a long time, following Shakespeare's example, now smart spirits are recognizing that not all that glitters is gold. The most amazing thing is that a clever woman is leading the way here and showing the entire English nation that one has to subject prejudices to reason and that one has to subject everything that serves to amuse the spirit to the judgment of a fine taste and the incontrovertible rules of art. It is Mrs. Lenox, a woman born in America, who is showing her countrypeople such an important model in this work" (my translation). According to Isles, "Gottsched's wife [...] owned a presentation copy of all three volumes of *SI*, sent to her by CL from London" (423 n.203).

12. On Lennox and Johnson's contrasting assessments of Shakespeare, see Karen Bloom Gevirtz, "Ladies Reading and Writing: Eighteenth-Century Women Writers and the Gendering of Critical Discourse," *Modern Language Studies* 33.1–2 (Spring-Fall 2003): 60–72; Susan Green, "A Cultural Reading of Charlotte Lennox's *Shakespear Illustrated*," *Cultural Readings of Restoration and Eighteenth-Century English Theater*, ed. J. Douglas Canfield and Deborah C. Payne (Athens and London: The University of Georgia Press, 1995), 228–57; and Kramnick.

13. Since this copy is not traceable in the Bodleian Library today, it is unclear whether this presentation really occurred.

14. Johnson "uses quotations from *SI* in his definitions of *wherever, whetstone,* and *wreath*" (Isles 424 n.206).

15. This is a reference to Garrick (among others), who had promoted Shakespeare in events such as the Jubilee at Stratford in 1769 (see Stone/Kahrl 577–85).

16. The original 1753/54 *SI* was duodecimo.

17. This probably would have been pasteboard; cf. Marks 36–37.

18. Lennox *did* start selling subscriptions—see the letter to an anonymous subscriber to six editions, #80.

19. It appears the edition never materialized.

20. In contrast to the list of booksellers in the previous proposal (#54), this one has only members of the *London* book trade. These booksellers all worked together frequently: Cadell and Dilly were in imprints together almost 200 times between 1796 and 1800, Cadell and Becket in about 100, Dilly and Hookham 60, and Dilly and Becket 31. However, there is only one other title where they *all* joined forces, the *Reports of the Royal Humane Society for the Years 1787 to 1789* that were probably published in

1790 ([London:] Printed for the Society, and sold by Cadell, Becket, [James] Robson, Hookham, Dilly, [Joseph] Johnson, and [George Sr., George Jr., and John] Robinsons, n.y.). The booksellers involved in Lennox's subscription edition are the following four:

- Thomas Cadell (1742–1802) started out as Andrew Millar's partner and later took over his business, while also collaborating with William and Andrew Strahan between 1780 and 1793. He knew many literary figures of the time, including Johnson and David Hume, and published works such as Edward Gibbon's *Decline and Fall of the Roman Empire* and Adam Smith's *Wealth of Nations*. Cadell established himself at 141, Strand in 1781. See Cynthia Guidici, "Cadell," in Bracken/Silver 33–38 and Maxted 37.
- See #54. By 1793, Edward had died, so this is his brother Charles Dilly, who published Boswell's *Life of Johnson*. See Daniel W. Hollis III, "Edward and Charles Dilly," in Bracken/Silver 97–102 and Maxted 66–67.
- Thomas Hookham worked from 145, New Bond Street until 1793 and from 15, Old Bond Street since 1792. He was known mostly as the proprietor of Hookham's Circulating Library, and had this edition of *SI* ever been published, it would certainly have appeared in that library. See Maxted 114.
- By now, Thomas Becket (see #54) had re-established himself at Pall Mall. See Maxted 17.

21. This also is an addition in Lennox's handwriting, but only on the Harvard copy. Since Boswell did not die until 1795, it appears this copy of the proposal was in Lennox's possession for several years.

79

Alexander Boswell
to Charlotte Lennox

[May 7, 1793[1]]

MS: Houghton Library, Harvard University, MS Eng 1269 (44)
Pages: 2
Edition: LC #40
Address: M[rs]. Charlotte Lennox
               N° 6 Great Tufton Street
               West[2]
Text:

Madam

   I had the honour of receiving
your Note this Evening & regret that circum:
:stances put it out of my power to be
so useful to you as I could wish. I am not
going <u>to</u> Scotland but just returned from
it.[3] If M[r]. Murray holds the Estate of Lennox
in Fee unrestricted by any Contract of
Marriage, Settlement, or deed of Entail[4]
I fear he may leave it to whom he
pleases, but in the event of his dying[5]
Intestate[6] your Relation would have
an undoubted claim if he is Heir at Law
as you inform me.[7] I shall not presume
to form any opinion upon the question

---

till I know its merits better but I
do not see what we could expect to

find in the Records & a Search is very
expensive. I can promise you little
accession of information but what I can
give you may expect when I have
the pleasure of seeing you which I shall
endeavour to do as soon as possible.

> I am
> Madam
> Your Most Ob[t]. Humble Serv[t].
> Alexander Boswell

Devonshire Street[8]
Tuesday Evening.

NOTES

1. Isles tentatively dates this letter as May 7, 1799 on account of the postmark, where he concedes the year is rather indistinct. However, Lennox refers to "the good Woman with whom I lodged in Tufton Street" (in Westminster, Rocque 19Aa and Horwood 33Ba) in her letter to Veronica Boswell of April 24, 1794 (#83), so the letter to Alexander must have been written earlier (see also n.5 below). In February 1793, Lennox still lived in Dartmouth Street (see #76 and #77), so the only available May is 1793. Furthermore, 1793 was clearly a year in which Lennox was in very close touch with the Boswell family, so I am dating the letter May 7, 1793, which was indeed a Tuesday.

2. Westminster.

3. Apparently, Lennox wanted Alexander Boswell to make legal enquiries in Scotland. This was most likely an extension of her husband's attempt to be recognized as the Earl of Lennox in the 1760s and 1770s based on claims about the Lennox family tree in the 14th and 15th centuries. The details are described in William Robertson, *Proceedings Relating to the Peerage of Scotland* (Edinburgh: Bell & Bradfute, 1790—this is a different Robertson from Lennox's correspondent), 335–36, 348–49, and 389–90. This source does not identify the Alexander Lennox in question as Charlotte Lennox's husband, but the critical consensus is that it was almost certainly him (see Isles 185–86 n.180, Kynaston 26–27, and Philippe Séjourné, *The Mystery of Charlotte Lennox* [Aix-en-Provence: Publications des Annales de la Faculté des Lettres, 1967], 20).

The estate of the Earls of Lennox had since come into the possession of James Murray (see #42 and correspondent's biography), who had no legitimate son. Lennox seems to have believed that her husband was the next heir to Murray and/or the Earls of Lennox, which would have meant that Alexander Lennox would have inherited the estate if Murray had died without a will. Almost certainly, nothing came of Lennox's efforts—at least there is no documentation of any further developments, and Murray willed his property to a natural (illegitimate) son. Lennox's claim was called "futile and preposterous" (John Riddell, *Inquiry into the Law and Practice in Scottish Peerages*, 2 vols. [Edinburgh: Clark, 1842], II 651).

4. These are all legal situations in which the estate would go someone *other* than the legitimate heir.

5. This suggests that Murray is not yet dead, i.e., that the letter was written *before* his death on April 30, 1799.

6. I.e., without a will.

7. My interpretation of this passage differs slightly from Isles's (185–86 n.180). I agree that Lennox is probably enquiring about the succession surrounding the Lennox estate, held until his death by James Murray. Lennox's request to Alexander Boswell suggests that she believed her family might have some claim to the estate, but the letter does not indicate to me that at this point Murray is dead. Therefore, I think Lennox's enquiry is more tentative—what *might* happen *when* Murray dies. In addition, since in 1793 Lennox was trying to find money to support her son, I believe that the "Relation" Boswell mentions is George Louis Lennox.

8. I can make no sense of this address. Since Alexander writes that he "just returned" from Scotland, it would seem he would be staying with his father at Great Portland Street (see #73).

80

Charlotte Lennox
to Anon.[1]

MAY 15, 1793

MS: Houghton Library, Harvard University, MS Hyde 10 (416)
Pages: 1
Text:

Sir

            I cannot dispense with myself from returning you once more[2] my thanks for your genteel[3]—— subscription for six copies of my book,[4] if such an example should be often followd [sic], my undertaking will be very successful

                —I am
                Sir
                Your obligd [sic] humble Servant
May 15.1793.   Charlotte Lennox

NOTES

1. This (male) correspondent remains unidentified. Since the subscription edition of *SI* was never published, there is not even a subscription list to provide possible addressees.

2. The previous thanks do not survive.

3. The gentry often subscribed to multiple copies of a work—not so much to have them all in their library but either to support the author or to give away their extra copies.

4. The subscription would have been for Lennox's new edition of *SI* (#78), which never appeared. Since subscriptions were sometimes considered a form of charity for authors, it is quite possible that Lennox would not have had to return the money in spite of not producing the book.

81

Charlotte Lennox
to [Richard Johnson[1]]

AUGUST 22, 1793

MS: Royal Literary Fund Archive
Pages: 2
Edition: Small 59
Text:

Sir,[2]

It is with great confusion that I take the liberty
                                          this
to importune You, who know me only by name, with ʌ application
and my distress may be easily imagind [*sic*], when it forces me to
break through decorums which I always wishd [*sic*] to observe[3]—
—but I am a Mother, and see an only child[4] upon the brink of
utter ruin. Driven as he was first, to desperation by a most
unnatural father; and then deserted, and left exposed to all the
evils that may well be expected from the dreadful circumstances
he is in—I would preserve him if I could—Alas! I do not pretend
to excuse his fault,[5] but if his story was candidly told, that
fault great as it is, would with the severest Judge meet compas
                                          used
-sion as well as blame—I have in vain ~~usuxd~~[6] my utmost
endeavours to mortgage the poor income I hold from a husband,
whose fortune I have made by the sacrifice of my own,[7] in order
to raise money to send this unfortunate Youth to my relations
in the United States of America,[8] who will receive him kindly.
—I have been informd [*sic*] Sir, that M[rs] Blair Your Daughter,[9]

234

is endeavouring to promote my subscription[10]—the generous efforts of that Lady, tho' they were to be as successful as Her most benevolent heart could wish, would come too late to preserve my unhappy son—the last ship that will go to
sail
America ~~will sail~~[11] till next March, will ∧ in a Week[12]—the money for the passage, must be paid before he goes on board, and the very lowest terms that are offered are out of my reach. I have been once releived [*sic*] by a benefaction from the Literary Fund;[13] if by Your interest Sir, I could procure some assistance in this hour of distress, my grateful heart will

---

will[14] be impressd [*sic*] with the strongest, and most lasting sense of Your goodness, to which I shall owe all the remaining comfort of my life. I am

> Sir
> Your Obligd [*sic*], and most
> Obedient Servant
> Charlotte Lennox

August 22 1793.
Doctor Johnson[15]

NOTES

1. This letter is ascribed to Richard Johnson by Small (59) without explanation. The ascription is likely because of the references to a Richard Johnson in #A1 and #A2. At the same time, there is a possibility that the letter is addressed to Alexander Johnson, the "Dr. Johnson" referred to in #A4, #A7–8, and #A10 as the chair.

2. The rendition here gives only the text written by Lennox. For the additional notes from the RLF, see below #A6.

3. The "decorums" probably include a woman not approaching a man for financial assistance.

4. George Louis Lennox had become an only child with the death of his sister Harriet around 1783/84.

5. How George Louis Lennox got in this trouble, and what exactly it was, is uncertain. The *Public Advertiser* 18201 (November 5, 1792): 4 had reported "A Felony" from the "Public Office, Bow Street": "Whereas, a man calling himself GEORGE LEWIS LENNOX, and affecting to be a Lieutenant in the 60th Regiment of Foot, now in the West Indies, stands charged with feloniously stealing at the La Sablonière [this word is difficult to decipher, and the last four letters look more like –nese, but the only hotel in Leicester Square is the Sablonière] Hotel in Leicester-square, sixty six Guineas in gold,

and a quantity of Shirts, Cravats, and Stockings, the property of Henry Sheares and John Sheares. Whoever will apprehend and secure him, or give such information at the above Office, as may be the means of apprehending him, shall receive a reward of TWENTY GUINEAS on his commitment to prison from the said Henry and John Sheares. The said George Lewis Lennox is about five feet six inches high, brown short hair, swarthy complexion, strong and well made, rather round shouldered, a mole near his left eye; is about the age of 21 years; sometimes wears a red coat, but had on when he went away a blue regimental coat [illegible] with red, green body coat lined with buff, and black cape red waistcoat, dark coloured pantaloon breeches, and half boots edged with yellow."

There is unfortunately no hard evidence that this is Lennox's son (the case never seems to have made it to the Old Bailey—perhaps because George Louis had left for America), but the age is approximately correct, and a felony of this order would certainly constitute a "fault." Two years previously, *Lloyd's Evening Post* 5215 (December 1, 1790): 7 and the *Public Advertiser* 17600 (December 2, 1790): 3 had reported a person called George Louis Lennox committing fraud in Aberdeen. These stories mention the individual drawing a draft "on a Mrs. Lennox, London," but do not clarify if that might be the subject of this volume.

6. This word, stricken out with two lines, might be a misspelling of "used." It begins with a "u" or "n," followed probably by an "s," and clearly ends with a "d."

7. Earlier in her life, Lennox had refused a position for herself and had instead asked the Duke of Newcastle to give one to her husband (see #42, #B6, and correspondent's biography for Mary Stuart, Countess of Bute).

8. This comment suggests not only that other members of the Lennox family had remained in the colonies when Lennox came to England in the 1740s, but that she knew enough about them half a century later to send her son to them.

It is unknown whether George Louis Lennox ever made it to the United States. However, the *Philadelphia Gazette and Universal Daily Advertiser* 11.1734 (May 2, 1794), [3] reported that there was mail for a "George Louis Lenox" in its "List of Letters, Remaining in the Post-Office, Philadelphia, May 2, 1794." There is no evidence that this was Lennox's son, but the timeline does fit.

9. The ODNB entry on the Richard Johnson identified as the recipient of this letter mentions several children he had in India (probably with an Indian native woman as mother) whom he wanted to see married in England. However, no records of these marriages or the women's married names survive.

10. This is certainly the (unsuccessful) subscription to *SI* (#78).

11. These words are only stricken through with one line.

12. The sailing season from Great Britain to America was relatively short in the eighteenth century, lasting approximately from the spring to the late summer.

13. Lennox had first received assistance from the RLF in May 1792; see below #A2.

14. The word "will" is indeed repeated at the top of the second page. It is not written as a catchword at the bottom of the first page.

15. This ascription is not in Lennox's hand.

82

Mary Gwyn
to Charlotte Lennox

[c. 1793–99[1]]

MS: Houghton Library, Harvard University, MS Eng 1269 (43)
Pages: 3
Edition: LC #39
Address: M[rs]. Lenox
Text:

Madam

I send the Opera which you
wish'd me to see[2]—and am sorry
to say I can not be of any
service on the occasion.
M[rs]. Bunbury[3] can not with
any propriety speak to the
Duchess of York[4] on the
subject—as she has already
mention'd to hr [*sic*] a work of
yours[5]—and for which we

collected subscriptions, which
work you do not now mention.[6]
give me leave to say; you
should put it in my power,
by publishing your first
book; to acquit myself of
the promises I made to

those, whose subscriptions
I receiv'd—before you Employ
me again.[7] I am
Madam with many good

wishes to you[8]
Your Obe[nt]. ser[vt].
  M Gwyn

NOTES

1. This letter was written after the *SI* proposal (1793) and before the death of Mary Gwyn's sister (1799).

2. The "Opera" to which Gwyn refers must be Lennox's *Philander*. The context suggests that Lennox was contemplating a subscription edition of this opera (see also Isles 184 n.173), but there is no other trace of such a project. Since *Philander* was received rather indifferently on its original publication, this subscription project indicates desperation on Lennox's part.

3. This is Mary Gwyn's sister Catherine, who married the artist Henry William Bunbury in 1771. Since Bunbury was a pupil of Francesco Bartolozzi, who engraved Reynolds's portrait of Lennox, this establishes another connection between Lennox and the extended Horneck family described in the correspondent's biography.

4. Henry William Bunbury (1763–1827; ODNB VIII 676–78) was groom of the bedchamber to Prince Frederick, Duke of York, George III's second son, which would have given his wife access to the Duchess, Princess Frederica of Prussia (1767–1820; see #78). Thus, Lennox was approaching a noblewoman for patronage at several removes: through her acquaintance Mary Gwyn, whose sister Catherine had a husband who worked for the husband of the noblewoman in question, the Duchess of York. Interestingly, Bunbury was involved in a project dedicated to the Duchess of York himself at this time (see #78).

5. The proposed subscription edition of *SI* (#78) was already dedicated to the Duchess of York. Apparently, Lennox had used the chain described above to approach her the first time.

6. This suggests that by the time this letter was written, Lennox had abandoned the subscription edition of *SI* (#78).

7. In other words, Gwyn is angry that Lennox is soliciting assistance in approaching the Duchess of York for the *next* project (*Philander*) when the *previous* one (*SI*) has not yet been published. As this letter and #80 above show, Lennox had succeeded in collecting some subscriptions.

8. Considering the content of the letter, the (formulaic) "good wishes" and the "Obent. servt." seem a bit ironic.

83

Charlotte Lennox
to [Veronica] Boswell[1]

APRIL 26, 1794[2]

MS: Beinecke Rare Books and Manuscript Library, Yale University, GEN MSS 89 (Boswell Collection), series I, box 26, folder 614 (C1727)

Pages: 1

Address: Miss Boswell
at James Boswell's Esqr
Great Portland Street
47
[in other hand:]
M^{rs}. Charlotte Lennox
28 April 1794

Text:

Dear Madam

                      Every one talks of the Wit the humour, the delicate, yet poignant strokes of ridicule displayd [sic] by Mr Boswel [sic] in his correspondence with his fair antagonist:[3] every one talks, because every one but me has read the letters—I shall be greatly obligd [sic] to him if he will afford me that pleasure by lending me the pamphlet in— which they are publishd [sic][4]—I am now settled for part of the— Summer in Chelsea[5]—change of air, has relieved me from most of my ailments but the heartach [sic],[6] and that I hope to get rid of in a little time, and to taste of peace before I die—Being now in the direct road to Ranelagh, I promise myself to have

the favour of a visit from you and Miss Euphemia[7] soon, in your
way thither. If Your Papa will be so good to lend me the—
pamphlet, and send it to Master Boswel [sic],[8] the good Woman with
whom I lodgd [sic] in Tufton Street,[9] will call on him for it, and
convey it safely to me—but perhaps Master Boswel [sic] may
like to take a Walk with it himself, and give me the pleasure
of his company at tea—I am engagd [sic] on Wednesday next
but any other day, I shall be happy to see him.
    I am with kind compliments to Mr Boswel [sic],[10] and Miss—
Euphemia

	Dear Madam
	Your obligd [sic], and
Saturday April 28	faithful humble Servant
[. . .] Ranelagh Walk[11]	
Chelsea	Charlotte Lennox

NOTES

1. The letter is addressed only to "Miss Boswell." James Boswell had three
daughters, but since the text of the letter refers to Euphemia (1774–1837) and
since Elizabeth (1780–1814) was still too young, the addressee must be Veronica
(1773–95).

2. The date clearly reads April 28 both under the letter and in the endorsement,
but April 28 was actually a Monday in 1794. Therefore, I concur with Waingrow that
the date should be April 26 (357).

3. The correspondence Lennox is referring to here is probably the exchange
between the poet Anna Seward and Boswell carried on in the *Gentleman's Magazine*
between October 1793 and January 1794 concerning remarks he had made in the *Life
of Johnson* (see Danzinger/Brady 254–56 and 278–79). Lennox is correct in asserting
that "every one talks" about the exchange: As Danzinger/Brady point out, the journal
also printed other "letters by supporters of both combatants" (279). By April 1794,
however, Lennox was behind the times: In February "the editor [of the *Gentleman's
Magazine*] expressed the wish to receive no further comments on the subject and
declared an end to the controversy" (279).

4. Lennox is probably requesting an individual issue of a magazine here, which
was commonly called a pamphlet in the eighteenth century. Boswell's contributions
to the controversy with Seward were published in the November 1793 and January
1794 issues of the *Gentleman's Magazine*.

5. This seems to be another summer residence of Lennox's (see #71).

6. It is uncertain what Lennox's "heartach" is. If her son George Louis left for America around August 1793, perhaps his absence is the source of her present heartache.

7. This is James Boswell's second child and middle daughter Euphemia.

8. This "Master Boswell" is James Boswell's son James, known as Jamie. Boswell's older son Alexander (Sandy) was in Scotland in early 1794, since Boswell addressed a letter to this son on February 29 as "To Alexander Boswell, Esq.,/ Younger of Auchinleck,/Edinburgh" (*Private Papers* XVIII 323) and wrote further letters in short succession on March 3, 13, and 17 and April 14 and 26 using the same address (XVIII 330). In contrast, then 16-year-old James was at Westminster School at the time (cf. Danzinger/Brady 58, 266), so it would make perfect sense for him to walk south to Chelsea.

9. See #79.

10. This is James Boswell Sr.

11. Unfortunately, the signs at the beginning of the address are illegible. Lennox's home at the time must have been a fairly new building: Ranelagh Walk, the short road near Chelsea Bridge (which crossed a dead arm of the Thames) and the Chelsea toll gate, is unnamed and unsettled as late as 1780, as can be seen in Carrington Bowles's *Reduced New Pocket Plan of the Cities of London and Westminster* [. . .] *Exhibiting the New Buildings to the Year 1780* (London: n.p., 1780). It can however be found in Horwood (31Db/32Ab).

84

Receipt (Mrs Martins[1] from Charlotte Lennox)

JUNE 15, 1795

MS: Houghton Library, Harvard University, MS Eng 1269 (51)
Pages: 1
Edition: LC #51
Text:

June 15.1795
   Received of M[rs] Lennox, two Shillings &
sevenpence halpenny [sic] in full for half a Years Interest
due upon her Promisary [sic] of five Ginneas [sic][2]
June 15 1795

NOTES

1. The receipt is endorsed on the back side (in what might be Lennox's hand),
"Mrs. Martins/Receipt." The individual in question could be a Mrs. Martin or a
Mrs. Martins and has not been identified.

2. If my math is correct, Mrs. Martins was charging 5% interest *per annum*, not
a bad rate in the eighteenth century. Lennox's taking out this loan shows both the
difficulty of her financial situation and Mrs. Martins's belief that she would get her
money back. No further records of this transaction exist.

85

Bennet Langton
to Charlotte Lennox

[c. 1795–97[1]]

MS: Houghton Library, Harvard University, MS Eng 1269 (46)
Pages: 1
Edition: LC #46
Text:

M[r]. Langton presents his Compliments to M[rs].Len-
nox; he is very sorry for his having appeared to neglect
his engagement today, according to what is mentioned
in the Note[2] that he received from her this afternoon,
which arose from a misapprehension, that he proposes
to take an early opportunity of waiting on M[rs]. Lennox
to explain.—
G[t]. George Street[3] Saturday Evening

NOTES

1. Isles offers "c.1785–1801?" for the present letter, but the address helps date
it more specifically. In August 1795, Langton was in Norwich. In his letter-book,
Langton's son Peregrine Langton-Massingberd writes that, "From Norwich [Langton]
again settled in London, hiring a house in Great George Street, Westminster—it was
that house which has the *West* end of it over an arch way into a small street leading to
the Abbey" (qtd. in *The Correspondence of James Boswell with Certain Members of
The Club*, ed. Charles Fifer [London: Heinemann, 1976] lxi). By December 4, 1797,

however, Langton "was listed as living at St. Marylebone, Middlesex" (ibid., lxii). For those reasons, the present letter must have been written between 1795 and 1797.

2. This note could have been written in response to the "engagement" with Lennox Langton missed. It no longer survives.

3. See n.1.

86

Anon.[1]
to Charlotte Lennox

[c. 1795–1801[2]]

MS:	Houghton Library, Harvard University, MS Eng 1269 (47)
Pages:	1
Edition:	LC #41
Address:	Mrs Lennox
	at M^r. Johnson's[3]
	N° 12 Ranelagh Street
	Pimlico[4]

Text:

Several Ladies who met Mrs Lennox at Mr Langton's[5] were astonish'd
to see a Gentlewoman's[6] hands in such horrid order—for God's sake
wash them & rub back the skin at the roots of the Nails

a hint from a friend[7]

NOTES

1. Because of the first two words, it is likely that this note was written by a woman.
Females present at Langton's in the time after 1795 included his wife Lady Rothes,
his daughters Mary, Diana, Jane, Elizabeth, Isabella, and Margaret, Frances Reynolds,
and Augusta Fielding (or Feilding), daughter of Sophia Fielding, chamber-woman
to Queen Charlotte (see Horace Pitt Kennedy Skipton, *John Hoppner* [London:
Methuen, 1905], 44).

2. The approximate dates for this letter are determined by Langton's return to
London in 1795 and his death in 1801. The dinner almost certainly took place in the
very last years of Lennox's life, "when illness and poverty must have made it difficult

for her to maintain the 'ladylike' standards of appearance demanded by this cruelly tactless correspondent" (Isles 416 n.181).

In contrast to the previous letter, this one does not specify at which London residence of Langton's the dinner occurred. After 1797, Langton lived at at least two different addresses in Westminster, and the dinner might have taken place at either of those as well as the George Street house.

3. The identity of this Mr. Johnson is unknown—the letter presents the same dilemma as #81. Isles suggests Alexander Johnson (416 n.182), but Alexander lived at 10 Charlotte Street, Portland Place (ODNB, XXX 231). At the same time, it seems unlikely that Lennox was living at Richard Johnson's since then she would not have had to address #81 to him in writing (though of course she could have moved in and out of his residence).

4. Pimlico is an area on the Northern bank of the Thames west of Westminster. The area was developed in the second half of the eighteenth century: Ranelagh Street does not exist in Rocque, but can be found in Horwood (22Bd).

5. On Bennet Langton, see #85 and correspondent's biography.

6. Calling Lennox a gentlewoman is a back-handed compliment here: On the one hand, it endows her with social standing; at the same time, the letter accuses her of being unwilling or unable to maintain the standards of gentility.

7. The tone of the note suggests that the author was hardly "a friend."

Royal Literary Fund Files

A1¹

Case File

Item:	This is the file folder holding Lennox's case file at the RLF.
Format:	The "Registered Case" files in the archives of the RLF are kept in folders (about 9½" × 12¼") with an identical printed grid (including the words "Year," "Authorship," etc.) for all cases on the front. "Registered Case" at the top and "Case=Book. Page" at the bottom are printed in a Gothic font. The number one of "Vol. 1" is on a small square of paper pasted on. At least four writers seem to have been involved in filling in Lennox's case:

- one wrote the top line,
- a second wrote the line from "1792" to "10 10 –" as well as all the works and their publication dates,
- a third added all the other information in the right column (and probably the word "Royalist" and the address at the top as well as the case authentication at the bottom, though these may be in different hands again), and
- a fourth added other years in pencil below 1792.

On the left inside of Lennox's folder, an unidentified hand has written (the rest of the folder is blank):

From Boswell's Life of Johnson LIV 1784

Tab. 2. Charlotte Lennox's Royal Literary Fund Case File (#A1)

Year	Authorship	Minutes Vol.	Minutes Page.	Grants Cur.No.	Grants Date.	Amount
1792 —93	1. Poems on several Occasions; (published under her maiden name of Ramsay) .... 8°.Lond.1747	1	22	13	May 4 1792} 1792} / Aug 1793	10 10 — / 12 12 —
1802 —3 —4	2. The Memoirs of Harriet Stuart Lond.1751					
	3. The Female Quixote .... 2 Vols. 8°.London.1752					
	4. Shakespeare Illustrated .... 3 Vols. 12°.Lond.1753					
	5. Memoirs of the Countess of Berci, taken from the French 2 Vols.12°.1756	for the express purpose of enabling her to send her son to Virginia + thence to Baltimore where the young man's friends reside"				
	6. Memoirs of Madame Maintenon, translated 1757				Nov 1793	1 1 —
	7. Henrietta: a Novel .... 2 Vols. 12°.Lond.1758				Jan 1802	10 — —
	8. Philander, a Dramatic Pastoral .... 8°.Lon.1758	"on account of her urgent distress"			Jan 1802	10 — — additional
	9. Ladies' Museum; a Magazine, begun in 1760–61, which extended to 2 vols. 8° v.-y.					
	10. Sophia: a Novel .... 2 Vols. 12°.Lond.1763				Mar 1802	7 7 —
	11. The Sister, a Comedy .... 8°.Lond.1769				Jan 1803	10 10 —
	12. Old City Manners, a Comedy .... 8°.Lond.1773	on account of her urgent distress			May 1803	13 13 —
	13. Euphemia; a Novel .... 4 Vols. 12°.Lond.1790				Oct 1803	
	14. Father Brumoy's Greek Theatre, translated, 3 vols 4°.Lond.					allowance continued
	15. Sully's Memoirs, translated .... 3 vols. (frequently reprinted in 8°.) 4°.Lond.	£1.1.0 a week to be paid			Nov 1803	8 8 —
	16. Memoirs of Henry Lennox; interspersed with Legendary Remains .... 12°.Lond.1804	till next meeting			Dec "	3 3 —

Case authenticated by
Rev W Beloe
Richard Johnson Esq
Lady Chambers

"I dined yesterday (said Dr Johnson) at Mrs Garricks'
with Mrs Carter, Mrs Hannah More + Miss Fanny
Burney. I know not where I could find a fourth,
except Mrs Lennox, who is superior to them all"
Dr Johnson wrote the dedication to the Earl of Orrery
of her "Shakespeare Illustrated" + Dr Goldsmith wrote
the Epilogue to her Comedy of "The Sisters"

Text:

Registered Case

№ 12.   Vol. 1

[Tab. 2 represents the text in the main body
of the RLF file which follows here.]

Royalist

M^rs. Charlotte Lennox, (daughter of Co^l. Ramsay, ∧ Governor of New York
in 1720.][2]

Address 56 Queen Anne St. East[3]

Born at New York ...... 1720[4]
Died in London .. Jany. 4th 1804

Case=Book. Page____[5]

NOTES

1. The material collected in this section comes from the files of the RLF, which consist of three parts conflated here. The first part is the folder in which the items in her file were kept. The front of this folder is the summary of her case, including some notes on her biography, a tabular version of her works, and a table with the dates and amounts of financial support she was given (#A1 and Tab. 2). The second part is the material inside the folder. This consists of various correspondence—between Richard Johnson, David Williams, William Beloe, William Boscawen, Lady Frances Chambers, and John Nichols—promoting her case, a number of receipts, and copies of minutes concerning her case. Among this material is one letter by Lennox, a thank-you note for money received, and one receipt signed by her. Also, this section contains two items concerning a request for information on Lennox from the United States in 1844. Finally, the third part contains the minutes of the RLF meetings in which Lennox's case was discussed, including the resolutions that were passed at these meetings. The resolutions, usually summarized in the left margin—as, e.g., "Case.12.Vol.1./Mrs Charlotte Lennox/£10.10" (#A4)—are written in a different hand and in blue ink instead of the black of the rest of the text. At the bottom (and not reproduced here), the minutes are signed by Thomas Dale, John Nichols, and/or Charles Symmons.

2. This list contains most, but not all of Lennox's works—for instance, her novel *Eliza* is missing (see Schürer). On the other hand, the list includes the *Memoirs of Henry Lennox* (London: Shurt, 1804), which are probably *not* by Lennox (Small 244–45). It is interesting to note that Lennox's translations *are* included under the heading "Authorship."

3. It is unknown when this address was added to the document. See also #A13.

4. On Lennox's birth date, see Carlile.

5. On Beloe, see #A9; on Johnson, #81, on Lady Chambers, #13. Since Lady Chambers was just returning to England in 1792, it is unlikely that these authentications were made when Lennox first applied to the RLF.

A2

Anonymous Letter of Recommendation
MAY 1792

Item: This is an anonymous letter of recommendation supporting Lennox's application for financial assistance from the RLF.

Format: The letter itself is written on the second and third page of a folded sheet (about 7½" × 9½"). The first page has three partially illegible names in the top left corner and the results of the vote on Lennox's application in the top right. The fourth page is blank.

Text:

D^r. Wighterian	May 1792—
Fitz Hugh	10 Guineas
M^{rs}. Ewart[1]	voted

Mrs Charlotte Lennox, Authoress[2]
of The Female[3] Quixote,
Euphemia, Eliza,[4] The Trans
lation of Sully's Memoirs,
Madame La Valiere's Me-
ditations &c.—Brumoire's [sic]
Greek Theatre, &c.&c.&c.&c...
is now Living, though at
an extremely advanced
age, & in very great want,
poverty & distress—She has
always been highly regarded
by people of the first distinction
& particularly so, by the late

Duke & Duchess of Newcastle,[5] by
(the Duchess's)
whose ∧ means she was enabled
to procure a Place in the Custom House for her husband

---

of considerable employment,
who died about three or four
years ago[6] & left his Unfortunate Widow without any other
certain dependence than
£
an allowance of 10. a year
as the Daughter of An Officer
of High Rank in the Army[7]

NOTES

1. These three names are very difficult to make out. None of them correspond with any names in the 1795 annual report of the RLF (see #81).

2. The handwriting in this letter looks similar to that of Lady Butler in the index and text of the Registered Case of the Chevalier D'Eon, but there is nothing else to connect Butler and Lennox.

3. "Female" is written above a struck-out illegible word.

4. This is one of the documents that support Lennox's authorship of that novel; see also #38 above.

5. See above #37.

6. This would indicate that Alexander Lennox died around 1788/89.

7. This is the only reference to a pension Lennox received as the daughter of an officer.

A3

Letter from Richard Johnson
to David Williams

[MAY 1792]

Item: This letter from Richard Johnson to David Williams is
             undated, but since the other material in this file is organized
             chronologically, it is reasonable to assume that it dates from
             May 1792. On the other hand, the letter may be a response
             to Lennox's own letter (#A6).

Format: The address is presented on the left inside of the folded sheet
             (about 7½" × 9½"); the text is on the right. The reverse is
             blank.

Text:

Rev^d. D^r. Williams[1]

Brompton Row[2]

M^r. Rich^d. Johnson presents

his compl^{ts} to D^r. Williams

       will

& begs he ∧ interest himself

in the unhappy case of M^{rs}.

Lennox, who he has just

recommended to the attention

of the literary fund——

Stratford Place[3]

~~Sunday~~ Saturday Eve^g.

NOTES

1. David Williams (1738–1816; ODNB LIX 154–59) was the founder of the RLF. Williams trained as a minister, but left the ministry in 1773 because he could not conform either to traditional Anglican theology and worship or to what he considered the Dissenters' intolerance and hypocrisy. Instead, he went into teaching and published a *Treatise on Education* (London: Payne, 1774) that promoted a pedagogy where students learned through participation rather than memorization. In the 1770s and 1780s, Williams continued to pursue liturgical and pedagogical reform in various institutional settings and publications. In 1786, he initiated the founding of the RLF, which was officially inaugurated in 1790. Because of his liberal *Letters on Political Liberty* (London: Evans, 1782), Williams was invited to Paris in 1792, but left after less than a year, disillusioned by the Revolution. Subsequently, he retreated from his radicalism as well the London literary scene. In 1802, he even wrote a report on Napoleonic France for the British government. His health declined in his last years, when he was supported by the RLF himself. He left a manuscript autobiography, "Incidents In My Own Life," that was not published until the twentieth century (ed. Peter France, Brighton: University of Sussex Library, 1980). The most recent biography is *David Williams: The Anvil and the Hammer* by Whitney R.D. Jones (Tuscaloosa: University of Alabama Press, 1986).

2. Williams lived at 23 Brompton Row, a newly developed street on the border of Chelsea and Kensington (Horwood 21Ad/Bc) from his return from France in 1793 until moving to Soho in 1805 (Jones 159).

3. Stratford Place, built in 1775 off Oxford Street (Horwood 12Ab), would seem to be Richard Johnson's address.

A4

Minutes

MAY 4, 1792

Item: Extract from the minutes of the RLF, I 22.
Text:

         Literary Fund Committee, & General Meeting.[1]
  May 4th 1792   Wood's Hotel, Covent Garden.[2]
         Present, Dr Johnson (in the Chair)[3]

Rev[d] Mr Gardner.	Geo. Jefferies Esq[r]
—D. Williams	Rev[d] Mr Naylor.
Cap[t] Morris.	Mr Ellis.
Col. Schaw.	Mr Rigaud.
Mr E. Brooke.	Dr Edwards.
Mr Deputy Birch.	W. Vaughan Esq[r]
Mr Deputy Nichols.	Major Gardner.
Col. Despard.	Mr Mitchell
Caleb Whiteford Esq[r]	Mr Salte[4]
Mr Bridel.	Dr Dale.[5]

N° 10.   A Letter[6] from Mrs Charlotte Lennox, who translated Sully's
Case.12.   Memoirs, & Brumoy's Greek Theatre, & authoress of several
Vol.1.   original Works, being read, signifying her very distressful
M[rs] Charlotte   Situation
Lennox
£10.10

  Resolved,   That a Donation of Ten Guineas be given to her; & that
         Cap[t] Morris be desired to convey it.[7]

NOTES

1. Lennox's case was discussed in General Meetings only three times (#A4, #A14, #A17). In all other cases, and especially towards the end of her life, decisions were made in meetings of the Extraordinary, Special, or Literary Fund Committee (presumably different names for the same committee).

2. "Wood's hotel and coffee house, Panton-square" (419) is listed under "Hotels, Taverns, Coffee Houses, &c. in London" in the third edition of Samuel Leigh's *Leigh's New Picture of London* (London: Leigh, 1819). Panton Square, Coventry Street (Roque 10Ca, Horwood 13Ad) is near Leicester Square in Covent Garden.

3. Alexander Johnson (bap.1716–99; ODNB XXX 230–31) was one of the founding members of the RLF. He grew up in Holland and was a physician by profession—he was internationally respected and one of the first advocates of resuscitation. Johnson, perhaps the brother of Richard Johnson (see #81), moved to London in 1773 and spent the rest of his life there. He was one of the vice-presidents of the RLF at least 1795–96.

4. With a contribution of £10 10s as a subscriber for life, Samuel Salte was also one of the vice presidents of the Fund. However, this could also be "William Salte, Esq. Poultry" (38), at £10 10s another subscriber for life, but only an "Other Subscriber."

5. The (only slightly more thorough) information on those present is gathered from the list of subscribers in the first report of the Fund, *An Account of the Institution of the Society for the Establishment of a Literary Fund* (London: Nichols, 1795). In addition to the personal information, the numbers and letters in parenthesis give the following information:

    I. page in the list of subscribers (35–39),
    II. status of subscribership (C = committee, T = treasurer, R = registers, O = other subscribers), and
    III. amount of subscription (1 = £1 1s, 2 = £2 2s, 3 = £3 3s).

Rev. John Gardnor, Battersea (35C1)

Rev. David Williams, No 23, Brompton-row (36C2)

Tho. Morris, Esq. No 54, Part-str. Grosvenor-sq. (36T1)

Lieut. Col. Schaw, Gibraltar (38O1)

Mr. E. Brooke, Bookseller, Bell-yard, Temple-Bar (36T1)

Mr. Deputy Birch, Cornhill (35C2)

Mr. Deputy Nichols, Red-lion-passage, Fleet-street (36R2)

[no Despard is mentioned in the reports of 1795 or 1797]

Geo. Jeffery, Esq. Throgmorton-street (37O1)

Rev. Mr. Naylor, Acton-road, Hammersmith (36C1)

[no Ellis is mentioned in the reports of 1795 or 1797]

J.F. Rigaud, Esq. No 71, Great Titch field street (38O1)

Mr. Edwards, Bookseller, Pall Mall (37O1)

W. Vaughan, Esq. Mincing-lane (36C3)

Major Garner, No 32, Bryanston-street (35C1)

Mr. Robert Mitchel, No 72, Newman-street (36C2)

Caleb Whitefoord Esq. No 2,
James-street, Adelphi (36C2)

Samuel Salte, Esq. Tottenham

Mr. Bridel, Stoke Newington (36O1)

Thomas Dale, M.D. Union-court, Old
Broadstreet (36R1)

According to the constitution of the Fund, a guinea (£1 1s) was the minimum annual contribution possible. The officers were elected as follows: "at noon, on the first Thursday in May, to meet the other Subscribers, annually, to chuse Registers, Treasurers, a Committee of twenty, and a Council of fifty, if the number of Subscribers at the meeting exceed a hundred; if not, the Subscribers to discharge the offices of the Council" (31). In the list of subscribers in 1795, no president is listed. There are five vice presidents, 21 members of the Committee, two Treasurers, two Registers, and 106 other subscribers—but no council seems to have been elected.

6. This letter is not preserved in the RLF file and no longer exists.

7. In the annual report of the Fund (repeated verbatim in several reports such as 1795, 1797, and 1799), it says as No. X: "May 4, 1792. A letter from a lady, the writer of several original works, being read, signifying her very distressed situation; it was resolved, that a donation of ten guineas should be presented to her, and that Captain Morris should be desired to deliver it" (9)—this is Lennox. As the report explains elsewhere, "Subscribers may have full information respecting the above cases by referring to the original minutes of the Society, in the possession of the Register.—To have printed the names of the persons relieved, or have given such descriptions as would be equivalent to naming them, would be a violation of that delicacy which alone can render gifts of the Society acceptable" (17). According to Lennox's thank-you note (#A5), Morris delivered the money.

A5

Thank-You Note by Charlotte Lennox

MAY 10, 1792

Item: This is a note in Lennox's hand thanking the RLF for their first "present" of ten guineas.

Format: The left side of the folded sheet (about 7½" × 9½") is addressed (with only the name) in Lennox's hand in the middle about three quarters down the sheet. The bottom left corner of the sheet is torn off, and there is a hole in the top left. Underneath and upside down, a different author has added Lennox's name and the year. The date and address above Lennox's text are also written in a different hand. The reverse is blank.

Text:

Capt Morrice

     Mrs Lennox—

     1792—

_____

           May <u>10.1792</u>

           To <u>Capt.</u> Morris[1]

Mrs Lennox presents her

respectful compliments to the

Committe [sic] of the Literary Fund, and

begs they will accept her grateful

Thanks for their present of ten

Guineas, which she received from

Capt Morrice[2]

NOTES

1. Thomas Morris (bap.1732–1818?; ODNB XXXIX 621–62), sometimes spelled "Morrice," served in the army for most of his adult life and spent ten years from 1757 to 1767 in the Americas. Among other exploits, he "managed to climb unscathed beneath the Niagara Falls" (ODNB XXIX 261). After retiring from active duty, Morris started writing and produced works such as *A Complete Collection of Songs* (London: Ridgway, 1786), *The Busy Bee* (London: Barr, 1790), and *Quashy, or, The Coal-Black Maid* (London: Ridgway, 1796). He performed the lead in *Richard III* in a benefit for the RLF, whom he served as a treasurer at least around 1795/6. He also recited poetry at the RLF's annual meetings, and published *A General View of the Life and Writings of the Rev. David Williams* (London: Ridgway, 1792).

2. Later, Lennox still signs receipts for money from the RLF (#A12), but this is the only thank-you note. In the RLF annual report for 1795, reporting back on the time between August and December 1792, it says: "it was resolved, that this Society expect to receive a letter of acknowledgement from those persons who should obtain relief" (10). If Lennox ever wrote any such letters after 1792, they no longer seem to exist.

A6

Letter from Charlotte Lennox to [Richard Johnson]

AUGUST 22, 1793

Item: This item is Lennox's letter #81 to Richard Johnson above.

Format: The letter is written on the front and the back of a
            sheet (about 7½" × 9½"). The words "Aug.22.1793/ To
            Dr Johnson." are added in one hand, the other comments in
            another.

Text[1]:

                    Aug.22.1793

Sir,   Aug. 1793.   To Dr Johnson.
        12 Guineas voted to send her Son to Virginia[2]
        Nov. 1793 , Guinea to be cons^d part of former Grant.

NOTES

1. For the full text of the letter, see #81 above. The RLF comments ("12 Guineas
. . . former Grant") are written above the first two lines of Lennox's letter.

2. In her letter, Lennox asks about sending her son to America. However, as the
minutes of the RLF meeting of November 29, 1793 (#A8) clarify, the passage went
via Norfolk in Virginia.

A7

Minutes

AUGUST 27, 1793

Item: Extract from the minutes of the RLF, I 36.

Text:

Literary Fund.

Extraordinary Committee held at Mr Alderman Boydell's Cheapside.

August 27th 1793.   Present, Dr Johnson (in the Chair).

Mr Alderman Boydell.	Rev[d] Mr Bracken.
Mr Deputy Nichols.	Mr Bridel.
Cap[t] Crookshanks.	Dr Dale.
Cap[t] Morris.[1]	

N[o] 24.   A Letter from Mrs Charlotte Lennox being read, stating her
Case.12.Vol.1   present distressed Condition, arising from the Situation of her
M[rs] Charlotte   Son; & requesting assistance from the Literary Fund:
Lennox

£12.12. Resolved, That the Sum of Twelve Guineas be allowed to Mrs Lennox
for the express purpose of enabling her to send her Son to Virginia: & that Care be taken that the Money be given to the
Captain himself, who is to take him over: but if her Son should
Vide Nov.29.   stay in England, the Money to be returned to the Society
1793

263

NOTE

1. In addition to the previous categories, there is one vice-president (VP) at this meeting. The participants are listed in the 1795 annual report as:

Mr. Alderman Boydell, Cheapside (35VP5)

Mr. Deputy Nichols, Red-Lion-passage, Fleet-street (36R2)

[no Crookshanks is mentioned]

Tho. Morris, Esq. No 54, Park-str. Grosvenor-sq. (36T1)

Rev. T. Bracken, No 112, Jermyn-street (35C1)

[no Bridel is mentioned]

Thomas Dale, M.D. Union-court, Old Broad-street (36R1)

A8

Minutes

NOVEMBER 29, 1793

Item: Extract from the minutes of the RLF, I 37.
Text:

Literary Fund Committee

Nov. 29th. 1793   Holyland's Coffee house. Strand.[1]
Present. Dr. Johnson (in the Chair).

Mr Salte.	Capt Morris.
Rev^d Mr Bracken.	Revd D. Williams
Rev^d Mr Naylor.	Mr Deputy Nichols
Mr E. Brooke.	Rev^d Mr Gardner
Mr Pugh.	Mr Bridel.
Mr FitzGerald.	Dr Dale.

And the Rev^d Mr Tasker as a Visitor.[2]

N°. 24 cont^d Dr Johnson having reported, that upon delivering to the Consul from
Case.12.Vol.1. Virginia, the Money granted Mrs C. Lennox for the purpose of
Mrs Charlotte sending her Son over to America, he found another Guinea would
Lennox   be absolutely necessary to pay for the Passage &c. from Norfolk
£1.1   in Virginia, where the ship he is to go in, was bound to Baltimore
             in Maryland, where the young Man's Friends reside, & that he
             had therefore advanced one Guinea for that purpose.

Resolved,   That Dr Johnson be reimbursed the Guinea so advanced.

NOTES

1. "Holyland's Coffee House, St. Martin's Lane" (352) is listed under "Hotels, Taverns, Coffee Houses &c. in London" in Leigh. St. Martin's Lane (Rocque 11Aa/b, Horwood 13Bc/d) is next to the Strand north of Charing Cross.

2. The individuals mentioned here for the first time are:

> D.H. Pugh, Esq. No 8, King-street, Cheapside (36C2)

> W.T. Fitz Gerald, Esq. No 19, Upper Seymour-st. (35C1)

> Rev. W. Tasker, Iddesley, Devon (39O1)

Rev. Tasker was himself a beneficiary of the RLF at about the same time; see above in the introduction.

A9

Letter from William Beloe
to John Nichols

January 14, 1802

Item: In this letter, William Beloe asks John Nichols to help in procuring assistance for Lennox.

Format: The letter is written on the front of a sheet (about 8" × 10"). The endorsement, "14 Jany. 1802/£10 voted," is added in a different hand. The reverse is blank.

Text:

14 Jany. 1802

   £10 voted

My dear Friend

I shall be much gratified & obliged if You
will endeavour to procure some assistance
from the Literary Fund, for Mrs Lennox
whose case & claims are mentioned in the
enclosed Paper[1]—It will be an additional
incentive to Y^r benevolence to know that she
is highly respected by the family of the late
excellent Bennet Langton[2]—Pray attend
to this as soon as possible—

     I am Yours truly[3]

     Beloe[4]

Jan 8. 1802

J Nichols[5] Esq

Red Lion Court[6]

Fleet St[7]

267

NOTES

1. It is not clear which, if any, of the other items in the RLF file this paper may be.

2. See #85. Langton had died in 1801.

3. This phrase is almost impossible to decipher—it might also be "Your servant."

4. William Beloe (1758–1811; ODNB V 37–39) was an ordained minister and master at several schools. He started publishing poetry in the early 1780s, and in 1793 he co-founded the conservative *British Critic*. He became rector of All Hallows, London Wall, in 1796 and a prebendary of Lincoln a year later. The climax of his career was his appointment as under-librarian at the British Museum in 1803, but he was dismissed because of supposed negligence in 1806. Beloe wrote *Anecdotes of Literature and Scarce Books,* 6 vols. (London: Rivington, 1807–12) and *The Sexagenarian, or, The Recollections of a Literary Life,* 2 vols. (London: Rivington, 1818), in which he described London literary life. He met Lennox at the house of the actress Mary Ann Yates (see #51; *Sexagenarian* I 401).

5. John Nichols (1745–1826; ODNB XL 788–95) was the most important printer and literary historian of the late eighteenth and early nineteenth century. He began as an apprentice to William Bowyer the Younger and became his partner in 1766. Nichols took over the business entirely on Bowyer's death in 1777. As a printer, Nichols earned substantial amounts of money with *Votes* of the House of Commons and the *Journals* of the House of Lords. Most importantly, he became sole publisher of the *Gentleman's Magazine* in 1780, immediately increasing its coverage significantly. Nichols used the *Gentleman's Magazine* to solicit biographical information on authors and throughout his career edited and printed the works or correspondences of over 100 writers. He served the RLF as an officer in various capacities, but particularly as a registrar, at least from 1795–1805. His career as a printer culminated in his being made master of the Stationers' Company in 1804. However, this was followed by a fracture of his thigh in 1807 and the destruction of his office and warehouse in a fire in 1808, with a loss of about £30,000. Nichols managed to recover both mentally and financially and went on to complete (with the help of his descendants) the two works of literary history he is best known for today: *Literary Anecdotes of the Eighteenth Century,* 9 vols. (London: Nichols, 1812–15) and *Illustrations of the Literary History of the Eighteenth Century,* 8 vols. (London: Nichols, 1817–58). These volumes offer an invaluable insight into the book trade of the eighteenth century. While there is no recent biography of Nichols, there is an assessment of his professional work in Albert H. Smith, "John Nichols, Printer and Publisher," *The Library* 5th series 18.3 (September 1963): 169–90.

6. These words are difficult to make out, but Nichols lived at Red Lion Court (Wheatley III 154–55), so that interpretation makes sense.

7. Fleet Street, the center of the book trade for much of the nineteenth and twentieth centuries, runs parallel to the Thames between the churches of St. Clementa and St. Paul (Rocque 12Aa, Horwood 14B/Cc).

A10

Minutes

JANUARY 14, 1802

Item: Minutes of the RLF, I 147.[1]

Text:

At an Extra[2] Committee of the Literary Fund, at the Prince of
Wales's Coffee House,[3] Jany 14. 1802

    Present Mr Boscawen, in the Chair
    Mr Williams.   Dr Gray.   Mr Nichols.
    Mr Pye.   Mr Gates.   Dr Symmons[4]

Case.12.Vol.1.

Mrs Charlotte   The Meeting having been called to take into Consideration the Case of

Lennox   Mrs Charlotte Lennox, which (at her age of 83) is extremely urgent;

£10

Resolved,   Unanimously that Ten Pounds be immediately presented to her; & that
Mr Beloe be requested to deliver it.

NOTES

1. This was a meeting with only one item on the agenda, so these are its entire minutes.

2. I.e., extraordinary.

3. "Prince of Wales Coffee House, Leicester Place" (353) is listed under "Hotels, Taverns, Coffee Houses &c. in London" in Leigh. Leicester Place was a recent development on the north side of Leicester Square (not in Rocque; Horwood 13Ac/d).

4. For Williams (#A3) and Nichols (#A9), see above. William Boscawen (1752–1811; ODNB IX 707) was by trade a lawyer, but by passion a poet. He translated

Horace, contributed to the *Gentleman's Magazine* and the *British Critic*, and composed poems for the annual meetings of the RLF almost every year. He was a member of the Committee or Council of the RLF every year at least from 1795 to 1805. Three of the other four individuals are listed as officers of the RLF in *Claims*, the annual report for 1802:

John Gray. LL.D. Somerset-place (256—Council—1)

H.J. Pye, Esq. Queen-square, Westminster (257—Committee—1)

C. Symmons, D.D. Upper James-st. Westm. (257—Registrer—1)

There is no mention of an individual called Gates.

A11

Receipt from William Beloe for RLF

JANUARY 15, 1802

Item: This is a receipt from William Beloe to the RLF for money to give to Lennox.

Format: The item is written horizontally on the front of a torn sheet (about 7" × 4"), with the reverse blank.

Text:

Jan. 15_ 1802[1]

Received from the Literary Fund, the
Sum of Ten Pounds for the Benefit
of Mrs Lennox—
                William Beloe

NOTE

1. From Lennox's RLF "Case File" (#A1 and Tab. 2), it seems that she received money twice in January 1802. Here, Beloe is receiving money from the fund which he will subsequently (#A12) pass on to Lennox.

A12

Receipt Signed by Charlotte Lennox

JANUARY 15, 1802

Item: This is a receipt for money received from the RLF via Beloe. Only the signature is in Lennox's hand.

Format: The item is written horizontally on the front of a torn sheet (about 7" × 3"). The sheet itself is torn three quarters to the right from top to bottom (between the letters "l" and "e" in Lennox's signature) and pasted together with a scrap against the back. On the back, a "D" can be discerned underneath the scrap, but everything else is torn off.

Text:

15.th Jany 1802.

Received from the Literary Fund by the hands
of the Rev^d. W^m. Beloe Ten Pounds[1]
       Charlotte Lennox[2]
 £10

NOTES

1. This would seem to be a receipt for the money Beloe received in #A11.

2. Lennox's hand in the signature is shaky, and the ink is blotchy—clearly Lennox was having trouble writing.

A13

Letter from Lady Frances Chambers to David Williams

JANUARY 20, 1802

Item: This is a letter from Lady Frances Chambers to David Williams telling him that, at the behest of the recently deceased Bennet Langton (see #85), she is trying to raise money for Lennox.

Format: The letter is written on the front and back of a sheet (about 8" × 10"). The first four lines are not in Chambers's handwriting.

Text:

Jan[y]. 1802
£10 additional[1]
Mar. 1802
7 guineas additional
Sir

The enclosed note[2] I was favour [*sic*] with the
end of last month in consequence of having been
desired by the late M[r] Bennett [*sic*] Langton to collect any
small sums of half guineas or less for the immediate relief
of M[rs] Charlotte Lennox who is in great distress for the
common necessaries of life & is too ill & now too old to
be able to assist herself in any way—she has not been
able to go out of her lodging these three months &
but today I have been informed that she is at a
cabinet makers in Dartmouth Street Westminster[3] but
I do not yet know the number tho I shall make
a point of seeing her in a few days.—I sent by the
person M[r] Langton appointed the little matter I had

273

collected[4]—and did not wish to apply to the Literary
Fund till I had his approbation—alas his recent
death & the distress of his family has for the present
left M[rs] Lennox's cause in my hands and I have
today

---

today sent a gentleman[5] who was going that way
with a note to M[r] Nichols—Sir Robert Chambers[6]
says that he means to subscribe two guineas a Year
to the charity & I mean to call & pay it in Pall Mall[7]
very soon[8]—in the mean time Sir I have the
pleasure to find that M[r] Johnson recommends
for the <u>first</u> time since he became a subscriber[9]
& I trust that something will be done for M[rs]
Lennox who has not any relations or friends
who seem to think that she has claims on them
—indeed I believe she has lost in her daughter
the only friend she had a claim upon[10]—
I am Sir Your obedient Humble Servant
Frances Chambers[11]
56 Queen Ann S[t] East[12] Wednesday Jan[y] 20th—1802
Rev[d] D[r] Williams

NOTES

1. This is probably in addition to the £10 already disbursed on January 15 (#A11 and #A12).

2. It is unclear what note Chambers is referring to.

3. The addresses here are confusing. At the bottom of the letter, Chambers gives "56 Queen Ann St East" as *her* address, but in #A1, this is given as Lennox's address. However, it seems clear that Lennox is actually *living* with an unknown cabinet maker in Dartmouth Street, Westminster (Rocque 18Ca, Horwood 23Ac) in 1802.

4. Apparently, Lady Chambers had collected money for Lennox and sent it to Langton via an unknown intermediary, "the person Mr Langton appointed." She did not want to apply to the RLF for more money for Lennox without Langton's approval. However, Langton had died in the meantime, so now Lady Chambers is taking it on herself to approach the RLF after all.

5. The identity of this gentleman is unknown.

6. Sir Robert Chambers (1737–1803; ODNB X 990–93) was a lawyer and law professor at Oxford, where he succeeded William Blackstone in 1766. From an early age, he was part of the literary circle around Johnson and the Thrale family. In 1774,

he married Frances Wilton and was appointed judge in the East Indies, so the couple moved to Calcutta. There, Chambers was meticulous in his opinions and worried about the application of English law to Indian subjects. He was knighted in 1777 and was confirmed as Chief Justice in 1791. During his time in India, Chambers was also interested in Orientalist scholarship, amassing an unparalleled collection of Sanskrit manuscripts and becoming president of the Asiatic Society of Bengal in 1797. In 1799, he retired and moved back to England, where his wife had gone in 1792. The most recent biography is *Sir Robert Chambers: Law, Literature, and Empire in the Age of Johnson* by Thomas M. Curley (Madison: University of Wisconsin Press, 1998).

7. Two of the places where subscriptions were received in 1802 were "HAMMERSLEY and Co. Pall-mall; DEVAYNES and Co. Pall-mall" (*Claims* 278). Pall Mall, off Piccadilly (Rocque 10Bb, Horwood 22Da), is one of London's most spacious streets. In the eighteenth century, it was known for fashionable houses and expensive shops.

8. Here, Lady Chambers seems to be suggesting a kind of horse trade: Her husband will subscribe to the RLF, who will support Lennox. The RLF did continue to support Lennox, but Chambers is not listed as a subscriber in any of the RLF annual reports—probably because he died in 1803.

9. This sentence is unclear to me, unless it means that (Richard?) Johnson had never before initiated support for an indigent author.

10. Harriet Holles Lennox, who died around 1783/84.

11. Frances Chambers, née Wilson (1759–1839) married Sir Robert in 1774, when she was only a teenager and he in his mid-thirties. However, Frances—known as Fanny—seems to have made a conscious choice in her spouse, including the fact that she had to move to India almost immediately. The match "turned out to be an ideal marriage," and Fanny was uninhibited in "her headstrong personality [and] artistic inclinations" (Curley 157–62, here 161). She had several children in India, one of whom died in a horrible shipwreck in 1782 (Curley 346–51). In 1792, Fanny returned to England to raise her children at home, and in 1799 Robert joined her. After his death in 1803, she promoted his memory with a memoir, by keeping his library and legal lectures, and generally by campaigning for his fame (Curley 533–40).

12. The Chambers lived in Queen Ann Street (also known as Foley Place; Wheatley III 138; Horwood 12A-C/a) near Cavendish Square at least as far back as 1774 (Wheatley II 67). See also n.3 above.

A14

Minutes

MARCH 18, 1802

Item: Extract from the minutes of the RLF, I 151–52
Text:

Literary Fund General Meeting & Committee.
Shakespeare Tavern, Covent Garden.[1] Thursday March 18.
1802.
Present, Lord Viscount Valentia[2]
     & afterwards   } in the Chair.
     His Grace the Duke of Somerset[3]

Case.12.Vol.1.
Mrs C. Lennox

    Resolved   That Seven Guineas be given to Mrs. C. Lennox: }
                       by Mr Nichols

£7.7.

NOTES

1. This is the tavern at the sign of Shakespeare's Head in Russell Street (Rocque 11Ba, Horwood 13Cc). This is also the inn where "the Beefsteak Society […] used to meet" (George Walter Thornbury and Edward Walford, *Old and New London,* new ed., 6 vols. [London: Cassell, {1879–85}], III 278).
2. This is Arthur Annesley (1744–1816), 8th Viscount Valentia and after 1793 1st Earl of Mountnorris (Samuel Egerton Brydges, *A Biographical Peerage of the Empire of Great Britain* (4 vols.; London: Johnson, 1808–17), IV 137–41. Annesley was a vice-president of the RLF at least 1802–5. His son George Annesley (1770–1844)

was 9th Viscount Valentia, but he was traveling in India 1802–6 (Charles Edward Buckland, *Dictionary of Indian Biography* [London: Swan Sonnenschein, 1906], 433–34).

3. Edward Adolphus Seymour, 11th Duke of Somerset (1775–1855; ODNB XLIX 875) was a scholar of science, mathematics, and history as well as a progressive landlord. He was elected member of many learned societies—the Royal Society, the Society of Antiquaries, the Linnean Society, the Royal Asiatic Society, the Royal Institution—and was president of the RLF 1801–38.

A15

Receipt from William Beloe
for William Boscawen

APRIL 17, 1802

Item: This is a receipt from Beloe to Boscawen for money previously (in January and March 1802) paid to Lennox.

Format: The item is written on a torn sheet (about 4" × 7"). The text on the front is written vertically, on the back horizontally on the right half of the (folded) sheet. On the front, the text starting with "Paid" is written in a different hand. On the back, "Mrs Charlotte/Lennox/Receits [*sic*]" is written in a different hand.

Text:

Rec^d of William
Boscawen Esqr from
the Literary Fund & for
the Benefit of M^rs
Lenox [*sic*] Seventeen
Pounds, Seven Shillings
      William Beloe

April 17 1802
Paid in March 1802 to Mr Beloe
& to Mrs Beloe[1]   5 B [illegible]
7.7   2 B [illegible][2]
£ 17.7   — 7 [illegible][3]
                £ 7.7 [illegible][4]

Mrs Charlotte
Lennox[5]

278

<u>Receits</u> [*sic*]
for
10 . __ by M^r. Beloe
10 . __ by M^{rs}.Beloe
<u>7. 7 by</u> M^r.B—
27. 7. 0

    WBeloe[6]

NOTES

1. The title before the name is difficult to decipher—it could be "Mr." or "Mrs." William Beloe married Mary Anne Rix (d. after 1817) in 1780 (ODNB V 38).

2. Here and in the line above, the "B" is followed by another (illegible) letter.

3. This word might be "Piece."

4. These are two (capital?) letters, the second of which is a B.

5. To the right, there is in two lines what reads like a "29" and an abbreviation, perhaps "Fry" for February.

6. This could also read "Baker"—cf. #A19.

A16

Minutes

Item: Minutes of the RLF, I 159.[1]
Text:

Case.12.Vol.1.
Mrs Charlotte Lennox
£10.10.

Extraordinary Meeting of the Committee of the Literary
Fund, at the Westminster Library, Tuesday Jan: 11.1803.
The distressed Case of Mrs Charlotte Lennox (Vide. Nos.[2]   )
being submitted to the Meeting;

Resolved,   That the Sum of Ten Guineas be given to Mrs Lennox; & that the Collec-
=tor be directed to pay the Money for her use, in such manner that
her Friends may think proper.

Resolved,   That this Resolution be submitted to the ensuing General Meeting
for its approbation.[3]

NOTES

1. This was a meeting with only one item on the agenda, so these are its entire minutes.

2. A large space is left open here, presumably to insert references to previous meetings or minutes, but the space remains empty.

3. See the following item #A17, where the resolution was approved.

A17

Minutes

JANUARY 20, 1803

Item: Extract from the minutes of the RLF, I 160.
Text:

Extraordinary General Meeting & Committee
of the
Literary Fund.
Crown & Anchor Tavern.[1] Thursday Jan: 20: 1803.
Present, Mr FitzGerald, in the Chair.

Revd David Williams.	Mr Boscawen.
Revd John Gardner.	Mr Hughs.
Rev^d Mr Yates.	Mr Griffin.
Dr Valpy.	Mr Rigaud.
Mr Pye.	Mr Stewart.
Mr Nichols.	Major Pye.
Mr Rivington.	Dr Anderson.[2]

Case.12.Vol.1.

Resolved,   That the Resolution of the Meeting of the 11th of Jany be confirmed;[3] & that

                           n
            Mrs Len ∧ ox's Case be taken into further consider-
Mrs Lennox   ation at the next Meeting.
resolution of last
meeting confirmed.

NOTES

1. The Crown & Anchor Tavern near the Strand on 37 Arundel Street was "noted for its social clubs and political meetings" (Wheatley I 480), so it is no surprise that the RLF met there. The tavern, which was turned into a private club in 1847, was

famous enough to be named on Horwood's map (14Ac). The Academy of Antient Music was also founded here in 1710. At least for the next year after this letter, the Crown & Anchor was the regular meeting place of the RLF Committee.

2. The individuals mentioned here for the first time are:

Rev. Richard Yates, Chelsea-college (257—Committee—1)

Charles Rivington, Esq. Hatton-garden (267—Other Subscriber—1)

John Griffin, Esq. Steward-street, Spital-fields (256—Council—1)

John T. Stewart, Gracechurch-street (256—Council—1; the only member of the Council with no title)

James Anderson, LL.D. Hammersmith (256—Committee—1)

There are several individuals with the last name Hughes listed among the other subscribers, but none of them is titled "Mr." There is no-one named Valpy listed, though this probably the "Rev. Dr. Valpy, Reading, Berks." listed in the 1805 annual report (38).

3. See previous item #A16.

A18

Extract of Minutes of RLF Meetings (1)

JANUARY 11, 1803 AND JANUARY 20, 1803

Item: This is a neatly written extract from the minutes of the meetings of the RLF on January 11 (#A16) and January 20 (#A17), specifically the resolutions adopted in the matter of assistance for Lennox.

Format: The extracts are written on the front of a sheet (about 7½" × 9"). The reverse is blank.

Text:

Extract from the Minutes

January 11.1803. Extraord^y. Meeting

"Resolved that the sum of Ten Guineas be given
"to M^{rs}. Lennox, and that the Collector be directed
"to pay the Money for her use, in such manner that
"her Friends may think proper."

"Resolved that this Resolution be submitted to the
"Ensuing General Meeting for its approbation."

January 20.1803 Ex^y. Genl. Meeting

"Resolved that the Resolution of the Meeting of the 11. of Jan^y.
"be confirmed, & that M^{rs}. Lennox's Case be taken into
"further consideration at the next Meeting"

A19

Minutes

AUGUST 20, 1803

Item: Minutes of the RLF, I 169.[1]
Text:

At a Special Committee of the Literary Fund, summoned to take
into Consideration an Application for Relief made by the Revd William
                            n
Beloe on behalf of Mrs Charlotte Len ʌ ox, held at the Crown & Anchor Tavern,
on Wednesday August the 20th 1803.

Present Mr FitzGerald, in the Chair
Mr Boscawen.   Dr Gray.
Major Pye.   Mr Grubb.
Mr Nichols.   Mr Desmond.
                       Dr Dale.[2]

A Letter from Mr Beloe to Wm Boscawen Esqr dated the 14th of July,
Case.12.Vol.1.   n
Mrs C. Lennox stating the distressed Situation of Mrs Len ʌ ox, being read;[3]
Resolved,   That one Guinea per week be paid by Mr Baker to Mr Beloe, or to
£1.1   whom he shall appoint, to be applied for the Benefit of Mrs Lenox, until
per week   the next ordinary Meeting of the Committee.

NOTES

1· This was a meeting with only one item on the agenda, so these are its entire
minutes.

2. The individuals mentioned here for the first time are:
    Edward Grubb, Esq. Great Queen-street, Lincoln's Inn Fields (257 —Committee—2)
    William Desmond, Esq. New Palace-yard (261—Other Subscriber—2)
3. This is #A22 below.

A20

RLF Resolution

SEPTEMBER 1803

Item: This seems to be a resolution adopted by the RLF, though
                         there are no minutes corresponding to it. However, the min-
                         utes of #A19 (August 20, 1803) are practically identical.

Format: The minutes are written on the front of a sheet (about 6¼ ×
                         8"). The main text seems to be in the handwriting of Thomas
                         Dale, with Nichols adding his signature. The matter on the
                         left (Aug. 1803/13 Guineas/at the rate/of 1 Guinea/a week)
                         is written in a different hand. The back (starting at the top)
                         appears to be written by Annandale. There is a date, "Sept^r
                         1803," written horizontally in the right margin in a different
                         hand. The address "To bring to M^r/Sutherland/ [illegible]/
                         Fleet" is added in pencil in yet another hand.

Text:
Aug. 1803
13 Guineas   Extraordinary
at the rate   Literary Fund ∧ Committee
of 1 Guinea
a week[1]   Crown & Anchor Tavern, Strand.[2]
                         July 20 1803
Resolved that One Guinea per Week
be allowed to M^{rs}. Charlotte Lenox [*sic*]
in consequence of her advanced Age
& Infirmities, till the next ordinary
Meeting of the Committee; & that

286

to pay
M^r. Baker[3] be desired ∧ that Sum
every week to the Rev^d. M^r. Beloe,
or such Person as he shall
appoint.

Thomas Dale[4] ⎤
⎬ Registrars
J Nichols ⎦

To Peter Mellish Esq^{r5}

M^{rs}. Lennox is not worse
in point of Health but has
entirely lost her memory.

W. Annandale[6]
for Mr Sutherland[7]

Septr 1803
To bring to M^r
Sutherland
        [illegible][8]
Fleet

NOTES

1. This is the beginning of *regular* support for Lennox.

2. See #A17 above.

3. *Claims* with the 1802 annual report lists (for 1801) one "EDMUND BAKER, *Collector, No. 1, James-street, Buckingham-gate, Westminster*" (277). Presumably the same person is mentioned in the 1805 annual report as "Mr. EDMUND BAKER, No 42, Broad-street, Golden-square, Receiver, and Clerk to the Committees, Treasurers, and Registrers" (51).

4. Thomas Dale (1748/9–1816; ODNB XIV 937) was born in Charleston, SC, but came to England as a child. He was an apprentice to an apothecary, but later became a physician. Also a "good linguist and classical scholar" (ODNB XIV 937), he was registrar of the RLF from 1790 until his death.

5. "Peter Mellish, Esq. Shadwell" is listed as a member of the RLF's Committee in the 1796 annual report (28) and "Peter Mellish, Esq. Brunswick-square" in *Claims* as one of three treasurers of the RLF (257).

6. I have not been able to identify this individual. There is no W. Annandale mentioned as an officer of, subscriber to, or contributor to the general fund of, the RLF in any of the annual reports.

7. The only Mr. Sutherland who seems to have been involved with the RLF is listed as a subscriber who joined in 1803 in the 1805 annual report (*An Account of the Institution of the Society for the Establishment of the Literary Fund* [London: Nichols, 1805]): "Alexander Sutherland, Esq. Queen-st. Westminster" (37). However, it remains unclear why he was involved with disbursing money, especially considering that (according to the minutes below) he was not even present at the meetings of the RLF.

8. This may read "Red Lion," but is almost impossible to make out. "Red Lion" would be Nichols's address; see above #A9.

A21

Receipt from Alexander Sutherland for Edmund Baker

SEPTEMBER 13, 1803

Item: This is a receipt from Alexander Sutherland for money received from Baker for Lennox.

Format: The item is written horizontally on the front of a sheet (about 7½" × 3"). The reverse is blank.

Text:

13th. Septr. 1803

Receiv'd from M^r. Baker Ten pounds
at Sundry times[1] on account of M^{rs}. Charlotte
Lenox [*sic*]

Alex^r. Sutherland

£10..—"—"—

NOTE

1. This again indicates that Lennox was receiving regular support starting in 1803.

A22

Letter from William Beloe
to William Boscawen

OCTOBER 1803

Item: This is a letter from Beloe to Boscawen asking him to support further financial assistance for Lennox. The letter was written in July 1803, but it is placed here because of the note from October 1803 stating that Lennox's allowance will be continued.

Format: The letter is written on the front of a sheet (about 7½" × 9"). The first three lines are written in a different hand. The back carries only the address "William Boscawen Esq."

Text:
Oct. 1803
allowance of 1 Guinea a week
to be continued

Dear Sir

    I must once more entreat your
Kind intersession¹ in [sic] behalf of
Mʳˢ Lenox [sic], whose infirmities have
progressively increased & whose circumstances
are greatly distressed—
Your recommendation to the Committee
will I know have its usual effect.
       I remain

Yours truly
July 14.   William Beloe

NOTE

1. This word is difficult to make out.

A23

Minutes

OCTOBER 20, 1803

Item: Extract from the minutes of the RLF, I 170.
Text:

Literary Fund Committee
Crown & Anchor Tavern. Thursday Oct. 20th.1803.
Present, Revd D. Williams in the Chair.
Rev^d Dr Symmons.
Rev^d Mr Yates.   Mr Sastres.
Mr Grubb.   Dr Dale.[1]

Case.12.Vol.1.   n
  Resolved,   That the Allowance voted to Mrs Charlotte Len ∧ ox, at the Extraordinary
              Committee on the 20th of August, be continued till the next Monthly
Mrs C. Lennox. Committee.
£1.1
per week.

NOTE

1. The only individual here not mentioned before is "Mr. Sastres." Although no such person is listed in *Claims*, this is almost certainly the "Francisco Sastres, Esq. His Sicilian Majesty's Consul, Upper Seymour-street" listed in the 1805 annual report (21—General Committee for 1804—1).

A24

Receipt from W. Annandale
for Edmund Baker (1)

OCTOBER 20, 1803

Item: This is a receipt from Annandale (for Sutherland) for money
               received from Baker for Lennox.
Format: The item is written on the front of a sheet (about 7½" × 3").
               The reverse is blank.
Text:

20ᵗʰ. Octʳ. 1803
Received from Mʳ. Baker three pounds
thirteen Shillings for Mʳˢ. Lennox
£3.13.   W. Annandale
                         for Mʳ. Sutherland

A25

Receipt from W. Annandale
for Edmund Baker (2)

NOVEMBER 16, 1803

Item: This is another receipt from Annandale (for Sutherland) for money received from Baker for Lennox.

Format: The item is written on the front of a torn sheet (about 7¼" × 4½"). The reverse is blank.

Text:

16th Novr. 1803
Received at Sundries from the Literary
Fund four guineas for the use of
M^{rs}. Lennox who continues much as
before.

          W. Annandale
          for M^r. Sutherland

A26

Minutes

NOVEMBER 17, 1803

Item: Extract from the minutes of the RLF, I 171.
Text:
                              Literary Fund Committee
                Crown & Anchor Tavern, Strand. Thursday Nov[r] 17th 1803.
                              Present, D. Williams, in the Chair.
                              Rev[d] Dr Symmons.   Mr North.
                              Rev[d] Mr Yates.   Major Pye.
                              Mr Boscawen.   Mr Gregg.[1]
Case.12.Vol.1.   n
  Resolved,   That the Allowance be continued to Mrs Charlotte Len ʌ ox, till
Mrs C. Lennox. the next Meeting of the Committee.
allowance con[td]

NOTE

1. There are two individuals mentioned here for the first time. The first is "Henry Gregg, Esq. Bedford-square" (256—Council—2). There is no "Mr North" in *Claims* or the 1805 annual report.

A27

Minutes

DECEMBER 15, 1803

Item: Extract from the minutes of the RLF, I 172.
Text:

          Literary Fund Committee
Crown & Anchor Tavern. Thursday Dec:15:1803.
       Present   Mr FitzGerald in the Chair.
       Mr Griffin.   Major Pye.
       Rev[d] Mr Yates.   Mr Grubb.
       Governor Franklin. Dr Dale.[1]

Case.12.Vol.1.

     Resolved,   That the Allowance to Mrs Charlotte Lenox, be
Mrs C. Lennox.   continued till the next Meeting*.
allowance continued.

              * Mrs Lenox died on the 3[d] of Jan[y] 1804.[2]

NOTES

1. The only individual mentioned here for the first time is "Governor Franklin, No. 17, Norton-street" (256—Council—1).

2. This line is at the bottom of the minutes. Since the period is clearly after the asterisk, it stands to reason that these minutes were written up after Lennox's death.

A28

Extract of Minutes of RLF Meetings (2)

November 17, 1803 and December 15, 1803

Item: This is a neatly written extract from the minutes of the meet-
                ings of the RLF on November 17 (#A26) and December 15
                (#A27), specifically the resolutions adopted in the matter
                of assistance for Lennox (including the asterisked notice of
                Lennox's death).

Format: The extracts are written on the front of a sheet (about 7½" ×
                9"). The reverse is blank.

Text:

Extract from the Minutes
Nov.17.1803.
"Resolved that the Allowance be continued to M^rs.
"Charlotte Lennox till the next meeting of the Committee."
Dec.15.1803
"Resolved that the Allowance to M^rs. Charlotte Lennox
"be continued till the next Meeting."*
"*M^rs. Lennox died on the 3rd. of Jany. 1804."

Receipt from W. Annandale for Edmund Baker (3)

DECEMBER 12, 1803

Item: This is a third receipt from Annandale (for Sutherland) for money received from Baker for Lennox.

Format: The receipt is written horizontally on the front of a torn sheet (about 6½" × 4"). The reverse is blank.

Text:

12 Dec[r]. 1803
Received from M[r]. Baker collector to
the literary fund four guineas for
the use of M[rs]. Lennox who still
continues very unwell, having in
addition to her former complaint
a Bad cough

W. Annandale

£.4.4—   for M[r]. Sutherland

A30

Receipt from W. Annandale
for Edmund Baker (4)

January 2, 1804

Item: This is a fourth receipt from Annandale (for Sutherland) for money received from Baker for Lennox up until her death.

Format: The receipt is written horizontally on the front of a torn sheet (about 8" × 4½"). The words "Collector of the Literary Fund" and "the Day of her Death" are added in a different hand (but probably both by the same). The reverse is blank.

Text:

      Collector of the Literary Fund

Rec^d. from M^r. Baker ⋀ three guineas

for M^{rs}. Lennox up to Jan^y

2^d. 1804[1] the Day of her Death

Jany. 2^d. 1804   W. Annandale,

                      for M^r. Sutherland

NOTE

1. While #A28 gives January 3, 1804 as the day of Lennox's death, this receipt offers January 2.

A31

Letter from George Palmer Putnam to RLF

MARCH 8, 1844

Item: This is a letter from Putnam requesting information on
              Lennox on behalf of an unnamed person in the United
              States. The letter is addressed to Octavian Blewitt, the sec-
              retary of the RLF 1839–84.
Format: The letter is written only on the right side of the front and
              left side of the back of a folded sheet (about 8¾" × 7").
              The other halves of the sheet are blank. In the top left
              corner, another hand has added "Ans.[d] 11.L,"[1] indicating
              that the letter was answered. Underneath that note, there
              is a reference, "12/1," that makes no sense to me. At the
              bottom of the front right side, the words "Mr. [or W]
              James/D Sutherland/[illegible]" are added in pencil and
              upside down by a different (third) hand.
Text:
              Stationer's Hall Court[2]
                    March 8. 1844
Sir,
        An official person at
Washington,[3] (U. States) has
written to me to obtain information if possible respecting
Mrs Charlotte Lennox, an
American lady,[4] & the author
of Several works, who lived
some years in England,
and died here in 1804.

300

Gorton's[5] Biog[l]. Dicty, I find,
states that she rec[d].[6] effectual
receiving assistance from this
Literary Fund, and I therefore

---

beg to enquire if you have
at hand any record respecting
her. I do not know the
exact purpose of the enquirer
—but should be glad to
send him whatever
information there may be,
accessible. If you could
conveniently favor me
with any such you would
much oblige, Sir
       Yours very respectfully
       Geo.P. Putnam
       (Wiley & Putnam)[7]
Octavian Blewitt[8] Esq.
Secty Literary Fund

NOTES

1. The last character is difficult to make out.

2. The Stationers' Company—a guild of members of the book trade with its own livery—was founded in 1403 and regulated the book trade in England for centuries. It administered copyright, bought and sold shares, and gave its members pensions. The Company's premises, which burnt down in the Great Fire in 1666 and were rebuilt in the same place, are near St. Paul's (Rocque 12Ba, Horwood 14Dc).

3. Unfortunately, the identity of this person is unknown. It is tempting to speculate that it might have been the American book collector James Lenox engaged in genealogical research, but Lenox was not living in Washington (see Greenspan 147–58 and 191–209 and Ezra Greenspan [ed.], *The House of Putnam, 1837–1872: A Documentary Volume* [Detroit: Gale, 2002=Dictionary of Literary Biography 254], 55–56).

4. This must refer to Lennox's time in the American colonies—looking at her life as a whole, it is difficult to consider her "American."

5. This word is difficult to decipher. However, "Gorton" is a likely reading considering the entry in John Gorton's *A General Biographical Dictionary*, 2 vols. (London: Hunt and Clarke, 1828): "a lady distinguished by a considerable portion of literary ingenuity, who was highly respected by Dr Johnson and Samuel Richardson. She was

born in 1720, at New York, of which her father, colonel James Ramsay, was governor, who sent her over to England to an opulent aunt for education. Her father died
soon after, leaving scarcely any provision for his family; and little is known of the
subsequent history of the subject of this article, except that she married a Mr Lennox,
and supported herself with her pen. [Here follows a list of Lennox's works with some
comments.] It is to be lamented, that with so much literary aptitude, united to great
private worth and respectability, she should be doomed to penury and sickness in
her declining years. She was however relieved very effectually by the Literary Fund
Society, towards the close of her life" (II 327). Especially since the word "effectual"
appears in both places, I am almost certain that the word in the letter is "Gorton."

6. I.e., "received."

7. These names are difficult to make out. From the address above, it stands to reason that the individual in question would be an official at the Stationers' Company,
but neither Cyprian Blagden in *The Stationers' Company: A History, 1403–1959*
(London: Allen & Unwin, 1960) nor Robin Myers in *The Stationers' Company
Archive: An Account of the Records 1554–1984* (Winchester: St Paul's Bibliog-
raphies, 1990) mentions anybody named Putnam or Puttnam. The minutes of the
relevant RLF meeting suggest that it must be the American publisher George Palmer
Putnam of the Wiley & Putnam publishers (see #A32 below).

After various other ventures in the literary marketplace, George Palmer Putnam
(1814–72) joined the firm of Wiley & Long in 1833, and in 1838 the firm was
renamed Wiley & Putnam. Between 1838 and 1848, Putnam spent most of his time
in London, where he ran a branch office of his New York publishers. In other words,
Putnam was living in London when the present letter was written—perhaps an
explanation for the Stationers' Hall address. In the 1840s, Putnam was a strong advo-
cate for copyright laws, which might explain his interest in Lennox, though I have
not been able to trace a US publication of any of her works in the 1840s or 1850s.
For information on Putnam, see Greenspan and Ronald Zboray, "Putnam, George
Palmer" in *American National Biography,* 24 vols., general editors John Garraty and
Mark Carnes (New York: Oxford University Press, 1999), XVIII 6–8.

8. Octavian Blewitt (1810–84; ODNB VI 209–10) pursued a medical career and
traveled in Spain, Egypt, Greece, Turkey, and Italy before becoming a writer for
travel guides and periodicals. He was elected secretary of the RLF in 1839. With this
and his position as under-secretary for literary patronage, Blewitt wielded great literary influence, which he used to promote moral rectitude and put the RLF's books in
order. He was secretary of the RLF until his death and had a reputation for being a
good Anglican and a kind patron.

A32

Minutes

MARCH 13, 1844

Item: Minutes of the RLF, IV 305 and 307.

Text:

At a Meeting
of The General Committee
of The Literary Fund Society
held at 73. Great Russell Street[1]
Wednesday, March 13. 1844

Case. Vol.	A letter was read from M[r]. G.P. Putnam,[2] of the firm of

Case. Vol.
M[rs]. C. Lennox
Letter from
the United States
respecting her

A letter was read from M[r]. G.P. Putnam,[2] of the firm of
Wiley and Putnam of New York,[3] requesting information
respecting M[rs]. Charlotte Lennox, an old Applicant of
the Society. The Committee, not feeling themselves at
liberty to communicate to a Stranger the records of
the Society, M[r]. Nichols undertook, at the request of
the Committee, to answer M[r]. Putnam's Letter from
documents in his private Library.

NOTES

1. In 1844, the chambers of the RLF were in Russell Street.
2. See items #A31 and #A33 above and below.
3. John Wiley and George Putnam worked together in Wiley's publishing house in New York from 1836–48. They published American authors such as Melville, Poe, and Hawthorne as well as British writers such as Dickens and Elizabeth Barrett Browning.

A33

Letter from [John Bowyer] Nichols to Octavian Blewitt

MARCH 18, 1844

Item: This is a letter from Nichols outlining his response to the previous letter to Blewitt and asking for permission to send it to Putnam.

Format: The letter is written on the right half of a folded sheet (about 8¾" × 7"). On the left half, in the same hand, it is addressed to "O Blewitt Esq."

Text:

My dear Sir

  I have abridged some
little am^t. of Charlotte
Lennox from the biographical works in my Library.[1] I have
ventured to say she was relieved
by the literary Fund, as that
is spoken of in all the accounts
of her, & that her Son also was
filled out for an employment[2]
in the American States.—
I have added that no farther
particulars can be gleaned
from these Records—Do
you approve of this, & is it
the fact?[3]—Sending letter,
to Mr Puttmann [*sic*], if you
approve of it.[4]
        Yours truly

[illegible] Nichols[5]

O Blewitt Esq   March 18

1844.

NOTES

1. Unfortunately, Nichols's actual letter to the person requesting information does not survive.

2. Not exactly—the RLF gave money to pay for George Louis's passage to the United States, not to set him up with a job there.

3. The preceding two sentences imply that Nichols is either uncertain about the amount of information available about Lennox or uncertain about how much of it should be shared. The minutes above (#A32) indicate that the RLF did not want to communicate sensitive information from its files to a "Stranger."

4. It appears Nichols responded with a letter that Putnam published much later, in 1869, in his *Putnam's Magazine.* In the section "Leaves from a Publisher's Letter-Book," Putnam includes an untitled and undated letter that starts, "SIR: I am sorry I cannot communicate any particulars relative to Mrs. Charlotte Lennox, except what appears in 'Nichols' Literary Anecdotes,' the 'Gentleman's Magazine,' 'Chalmers' Biographical Dictionary,' &c. She was an active member of the literary world for a long series of years." The bulk of the letter is a summary of Lennox's early life and a long and slightly annotated list of her publications. In one place, the author of the letter writes, "Her latter years were clouded by distress; and it is mentioned in the printed notices of her, that she was relieved by the Literary Fund; but no additional particulars of her are to be gleaned from their books" (*Putnam's Magazine* n.s. 4.23 [November 1869]: 558–59, here 558).

The letter is signed "B. NICHOLS," to which *Putnam's Magazine* adds a footnote: "Author of 'Literary Anecdotes of the Eighteenth Century,' in 16 vols. 8vo. At this time he was about eighty years old, and remained as a connecting link with the days of Dr. Johnson, Goldsmith, and Reynolds" (559). Since the letter is undated, this biographical notice is difficult to understand. If this is a letter Putnam received in 1844, this could clearly not have been John Nichols, who died in 1826. Similarly, there is no reason John Nichols would sign "B. NICHOLS." At the same time, John Bowyer Nichols was only 65 in 1844, and he was hardly a "connecting link with the days of Dr. Johnson, Goldsmith, and Reynolds." Perhaps Putnam misremembered or was trying to claim a connection that was simply not there.

5. The initial preceding the last name is impossible to make out, but there is a good chance this is John Nichols's son John Bowyer Nichols (1779–1863) or his grandson John Gough Nichols (1806–73). Two Nichols were present at the RLF meeting at which this case was discussed (see above #A32): J.G. Nichols, presumably John Gough, and a "Mr. Nichols." Since John Bowyer was registrar of the RLF at that time, it is likely that he is "Mr. Nichols"—see also the previous footnote.

Miscellaneous Publications

"On Henrietta Holles Lennox 17"

[1782–83?[1]]

MS: Houghton Library, Harvard University, MS Eng 1269 (50)

Pages: 2

Edition: LC #49

Text:

On Henrietta Holles Lennox 17

Stop ye gay tenants of the fleeting day

Who careless bask in life's uncertain ray

For serious counsel some few moments save

And take a lesson from this early grave

O stop! Nor check the sympathizing tear

Youth beauty wit & Elegance lie here

In youth in beauty mark how vain to trust

Mark that fair frame now mould'ring in the dust

Would you like her on Wings of Seraphs rise

~~But this life on Seraphs Wings you fly~~

Let Virtue sign your passport to the Skyies

NOTE

1. This poem is dated as if it were written when Harriet Holles Lennox (*1765) was 17.

B2

Six Poems on Mrs. Lennox

[c. 1782–1804?]

MS: Houghton Library, Harvard University, MS Eng 1269 (49)
Pages: 4
Edition: LC #50
Text:
[I.¹]

             an Alcove in
     Wrote in ∧ Richmond Gardens anonimous [*sic*]
To these soft shades the muses oft retire,
For here the brittish Sapho [*sic*], loves to stray,
Here her fair breast, the tuneful Nine inspire;
And all unite to form her moral lay.

     Wrote underneath anonimous [*sic*]
Dear Poet pray tell us, if any cure lyes
In her fine moral lays, for wounds made by her eyes.

     answerd
                        blaze
Should the flames burn too fiercely, that ~~live~~ in her
                               (eye,
Each pitt in her face, will a cooler supply.

     answerd
In these lines that would rob thee of beauty's soft
                               (grace,
How easy the spite of a female to trace;
But this malice so witty, this satire so keen,
To defeat it of L··x, thou needst but be seen.

[II]
Sent to M^{rs} L by an unknown who happened to see
                                    in Windsor Forest
her riding on horseback in the dress of a country
Girl with a basket on the pommel of her saddle

Of old the fabled Goddesses have been
Often in private with their Votaries seen.
But the coy muses still have kept their state
Hid in Pierian Groves their soft retreat
Yet Windsor's shades they surely haunt for here
Clio did once in Le— form appear
In   rustic fair
∧ but a gown the soft ∧ disguise
I saw the latent Goddess in her eyes
And would have worshipped, but she fled my sight
Had she been mortal I had stopd her flight.

                                    anonimous [*sic*]

[III]
                 Copied from a newspaper anonimous [*sic*]²
While Ladies from our Sex usurp the bays
And some write histories, and some write plays
Where's now the glowing page, the moral vein
The Soul of wit that breathes in Charlotte's strain
Oh happy genius that so oft has shown
Each pow'r of judgment, fancy wit thy own
Why silent now—to fame prefering ease
Careless of pleasing 'cause thourt sure to please
Fame by all others courted thee pursues
And will't thou still her envied wreaths refuse

[IV]
Copied from a Magazine³
   On reading poems by Mrs L··x publshd when
   she was not 14 years old
Admiring Greece that boasts the Sapphick Muse
To Thee a second wreathe would not refuse
But Brittain emulous of grecian fame
Does equal honours for her Sappho claim
Her genius sure thy youthful Court inspires
But breathes into thy manners purer fires
~~Thy eyes into our souls~~

312

While thy bright eyes into our souls convey
The sweet distress of thy melodious Lay

Anonimous [sic]

[V]

 Copied from a news paper upon reading
 Mrs Maccaulay's writings, and seeing a
 p^{r4} of Ruffles workd by M^{rs} L for her husband
How each in her mistaken task delights!
L··x works Muslin and Macaulay writes

anonimous [sic]

[VI]
In
one of
Churchil poem—
If wit into the scale be thrown
We boast a Lennox of our own[5]

NOTES

1. The Roman numerals are added to make the distinctions between the six poems more clear.

2. This is an imperfect transcription of the poem "To Mrs. CHARLOTTE LENNOX" published in the *Gazetteer* 11013 (June 28, 1764): 1.

3. This is an imperfect transcription of eight lines from the 16-line poem "*To Mrs Charlotte Lennox. On reading her Poems, printing by Subscription, in one Vol. 8vo, price 5 s,*" signed by the unknown E.N. and published in the *Gentleman's Magazine* 20 (November 1750): 518.

4. pair

5. This is a misquotation of a poem by Charles Churchill (1731–64). In Book II of "The Ghost" (1762), Churchill writes,

 If wit into the scale is thrown,
 Can boast a Lennox of our own
 (*Poems of Charles Churchill,* ed. James Laver, 2 vols. [London: Methuen, 1933], I 93)

The context here is not entirely positive about Lennox: The poem is saying that Lennox should be praised for her wit, but also that she is a Modern—while the Ancients are valued more highly overall.

B3[1]

"Elegy, in Imitation of Shenstone, on Mrs. Yates"

JUNE 1783

Editions: *British Magazine and Review* 2 (June 1783): 461.
              Edinburgh Weekly Magazine 58 (October 2, 1783): 18.
              Whitehall Evening Post 5586 (July 15, 1783): 4.

Text:

ELEGY,
IN IMITATION OF SHENSTONE,
ON MRS. YATES.
WRITTEN BY MASTER GEORGE LENOX,
AT ELEVEN YEARS OF AGE*.

* This young Gentleman is the son of Mrs. Lenox, the celebrated Author of the Female Quixote, and other well known literary productions.[2]

AH! Strephon, your strains are too gay!
They ill suit the poor tortur'd mind;
I wish not to see the bright day,
For Calista has prov'd most unkind.
She despises the heart she has won,
And laughs at the pains I endure:
Ah! Strephon, your friend is undone,
Since for love there, alas! is no cure.
Yet surely I cannot be blam'd,
Tho' I yielded my heart up her prey:
Far and near has her beauty been fam'd,
And Calista's the theme of each lay.
Jove gave to her figure such charm
Of grandeur and softness combin'd;
But, oh! ere I saw that fair form,

Would to Heaven that I had been blind!
Her eyes have such softness and fire
As my pen can never express;
At once they excite soft desire,
And at once the loose passion repress.
Ah! gaze not upon them, ye swains,
Each glance wing'd with poison will fly;
The Goddess will laugh at your pains,
And despises the heart-breaking sigh.
From her lips, Gods! what nectar is press'd;
For I their soft witchcraft have prov'd,
When fondly she lean'd on my breast,
And swore that like Edwin[3] she lov'd.
But where are your vows, perjur'd fair?
And where are the oaths that you swore?
Alas! they are melted in air,
And shall charm the lost Edwin no more!

NOTES

1. The following poems and stories (#B3–B14) are transcribed from whatever was their first publication. Typographical errors are silently corrected. There are some differences in capitalization, spelling, and punctuation between the various versions, but only significant variants between the first and later versions are given in footnotes. Here, I have annotated only names and places, not passages that pose difficulties for interpretation because of their poetic language or eighteenth-century concepts.

2. This footnote is not included in the edition of the poem in the *Edinburgh Weekly Magazine,* since there it was published *after* George Louis Lennox's poem *Laura.* Also, it is notable that here his name is given only as "George Lenox."

3. "Edwin" seems to have been the persona George Louis Lennox took on for his poetry (if he was indeed the author)—see also below #B11.

B4

"Laura"

July 1783

Editions: *British Magazine and Review* 3 (July 1783): 49–50.
            Edinburgh Weekly Magazine 57 (September 25, 1783): 401.

Text:

LAURA; A TALE.
BY MASTER GEORGE LEWIS LENOX,
ELEVEN YEARS OF AGE.

WHILE war's fierce standards wave upon the plain,
Oft do our virgins mourn a lover slain;
Oft the fond bride her husband's death deplore,
And parents part with sons, to meet no more.
Ye hapless train, who have these sorrows known,
In hearing Laura's woes, forget your own;
Lament the fate, the matchless truth revere,
Of Laura bleeding on her lover's bier.
Ye British youths, pour the lamenting strain
O'er Henry, in the cause of Britain slain.
Where Sol's fierce rays through shady vallies beam,
And gentle Iber rolls his silver stream,[1]
There liv'd a gentle maid, unknown to fame,
In beauty rich, and Laura was her name.
All-bounteous Heaven had adorn'd her mind
With ev'ry charm that captivates mankind;
Virtue in her fair breast had fix'd her throne,
And Wisdom call'd the blooming maid her own.
Amid the youths who sigh'd at Laura's feet,
Would Henry oft his love-sick tale repeat;

By manly charms distinguish'd from the rest;
The first in power, as in worth, confess'd,
Laura, whose noble mind shunn'd all disguise,⎤
Check'd not the melting softness in her eyes, ⎬
And scorn'd o'er a fond heart to tyrannize. ⎦
She fix'd the day, she nam'd the happy hour,
When he should lead her to the nuptial bower.
'Tis vain with the decrees of Heaven to strive;
That hour, 'twas fated, never should arrive!
For while the maids prepare the choral lay,
And rural sports, to celebrate the day;
While Henry, panting for his Laura's charms,
Expects the morn that gives her to his arms;
And Laura, with sweet virgin modesty,
Shuns the triumphant gaze of Henry's eye;
Ah, luckless pair! see, each fond wish is lost;
The treach'rous Frenchmen land on Jersey's coast!
With fire and sword our hated foes invade
The soft recess of Jersey's peaceful shade;
Like lions, rush at midnight on their prey,
Whilst rape and murder mark their ruthless way.
At length young Henry led a chosen train,
To oppose the wild invaders on the plain:
His martial ardour fired every breast;
The lover and the soldier shine confess'd.—
On, on, my friends! (he cried) maintain your right!
For honour, love, and liberty, we fight!—
On every side the trembling cowards fly,
And leave the field to us and victory.
But Henry fell a bleeding sacrifice,
And in his country's quarrel nobly dies.
His comrades, weeping, place him on a bier,
And to his aged sire the hero bear.

But, oh! what tongue to Laura shall relate
The sad conclusion of her lover's fate!
Already the dire news had reach'd her ear;
She flies to know the truth, half frantic with her fear!
Loose and dishevell'd was her auburn hair,
Her zone ungirt, and all her bosom bare;
It's [sic] dazzling whiteness she deform'd with blows,

And round her wild, inquiring eyes she throws!
At length she casts them on the sable bier,
And sees the hapless youth extended there!
Clos'd were those charming eyes, which could impart
The softest passion to the virgin's heart;
Lifeless those lips, which oft to hers were prest;
And cold as adamant his bleeding breast!
That breast which felt for her the purest fire
That beauty, youth, and virtue, could inspire!
Awhile in stupid sorrow fix'd she stands,
And on her ivory bosom folds her hands;
But madness kindling, as she view'd the youth—
Henry, (she cry'd) I come to prove my truth!
Then from her side a ready dagger drew,
Which in her own heart's blood she did embrue!
All flew with one accord to aid the fair;
Who, bleeding, fell upon her lover's bier!—
Your help is vain! (the panting virgin cried;)
And then, without a struggle, sigh'd, and died!
Still to their tomb the weeping maidens bring
The earliest tribute of the blooming spring;
And still do Jersey's bards, in flowing verse,
The mournful story of their loves rehearse;
Bid melting virgins weep at Laura's name,
And Henry's deeds transmit to lasting fame.[2]

NOTES

1. The *Edinburgh Weekly Magazine* has "her silver stream."

2. Since "Laura" was the first poem by George Louis Lennox to be published in the *Edinburgh Weekly Magazine*, it has the footnote, "* *This young gentleman is the son of Mrs Lenox, the celebrated author of the Female Quixotte* [sic]*, and other well known literary productions.*"

B5

"Sylvana"

August 1783

Editions: *British Magazine and Review* 3 (August 1783): 136.
             Edinburgh Weekly Magazine 58 (October 29, 1783): 114.
Text:

SYLVANA; A PASTORAL.
BY MASTER GEORGE LEWIS LENOX*.
* This beautiful little Pastoral, though now first published, was actually written near a twelve-month since, when Master Lenox was only in his TENTH
year. The succeeding Verses on his Sister are a later production.

IN yonder fair vale, where the rivulet flows;
Where the primrose, the violet, the daffodil blows;
In a neat little cottage, with thatch cover'd o'er,
Hear the cackling of poultry that feed by the door:
'Tis there that Sylvana, once lively and gay,
Sighs through the long night, and in tears spends the day!
In vain the sun rises each mortal to chear;
She hangs her fair head, and his beams cannot bear:
In vain cooling rains the sweet flowers restore,
They bloom in Sylvana's soft bosom no more!
The lambkins no longer she tends in the vale,
Neglected they roam thro' each brake and each dale,
To the fox, to the wolf, to the robber a prey,
For Sylvana's more lost, more neglected, than they!
Ye maids of the village, so blooming and fair,
By Sylvana's fate warn'd, of Palemon beware!

In his form every grace, every charms is combin'd,
All heaven his face, but all hell in his mind:
So shines the false glow-worm, our hopes to destroy;
O'er marshes and bogs thus it leads the fond boy,
Till, plung'd in the mire, it leaves him to moan,
That e'er he should be by his folly undone.

B6

"On Miss Lennox"

AUGUST 1783

Editions: *British Magazine and Review* 3 (August 1783): 136.
             Edinburgh Weekly Magazine 58 (October 29, 1783): 114.

Text:

ON MISS LENOX.
BY THE SAME.[1]

SHE's just turn'd sixteen, with a figure not mean,
And a face where 'tis certain no folly is seen:
To speak nothing but truth, her complexion is fair;
Gay, sprightly, but yet unaffected, her air.
Her eyes are not practis'd your bosom to melt,
But they stream for the woes which another has felt.
This, Charles, is her form; which, if ever you see,
You will not say has been much flatter'd by me.
'Tis true that the fates have my Harriet denied
The splendor of fortune, and trappings of pride:
Yet much to be priz'd are the blessings they sent;
They withheld from her riches, and gave her content.
The sneers of the world her mind is above;
She sighs not for beauty, and dreams not of love:
The truth is, she has been so cleverly taught,
She thinks our whole sex is not worth a groat!

Declares we are made up of folly and lies;
And, proof 'gainst each art, man she proudly defies.

NOTE

1. This poem immediately follows "Sylvana" in both the *British Magazine* and the *Edinburgh Weekly Magazine*.

B7

"Verses, Occasioned by Repeatedly Seeing the Astonishing Poetical Productions of Master George Louis Lenox"

SEPTEMBER 1783

Editions: *British Magazine and Review* 3 (September 1783): 207.
            Edinburgh Weekly Magazine 58 (November 27, 1783): 271.

Text:

VERSES,
OCCASIONED BY REPEATEDLY SEEING THE
ASTONISHING POETICAL PRODUCTIONS
OF
MASTER GEORGE LOUIS LENOX,
AGED ONLY ELEVEN YEARS;
WITHOUT A SINGLE COUPLET FROM CON-
GENIAL MERIT, IN PRAISE OF A GENI-
US WHICH WAS PERHAPS NEVER EQUAL-
LED AT THE SAME AGE.

WHILE generous bards wake the funereal lyre,
Round a lost Youth his country saw expire,
And o'er his urn the deathless trophies raise,
Shall living Genius want the Sun of Praise!
Alas! poor Chatterton! tho' every Muse
Thy verdant sod incessantly bedews;
Tho' man repents him, and tho' angels mourn,
From the¹ low bed thou never shalt return!
Yet shrill I hear thy godlike spirit call—
Let not on me the gems of pity fall;
But kindly turn from my much-honour'd shade,
And give to living worth your future aid:

Nurture young Genius; nor suspect it's [*sic*] power,
Lest mean suspicion blast the promis'd flower.
The tender plant, that hastily uprears
It's [*sic*] pregnant blossom ere the spring appears,
Left to the wintry winds, and frowning skies,
Too precious gift! alas, too surely dies!
Lo! infant Lenox claims your fostering care;
Shine out, bright Sun! the beauteous floweret chear!
Shall he who pens, in such delightful lays,
The praise of others, not himself have praise!
While in my ear these[2] generous accents ring,
Madly I grasp the lyre, and vainly strive to sing!
Ah! take it, Seward, Hayley, Mason, Pye,
Nor let our little floweret droop and die!

      SEPT. 30, 1783.   H——.[3]

NOTES

1. The *Edinburgh Weekly Magazine* has "thy."

2. The *Edinburgh Weekly Magazine* has "those."

3. In the *Edinburgh Weekly Magazine* publication, the poem is neither signed nor dated.

B8

"Verses Written in the Character of an Unfortunate Young Lady"

September 1783

Editions: *British Magazine and Review* 3 (September 1783): 207.[1]
            Weekly Entertainer 8.187 (July 31, 1786): 120.

Text:

VERSES
WRITTEN IN THE CHARACTER OF AN UN-
FORTUNATE YOUNG LADY.
BY MASTER GEORGE LOUIS LENOX.

BY twenty racking cares possess'd,
In vain I try to close my eyes;
Peace long has fled this tortur'd breast,
And Sleep, her lov'd companion, flies.
Once I could undisturb'd remain,
Tho' tempests rent the troubled air;
The roaring winds have rag'd in vain,
I slept secure, and knew no fear.
The watch has call'd that dreadful hour
When spectres leave their earthly bed,
Some favourite spot to wander o'er,
Or hover round the guilty head.
Now witches mutter o'ver their spell;
And, ah! what means that mournful toll!
Oh, 'tis the neighbouring abbey-bell,
Rings for some poor departed soul!

These terrors now no more annoy,
No longer fill my breast with fears;
For here I sit, and here enjoy
The mournful privilege of tears.

NOTE

1. In the *British Magazine*, this poem immediately follows the previous one (#B7).

B9

"Annette"

OCTOBER 1783

Editions: *British Magazine and Review*
              3 (October 1783): 266–70 and
              3 (December 1783): 420–24.
              Hibernian Magazine
              December 1783: 645–48 and
              June 1784: 312–15.
              Edinburgh Weekly Magazine
              58 (December 18, 1783) and
              59 (January 1, 1784): 8–9.[1]
              New Novelist's Magazine[2] 1 (1786): 187–94.
              Gleaner 1 (1804): 320–29.

Text:

ANNETTE.
A FAIRY TALE.
BY MASTER GEORGE LOUIS LENOX.

As the newly-married wife of an opulent country farmer, in the ever memorable reign of Henry the Great,[3] was strolling through the delightful valleys of Vincennes, a stag pursued by the hounds flew for protection to her feet; and, looking in her face with eyes streaming in tears, seemed to implore her pity and assistance. Annette, whose tender and humane disposition was expressed in every line of her engaging countenance, raised the poor animal in her delicate arms; and, the hunters now approaching, addressed herself to him who seemed the principal, in these words.

'The poor stag you are looking for, has flown to me for protection; but, as I am unable to afford him that, all I can do is to become a petitioner in his behalf: I will not presume to censure your diversions—but let me entreat you, gentlemen, instead of sacrificing the poor trembling animal to your dogs, bestow him upon me; and, be assured, I shall always remember your kindness with gratitude.'

The young hunter, who regarded the blooming Annette with that admiration which a young pleasing woman always inspires, immediately replied—'Be under no apprehensions, Madam, for your dumb client: whatever you protect must be sacred; and I shall think the loss of our diversion amply repaid by an opportunity of obliging you.' Annette, perceiving the young gentleman wished to improve this opportunity, made no other reply to his compliment, than a respectful curtsey; and, hastily striking into a grove of poplars, was out of sight in a moment. As soon as she arrived at the farm, she was met by her husband, with looks full of the most anxious solicitude, her long stay having alarmed him. Annette excused her absence, by her adventure; and, having seen the poor stag taken proper care of, sat down to a light repast: after which she retired to enjoy the united blessings of Hymen and Morpheus, in the fond arms of her enraptured Beauville.

The sun darting his beams through the white curtains of Annette's bed, rouzed them next morning from their innocent slumbers to their different employments. Beauville, with a tender kiss, left his fair bride, to attend the labours of the vintage; while the cares of the dairy and farm demanded the presence of Annette: but first, with her lap full of acorns, she hastened to that spot in her garden which she had alloted for the stag. But how great was her surprize, when, instead of her quadrupede friend, she beheld a beautiful young lady, of a most majestic figure, who held in her hand a silver wand! 'Approach my presence,' said she; 'and behold, in the stead of that poor stag whom your humanity rescued from a painful death, the Fairy Orinda, who longs to convince you of her gratitude and affection: ask, therefore, your reward, and enjoy it to the utmost of my power.'—'For myself, gracious lady,' returned Annette, when she had recovered herself a little, 'I desire nothing; my wishes are few, and those amply gratified by the blessings I at present possess: but I find,' continued she, with a modest blush, 'there will be others for whose happiness I must provide. Let me therefore intreat, that whatever kind intentions you have formed in my favour, may be extended to my infant.'—'Beauty, wealth, power, and virtue, are in my disposal,' replied the Fairy; 'chuse wisely, and be gratified.'—'Oh, Madam!' exclaimed Annette, casting herself at the feet of Orinda; 'since you have given the rein to my wishes, pardon the fondness of a mother that dictates them. If my child proves a daughter, endow her with the inestimable blessing of beauty; let her be the object of universal admiration; powerful from her charms, and great by her marriage: if a boy—' 'Your wishes are accomplished,' interrupted the Fairy; 'for the child with which you are pregnant, is a daughter, who will live to repent, in bitterness of soul, her mother's ill-judged choice! and to convince the world, that the united advantages of beauty, rank, and power, may increase, but cannot procure happiness!' At these words she disappeared, leaving Annette more pleased with the promise that her desires should be complied with, than alarmed by the prediction that accompanied that promise. Her mind was full of a thousand agreeable ideas, when she perceived her husband approaching, and flew with the utmost alacrity to acquaint him with the metamorphosis of her stag, and the future greatness of her daughter, whose matchless beauty, she assured him, would raise her to the most exalted station. Beauville, who possessed an excellent understanding, could not be persuaded to believe his wife's story; and, fearing her head was a little disordered, advised her to retire to her apartment, and take a little rest. Annette, provoked at her husband's incredulity, which she saw it was in vain to combat, complied with his request, that she might be at liberty to indulge her own agreeable reflections; as she plainly perceived she could derive no additional pleasure from communicating them to Beauville: and, during the remaining months of her pregnancy, she resolved never again to speak to him on the subject, but let time prove the truth of her assertion.

At length the wished-for time arrived, and Annette was delivered of a girl, whose dazzling beauty almost staggered the faith of Beauville with regard to what his wife had told him. Highly as the expectations of Annette had been raised, and extravagant as her wishes were, the beauty of little Eloisa exceeded both. Often would she exclaim when she hung with rapture over her cradle, or pressed her to her bosom in an extasy of delight—'If my girl is thus lovely in infancy, what will she be as she grows up, when all the advantages of education are added to her charms! Well might the Fairy promise her greatness; the throne of Henry is hardly worthy of her!' Beauville, too, beheld his little girl with admiration, and wished her mind might be as perfect as her person.

Annette was now far advanced in the eighth month of her second pregnancy; and, walking one evening with her husband in that valley where her adventure commenced, she beheld Orinda approaching them: 'Well,' said the Fairy, 'your wishes have been complied with; it is but just, the same indulgence should be granted to your husband, whose good understanding will no doubt instruct him to make a better choice.—Behold in me,' continued she, addressing herself to Beauville, who stood torpid with amazement, 'the Fairy Orinda; who promises to bestow upon your second daughter whatever you shall think most conducive to her happiness.'—'Great lady!' returned Beauville, recovering himself a little; 'when mortals are allowed the privilege of chusing for themselves, their choice generally proves how unfit they are to be trusted: what my child may think happiness, I know not; with some it consists in riches—with others it centres in beauty, and with some in power—but of this I am certain, that, if she is good, she never can be unhappy: be pleased, therefore, to bestow upon her the love and practice of virtue. I ask no greater blessing; convinced that, in that, she possesses the means of attaining every other.'—'How wisely you, Beauville, have used the privilege of chusing,' replied the Fairy, with a smile of pleasure, 'every action of your daughter's life will prove!' Saying this, she disappeared; and Annette, with an air of triumph, asked her husband if he would now suppose her a visionary. 'Indeed, Annette,' returned he, 'I know not what to think; my senses are bewildered: and I can hardly believe but what I myself have been witness to is an illusion!' [4]

Soon after this, Annette was delivered of another daughter; not, indeed, so exquisitely beautiful as Eloisa, but possessed of just charms sufficient to render her engaging and agreeable. Though Beauville felt the fondest affection for both his[5] children, it is not surprizing he should attach himself particularly to Adelaide; the meekness and docility of whose disposition appeared even in her infancy, and promised to fulfil all the expectations Orinda had raised. As soon as she was of an age to profit by his instructions, Beauville dedicated every leisure moment to the improvement of his favourite's mind; whilst Annette was absorbed in equal cares for the person of Eloisa; the morning sun was not suffered to dart his beams on her fair face, lest he should sully the delicacy of her complexion; while Adelaide was taught to preserve the bloom of health by early rising, and moderate exercise. No expence was spared for the education of both the girls; though the manner in which they received it was different. Eloisa was instructed to consider the accomplishments of music, drawing, and dancing, as the only parts of education she ought to attend to; Adelaide was taught to prize them only as they contributed to embellish the far more valuable endowments of the mind. Eloisa was told she was a divinity; that Paris was the sphere in which she ought to shine; and that her beauty would raise her to a principality; Adelaide was taught, that perfect happiness was only to be found in private life, and domestic pleasures. Both parents succeeded in their endeavours: for, at the age of sixteen, Eloisa was a finished coquet;[6] Adelaide a perfect mistress of every useful and elegant acquirement, alike fitted to shine in a court or adorn a cottage. It was at this period of time that the young Countess De St. Martin arrived at her seat near Vincennes: and, having heard the most extravagant praises of the beauty and accomplishments of Eloisa De Beauville, she resolved to cultivate an acquaintance with her; and accordingly dispatched a billet, requesting hers and her sister's company at an entertainment she proposed giving to some people of fashion, at her seat. The invitation was respectfully accepted, and the time she named impatiently expected by Eloisa; who, as well as her mother, considered it as the opening to her future greatness. At length, the important day arrived; and, after four hours spent at the devotions of the toilette, Beauville handed his daughters into the chaise, which the countess had politely sent to conduct them to her house. Upon their arrival at the Hotel De St. Martin, they were met by a young gentleman of a most elegant appearance, who conducted them into a magnificent saloon, where the countess and her friends were sitting: 'Sister,' said the young gentleman, leading Eloisa and her sister towards the countess, who rose to receive them, 'I have the honour of presenting to you two young ladies, of whom you have heard so much and so little: so much, that curiosity was raised to the highest pitch; yet so little, when compared with their deserts!' The countess, with an elegant compliment, acquiesced in the justness of this remark; and conducted her fair visitors to a seat, where the eyes of the whole company were immediately turned upon them. Eloisa, conscious of her charms, and triumphing in the effect she knew they would produce, bore the gaze with an easy, unembarrassed air; and contrived, by every look and gesture, to discover some new grace. Adelaide, whose cheeks glowed with modest blushes, cast her eyes upon the ground; and, by that evident appearance of innocence and sensibility, interested every heart in her favour: Eloisa, it is true, was regarded with admiration; but Adelaide, the sweet blushing Adelaide, excited tenderness, respect, and esteem. Among those who particularly distinguished Eloisa, was the Duke De Biron, and the Chevalier De Versorand. The duke possessed few advantages besides his high rank and princely fortune; the chevalier was young, noble, and charming in the highest degree, but his fortune very little above mediocrity. Both were enamoured with Eloisa; and both languished to possess her, but in a different manner: the duke resolved to solicit her for a mistress; and, from her situation, had no doubt of success. Versorand, who fancied her all perfection, could not admit a thought that implied a doubt of her virtue; and would have thought himself the happiest of mankind in the title of her husband.

Such were the gentlemen who surrounded the chair of Eloisa, and by a thousand nameless assiduities discovered the passion she had inspired them with.

While these were offering up incense at the shrine of beauty, Monsieur De Bercy, the brother of Madam De St. Martin, no less captivated by the modest charms and unassuming merits of Adelaide, was endeavouring to inspire her with a passion which, from the first moment she beheld him, had been gaining ground in her bosom; and never, sure, was any one more worthy a tender and sincere attachment than Monsieur De Bercy: possessed of every requisite to please, he had youth, elegance, wit, and high birth; with the most noble, tender, and benevolent disposition. Being the youngest of a numerous family, he had not, indeed, a great fortune to offer; but what he possessed was sufficient to answer every purpose of ease and happiness. Adelaide was too prudent to acknowledge on affection so rapidly conceived; but while he was breathing the most tender vows in her ear, a few unguarded sighs convinced M. De Bercy that he was not totally indifferent to her: but it was now far advanced in the evening, and both sisters heard the carriage announced with concern.

Madam De St. Martin, equally delighted with both, promised soon to return their visit; and gave them a general invitation to her house during her continuance at Vincennes: the Duke De Biron and Monsieur De Bercy conducted them to the chaise; where they left them with sighs of regret.[7]

On their arrival at the farm, Annette flew to demand an account of their adventures; and, upon hearing the particular attention which the Duke de Biron[8] had paid to Eloisa, she considered the promises of the Fairy as accomplished; and, having wished her joy of her approaching greatness with as much confidence as if the marriage-articles had been already signed, she dismissed her to her repose; where Fancy continued the scene, and represented the Duke de Biron casting his fortunes at her feet.

While Eloisa, wrapt in the arms of Morpheus, was enjoying her ideal greatness, the gentle bosom of Adelaide was filled with a thousand tender disquietudes. Monsieur de Bercy was charming; she had found him but too much so: he had acknowledged for her the most tender and delicate passion; 'But, alas!' said she to herself, as she lay restless by the side of her sister, 'what can I hope from that passion, even if it be real? Will his friends, noble and powerful, will they consent to his union with a poor nameless girl? The expectation would be madness; and I must expel this invader from my bosom while it is in my power.'

Adelaide, having resolved never to think of De Bercy as a lover, endeavoured to compose herself to sleep; but, alas! a dream, in which she beheld him at her feet with that insinuating softness which he possessed in so eminent a degree, offering up the most ardent vows of love, broke all her prudent resolutions, threw her into a fit of tenderness, and convinced her, waking, that however rapidly her passion had been conceived, to conquer it must be the work of time.

Such was the situation of her mind, when a servant entering the apartment, informed them it was far advanced in the day; and that a gentleman, whose name she presented, had called to enquire after their health. The heart of Eloisa glowed with transport; when, eagerly snatching the card from the hands of the maid, she read the name of De Biron, this early visit realized her hopes, and confirmed her expectations.

The next morning the Countess De St. Martin sent to inform them, that herself, and her brother, and Monsieur De Versorand, proposed passing the afternoon at the farm. Annette, upon receiving the message, flew to prepare for the reception of her visitors, while her daughters retired to the devotions of their toilette.

Eloisa, having added every advantage of dress to a figure that required no additional graces, sat before her glass, exulting in the consciousness of her charms: but never before did Adelaide experience so ardent a desire of attracting; she even borrowed part of her sister's coquetry; and her handkerchief was so contrived as to discover, while it seemed to hide, all the beauties of her neck and bosom; her head-dress so judiciously fancied, as to give more languishing softness to her countenance; and casting a look on her arms, which were delicately fair, black velvet bracelets were contrasted to their whiteness. But, in the midst of these preparations for conquest, this reflection darted upon her mind, 'For what purpose am I so desirous of adorning my person? I cannot hide from myself that it is from a desire of pleasing Monsieur de Bercy; while reason, prudence, and duty, command me to banish from my own bosom a passion which can never have the sanction of his friends, and discourage instead of exciting it in his.'

Thus conscience spoke; and Adelaide, ever accustomed to obey that faithful monitor, altered, but not without some rebellious sighs, the whole plan of that dress which had cost her hours in accomplishing: and now, having consulted only decency in her appearance, she quitted her dressing-room, more glorious, in this conquest of her passions, than Alexander in subjecting the world.

Early in the afternoon the expected visitors arrived. The chevalier, to whom the desire of pleasing had given new graces, never appeared to more advantage; he seized the first opportunity of addressing Eloisa on the subject of his passion; her heart confessed his charms, and pleaded powerfully in his favour. For a moment she forgot all her predicted grandeur; and he had almost drawn from her an avowal of her sentiments, when the door opened, and the Duke De Biron was announced. At that name, Versorand, what became of thy hopes? Cupid himself had assisted thee in the siege of her heart; and, at the very moment when it was surrendering to the victor, Pride and Vanity arrive with fresh supplies, and Cupid is forced to an ignominious retreat!

The duke, whose visit was professedly to enquire after the health of the young ladies, having, in a polite compliment, addressed himself to them both, drew his chair next Eloisa; and dedicated his attention, for the rest of the evening, solely to herself. But the chevalier, who was but too well acquainted with his sentiments for her, by throwing himself negligently on the back of Eloisa's chair, effectually prevented the duke from making any formal declaration of his passion.

In the mean time, Monsieur De Bercy beheld the altered behaviour of Adelaide with surprize and concern. 'Ah, Mademoiselle!' said he, when he had an opportunity of speaking to her without observation, 'in what have I been so unfortunate as to offend you? What can have occasioned this sudden and cruel change in your behaviour!'—'I am sorry, Sir,' replied Adelaide, 'my behaviour should ever have been so imprudent as to render a change necessary.'—'I understand you, Madam,' returned De Bercy; 'you repent of the favour you was pleased to shew me at my sister's: it was, indeed, an happiness which monarchs might envy me; and, no doubt, reserved for some more deserving—' 'Hold, Sir,' interrupted Adelaide, with a sigh, which she in vain endeavoured to suppress, 'do not wrong me with that suspicion; my heart does justice to your merits; overflows with gratitude for the generous passion with which you honour me; and, had it the sanction of your friends, the whole study of my life should be to render myself deserving of it: but, without that sanction, Sir, which, in my humble situation, it would be madness to expect, I am determined never more to hear you on this subject.' Monsieur de Bercy was eager to reply, but she prevented him—'You know the terms, Sir, upon which only I can comply with your desires: if they are practicable, let your next application be to my father; if, as my reason convinces me, they are not, I must insist, Sir, upon your never renewing a suit, which a moment's reflection determined me to reject.'

At the conclusion of this speech, Adelaide rose from her chair, as well to avoid any farther conversation with her lover, as to conceal from him those emotions which were but too plainly expressed in her countenance. Soon after this, the countess took her leave, having continued her visit to so late an hour as to give the Duke de Biron no pretence for lengthening his.

Versorand, who had in vain endeavoured to catch a parting glance, retired in an agitation, of which those only who have felt the pangs of unsuccessful love are capable of judging; while Bercy, whose passion for Adelaide was now increased to adoration, ventured to confide his secret to the countess, whose excellent understanding and good heart, he knew, rendered her superior to low and interested motives. Madame de St. Martin, who was no stranger to the amiable disposition of Adelaide, and who justly conceived that virtue was the best security for happiness, applauded a passion which had so worthy an object; and promised to use her best endeavours to procure the consent of his relations to his addressing her.

In the mean while, the Duke de Biron, whom the imprudent behaviour of Eloisa had filled with the most sanguine hopes, had no sooner arrived at his house, than he sat down, late as it was, to write her those proposals which the unremitted attention of the chevalier had prevented him from declaring in person. Having finished his letter, he delivered it to his valet, with no other precaution than that of giving it into the hands of Eloisa's maid only; for he considered his offers as too splendid to be rejected even by Beauville himself, should the letter happen to fall into his hands: and so indeed it did; for the girl, to whom it was entrusted, and whom the repeated injunctions of Eveille to deliver it privately, led to suspect the nature of the billet, impelled either by the rectitude of her own heart, or the force of that destiny which was now preparing to gratify the wishes of Annette, discovered the whole transaction to her master; who, having read the letter with the indignation it deserved, flew to the apartment of his daughter, and tossing it on the table before her; 'I know not, Eloisa,' said he, 'how far your own imprudence has occasioned this insult; but I think it necessary to inform you, that the moment I perceive your conduct deviate from the strictest rules of propriety, I will confine you in a place where your coquetry shall want objects, and your beauty bloom in vain.' Eloisa trembled at the conclusion of her father's speech; and hastily opening the paper that had occasioned it, found the contents as follow.

'CHARMING ELOISA,
'We were so narrowly observed last night by the Chevalier de Versorand, that I could only express my admiration of you in general terms: painful restraint to a heart captivated like mine, and languishing to pour forth it's adorations at your feet! But though my tongue was silent, my eyes, I am sure, plainly declared the state of my heart; and, if I may believe the expressive language of yours, the divine Eloisa is not insensible to my passion. It is in this flattering hope that I have presumed to address you; to implore permission to wait on you, and cast my fortune at your feet: dispose of it as you please, Mademoiselle; for it is yours as entirely as the heart of the passionate

BIRON.
'My servant will attend this evening for your answer: suffer me to hope it will be propitious to my wishes; and contain permission to place you in a stile of life for which your beauty and elegance have so evidently designed you.'

Eloisa, overcome by grief and confusion upon reading a proposal so very different from her expectations, threw herself back in her chair, and indulged, for a moment, the sorrows which oppressed her, in a flood of tears. At length, recovering herself, 'I did not, Sir,' said she, 'need any threat to force me to a sense of my duty: I feel but too sensibly the affront that is offered me; and only wait[9] your permission to resent it as I ought.'—'Leave the care of resenting this insult to me,' returned Beauville, 'and let your conduct be so guarded as to prevent a repetition of it for the future.' He then hastened to the duke; and in a respectful, but preemptory stile, desired him to desist from a pursuit so injurious to the honour of his daughter; 'and which,' added he, 'rather than she should be in any danger of complying with, I would confine her for ever within the walls of a cloister.' Biron, who, from the determined virtue of Beauville, of which he had had no conception, and the noble scorn with which he rejected all his offers, found he never could possess Eloisa in an unlawful way, quitted his villa at Vincennes, and endeavoured to forget his recent passion in the hurry and dissipation of Paris. But in vain did he try, by every means which his reason could suggest, to banish the charming idea of Eloisa: all pleasures became distasteful, because she did not share them with him; all beauty insipid, for he had seen perfection. His mind was torn by a thousand contending passions, when Eveille, whom he had left at Vincennes, with orders to observe, and give him the earliest intelligence of what passed at the farm, acquainted him that the Chevalier de Versorand had renewed his addresses; that they were approved by Beauville, accepted by Eloisa, and a marriage was soon expected to take place.

This information fixed the wavering resolutions of Biron, and determined him to sacrifice his pride to his love. He flew with the most eager impatience to Vincennes; implored, at the feet of Eloisa, her pardon for his former offence; and offered to repair it by an instant marriage. It was in vain that Beauville pleaded the prior engagement, and his word pledged to Versorand; the prayers of Eloisa, the impetuosity of Annette, carried all before them: the chevalier was discarded, and the Duke de Biron united to Eloisa, whose nuptials were soon followed by the far more auspicious ones of Adelaide and Bercy; those relations who might have refused their consent to a marriage with the amiable daughter of Farmer Beauville, thinking themselves honoured by an alliance with the sister of the Duke de Biron.

In the full enjoyment of every blessing that virtue merits, and which love bestows, let us leave them, to attend Eloisa in that exalted station to which she was now advanced. Scarce a month elapsed, before the duke conveyed her, with a magnificence suiting his rank, to Paris; which soon resounded with the fame of the beautiful Dutchess de Biron, whose empire over both sexes was unbounded; for while she was the universal idol of the men, the ladies acknowledged her the standard of taste, and arbitress of fashion.

It was now, when every virtue was absorbed in pleasure, every reflection drowned in dissipation, that Versorand, whom her perfidy had cured of his reverence for her mind, though his heart still languished for the possession of her person, renewed his former passion, but not with the same success; for Eloisa, who had before sacrificed her inclination to her interest, now, with far less reluctance, sacrificed her duty to her desires, and engaged in a commerce with the chevalier, which, notwithstanding all their caution, was soon reported to the duke.

The duke was more shocked than surprized at this intelligence; the dissipated and unguarded conduct of Eloisa having long given him reason to dread some imprudence. He, however, confined his indignation to his own breast till he should have more positive proof of her disloyalty than mere report; and, for that purpose, employed his valet, of whose fidelity he was well assured, to watch the conduct of the dutchess, and find how far she was culpable.

Eloisa was not long before she gave them the opportunity they wished; and Eveille traced her to an house, which he knew belonged to a woman who had formerly been nurse to the chevalier; who soon after entered it himself. Eveille had now seen enough to justify suspicion, and instantly acquainted his master with the result of his observations. The resentment which Biron had so long suppressed, now burst forth with redoubled violence; and wrapping himself up in his cloak, he commanded Eveille to conduct him to the house; the door of which being opened, he rushed forwards with an impetuosity which the weak efforts of an old woman in vain endeavoured to prevent; and, bursting open the door of an apartment which he found locked, he beheld Eloisa breathless on the floor, and Versorand prepared to defend himself: but in vain did he parry the furious thrusts of his antagonist, from whose avenging arm he soon received the punishment due to his crime. At that moment Eloisa recovered from her swoon, to behold that lover, for whom she had sacrificed her hopes, weltering in his blood, and the room filled with people, who were the witnesses of her disgrace. 'The infamous accomplice of thy crime,' said the duke, pointing to Versorand, 'has expiated his crime by his death. But, oh! thou serpent! whom I have nourished in my bosom, whom no principle of virtue could restrain, no sentiment of gratitude bind, what punishment can an injured husband inflict upon thee that is equal to thy deserts! I will not stain my sword with thy polluted blood, I will not immure thee for ever within the walls of a convent—for either of which I have the sanction of the laws—but leave thee to the vengeance of an offended God, and the internal reproaches of thy conscience!'

Eloisa, pale, trembling, confounded, fled from the presence of her injured husband; and, almost without being sensible of it, took the way towards Vincennes. Terror and despair gave her wings; and she arrived before sunset at the farm. 'Behold,' said she, casting herself at the feet of her father, 'a wretch, whose crimes have undone her! I left this happy roof with every smiling prospect open to me; secure in innocence, and flourishing in prosperity: I return to it a poor, miserable outcast; my peace lost, my hopes blasted, and my reputation murdered. All that would make life dear to me, is vanished; and what I now, with tears of heart-felt anguish, implore from your mercy, is, that you will not cast me out to beggary and contempt, but kindly guide me to some sheltering cloister, where I may employ the poor remains of life in penitence and prayer!'

Beauville, lost in astonishment and grief, was prevented from a reply by the sudden appearance of Orinda. 'Behold,' said she, addressing Annette, with a frown which clouded even celestial beauty; 'behold the fatal effects of your indulged desires!—Yet think not, Eloisa, the imprudence of your mother extenuates your crime; or that, to fulfil my predictions, I have led you into errors. Oh, no! I did but leave you to the guidance of those passions which are inherent in your nature. 'Tis true, had Annette preferred virtue to beauty, and innocence to grandeur, my art could have prevented the commission of thy crimes, by placing thee in a station where those passions would have lain dormant, because no temptations would have assailed them. Go, therefore, fair unfortunate; mourn within the melancholy inclosure of a cloister the pride that has misled, the love that has undone thee! There let thy tears wash out thy stain; thy penance expiate thy offences! So shall the Almighty, whose gates are never barred to the repentant sinner, at length behold thee with an eye of mercy, calm all thy soul, give comfort to thy afflictions, and bestow, amidst the gloom of a monastery, that peace from which thou art excluded in the world.—But, for Adelaide,' continued the Fairy, 'life reserves her choicest treasures; not in the wild attainments of ambition, but in the heart of her husband, the duty of her children, the esteem of the virtuous, and the approving plaudits of her conscience!"

NOTES

1. I have not seen the first installment of the *Edinburgh Weekly Magazine* publication. On March 4, 1784, the magazine published a notice: "The *Fairy Tale,* by Master Louis Lenox, which was begun some numbers ago (and for the conclusion of which some of our readers may be impatient), is not yet finished by the young author; though by a note in the British Magazine for November (from which publication we extracted it) he had promised to conclude it as about the last holidays" (296). Apparently, the editor was not aware of the conclusion in the December issue of the *British Magazine.* Indeed, the end of the story was never published in the *Edinburgh Weekly Magazine.*

2. The short-lived *New Novelist's Magazine* also published two works by Charlotte Lennox. "The Tale of Geneura. From the Italian of Ariosto" (1 [1786]: 95–102) was a reprint of the chapter "The Tale of *Geneura: From the* Italian *of* Lodovico Ariosto, *in the Fifth Book of his* Orlando Furioso" from *SI* (III: 231–56). This story is considered a source for Shakespeare's *Much Ado About Nothing.* The other work in the *New Novelist's Magazine* was "The History of the Count de Comminge. Supposed to be Written by Himself. Translated from the French. By Mrs. Lennox" (2 [1787]: 275–301, with an engraving), originally published in Lennox's translation of *Berci* (II 135–227; see also #24).

3. This is Henri IV (1553–1610), who was the first French king from the house of Bourbon from 1589 to 1610. Lennox knew much about his reign since she had translated the memoirs of his chief advisor, the Duke of Sully. She had excerpted

the history of Henri's mistress Gabrielle d'Estrées, Duchess of Beaufort, in her *LM* in 1760.

4. The first installment of the publication in the *Edinburgh Weekly Magazine* ends here; the second begins with the following paragraph.

5. The *Edinburgh Weekly Magazine* has "her" instead of "his."

6. The *Edinburgh Weekly Magazine* has "coquette"; all four other versions have "coquet."

7. The first installment of the version in the *British Magazine* and the *Hibernian Magazine* ends here; their second installments start with the following paragraph. The second and last installment of the story in the *Edinburgh Weekly Magazine* ends here as well.

8. At this point, the *British Magazine* switches from "De Biron" to "de Biron," though the change is not consistent.

9. The version in the *Gleaner* has "want" instead of "wait."

B10

"Verses on a Beautiful Young Lady"

OCTOBER 1783

Editions: *British Magazine and Review* 3 (October 1783): 297.
         Weekly Entertainer 8.202 (November 13, 1786): 477.
Text:

VERSES
ON A BEAUTIFUL YOUNG LADY, DANGE-
ROUSLY ILL.
BY MASTER GEORGE LOUIS LENOX.

MY wounded heart for Mira grieves,
And no fond hope my soul relieves!
Ah, no! abandon'd to despair,
And suffering with the hapless fair,
To Heaven I raise my streaming eyes,
But no kind angel hears my cries.
Methinks I see the lovely maid,
On the dire bed of sickness laid;
I see her fix her languid eye,
And now I hear a saintly sigh;
I see her robb'd of every grace,
And death triumphant in her face;
I view her frantic mother's fright,
While tears obscure her sister's sight.
Ye gods! if Virtue be your care,
The truest of her votaries spare;
Have pity on her blooming youth,

Her innocence, her spotless truth;
Restore her to a mother's care,
Hear a distracted lover's prayer;
Oh! give her to her sister's love,
And let the tears of thousands move;
For she to every heart was dear,
And all partook her parent's fear!
Will no kind angel intercede;
None stop the shaft that is decreed
To fall on her devoted head,
And number Mira with the dead?
Upon the wicked turn it's [*sic*] rage,
But spare the wonder of the age!

B11

"Verses Addressed to the Prime-Minister"

November 1783

Editions: *British Magazine and Review* 3 (November 1783): 379.
                          Edinburgh Weekly Magazine 59 (March 4, 1784): 289.

Text:

VERSES
ADDRESSED TO THE PRIME-MINISTER FOR
THE TIME BEING.
BY MASTER GEORGE LOUIS LENOX.

WHILE grateful Britons sing their ——'s[1] praise,
And thousands greet him with their loud acclaim;
Let not young Edwin[2] think his artless lays
Can please his ear, or consecrate his fame.
His monarch's favour, and his country's love,
His glorious toils with interest will repay;
And —— shall all the soft contentment prove
Which an applauding conscience can convey.
Envy will fling her poison'd shaft in vain
Against the heart that honour fortifies;
And Adulation, with her fawning strain,
Our ——'s noble bosom must despise.
But ne'er did Edwin prostitute his pen,
The vile oppressor of the poor to praise;
Nor have the deeds of the great, but wicked men,
E'er been recorded in my humble lays.
Sacred to Virtue still has been my lyre;

She guides my actions, she inspires my song;
To her I owe the soft poetic fire,
And to her votaries all my strains belong.
And, oh! when Edwin moulders in the grave,
Himself, his verse, his actions, all forgot,
Virtue her ——'s name from Time shall save,
And never-fading glories be his lot!

NOTES

1. There were three Prime Ministers in 1783: William Petty FitzMaurice, 2nd Earl of Shelburne until February, William Henry Cavendish Bentnick, 3rd Duke of Portland, for most of the year, and William Pitt the Younger from December. Since the person in question here must have two syllables to his last name, it must be one of the first two. Since the poem came out in November, it is probable that the Prime Minister alluded to is Bentnick.

2. See #B3 above.

B12

"Verses, to a Young Married Lady"

DECEMBER 1783

Edition: *British Magazine and Review* 3 (December 1783): 455–56.
Text:

VERSES,
TO A YOUNG MARRIED LADY, WHO RE-
GRETTED THE WANT OF CHILDREN.
BY MASTER GEORGE LOUIS LENOX.

AND would Amanda wish to share
A mother's joy, a mother's care?
Alas! my fair, you little know
How small the bliss, how great the woe!
And first, with many a torturing fear,
With many a groan and pang severe,
Nine months the burden you must bear.
The pangs of child-birth safely o'er,
How many miseries are in store!
Nature, perhaps, with liberal grace,
Gives to the boy an angel's face;
Perhaps, too, she may give a mind
Just, noble, tender, and refin'd.
The mother forms, with anxious care,
The growing virtues of her heir;
Beholds the seeds of knowledge shoot,
And glories in the promis'd fruit:
But hardly can she taste this joy,

Ere fell disease her hopes destroy.
Now guess her agonizing fears,
While death in different shapes appears!
But Heaven, in pity to her prayer,
The little innocent may spare.
Her infant dangers safely o'er,
She dreads what may be yet in store;
And sees him reach, with doubt and fear,
This crisis of his eighteenth year:
And now farewel [*sic*] to every joy,
A foreign land demands her boy;
A sailor, he must tempt the main,
Or fight on the embattled plain.

In vain the wretched mother mourns;
He goes—and, ah! no more returns!
Or, haply, Fortune may bestow
A kind exemption from this woe;
Nor commerce bear him o'er the main,
Nor honour to the martial plain;
But, to an easy fortune heir,
Secure he breathes his native air:
See pleasure now his mind engage,
The ruling passion of the age;
See beauty spread each tempting art
To win his young unguarded heart;
See artifice, like friendship dress'd,
Share his unsuspecting breast;
See him, with many a heart-felt sigh,
His very virtues misapply:
He is not tender now, but loose;
No longer generous, but profuse.
Now charm'd by women, now by play,
His health, his fortune, cast away,
The ruin'd youth his mistress flies;
The friends who shar'd his wealth, despise; }
And, worn by grief and pain, he dies!

B13

"The Fate of Sophia"

APRIL 29, 1784

Editions: *Edinburgh Weekly Magazine* 60 (April 29, 1784): 136.
                Wit's Magazine; or, Library of Momus 1 (1784): 75–76.
Text:

THE FATE OF SOPHIA.
BY MASTER GEORGE LOUIS LENOX,
ELEVEN YEARS OF AGE.

AT the foot of a willow, Sophia reclin'd;
Her beautiful bosom was fann'd by the wind;
Her eyes in all Venus's fires were dress'd,
Her breath sweeter far than the roses she press'd:
Her fair hands she clasp'd, and thus mournfully cry'd—
"Must my suit, Queen of Love, be for ever denied?
Ah! mindful the pangs for Adonis you bore,
Some ease to this poor tortur'd bosom restore!
What can I have done all this anguish to prove?
Since my flame is presumptuous, ah! why should I love?
'Midst the youths of the court I securely have stray'd;
For what were their charms to an innocent maid?
But when I the noble Augustus beheld,
In vain the soft tyrant your son I repell'd:
Who, goddess! can gaze on those beautiful eyes,
And amorous thoughts and soft wishes not rise?
Ah! why was their poison imparted to me?
From the hateful contagion why did I not flee?

Ah, why, cruel goddess! but that you decreed
With Love's hopeless pangs this heart ever should bleed.
I ask you not his gen'rous bosom to fire,
And to make me the object of lawless desire;
The heart I have lost is all I require.
But, alas! can I hope my suit to obtain,
When thy favourite Sappho has pleaded in vain?"
Thus she: and the goddess, who heard from the skies,
From a cloud breaking forth, stood reveal'd to her eyes.
In her right hand a glittering arrow she bore,
Round her bosom the powerful cestus she wore.
"Why," said she, "will Sophia dissemble with me;
From the pangs I've inflicted you would not be free?
But dry up those tears, those soft sighs restrain;
No longer those sighs or those tears shall be vain.
This arrow from Cupid's full quiver I bear
To plunge deep in the bosom of ——'s gay heir.
That done, with a passion like your's he shall burn,
And every pleasure of love he'll return."—[1]
Here paus'd the bright Goddess; nor waiting reply,
In a moment she soar'd beyond reach of the eye.
The astonish'd Sophia beheld her depart,
All Cupid's soft transports possessing her heart:
But few were those transports, and short was their date;
For Diana, to save from dishonour the maid,
From her quiver unwillingly drew forth a dart;
And, averting her eyes, wing'd it on to her heart;
Which, true to the hand, thro' each artery flies,
And the charming Sophia immaculate dies.

NOTE

1. In the *Wit's Magazine,* the line reads, "And every pleasure of love be your own."

B14

"The Duke of Milan"

1786

Edition: *New Novelist's Magazine* 1 (1786): 351–69.
              Weekly Entertainer
                      9.225 (April 23, 1787): 387–94;
                      9.226 (April 30, 1787): 409–14;
                      9.227 (May 7, 1787): 433–38;
                      9.228 (May 14, 1787): 457–61;
                      9.229 (May 21, 1787): 481–86; and
                      9.230 (May 28, 1787): 505–9.

Text:

THE DUKE OF MILAN
BY MASTER GEORGE LOUIS LENNOX.

At the death of Alphonso, Duke of Milan, who, from his many virtues, had attained the surname of The Good, his nephew, Lothario, succeeded to the dukedom. This young prince had been educated in the court of France, and imbibed all the levity of disposition which so eminently distinguishes that nation. With a person most exquisitely charming, he possessed a mind adorned with every noble quality; but so immersed in pleasure and dissipation, that his virtues seldom appeared, while his follies and imprudence were the universal talk of Milan.

But none of his faults were more severely felt by his subjects than his attachments to the fair sex, none of whom he considered as too high to be attempted, or too mean to seduce: hence did many of the most distinguished nobles of his court behold their daughters dishonoured, and their illustrious blood stained, by that very prince in whose defence they willingly would have shed the last drop of it; while the industrious mechanic, and honest citizen, saw their children torn from virtue and reputation, to satisfy the desires of a voluptuous youth, whose roving heart celestial beauty could not have fixed.

About two miles from a hunting-seat to which the duke frequently retired, in a house which Don Quixote might have mistaken for an enchanted castle, Don Ferdinand de Velasquis, a gentleman of high fortune and noble birth, had immured his only daughter; not from any principle of prudence, or any distrust of her virtue, but from the effects of tyranny and caprice which had actuated him during a life of fifty years, and which had occasioned the death of an amiable woman, to whom he owed the birth of Evadne. This young lady had nearly attained her nineteenth year; her person was elegantly formed; and her features, though not regular enough to be called beautiful, had an air of softness and sensibility diffused over them, which rendered her infinitely charming.

The education of this fair prisoner had been entrusted by Don Ferdinand to the care of an old gouvernante, who had formerly attended his sisters in that capacity, and whose disposition perfectly agreed with his own. Some business of importance happening to demand the immediate presence of Don Ferdinand at Verona, he took as affectionate a leave as his temper would permit of Evadne; and giving Marcella, which was the name of the governess, strict orders not to suffer his daughter to stir beyond the walls of the castle till his return, set out for that place.

For some days his orders were punctually observed; but one morning Evadne perceiving her governess in a better humour than ordinary, ventured to intreat her to take a walk in some beautiful meadows which were at a small distance from the castle. Marcella, after some reluctance, complied, more to indulge her own inclinations than gratify the desires of her charge. The spring was now advanced; and the morning being uncommonly pleasant, they were led to prolong their walk till they insensibly came within sight of the gardens of Lothario. Marcella thinking it imprudent to go any farther, commanded her young lady to return; and Evadne, who knew her temper would brook no contradiction, though unwillingly, was obliged to obey: but they had not proceeded far, before they were agreeably surprized by a chorus of hunting instruments; after which a stag flew rapidly by them, and took shelter in a neighbouring wood; whither it was followed by a party of very elegant horsemen, among whom Marcella easily discovered the Duke, and immediately pointed out her young sovereign to Evadne, whose eyes pursued him to the inmost recesses of the wood. 'Come, Madam,' said Marcella, alarmed at the eager attention with which she surveyed him, 'let us hasten to the castle, for I already repent of the indulgence I have shewn you.'—'Nay, pr'ythee, dear Marcella,' returned she, with an emotion she could not conceal from the penetrating eyes of her governess, 'oblige me with a few moments longer: it is long since I visited this sweet spot; and I cannot so soon leave it without regret.'—'Your reluctance to quit it now,' replied Marcella sternly, 'is a sufficient reason for my not trusting you here again; but, if you do not follow me this moment, I will acquaint Don Ferdinand with the little attention you pay to his commands, and resign my trust to one who can better enforce your obedience.'

Evadne, terrified at her menace, immediately complied, quite pensive and melancholy. She followed to the castle; but, alas! that peace and serenity of mind which were wont to render even that solitude delightful, were fled for ever! Discontented with herself, it was impossible for any thing to afford pleasure. Her table was furnished with magnificence, but the viands went almost untasted from it: her books were neglected; her lute cast aside; and, wandering all day through the woods that surrounded the house, she gave herself up to a hopeless and unconquerable melancholy. It was in vain that Marcella used every endeavour her understanding could suggest to discover the secret that preyed on the mind of her charge; her short and sullen answers to all her enquiries served only to discover the disorder of her mind, but without giving any light as to the occasion of it. Marcella, perceiving her health daily declined, thought proper to hasten the return of Don Ferdinand, by acquainting him with the condition of his child; and as he really loved her with uncommon tenderness, this account was sufficient to bring him instantly to Milan. Evadne received him with a transport that dissipated for a while the gloom that hung over her spirits, lighted all her countenance into smiles, and diffused an air of chearfulness around her; but the momentary effusion of joy soon subsided, and Don Ferdinand discovered his daughter laboured under a dejection of mind which neither tenderness could assuage, nor threats terrify her into disclosing. Alarmed at the condition to which he saw her reduced by the ravages this obstinate melancholy made in a constitution naturally delicate, he one day sent for her governess into his closet; and, contracting his brows with a frown still deeper than that which usually overspread them—'Marcella,' said he, 'when, at my departure for Verona, I consigned my daughter to your care, the soft tranquillity of her mind was well expressed by the bloom that overspread her countenance, and the brilliancy that sparkled in her eyes. At my return, I found her pale and emaciated in her person; wandering and distracted in her behaviour; and, to all appearance, labouring under the pressure of some fatal secret which all my efforts prove ineffectual to discover. Now, answer me truly; for on truth alone depends your safety. Do you remember my last orders at our parting?' Marcella trembled at these words; but, concealing her emotions under an appearance of surprize, immediately answered—'Most assuredly, my lord; they have never been one moment absent from my mind.'—'If this is true,' returned Don Ferdinand, 'what means the condition in which I behold Evadne? and if it is not, own to me, thou wicked deceiver, in what manner thou hast deceived me; own it this moment, or expect the severest effects of my resentment.'—'My lord,' replied Marcella, affecting an air of conscious innocence, 'your threats can have no effect on me, because I have not deserved them. I am incapable of deceiving any one, much less your lordship, to whom I am under such infinite obligations, as must bind my gratitude to the most rigorous performance of your will. The melancholy situation of my lady has filled me with astonishment and concern; but be assured, my lord, no vigilance has been wanting on my part, however ineffectual it has proved, to discover the cause; which, I am inclined to believe, proceeds rather from a distemper of the body than any disorder of her mind.'

Evadne entering the apartment at this moment, prevented her father from making any reply. 'I have the pleasure to acquaint you, my lord,' said she to Don Ferdinand, 'that the pictures you have so long expected from Verona are at last safely arrived: the messengers are below, and wait your pleasure.'— 'Go, Marcella,' exclaimed Don Ferdinand, extremely pleased at this news, 'let them be brought immediately into my chamber.—And do you stay, Evadne,' continued he, seeing his daughter about to depart, 'I must have your opinion of my purchases; which are, I assure you, the productions of our greatest Italian masters.'

The pictures being opened, the first that was taken out proved to be the celebrated Judgment of Paris on Mount Ida. The different characters of the contending goddesses were so beautifully marked on their countenances, and the conflicting passions that actuated the bosom of the royal shepherd so exquisitely depicted, that Evadne could not forbear the most lively expressions of admiration.

Don Ferdinand next directed her attention to a painting of our Saviour weeping over the grave of Lazarus; and in this piece the artist,[1] animated by an holy enthusiasm, seemed to have outdone himself: the person of the sacred Jesus was represented as beautiful in the excess, but it was that kind of beauty which soared above mortality. Peace and good-will to man beamed in every feature of his divine countenance; his eyes were fixed on the sepulchre of Lazarus, while the tears that fell gently from them attested the high worth of the deceased. On his right-hand stood Mary. Her hair, which streamed unbraided down her shoulders; and the deadly paleness that overspread her face; proved how intense her affliction had been: her hands were clasped in a supplicating manner; and her eyes turned on our Saviour, with a look that at once expressed her confidence in his power, and her hope from his mercy.

Evadne continued for some moments in silent contemplation of this finished piece; and the bursting into a flood of tears, gave a glorious testimony of the master's skill. 'My Evadne,' exclaimed Don Ferdinand, 'if you are so much affected with this piece, I believe I must not venture to show you the Crucifixion at present. But, in the mean while,' continued he, 'give me your opinion of this young gentleman.' A blush of the deepest crimson overspread the cheeks, and an universal tremor seized the frame of Evadne; when, casting her eyes on the picture which her father held, she recognized the features of the Duke of Milan. This emotion, however, was not observed by Don Ferdinand, who was taken up in wiping off some dust which covered one of that prince's beautiful eyes. 'Well, Evadne,' said he, 'how do you like our sovereign?'—'He is very handsome, Sir,' returned his daughter: but her lips faultered so when she pronounced this, that Don Ferdinand, who could not understand her, obliged her to repeat it again. 'It is true,' replied he, 'this prince is very handsome; and, had he no more faults in his mind than he has in his face, he would be a paragon of human excellence.'—'And if,' exclaimed Marcella pertly, 'he had as many blemishes in his face as he has vices in his heart, he would be an epitome of human deformity.'—'You know, Marcella,' replied Don Ferdinand, 'we have always disagreed in this point. Lothario has faults, and great ones, if we consider the pernicious consequences of licentiousness in a prince; but he has likewise such virtues as will overbalance all his crimes; and one day, I doubt not, do more good to his country than his vices have ever done harm.'

If Evadne was confused before, this conversation did not serve to decrease it: therefore, complaining her head was affected with the passion of tears she had fallen into, she desired leave to retire to her apartment.

Her governess, who had carefully observed her behaviour, was now convinced of what she before only suspected, that the duke her sovereign had made an impression on the heart of Evadne: but this discovery she resolved to confine to her own breast, well knowing that she herself only was to blame for the accident by which her charge had seen him. It was indeed true, that Evadne, from the moment in which she beheld the prince, had conceived for him a passion as violent as it was hopeless. In vain did her reason, her virgin delicacy, combat this fatal tenderness which Lothario was truly so capable of inspiring; her weak frame was not equal to these conflicts; and a severe illness, which confined her for fourteen days to her bed, was the consequence of her struggles. Her youth, however, favoured so much the skill of her physicians, that soon after that period they pronounced her out of danger; and it was not long before she was able to take the exercise of riding, which had been particularly recommended to her. To ride beyond the limits of her own park was an indulgence to which Evadne had not been accustomed; and she enjoyed the privilege which was permitted her of sometimes passing those bounds with the utmost delight. It was in one of these short excursions from the castle, that Evadne, who had galloped a considerable way before the servants who attended her, perceived herself in the most imminent danger of her life, without any one being near to give her the least assistance. The morning had proved uncommonly sultry; and the grooms having neglected to give water to the horse which Evadne rode, the poor animal, fainting with thirst and fatigue, flew rapidly to a brook he perceived at a distance, and plunged immediately into it, notwithstanding all the efforts of his terrified rider. A momentary suspension of her senses delivered her from the horrors she had suffered.

Evadne, on her recovery from this state of insensibility, perceived herself in a magnificent apartment, extended on a bed, and surrounded by people who were absolute strangers to her. A young gentleman, of a most noble figure, was kneeling before her, and chafing one of her hands; while the other was grasped by a gentleman, who, from the gravity of his appearance, she concluded was a physician. The young gentleman, who had with great eagerness watched her recovery, respectfully kissed the hand which he held; and, having congratulated Evadne on her safety, begged to know in what manner he might be farther useful to her. 'From this, Sir,' returned Evadne, gently disengaging her hand, 'I must conclude that the life I enjoy is in consequence of your strenuous exertions; pardon me, therefore, if my acknowledgments are unequal to so great an obligation. My senses are disordered, and I hardly know what I say; but if you will have the goodness to send to my father, he shall thank you for me and himself.'—'Be pleased, Madam,' returned he, 'to acquaint me with the name of him who has the happiness to be so nearly related to you, and your commands shall be immediately obeyed.'

Evadne having acquainted him with a name to which indeed he was no stranger, he bowed respectfully, and retired; carrying with him the physician, who declared the lady wanted nothing but a little rest to restore her entirely.

Evadne was now left to the care of two elderly women; one of whom, in the name of her master, desired she would be pleased to consider that place as her own, and every one in it as her servant. 'You will do me a great kindness, Madam,' returned Evadne, 'if you will acquaint me with the name of the gentleman I am so much obliged to, and by what means I came to be conveyed to his house.'—'All that I know, Madam,' replied the duenna, 'I will with pleasure relate to you. The name of the young gentleman is Don Louis de Montalis; he is the last descendant of that noble family, and thought to possess a great share in the affections of our sovereign.'

This circumstance weighed a great deal with Don Ferdinand; who, upon being informed of the accident that had happened to his daughter, hastened to the house of Don Louis, and mingled with his expressions of gratitude for the service he had rendered Evadne all that respect and consideration which is so lavishly paid to the favourites of princes. Finding the young lady was not in a condition to be removed, and that Don Louis seemed charmed with an opportunity of accommodating her in his house, he sent for her governess, and some of her women, to attend her; himself spending great part of his time with her, which Don Louis endeavoured to make as agreeable as the unfortunate circumstance that brought them there would admit. Meanwhile, Evadne continued to grow gradually worse; and the fever, which had now mounted into her brain, revealed the secret she had so carefully concealed: she called continually upon the name of Lothario, whom she sometimes imagined at the feet of her bed; at others, in the meadows where she first beheld him. She conjured her father, with floods of tears, to give her hand to the Duke of Milan. It was in vain that Marcella endeavoured to prevent these incoherent expressions from reaching the ear of Don Ferdinand; for Evadne herself defeated the precautions of her governess, and confessed so much in her fits of raving, that Don Ferdinand determined to dismiss Marcella from a charge of which she had so ill acquitted herself. It was in vain that the afflicted governess complained and implored; Don Ferdinand was inexorable; and having presented her with fifty ducats, desired he might never see nor hear of her more. The disorder of Evadne now drew near it's crisis; which appearing favourable for her, her physicians in a short time pronounced her out of danger: but the fever had left her in a state of such total weakness, that it required several weeks to restore her to a degree of strength sufficient to bear the being conveyed in a litter to the castle of her father. When her senses began to be a little settled, she was astonished at the dismission of her governess, and the coldness that appeared in the behaviour of her father. She frequently required[2] the reason of it from the women who were appointed to attend her, but could never obtain the smallest satisfaction.[3]

Evadne, after her illness had obliged her to continue two months at the house of Don Louis, began to recover her health and strength so fast, that she hourly expected orders from her father to prepare her for departure to the castle of Velasquis: but this event was not to take place so soon as she imagined; for one morning Don Ferdinand entered her apartment, and commanding her women to retire, addressed her in the following manner. 'You have, no doubt, Evadne, observed the alteration of my behaviour to you within these two months; I am now to account to you for that change, and point out the only method by which you can regain my favour.' Evadne, whom astonishment kept silent, making no reply, Don Ferdinand proceeded—'I am not displeased at this confusion, it shews you at least sensible of your crime, and that is one step towards mending.'—'If you think, my lord,' exclaimed Evadne, 'that my silence proceeds from any consciousness of my guilt, you are deceived. Horror and surprize deprived me of the power of speaking;

but I am not conscious of having committed any crime that should occasion that alteration in your behaviour to me which you mention; and I have good reason to be surprized both at that and your lordship's present discourse to me.'—'Intolerable insolence!' replied Don Ferdinand; 'how dare you, contaminated as you are with the vilest inclinations, to assume the just indignation of suspected innocence?'—'Gracious Heaven!' exclaimed Evadne, 'what is it I hear?'—'This,' returned her father, starting from his chair, 'that your mad passion for your prince is no longer a secret; and you will soon be as contemptible in the eyes of the world as you are now in those of your family.' Saying this, he tossed to her a miniature picture, which in those hours she was unobserved she had copied from the original, and had these lines inscribed on the back—

'With such a sweetness youthful Paris smil'd,
'Such were the looks that Helen's heart beguil'd;
'Had honour fed the flame that warm'd each breast,
'How blest the lover, and the fair how blest!'

This shock, so severe and unexpected, Evadne was unable to support; and would have sunk on the ground, had not the father, alarmed at the deadly paleness that overspread her face, conveyed her in his arms to a chair. 'I meant not, Evadne,' said Don Ferdinand, in an altered tone, when she was sufficiently recovered to attend to him, 'to have given your spirits such a shock, had not you brought it upon yourself by a duplicity which is always the attendant on guilt. Your presumptuous passion for the Duke of Milan is a fact which your artifice can no longer conceal. Whether you would be any farther criminal, is doubtful; both my honour and duty call upon me to prevent it: it was therefore my firm intention, as soon as your health was established, to convey you to the monastery of which my sister is abbess; but this resolution has been staggered by the noble and disinterested offers of the gentleman in whose house you are. Don Louis de Montalis is pleased with your person, and solicits your hand as eagerly as if he was ignorant of the honour he confers upon us by accepting it.'

Evadne, who had impatiently waited a pause in her father's discourse, now cast herself at his feet, and, with her eyes drowned in tears, besought him to hear what she had to say in her defence.

Don Ferdinand having signified his consent by a silent nod, Evadne proceeded thus. 'If I understand your lordship rightly, you have accused me of entertaining a criminal passion for my sovereign, on no other ground but that you have found his picture by my hand. If you be pleased to reflect a little, my lord, before you condemn me, you will know that you might with equal justice suspect me of an inclination for his Catholic Majesty; for I have also copied the pictures of both those princes. The verses you have read are applicable only to the character of the Duke of Milan; but breathe no sentiment that could possibly justify your suspicions of me.'

Evadne would have proceeded; but Don Ferdinand interrupted her—'I will hear no more, Evadne: your arguments are too weak to remove my suspicion; the only way by which you can do it effectually, is to receive the addresses of Don Louis, with that politeness and gratitude he so well deserves from you. He will visit you this evening; and your behaviour to him will determine my conduct towards you.' At these words Don Ferdinand retired, leaving Evadne in an agony of grief which she had with difficulty repressed in his presence. Matilda, her favourite woman, alarmed at the deep sighs she heard her utter, burst into the apartment, and finding her almost suffocated with passion, used every proper method for her recovery, without calling her other attendants to witness their mistress's affliction.

Evadne having now regained her senses, broke out into the most bitter complaints of her fortune; but was interrupted by her maid, who represented to her, that every word she inconsiderately dropped might be conveyed to the ears of her father. 'Ha!' exclaimed Evadne eagerly, 'have I then spies about me?'—'I am afraid, Madam,' returned her maid, 'there are some about you who are not ashamed of executing that office.'—'It is well,' said Evadne, haughtily, 'my conduct and sentiments are both so free from guilt, that those who will carry complaints of me must endanger their souls by falshood [*sic*]. But tell me, Matilda, for you seem well informed, what was the mystery of Marcella's dismission; and let me know the incendiary you mentioned, that for the future I may avoid him.'—'Madam,' replied Matilda, 'I would long ere now have acquainted you with all I know, had I not dreaded being obliged to repeat circumstances which I was certain would give you offence.'— 'Speak freely,' interrupted Evadne; 'I solemnly declare nothing you say shall draw my resentment on you.'—'On that assurance, Madam' said Matilda, 'I will conceal nothing from you. But this is no place for free discourse; if you will allow me the honour of attending you in the garden, we may there speak with more safety.'—'I must attend my father at his dinner,' returned Evadne; 'when that task is over, you will find me near the grotto.'

At table, Don Ferdinand preserved the same cold civility which he had long affected to his daughter; and she, on her part, assumed the air of a person who considers herself wronged. She seized the first opportunity of retiring; and, flying to the grotto, found her faithful Matilda had been there before her. She instantly claimed her promise; and the girl addressed her in these words.

'There are some hearts, Madam, so naturally depraved, that no benefits can attach, and no gratitude bind them; wretches who, to gain a paltry advantage, would slander the fairest reputation: of these, I am sorry to say, we have an instance in our family. Jerome, who had the honour to be steward to my lord for a series of years, has had so many proofs of his lordship's suspicious disposition, that he knows he cannot please him better than by watching every motion in the family, which he always conveys to his ears. He was, indeed, ignorant of your excursion with Marcella; but he filled my lord's head with suspicions she had not done her duty in his absence. From this charge, however, your governess had the good fortune at that time to clear herself. He next marked your ladyship for a victim; and, observing you frequented the picture-gallery, he constantly retired to an apartment which commands a full view of it, when you was there. He observed this conduct for a fortnight; and the morning that your horse was so unfortunately neglected, he took advantage of your absence to demand a private audience. Sebastian, my lord's valet, happening to be in an adjoining apartment, heard all that passed; with which he instantly acquainted me, recommending it earnestly to inform you. These were the words he related; pardon me, Madam, for being obliged to repeat them—

"Your lordship has had so many proofs of my zeal and attachment to your noble family, that I hope you will not doubt me, when I assure your lordship that the illness of my dear young lady afflicted me very sensibly: her disease appeared plainly to be on her mind;[4] and what could affect the mind of a young lady, bred in such retirement that she has never been beyond these walls, unless in your lordship's company? I have observed her for a considerable time retire constantly, at one part of the day, to your lordship's picture gallery, where she spent many hours. I have, unseen, taken the liberty to watch her;[5] and this was her behaviour: as soon as she entered the room, she secured the door, and drawing a chair towards the celebrated portrait of the Duke, she folded her hands, and for some time contemplated it; then starting from the chair, she appeared to be speaking with great emotion, but what she said I was not near enough to hear: however, after another fit of silent contemplation, she pulled from her bosom what appeared to be a miniature picture, and comparing it earnestly with the portrait of the prince, she pressed it to her lips with an air of respect mingled with tenderness. This is the scene, my lord, to which I have been witness for fourteen successive days. My duty to your lordship, and respect for my young lady, called on me to acquaint you of what your lordship may receive ocular demonstration whenever you think fit."

'To this discourse, Madam, Sebastian says it was some time before my lord made any reply; and when he did, he was so much agitated, that it was with difficulty he was understood. He commanded Jerome to acquaint no one with what he had seen; and desired, the next time you visited the gallery, he might be conducted to a place where he might observe you: he commended the fidelity of the steward, which he promised should not go unrewarded; and then desired to be left alone.

'Sebastian had hardly concluded this relation, when the grooms who had attended you in your airing, with countenances expressive of the utmost horror, and their horses all covered with foam, being conducted to my lord, informed him that your horse had galloped with such impetuosity as to make it impossible to keep near you; that he at last appeared to take fright, and got entirely out of their sight. They added, that they had spent two hours in fruitless search of you, and were now come to take his lordship's commands. It is impossible, Madam, to give you a just idea of the horror that took possession of Don Ferdinand at this account. It occurred to him immediately that the animal might possibly have thrown you into some of those rivulets that flow through his park. Orders were instantly given to have all the ponds drained: and, during the interval, my lord your father remained locked in his closet; where, though many endeavours were made, no one could gain admittance. At last, Madam, a gentleman arrived with a letter from Don Louis de Montalis, and rejoiced us all with the happy news of your safety. Don Ferdinand, loading him with presents and caresses, set out with him for the seat of Don Louis; and soon after Marcella, Leonora, and myself, were commanded to attend you: there we found you, my dearest lady, in the paroxisms [sic] of a fever, which at last mounted into your brain; and in that unfortunate delirium you uttered many things that served to enflame your father's mind, and corresponded with the assertions of his steward.

'I had forgot, Madam, to mention one circumstance. Some time after my lord's departure, one of our servants, walking through the parks, found a miniature picture of the Duke of Milan, fastened to a string of pearls which he knew had belonged to your ladyship: this picture he delivered to Jerome, who had it immediately conveyed to my lord. These circumstances, Madam, had so strong an effect on your father's mind, that he at last dismissed Marcella entirely from his service, loading her with many reproaches for her ingratitude. Your governess, Madam, in vain pleaded her innocence; my lord was inexorable. Roderiga, by Jerome's recommendation, has succeeded to her place; a woman without any qualification to fit her for so honourable a trust; she is despicable in her birth, and in her manners, and has that aversion to youth and loveliness which is common to people who are deprived of those advantages: she will therefore do your ladyship all the ill that is in her power; and I am sorry to say my lord gives her but too many opportunities.'[6]

Matilda here ended her discourse; and Evadne, who had listened in silence and confusion, was going to reply, when a servant, who had wandered over the garden in search of her, informed her that his lordship desired to introduce her to his new acquaintance, Don Louis de Montalis. Evadne turned paler than death, but instantly obeyed the mandate of her father; and, leaning on the arm of her maid, proceeded to the house. She employed this short interval of thought in forming the plan of her future conduct; and finding, from what she had heard, that every thing was lost with her father if she refused to comply with his will, resolved to make a trial of Don Louis's generosity. These reflections brought her to the door of the apartment, where she was met by her father; who, seizing her trembling hand, presented her to Don Louis. The ardour with which he saluted, and the rapture with which he surveyed her, gave Evadne no good prognostick[7] of success; she, however, behaved with a tolerable degree of propriety, till her father, under pretence of business, quitted the room.

Here her courage totally forsook her, her bosom heaved, her eyes filled with tears, and she turned pale and red alternately. Don Louis, apprehensive of her fainting, though ignorant of the cause of her disorder, drew her gently to the window; and finding some water in the room, he eagerly pressed her to drink it. She complied, almost insensibly, but soon experienced the good effects: she recovered her breath, and some degree of calmness; which Don Louis perceiving, instantly took advantage of—'I have been so fortunate, Madam,' said he, 'to have been in some measure the means of preserving this beautiful form from an early and melancholy death. I must now,' proceeded he, casting himself at her feet, 'become a petitioner to you, Madam, to bestow life on a man who only desires to spend it in your service. I adore you, beautiful Evadne; your father has authorized my passion, but it remains with you to confirm my happiness, or reduce me to despair.'—'Heaven forbid,' returned Evadne, rising from her chair, 'that the happiness of any one should depend upon so wretched a creature as myself! Alas, my lord, you kneel to me, when I meant to become a suppliant to you; to implore you, by that honour and humanity which so gloriously distinguishes your character, to spare an unhappy young creature the fury of her relations, too violent and too ungovernable to be trusted.'—'Ah, Madam,' replied Don Louis, 'what is this you desire? what dreadful task are you going to impose on me?'—'This, my lord,' said Evadne, 'that you renounce a maid who is unworthy the honour you designed her. The court of Milan abounds with blooming beauties; among them, my lord, fix your choice, it will do honour to the proudest of them; but for me, my heart is insensible of love; death would be preferable to the marriage bed, and death I must expect, if I disobey the commands of my father.'

Here Don Ferdinand burst into the room, and would, in all probability, have verified the words of his daughter, had he not been prevented by Don Louis; but his tongue was under no restriction, and he loaded her with the barbarous invectives and threats. Don Louis, almost distracted with grief, made him perceive that his victim lay senseless at his feet; but his rage was too great to be moved even at that sight, and he declared, that if in that fit she expired, she carried his curse to the regions of eternity.

Don Louis, having summoned his attendants, conveyed her in his arms to her apartment; and having seen the methods of recovery practised with success, he returned to calm Don Ferdinand. Evadne, it is true, opened her eyes, but it was only to close them on the light with horror; her lips, too, recovered their colour, but not one word proceeded from them to those about her; and she appeared resolved, in this silent melancholy, to refuse all nourishment and assistance. Don Louis was inconsolable; and, rather than see her in this condition, was on the point of renouncing all his hopes: but her father was still inexorable; declaring, with bitter imprecations, that unless she was the wife of Don Louis, he should behold her death with pleasure.

Evadne continued two days in a very weak condition; when Matilda, whose grief for her lady had been equal to that of the most tender mother, perceiving Roderiga leave the room, approached the bed, and tenderly kissing her hand, which she bathed with her tears—'Why, my dearest lady, will you abandon yourself to this fatal melancholy, while there are yet means left for your deliverance from a marriage so disagreeable to you?'—'Oh, that there were!' said Evadne, eagerly: 'though I can never be happy; yet, in that case, I should be less miserable.'—'Suppose, Madam,' pursued Matilda, 'that we should be able to prove to your father that Don Louis is engaged to another lady.'—'Is it possible!' said Evadne, 'that there can be any grounds for a suspicion so dishonorable to Don Louis?'—'There are,' replied Matilda; 'and, before two days are elapsed, I hope to gain a perfect knowledge of the affair.'—'Tell me now, at least,' said Evadne eagerly, 'all that you know.'— 'It is not more than two hours ago,' said Matilda, 'when, as I was walking in a close alley of these gardens, I was accosted by a lady, all covered with her veil, who seemed to be in great agitation as she approached me; and, without any preface, enquired if I belonged to the daughter of Don Ferdinand de Velasquis. I replied—"Yes, Madam, I have that honour."—"Then you can inform me," replied she, "whether she has consented to marry Don Louis de Montalis."—"There is no doubt, Madam," replied I, "but my lady will act conformably to her duty." The lady, at these words, striking her forehead vehemently, exclaimed—"Base, perjured Don Louis!—Wretched, undone Louisa!" and, turning from me, hastily quitted the alley. I would have followed her, but Don Ferdinand that moment appeared in sight; and I, to avoid him, took another way into the house.'—'We must find out this lady,' said Evadne, who perceived some gleam of hope in what her woman had told her. 'Leave that to me, Madam,' replied Matilda, in a chearful accent: which so greatly comforted Evadne, that, upon receiving a message from her father, enquiring if she was able to be removed to the castle, she sent him word she was ready to attend him when he pleased.

Don Ferdinand appointed the cool of the evening for this little journey. Evadne, whose spirits were somewhat revived by what she had heard, found herself strong enough to take a walk in the gardens; and, leaning on her faithful Matilda, she, at her desire, directed her steps to that sequestered part of them where she had seen the distressed lady.

This strange adventure afforded them matter for a long conversation; when suddenly they were interrupted by a quick and unequal step behind them. Matilda, turning to see who it was, exclaimed—'Oh, Madam, here she is! here is the lady!' Evadne immediately stopped, and waited her approach, trembling, and anxious for the event of this encounter. The lady gazed on her in silence for a minute; then, addressing herself to Matilda, asked her if it was not the daughter of Don Ferdinand whom she saw. 'You are not mistaken, Madam,' said Evadne; 'I am Evadne.'—'You are, then, that happy fair one,' pursued the stranger, 'who are in possession of the heart of Don Louis de Montalis.'—'I do not consider it as a happiness, Madam, to be in possession of the heart of Don Louis; he is my father's choice.'—'And not your's, Madam?' eagerly asked the stranger. 'Is it possible that you can be so indifferent to him as you would be thought?'—'It is not only possible, but strictly true,' replied Evadne. 'I am not the less miserable,' answered the lady; 'for, oh too lovely rival! he who has worn your chains can never cease to be your lover.' Then throwing off her veil, she discovered a face extremely beautiful, but pale and wan; and raising her fine eyes, streaming with tears, to heaven—'Oh, pardon,' cried she vehemently, 'pardon the effects of a despair I am not able to conquer!' Then turning them upon Evadne, with a look so wild as made her tremble—'Tell your intended bridegroom, Madam,' said she, 'that you have seen the deceived, abandoned Louisa; and bear this message to him, that revenge would have carried this dagger to his heart, but love directs it to my own.' And that instant, with a poniard she held concealed, she aimed a furious blow at her breast.

Evadne, guessing her intention from her last words, seized her hand the same instant; and, with the assistance of Matilda, forced the poniard out of it: then, gently supporting her in her arms, led her to a covered arbour, and seating herself by her, conjured her to calm her mind, and depend on the inviolable promise she made her never to be the wife of Don Louis. Louisa, rescued from the abyss into which she was going to plunge herself, began to feel all the horror of her design: tears of remorse flowed from her eyes, which were ardently raised to heaven, while inly[8] she poured out fervent prayers for pardon of her rash attempt.[9] Evadne encouraged these new dispositions by every argument that her piety and good sense could furnish her with. Louisa, convinced by her reasoning, and consoled by her promises, embraced her affectionately, calling her Angel of Peace, her preserver; 'and, oh!' added she, 'but that I am unworthy, I would say, my truest friend!'

Evadne, repeating her assurances of tenderness, and regard to her interests, begged to be informed of as much of her story as she thought fit to communicate. 'I can have no reserves to you, Madam,' replied the lady. 'My name is Louisa de Lira; my mother died in bringing me into the world; and the Marquis de Lira, my father, survived her but two years, leaving me heiress to a very considerable estate. I was brought up with great care[10] and tenderness by my grandmother, with whom I have constantly resided at our family seat, about five leagues from Milan. I never was at court but once; and there Don Louis saw me: he felt, or feigned, a passion for me; he solicited my grandmother's consent to our union; for mine, alas, he too soon obtained! The marchioness, sensible of the advantage of such an alliance, accepted his offer with apparent satisfaction. While preparations were making for our marriage, my grandmother sickened and died. Alas, this stroke was every way fatal to me! Decency required that our marriage should be suspended for some months. Don Louis murmured at this delay; and every visit he made for some time afterwards, his impatience for our union seemed to increase. But a strange alteration soon took place: his visits became less and less frequent, his behaviour more and more indifferent and constrained; he no longer pressed for the completion of our marriage; he scarce deigned to make any excuse for the long intervals between his visits; and for some time past has totally neglected. To my letters he returned only verbal answers, made up of cold compliments and slight excuses. I now perceived I was no longer beloved, that I was forsaken and despised. Guess my grief, my distraction, my despair! My faithful Maria brought me the first news of his intended marriage with you. She confirmed me in my resolution to force an interview with my perjured lover; she provided me a private lodging here in the neighbourhood, to which I came, attended only by her and an old confidential servant of my father. I passed for the widow of an officer, who had affairs to solicit at court; and, by means of a bribe to the head gardener of Don Louis, got permission to walk when I pleased in these gardens, which I pretended to admire greatly. The intelligence I received here of Don Louis's violent passion for you, and your father's willingness to conclude your marriage with him, deprived me of all hope of regaining his heart. Despair now wholly possessed me; and all my thoughts ran upon procuring an interview with him, and dying, by my own hand, in his sight. You know the rest, Madam. I am your convert: never more will I raise an impious hand against my own life, but wait for my release from Heaven; and sure, if I divine aright, I shall not wait long for it.'

Evadne gave some tears to this affecting relation; and after a short pause, during which she was considering how to assist her, she fixed on a plan which seemed to promise something favourable for them both. Embracing her, therefore, with great kindness—'Be comforted, beautiful Louisa,' said she; 'I foresee a happy end to your misfortunes. You shall, if you please, accompany me to the castle of Velasco, whither I am going this evening; and accept of my apartment for your residence till there is some change in your affairs. I will take a proper opportunity to acquaint my father with your claim to the hand of Don Louis, which will put an end to his pretensions to me; and I doubt not but the representations Don Ferdinand will make him of what his honour and reputation exact of him with regard to you, will have due weight. Your beauty, and continued attachment to him notwithstanding his perfidy, will do all the rest.'[11]

Being unwilling to trust her out of her sight in the present perturbation of her spirits, she proposed to return with her to her apartment in Don Louis's palace, where she might remain concealed till the time of their setting out for the castle; when, covered with her veil, she might pass for one of her women and follow her, with Matilda, in the carriage appointed for the use of her attendants; all of whom, except that faithful confidant, she would immediately send away, her governess being, by her father's order, gone some hours before, that she might be ready to receive her. Louisa, with many acknowledgements for her kindness, agreed to every thing she proposed. They passed unobserved into Evadne's chamber; and the hour appointed by Don Ferdinand being now come, Evadne attended his summons. Don Louis, with many a deep-drawn sigh, led her to the chariot; her father placed himself beside her; and Don Louis, after asking permission to wait on them the next day, took his leave.

Matilda found no difficulty in conveying Louisa to the castle; and Evadne, soon after she came there, had the pleasure to see her enter her apartment. She ordered a chamber next her own to be prepared for her, being under no apprehensions of the prying Roderiga, who had taken to her bed immediately after her arrival; and her distemper being by the physician pronounced the small-pox, which Don Ferdinand never had, none but her nurses were permitted to go near her.

Evadne and her friend having formed their plan of proceeding, waited impatiently for Don Louis's visit; Evadne, animated with pleasing hopes that all would end favourably for them both: but it was not so with the unhappy Louisa; she feared much, and hoped little. When Evadne was summoned by her father to receive the visit of Don Louis, the agitation of Louisa was so great, that she was near fainting. Evadne comforted and encouraged her; but was herself at that moment under some inquietude. However, she received the passionate address of Don Louis with an air of indifference, though to her father's explicit declaration of his resolution to give her hand to him in a few days she paid respectful attention; but when, in consequence of this declaration, he presented her hand to that young nobleman, who, kneeling, prepared to receive it, she drew it back; and looking steadily at him—'Are you sure, my lord,' said she to the now alarmed lover, 'that there is no transaction of your life that will render it impossible for my father to make you his son-in-law?'—'What to do you mean, Evadne?' said Don Ferdinand impatiently, while Don Louis's confusion kept him silent. 'I mean, Sir,' replied Evadne, 'that Don Louis cannot be my husband, because he is contracted to another lady, who is his equal in birth, and whose beauty and constant affection for him, notwithstanding his cruel desertion of her, merit all his love, gratitude, and esteem.'—'Is this true, my lord?' said Don Ferdinand, in a stern accent. 'Before I answer that question, my lord,' replied Don Louis, 'I beg this young lady will please declare from whom she had this intelligence, and what proofs she has received that it is not false.'—'That is but reasonable,' returned Don Ferdinand; 'tell us, then, Evadne, from whom you heard this story.'—'Alas, my lord!' said Evadne, 'I have a tale to tell, that, if Don Louis has not cast off all humanity, must melt his very soul.' She then related her accidental meeting with the daughter of the Marquis de Lira, the affecting relation that unfortunate young lady had given her, Don Louis's engagement with her, and the desperate attempt that, prompted by despair, she had made on her life, which, with the assistance of Matilda, she had been fortunate enough to prevent.

Don Ferdinand was greatly moved at this relation, and beheld Don Louis with a fierce and accusing look; which was instantly softened to compassion, when he saw a deadly paleness overspread his face, and tears stealing fast from his eyes, as he leaned his head against the tapestry, willing, as it should seem, to conceal his emotion.

Evadne thought this a favourable moment for compleating her design. She flew with eager haste to Louisa, who, pale and trembling, waited the event. 'Come, friend, come,' said she, taking her hand, and obliging her to rise from her chair, 'this is the crisis of your fate. Don Louis has heard the story of our meeting; he seems touched; come and compleat the work.' Donna Louisa, abashed, silent, and irresolute, hung back; but Evadne forcing her along, led her, all covered with blushes, into the room where she had left her father and Don Louis. Her appearance had so powerful an effect on the heart of Don Louis, agitated as it was with various conflicting passions, that, unable to support himself, he fell almost senseless on a sofa that was near him. Louisa thought him dying; she uttered a dreadful scream, and sunk down in a fainting fit at his feet. Evadne and her women were busy in endeavouring to assist her, while Don Ferdinand employed his charitable cares on Don Louis. That young nobleman soon recovered; but Louisa remained so long in a state of insensibility, as to make it doubtful whether she was not really dead. Don

Louis, kneeling by her, supported her in his arms, passionately exclaiming against himself for being the cause of her distress, and watching the returns of life in an agonizing suspense. At length she opened her eyes, and the first object they fixed on was her lover, bathed in tears, and holding one of her hands, which he often pressed ardently to his lips. 'Can it be!' said she, faintly, still gazing on him. 'Do you not then hate me?'—'No, no!' cried he eagerly; 'I love you more than ever. Say only that you pardon me, and will continue to love me.'—'Alas! can I help it?' replied she, hiding her glowing face in the bosom of the tender Evadne, who hung over her, and softly whispered her congratulations on the happy effect of her scheme. Don Ferdinand thought proper to put an end to this soft scene, which grew a little tiresome to him. 'Since our lovers are reconciled,' said he to Evadne, 'we will now go to supper; after which, I shall be happy to sign your contract of marriage, Don Louis, with this charming young lady. Her father was my friend, and I must love her on his account as well as her own.' Saying this, he led Don Louis out of the room.

Evadne, whose situation was much mended by the happy termination of her friend's affairs, embraced and congratulated her with great tenderness; and Louisa mingled with her acknowledgments the warmest professions of eternal friendship.

In the mean time, Don Ferdinand, who, with very high notions of honour, possessed great benevolence of heart, took great pains to confirm Don Louis in the design he had formed to do justice to Louisa. His apologies for his past conduct to that young lady, and his presumption in addressing Evadne, though weak, he seemed to take in good part, not being willing to quarrel with the favourite of a prince; and although it was impossible for him to continue to esteem him, yet his behaviour betrayed no alteration in his sentiments.

When the ladies appeared at supper, Don Ferdinand took care to turn the conversation on indifferent subjects; but, before they separated for the night, he forgot not to have a contract of marriage drawn up; which Don Louis signed very chearfully; and which was witnessed by Don Ferdinand and his daughter: and a few days afterwards the marriage was celebrated with great pomp, the Duke of Milan himself assisting at the ceremony; upon which account Evadne, at her own desire, was excused from being present.

Don Ferdinand saw all the merit of this sacrifice; but although he drew from thence a favourable presage of her virtue and prudence, yet he neglected no means of providing against any indiscretion her fatal attachment might unwarily lead her into. He engaged a duenna of established reputation for the strictness of her discipline; who being, besides, a woman of good birth and education, he doubted not but she would make herself agreeable to his daughter, if her inclinations were not at war with her duty. To Signora Mencia's care, therefore, he confided her; and the young lady, who had no wish for more liberty than she enjoyed, was so far from disliking her watchful governess, that she took pleasure in her conversation, and treated her with kindness and respect.

Don Ferdinand, from time to time, enquired how his daughter passed her hours when she was not with him; and if she was chearful and contented. Signora Mencia, who was charmed with the sweetness of her temper, gave her those praises to which she was so justly entitled; but acknowledged, that she was melancholy, often so absent that she appeared not to hear any thing that was said to her, and seemed to relish no amusement but reading, or a solitary walk in the most retired part of the spacious park that surrounded the castle. 'This inclosure,' she added, 'seems to bound all her desires.'

Don Ferdinand was greatly affected at this account: he found her mind had received an incurable wound; he could not depart from his maxims with regard to the necessary restraints on female liberty; but he encouraged the visits of Donna Louisa, with whose society she seemed pleased, and sometimes permitted her to take the air in her company.

Evadne, pressed by this tender friend to unbosom her griefs, had, with many blushes, confided her secret to her. She shewed her the picture she had copied, with the lines wrote under it: and, having got over this painful step, indulged herself in talking of the duke; lamented her own weakness, in that she had entertained a passion for a man whom she could never hope to have for a husband; and often declared her resolution to take the veil, if her father would consent to it, and his consent she, one time or other, hoped to procure. Louisa neither soothed nor condemned her unhappy attachment; but sought, by every means in her power, to detach her thoughts from the fatal object that engrossed them: she acted the part of a true friend; except that, like a fond wife, she could not keep Evadne's secret from her husband, but imparted it to him as to another self, not doubting that he would observe an inviolable secrecy.[12]

Don Louis, who was now quite cured of his passion for the charming daughter of Don Ferdinand, was pleased with the news; and, eager to communicate it to his young amorous sovereign, he engaged his wife to procure him a sight of the picture, being willing to produce proofs of the pleasing tale he had to tell. Louisa, not guessing his intention, easily contrived to gratify him; and Don Louis, as if in a playful humour, put it in his pocket, saying, the verses were so pretty, he would read them over till he had fixed them in his memory; and ran away without heeding her earnest entreaties to return it. He easily found means to procure a private conversation with the duke, who listened with rapture to the soft tale of a young and noble beauty dying for love of him; and although on such occasions he was credulous enough, having been, indeed, but too successful with the fair, yet the testimony of his picture, drawn by so charming a hand, and the tender verses beneath it, increased his satisfaction. He kissed the verses a thousand times, and took a copy of them himself. And now the means of procuring an interview with the fair one were discussed: Don Louis laid before the impatient prince the difficulties they had to surmount, not only from the rigid maxims of Don Ferdinand, but the reserve and modesty of the young lady. The duke allowed there was some room for apprehension with regard to the severe father; but he laughed at the notion of being intimidated by the reserve of a young lady, whose heart was occupied by a violent passion, which her tongue had ventured to confess: he therefore insisted upon his confidant's managing a private interview for him, and would hear of no difficulties.

Don Louis, anxious to oblige him, sounded his wife at a distance; but perceiving she was not at all disposed to favour his views, he durst not venture to open himself clearly: chance, however, favoured him more than he had reason to expect. Louisa, having received the picture from him, went to pass the afternoon with Evadne, in order to put it in the place she had taken it from.

Don Ferdinand came into his daughter's apartment soon afterwards; and observing her to look paler and more melancholy than usual, proposed her taking an airing in the coach, since Donna Louisa was with her to bear her company; for Signora Mencia was indisposed, and kept her chamber. The coach was ordered; and in the mean time Don Louis came in, who hearing of their intended excursion, informed himself particularly of the route they were to take; when suddenly pretending to recollect an engagement, he hastily took leave, and flew to the palace.

He found the duke just risen from table; and, giving his highness a significant glance, the prince drew him aside to a window. 'You look,' said he to his confidant, 'as if you had some good news to tell me.'—'The best in the world, Sir,' replied Don Louis. 'Your highness may, if you please, not only see the charming Evadne this afternoon, but may have an opportunity of speaking to her. I left her preparing to set out with my wife for the forest, where they propose[13] to walk this evening.' The duke instantly called to a page, to order his horses to be saddled.—'You shall ride with me this afternoon, Montalis,' said he aloud to Don Louis; 'we will then talk over this business.' The duke discovered great impatience to be gone; and as soon as he was told his horses were ready,[14] mounted instantly, as did Don Louis; and, attended only by one of the duke's equerries and a footman, both of whom were ordered to follow at a distance, they took their way to the forest; but kept out of the high road, to avoid being seen.

In a few minutes Evadne's coach appeared. The duke, losing all caution in his eagerness to see her, was for galloping up to the carriage; but Don Louis stopped him, telling him that the ladies intended to alight, as soon as they came to the forest, in order to walk there; but, if they shewed themselves to them, it would prevent them, and his highness would lose an opportunity of speaking to them. The duke agreed he was in the right, and continued to keep the bye-path, till he saw the coach stop at the entrance of the forest. He was near enough to have a full view of the elegant form of Evadne as she alighted from the coach; but he could not distinguish her features. 'Ah, Montalis,' said he, gazing on her as she moved slowly along, leaning on Donna Louisa, 'if the charms of her face equal those of her figure, I am a lost man!'

The ladies had now entered the wood; and the duke's attendants being by this time come up, he and Don Louis alighted, and leaving their horses to their care, took another path, but which led them within view of that the ladies had pursued. The duke and his companion concealing themselves behind the trees, Evadne and her friend passed very near them. She looked more beautiful that day than usual; the air and exercise had brought back the roses in her cheeks; but her languid motion, the soft melancholy that appeared in her countenance, and the plaintive sweetness of her voice, (for she was speaking to Louisa) proclaimed her mind to be ill at ease; which, although it deprived her charms of the graces that vivacity gives, yet made them more interesting and attractive, particularly in the opinion of the duke, who was so highly flattered by the cause of that gentle languishment. 'Montalis,' cried he, 'she is an angel!' These words, pronounced in an eager tone, struck the ears of both ladies, who, in some terror, instantly turned back; and were hastening to the place where the carriage and servants waited for them, when the duke, in agonies lest he should lose this opportunity of accosting her, quitted his stand, to follow her.

Evadne, who had now a full view of him, exclaimed—'Ah, Louisa, see who is there!' and ran as fast as her strength would permit her, in order to gain her carriage. The duke followed with more swiftness, and soon overtook her. 'You fly me, charming Evadne,' said he, gazing on her with increased admiration; 'what is it you fear?' Evadne, pale, trembling, and not daring to meet his passionate glances, made a deep curtsey,[15] and attempted to pass by him; but the prince, throwing himself at her feet—'Stay only one moment,' said he, 'till I have assured you that I love, that I adore you!' At the same time, seizing one of her hands, he gave it a thousand kisses. Evadne, shocked at this liberty, of which she instantly divined the cause, drew her hand indignantly from him. 'Forbear to insult me, my lord,' said she, 'with a declaration which the daughter of Don Ferdinand is not permitted to hear from her sovereign.' She turned haughtily from him as she pronounced these words; and, deriving new strength from the anger that now filled her breast, she rather flew than ran to gain her coach; and, throwing herself into it, waited for Louisa's coming without casting a look that way. Don Louis led his wife to the coach, making a short compliment to Evadne, which she returned with a silent inclination of the head; and they drove away.

Evadne now gave free course to her tears, often repeating—'Cruel friend, you have betrayed me!' Louisa, conscious of the fault she had committed in trusting her husband with Evadne's passion for the duke, who, she doubted not, had revealed it to him, attempted not to excuse herself, but wept in silence. When they came to the castle, Evadne, complaining of indisposition, took leave of Louisa with a cold politeness, and retired to her apartment.

Louisa returned home very much mortified at the consequences of her indiscretion. The duke detained Don Louis at the palace till late in the evening, talking of Evadne, with whom he was actually become passionately in love; and as in that passion, if one hopes all, one fears all likewise, he suffered great inquietude from the steady resentment discovered by that young lady, which promised little probability of his succeeding in his designs upon her. Don Louis, like a true courtier, flattered his wishes, and engaged himself, body and soul, in the service of his schemes. The duke charged him with an ardent billet to the fair one, which Don Louis promised him should be conveyed to her the next day by his wife, who possessed all her confidence. It was in vain that he attempted to prevail on Louisa to be the bearer of this billet; she bitterly lamented her folly in trusting him with the secret of her friend, which he had made so bad a use of, and vowed she would not be accessary to the duke's designs. Don Louis was offended at her obstinacy; he expostulated, soothed, and was angry, by turns; all was ineffectual, and at length they parted for the night in great disgust. Don Louis retired to his own chamber, to contrive some means of gratifying his master; and Louisa to her's, to weep at the double misfortune of having offended her husband and her friend. She had not courage enough to wait on Evadne the next day, and only sent to enquire after her health. But Don Louis, enterprizing and sanguine, took a resolution to pay a visit to Don Ferdinand, and to contrive some means of delivering the duke's billet himself. Beyond his hopes, he found Evadne in her father's apartment. She put some constraint on herself, in order to behave to him with her usual politeness, to prevent her father's observation. Don Louis was beginning to fear he should have no opportunity to give her the duke's billet; when a letter being brought to Don Ferdinand, he went out of the room to speak to the messenger; and Don Louis seized that moment to tell her he brought an apology from the duke, who was in despair for having offended her; at the same time presenting her the letter. 'I accept his highness's apology from your mouth,' said Evadne; 'I receive no letters unknown to my father.'

Don Louis intreated her not to put such an affront on his sovereign as to refuse receiving his letter, and again offered it. Don Ferdinand's sudden entrance so disconcerted him, that the letter fell out of his hand. He ran up to him, in order to divert his attention, leaving Evadne to manage it as well as she could. She dropped her handkerchief upon it, and a moment afterwards took up that and the letter, and put both into her pocket, Don Ferdinand not having the least suspicion of what had happened. Don Louis took his leave soon after, charmed with his success so far; and Evadne retired to her chamber. Her inclinations prompted her to read the billet, but she checked the thought, as inconsistent with her duty; and, sensible how necessary it was to convince the prince that she was not disposed to give him any encouragement, she could think of no other means of returning the letter than sending for Donna Louisa, against whom her resentment was still very high. Louisa with joy obeyed the summons. 'See, Madam,' said Evadne, shewing her the prince's letter, 'see the consequence of your betraying my unhappy secret! the prince despises me, and scruples not to affront me with his licentious pursuits. Don Louis, too, is not ashamed of being assistant to his designs, and acts a part unworthy of his birth: he was the bearer of this letter. But take it, Madam, take it back to him. It was to do me this small service that I took the liberty to send for you.'—'Yes, Madam,' replied Louisa, receiving the letter, 'I will obey you. Don Louis cannot be more offended with me than he is already for my opposition to his will, by refusing to give it you myself. He no longer loves me, Madam,' pursued she, 'he has banished me from his sight.' Her tears interrupted her speech. Evadne threw herself upon her neck, and mingled her tears with her's. 'Oh, you have suffered too much for your indiscretion,' said she, 'if Don Louis is unkind to you; for well I know your fondness for him.'—'Then you pardon me, dear Evadne?' said Louisa, returning her embraces. 'I do,' replied Evadne; 'and I am now convinced of your virtue. Don Louis, depend on it, however he may seem to resent your not complying with his request, will in his heart esteem you the more for it. Lose not a moment, then, my dear friend, to return this letter; I am miserable while the duke is ignorant of my resolution never to admit his insidious importunities.'

Louisa departed to execute her commission. She inclosed the duke's letter in a blank cover to her husband; who, very much mortified, repaired to the duke, to acquaint him with his ill success. That young prince, whose passion for Evadne was increased by the obstacles her virtue and modesty threw in his way, was resolved to employ every means his rank and power could furnish him with to accomplish his designs. He knew Don Ferdinand was ambitious, and had been too much neglected by his predecessors, in whose armies he had served with great reputation. He now caused him to be told that he destined him for the command of a body of troops which were to be sent into Catalonia, to join the army of the Archduke[16] there; but, at the same time, he employed one of his emissaries to corrupt Evadne's governess, who tendered her a large sum of money, and a promise of future rewards, if she would prevail on her lovely charge to admit of an interview with him. Signore Mencia, steady in her trust, refused the bribe, and acquainted Don Ferdinand with the offer.

Thus instructed in the duke's intentions by the splendid promotion he offered him, which were plainly to facilitate his access to his daughter, by sending him to a distance from her; he waited on the duke, and with much respect, in which, however, was mingled a certain air of discontent, he excused himself from accepting the distinguished command he offered him, on account of his declining years, and increasing infirmities; and this so steadily, that the duke saw it was in vain to press him.

All these circumstances came to the knowledge of Evadne, by means of Donna Louisa, to whom the governess had imparted them. Her resolution to reject the duke was fixed and immoveable; but her passion for him, flattered by those proofs of his attachment to her, gained strength every day; her delicate frame sunk under the strong emotions of her mind, and her health was visibly declining. Don Ferdinand, though subject to violent gusts of passion, was nevertheless an affectionate father: convinced of her strict adherence to her duty, he no longer reproached her with her misplaced passion, but lamented in silence the fatal effects of it on her constitution, which was evidently impaired.[17]

The duke, not discouraged by the failure of all his schemes hitherto, prepared a new trial for the tender, drooping Evadne. Learning that she passed many hours in the deepest solitude of the spacious park[18] that belonged to the castle of Velasco, he prevailed on the keeper, by a large bribe, to conduct him in disguise to the place she most frequented. He was fortunate enough to meet with her there alone; she was seated under the shade of a large tree, with a book in her hand. He stood still for a few moments, gazing on her with a fixed attention: he perceived, that although her eyes were on her book, yet she either did not read, or reading did not detach her thoughts; for she often sighed deeply, and often wiped off a falling tear. These marks of her extreme sensibility, joined to her paleness and languor, affected the duke with the strongest emotions of pity, love, and admiration. Could he hope to prevail over such purity of sentiment, that made her a willing sacrifice to what she conceived to be her duty! He had, indeed, but little hope; but the tyranny of his passion compelled him still to new attempts to move her: he quitted his station, and advanced slowly towards her. At the sound of his steps she raised her eyes; and, not knowing him in his disguise, she supposed he was one of the keepers, and discovered no marks of surprise. She knew him immediately, however, on his nearer approach, and rising hastily, would have fled; but the duke, catching hold of her robe, threw himself at her feet, and implored her only to hear him for a few moments. In this suppliant posture, tears trembling in his eyes, and, above all, his respectful reserve,[19] not daring to touch her hand, but passionately kissing the hem of her robe, the young, the beautiful, the princely Lothario, was an object too dangerous for a virtue less confirmed that Evadne's: she would not meet the powerful language of his eyes; she turned away her head; and, almost sobbing with the violence of his emotions—'Oh, why,' said she, 'will your highness thus continue to pursue an unfortunate maid, whom you may make wretched, but never guilty? Alas!' pursued she, unable to restrain her tears, 'you may tear, you may rend my weak heart in pieces, but you can never make it forget it's duty!' As she uttered these words, their passionate import not being then perceived by herself, she made so violent an effort to free herself from his hold, that she succeeded; and fled with such surprizing swiftness, that the duke, apprehensive of being discovered, durst not attempt to overtake her. He remained some moments fixed like a statue in the place where she had left him, her animated speech still sounding in his ears: it acknowledged her tenderness; but, at the same time, it shewed her virtue to be impregnable. Pensive and melancholy, but more in love than ever, he gained the keeper's lodge; then, throwing off the great coat in which he had wrapped himself, he joined his equerry, who waited for him at the gate with his horse, and proceeded to his palace; where, as soon as he arrived, he shut himself up in his closet, and would be seen by nobody but Don Louis, to whom he imparted his adventure.

In the mean time, Evadne appeared in such agitation when she returned to her apartment, that her governess, greatly alarmed, eagerly enquired the cause. Evadne, throwing herself on a couch, complained of a violent headache, and desired to be left alone, that she might endeavour to get some sleep. Signora Mencia withdrew to the farther end of the room, where she heard her often sigh profoundly: she would not, however, importune her for the present with any farther questions.

Evadne had now leisure to reflect on what she had said to the duke. She was almost distracted to find that it contained a confession of her weakness, for which she concluded he must despise her. To lose his esteem, which was all she pretended to, was a misfortune she was not able to support; and now nothing but the veil, she thought, could free her from self-reproach, and restore her to the good opinion of the duke. Her resolution thus suddenly formed, she called her governess, and related to her how she had been surprized with the sight of the duke in the park; declaring, that his continued importunities made her miserable, and would, in the end, be injurious to her reputation. She entreated her, therefore, to acquaint her father with what had happened; and to represent to him that her health, which he could not but perceive was daily declining, could only be restored by the tranquillity of a cloister, and she earnestly implored him to approve of her resolution to take the veil.

Signora Mencia, who thought that in her situation, the victim of a hopeless passion, and the object of the libertine pursuits of the very prince she loved, but whom she had virtue enough to resist, a convent was her only resource, accepted the commission.

Don Ferdinand was struck with admiration at her conduct on this occasion, and exclaimed—'She is a noble girl! I will never constrain her.' He hastened to her apartment; and, tenderly embracing her, told her she was the mistress of her own fate; that if a monastick life was her choice, whatever pain it might give him to part with her, he would not oppose it. Evadne thanked him for this concession with an ardour of gratitude that melted him into tears. She wept much herself; a thousand different emotions agitated her breast: but her resolution was fixed; and it was settled, that in a few days she should retire[20] to the convent of the nuns of St. Anne, of which a sister of Don Ferdinand was superior, and there enter upon her noviciate.

Donna Louisa, whom she immediately acquainted with her design, heard it with the deepest concern. It was in vain to oppose it by her tender expostulations. She returned home all in tears; of which Don Louis enquiring the cause, was no sooner acquainted with it, than he hastened to the duke with the alarming news. That prince, struck as with a thunderbolt, remained for several minutes silent and immoveable; then suddenly exclaimed—'Oh, Montalis, if Evadne once enters the gate of a convent, she is lost to me for ever!'—'We must think of some means to prevent it, Sir,' said the ready courtier. 'Your highness may command my services.' The duke, lost in thought, heard not what he said. Don Louis repeatedly assured him, that there was nothing he would not attempt to prevent the misfortune his highness so much apprehended.

The duke, rouzed from his reverie by the continued importunities of his confidant, desired to be left alone. Don Louis instantly withdrew; and the young enamoured prince, after passing many hours in great agitation of mind, at last yielded to the force of a passion he was not able to conquer, and resolved to become the lawful possessor of the object of his affections. Having taken this resolution, he was so well convinced of it's justice and propriety, that he was amazed he had so long delayed his own happiness, when the means were in his power. It was now necessary to acquaint Don Ferdinand with his design; but he would not employ Don Louis on his occasion. The complaisant minister of his irregular desires did not now appear a proper person to bear his honourable proposal to the father of his intended bride; he therefore sent one of the gentlemen of his bedchamber to the castle of Velasco, with a message to Don Ferdinand, requesting his immediate attendance at the palace.

That nobleman, although persuaded that some new insidious proposal was to be made him, yet delayed not to obey the commands of the prince. He was introduced into his closet, where he found him alone. The duke accosted him with an air of friendship and affability which lost all it's merit with prejudiced Don Ferdinand; who, in a kind of sullen silence, waited to know his pleasure. 'Don Ferdinand,' said the duke, 'when I offered you the command of my army in Catalonia, you gave very good reasons for declining to accept it; but the proposal I have now to make you, will, I flatter myself, be liable to no objections.' Don Ferdinand bowed profoundly low, but was still silent. The duke could not be displeased with a reserve so honourable in his circumstances. 'Dismiss your prejudices,' pursued the young prince; 'I acknowledge they have not been ill-founded. I am going to convince you that I deserve your confidence. Your daughter—' 'My daughter, Sir,' interrupted Don Ferdinand hastily, 'devoted to God, this day will shut herself up in a convent for life.'—'Heaven forbid!' exclaimed the duke passionately; 'she is worthy to grace the first throne in the universe; and when I offer her my hand, I offer her a gift below her merit. It was to tell you this that I sent for you. I shall this day acquaint my council with my resolution to wed Evadne; after which, I trust,[21] you will have no scruple to present me to her, and engage her consent to my happiness.'

Don Ferdinand, overcome with surprize and joy, cast himself at the duke's feet; and, kissing his hand with disordered eagerness, expressed his grateful sense of the honour designed his daughter in few but emphatical words. The duke raised him, and affectionately embracing him, said with a smile— 'Excuse the ardour of a lover; I am impatient till you procure me the consent of Evadne. The hour approaches when I am to meet my council; I shall communicate my intentions to them immediately; and to-morrow morning I expect you will return here, in order to conduct me to your daughter.' Don Ferdinand, at his departure, would again have kissed the duke's hand, who prevented him by another embrace.

Every thing passed in council agreeably to the duke's wishes. His subjects earnestly desired to see him married; and though this alliance brought him no accession of power or riches, yet, as the lady's birth, beauty, and virtue, were universally known, no reasonable objections could be found against it.

Don Ferdinand, with proper precautions, acquainted his daughter with her good fortune; in which, considering nothing but the happiness of being united to the object of her affections, and who by this generous act was now deservedly so, her joy was rational, calm, and unaffected.

When her father presented the duke to her the next day, her blushes and soft confusion deprived her of no part of that dignity which she derived from the noble sentiments that had influenced her conduct, and filled her mind with the permanent satisfaction of conscious rectitude. The duke's address, though ardent, was as respectful as to a princess.

The now Dutchess of Milan promoted her former prudent and virtuous governess to an honourable post about her person; Donna Louisa, as she well deserved, continued to possess the first place in her friendship and esteem; and the duke, well acquainted with the worthiness of that lady's character, took pleasure in distinguishing the friend of his adored Evadne with every mark of favour.

It was not so with Don Louis; he came to court, and was treated with a cold politeness: and this distinction between the reception given to his wife and him, served to shew him the mortifying difference between the supple courtier who flattered the passions of his prince, and the duteous subject who dared to oppose them.

NOTES

1. The *Weekly Entertainer* has, "in this the artist."
2. The *Weekly Entertainer* has, "acquired."
3. The first installment of the publication in the *Weekly Entertainer* ends here.
4. The *Weekly Entertainer* has, "in her mind."
5. The *Weekly Entertainer* has, "all her motions."
6. The second installment of the publication in the *Weekly Entertainer* ends here.
7. The *Weekly Entertainer* has, "no great prognostick."
8. The *Weekly Entertainer* has, "inwardly."
9. The *Weekly Entertainer* has, "for her rash attempt."
10. The *Weekly Entertainer* has, "with care."
11. The third installment of the publication in the *Weekly Entertainer* ends here.
12. The fourth installment of the publication in the *Weekly Entertainer* ends here.
13. The *Weekly Entertainer* has, "the purpose."
14. The *Weekly Entertainer* has, "as his horses were ready."
15. The *Weekly Entertainer* has, "a curtsey."
16. The *Weekly Entertainer* has, "Archbishop."
17. The fifth installment of the publication in the *Weekly Entertainer* ends here.
18. The *Weekly Entertainer* has, "the solitude in the spacious park."
19. The *Weekly Entertainer* has, "his reserve."
20. The *Weekly Entertainer* has, "it was settled, she should retire."
21. The *Weekly Entertainer* has, "which I hope."

B15

"On the Death of Miss Henrietta Hollis Lennox"

1793

Editions: *A Collection of Interesting Anecdotes, Memoirs, Allegories, Essays, and Poetical Fragments.* By Mr. Addison [pseudonym]. London: Printed for the Author, 1793. 180–81.[1]

Text:

ON THE DEATH OF
Miss HENRIETTA HOLLIS LENNOX
DAUGHTER OF THE CELEBRATED MRS. C. LENNOX.

So blooms the rose, when vernal gales,
Their soft enlivening influence shed:
So, when a noxious blast prevails,
It droops, and all its beauties fade.
Ah! short-liv'd flower, ah! hapless fair!
Alike your charms, alike their date!
Flow, flow, my tears, on Harriet's bier,
Sweet victim of an early fate!
Say, shall th'impassioned bosom grieve,
At angry heav'n's too partial doom,
That blasted all our hopes, and gave
The spring of beauty to the tomb.

Or shall we, with faith's steady eye,
View thee thy kindred angels join;
An inmate of thy native sky,
Whilst heav'n's eternal year is thine.[2]

NOTES

1. Various versions of this compilation were published between 1793 and 1797, most of which included this poem. The poem is transcribed from its first publication—later ones only differ in small details.

2. At the proof stage of this manuscript, I discovered that this poem had also been published anonymously in the *Town and Country Magazine* 19 (March 1787): 138 under the title of "*On the Death of a Young* LADY." In that publication, the poem ends (as it grammatically should) with a punctuation mark.

Appendices

Appendix I

List of Correspondents

The numbers in this list refer to numbers of items, not page numbers.

	from Lennox	to Lennox
Anon.	80	86
Birch, Thomas	33	
Boswell, Alexander		79
Boswell, James	73, 76	77
Boswell, Veronica	83	
Boyle, John, Earl of (Cork and) Orrery	31	13, 35
Clerke, Lady Lydia	61, 63	
Colman, George		43, 44, 45
Dodsley, James	71, 74	75
Garrick, David	41, 51, 52, 57	17, 29, 36, 50
Gwyn, Mary		82
Harte, Walter		32
Hawkesworth, John		23, 48
Hunter, Dr. William	55	
Johnson, Richard	81	
Johnson, Samuel	5, 8, 10, 59, 64, 65	1, 9, 11, 15, 16, 24, 25, 27, 56, 66, 67, 68
Jones, Mary		19
King, Walker	69	
Langton, Bennet		85
Lennox, Alexander	60	
Millar, Andrew	20, 21	

Appendix II

Short Biographies of Correspondents

Thomas Birch (1705–66; ODNB V 802–4) was born into a Quaker family but later took orders in the Church of England and worked as a cleric in various holdings for most of his life. At the same time, he was a historian and biographer, producing significant works such as the *Life of the Right Honourable Robert Boyle* (1744) and a *History of the Royal Society of London* (1756–57). He also served as tutor and friend to Philip Yorke, Lord Royston. His most important contributions to the world of literature, however, were his numerous entries in the *General Dictionary, Historical and Critical* (1734–41). His voluminous papers, including correspondence with many literati of his time, are held at the British Library. There is a rumor that Birch taught Lennox Latin early in her time in London (Philippe Sejourné, *The Mystery of Charlotte Lennox* [Aix-en-Provence: Publications des Annales de la Faculté des Lettres, 1967], 17)—perhaps based on the fact that his papers include one of the poems published in *Poems* in English as well as Latin—but nothing else to back up the idea.

The only monograph on Birch is Albert Gunther, *An Introduction to the Life of the Rev. Thomas Birch* (Halesworth: Halesworth Press, 1984).

Alexander "Sandy" Boswell (1775–1822; ODNB VI 726–27) was the third child and oldest son of James Boswell. He was first educated at the family estate in Auchinleck and at an academy in Soho Square in London. After his mother's death in 1789, Alexander attended Eton College, and he entered Edinburgh University in 1795. Though trained as a lawyer, Alexander spent most of his life on literary and political pursuits. He published many songs and poems, even establishing a press at Auchinleck in 1815. From 1816 on, he was a Member of Parliament for the Tories. During the same period, he supported Scottish landowners and participated in subduing political unrest in Scotland. He died in a duel and left his estate in great debt.

Information on Alexander Boswell is included in biographies of his father. *Half a Millennium of Boswells of Auchinleck* by David Boswell (Bath: N.p., 2004) tells the story of the duel that ended his life. Alexander Boswell would have met Lennox through the circle around his father.

James Boswell (1740–95; ODNB VI 729–42) was a famous Scottish lawyer and man of letters. Born in Edinburgh, Boswell briefly came to London in 1760 and almost immediately joined literary and political circles, but was recalled to Scotland. In 1762, he returned to London, finally meeting his idol Samuel Johnson on May 16, 1763. Subsequently, Boswell studied law and went on a Grand Tour, immortalizing part of his trip in his *Account of Corsica.* From 1766 on, he practiced law in Edinburgh but continued to visit London and meet Johnson regularly. In 1769, Boswell married his cousin Margaret Montgomerie Boswell (c.1738–89), with whom he had seven children, five of whom survived: Veronica (1773–95), Euphemia (1774–1837), Alexander (1775–1822), James (1778–1822), and Elizabeth (1780–1814). However, throughout his life he was known—and celebrated—for his infidelity and affairs. In 1773, Boswell went on a trip with Johnson that he later described in the *Journal of a Tour to the Hebrides.* Soon after Johnson's death in 1784, Boswell moved to London. In 1791 he published his biography *Life of Johnson* to great acclaim.

Lennox probably met Boswell through Johnson. Since Boswell spent much of his time until 1785 in Scotland, however, they could not have been very close. There is no evidence that Lennox tried to contact Boswell any time between Johnson's death in 1784 and the letter of 1792, eight years later.

The standard biographies of Boswell are Frederick Pottle's *James Boswell: The Earlier Years, 1740–1769* (London: Heinemann, 1966) and Frank Brady's *James Boswell: The Later Years, 1769–1795* (London: Heinemann, 1984). In addition, recent significant biographical works include Roger Hutchinson's *All the Sweet Beings: A Life of James Boswell* (Edinburgh and London: Mainstream, 1996), and Peter Martin's *A Life of James Boswell* (London: Weidenfeld & Nicolson, 1999).

Veronica Boswell (1773–95) was the eldest child of James Boswell, and he celebrated her birth with letters to eleven friends (Peter Martin, *A Life of James Boswell* [London: Weidenfeld & Nicolson, 1999], 290). Boswell frequently traveled to London, so Veronica grew up with her mother in Scotland, but apparently James was still a devoted father, concerned about her Scottish accent and appreciative of her harpsichord playing. From 1786–89, Veronica attended a boarding school in London, but when her mother died in 1789, she was the only child of Boswell's to stay at the family seat in Auchinleck. Subsequently, she came to London again and was part of the celebrations of the success of the *Life of Johnson*. Some of her contemporaries considered her uncouth and impolite. In 1794, Veronica accompanied her father back to Auchinleck, where she nursed him through his final illness. However, she died only four months later at the age of 22 of consumption.

Some biographical information on Veronica Boswell is included in biographies of her father, particularly Peter Martin's *A Life of James Boswell* and Frank Brady's *James Boswell: The Later Years 1769–1795*. In addition, there are many references in the Yale Editions of the Private Papers of James Boswell. Veronica probably met Lennox through the circle around her father and Johnson. Lennox first mentions "the Ladies of your family" to James Boswell in 1792 (#73).

John Boyle, fifth Earl of Cork, fifth Earl of Orrery, and second Baron Marston (1707–62; ODNB VII 82–83) was born into the courtly family of Charles Boyle, fourth Earl of Orrery, and reunited the lines of Cork and Orrery when a relative died in 1753. He was educated at Christ Church and spent some time in Parliament, but is best known for his literary endeavors. From 1731, Orrery was friends with Swift and in 1751 published the commercially successful (and surprisingly critical) *Remarks on the Writings and Life of Dr Jonathan Swift*. Orrery was also friends with Alexander Pope and Samuel Johnson, whom he wanted to patronize (and sided with against Lord Chesterfield) but was unable to for lack of money (and perhaps because Johnson had little respect for him). The two started corresponding towards the end of 1751. Orrery pursued literary fame by publication or association his entire life, but never quite succeeded.

Lennox almost certainly became acquainted with Orrery (whether they ever met or merely communicated remains unknown) through Johnson. Orrery was part of the effort to get *FQ* published, and later he contributed large parts to Lennox's *Brumoy*. In turn, Lennox dedicated that book (in a dedication written by Johnson) to Orrery.

Mary Stuart, Countess of Bute (1718–94) was the daughter of Lady Mary Wortley Montagu and her husband Edward. Mary married John Stuart, third Earl of Bute (1713–92; ODNB LIII 173–79) in 1736 against her mother's wishes, but the two later reconciled. Apparently, "[t]he marriage proved a happy one" (James Alexander Lovat-Fraser, *John Stuart, Earl of Bute* [Cambridge: University Press, 1912], 3), and it produced five sons and six daughters. Mary accompanied her husband's political rise (he was Prime

Minister from May 1762 until April 1763) and subsequent fall (when his government was replaced by the Newcastle/Rockingham faction, see #42) with equal grace: "Taking without elation her husband's rapid rise to high station, and brief reign of power, she also bore with composure the long martyrdom of popular persecution. With an unobtrusive heroism, she sought to shield Lord Bute from the most painful results of vindictiveness" (Violet Stuart Worley [ed.], *A Prime Minister and His Son* [London: Murray, 1925], 220–21).

Like most aristocrats, the Butes engaged in patronage, and there is a good chance that Lady Bute was involved in its administration. However, since Lennox had been patronized by the Newcastle/Rockingham faction, this application for permission to dedicate a work to her (#58) was unlikely to succeed.

Lydia Clerke (1740–1814), originally from Gosport, married Sir John Clerke in 1762. John Clerke "was a midshipman in the Royal Navy by 1748, had a distinguished naval career in African, Indian, and home waters, was knighted on 31 January 1772, and died in active service in the East Indies" (Isles 427 n.216). He became Commander on March 9, 1759, and Captain on May 26, 1761. Clerke served as captain of the *Prudent* from 1771 and in 1772 was ordered to reinforce Rear Admiral Harland in the East Indies. At some time there, he removed to the *Dolphin* because the *Prudent* had been ordered back to England. According to *The Commissioned Sea Officers of the Royal Navy 1660–1815* (ed. David Syrett and R.L. DiNardo; [Aldershot: Scolar Press for the Navy Records Society, 1994], 85), Sir John Clerke died on October 11, 1776. By that time, he was apparently heavily in debt due to speculation and/ or smuggling. In contrast, Lydia Clerke was apparently a warm person with a large group of friends and correspondents, male and female. She "remained a widow for 14 years, but, on March 26, 1790, she married Joseph Townsend" (Berg, "Letters" 65).

Though none of her own letters have survived, Clerke as a recipient of much correspondence is at the center of Temma Berg's *The Lives and Letters of an Eighteenth-Century Circle of Acquaintance* (Aldershot: Ashgate, 2007).

George Colman the Elder (1732–94; ODNB XII 761–66) was an author, theater manager, and lawyer. He pursued a career in law for a few years at the urging of his guardian, but soon switched to literature. His periodical *The Connoisseur* (1754–56), co-written with Bonnell Thornton, was a big success. During 1763–67 he worked with David Garrick (see #17) at the Drury Lane Theatre. They collaborated in *The Clandestine Marriage,* probably Colman's most successful piece. In 1767, Colman took over the Covent

Garden Theatre and stayed there for a decade. The first three years were rocky since his investors, who knew nothing about drama, kept interfering in the management and even sued him. The failure of Lennox's *The Sister* falls into this period and was specified as an item in the law suit. However, Colman's fortunes improved, and the partners reconciled. He managed the Haymarket from 1777 until his retirement in 1789. Towards the end of this period, he cooperated with his son George Colman the Younger. In all three theaters, Colman managed the house, but also produced his own plays with some success. In addition, he wrote literary criticism. His private life was unusual in that he lived with at least two women of damaged reputation—one the mother of his son.

Information about Colman is available in two biographies: *George Colman the Elder* by Eugene Page (New York: Columbia University Press, 1935) and *Memoirs of the Colman Family* by Richard Brinsley Peake (2 vols.; London: Bentley, 1841). Colman could have met Lennox through Garrick, or she could have approached him independently about producing *The Sister*.

James Dodsley (1724–97; ODNB XVI 433–37), bookseller, always stood in the shadow of his older brother Robert (1704–64; ODNB XVI 432–33). Robert had established himself as a bookseller by 1729, and James joined him around 1742. The two were listed together in imprints from 1753 on, and James Dodsley took over the business when his brother retired in 1759, leading the firm for another thirty years. Dodsley profited from the copyrights Robert had accumulated, but also added works he acquired himself, such as Sterne's *Sermons of Mr. Yorick,* Anstey's *New Bath Guide,* Burke's *Reflections on the Revolution in France,* and Lord Chesterfield's *Letters to his Son.* In contrast to his brother, James was not an author himself and not as innovative in his business practices. Nevertheless, he retired in the early 1790s with an estimated immense wealth of £70,000.

James Tierney has written "R. Dodsley, R. and J. Dodsley, J. Dodsley," in Bracken/Silver 106–22. In addition *The Correspondence of Robert Dodsley,* ed. James Tierney (Cambridge: Cambridge University Press, 1998) and *The Rise of Robert Dodsley: Creating the New Age of Print* by Harry Solomon (Carbondale: Southern Illinois University Press, 1996) contain information on James. The Dodsleys published Lennox's *Sully,* so they would have been acquainted as early as 1755. However, Robert Dodsley does not mention Lennox a single time in his surviving correspondence.

David Garrick (1717–79; ODNB XXI 527–37) came to London with Samuel Johnson in 1737. After a brief stint as a law student, he commenced his spectacular acting career in 1741, introducing a naturalistic acting style to audiences bored with French mannerisms. After a period in Dublin, he took over Drury Lane Theatre—one of only two licensed theaters in London after the 1737 Licensing Act—in 1747. There, he went about reforming acting, stage, and audience, but most importantly re-introduced Shakespeare to the public with great critical and financial success. He wrote several original plays and adaptations of many others—and was a prolific letter-writer—but his crowning achievement was the Shakespeare Jubilee in Stratford (and later London) in 1769, a dramatic unveiling of a statue of the Bard. After Garrick retired in 1776, he remained popular in literary circles until his death three years later.

Lennox almost certainly would have been introduced to Garrick by Johnson. On the other hand, Garrick quite likely saw Lennox on stage between 1747 and 1749—perhaps before she knew Johnson. In a letter of September 3, 1748, Horace Walpole writes:

> I am just come from a play at Richmond,[1] where I found the Duchess of Argyle and Lady Betty Campbell and their court; we had a new actress, a Miss Clough;[2] an extreme fine tall figure and very handsome; she spoke very justly and with spirit. Garrick is to produce her next winter, and a Miss Charlotte Ramsay, a poetess, and deplorable actress.[3] Garrick, Barry[4] and some more of the players were there to see these new comedians; it is to be their seminary. (*The Yale Edition of Horace Walpole's Correspondence,* 48 vols., ed. W.S. Lewis [London: Oxford University Press, 1937–83], IX 74)

Recent literature on the actor includes *Shakespeare and Garrick* by Vanessa Cunningham (Cambridge: Cambridge University Press, 2008), *Garrick* by Ian McIntyre (London: Lane/Penguin, 1999), *David Garrick: A Biography* by Alan Kendall (New York: St. Martin's Press, 1985) and the seminal *David Garrick: A Critical Biography* by George Winchester Stone, Jr. and George Kahrl (Carbondale: Southern Illinois University Press, 1979). George Kahrl and David Little edited *The Letters of David Garrick* (3 vols.; Cambridge, MA: Belknap Press, 1963) before the letters included here were discovered.

Mary Gwyn (1753–1840) was the younger daughter of Captain Kane Horneck and his wife Hannah, from Devonshire. She and her sister Catherine (1750–99) were considered great beauties. When Captain Horneck died in 1769, Edmund Burke became their guardian. Mary married Colonel Francis Edward Gwyn in 1778. She was close with Oliver Goldsmith as a young woman (she traveled to France with him, her sister, and her mother), and, as late as the 1820s, she was interacting with literary figures such as William Hazlitt.

Most information on Mary Gwyn comes from Ralph Wardle, *Oliver Goldsmith* (Lawrence: University of Kansas Press, 1957), 172–73 and

207–10, John Forster, *The Life and Adventures of Oliver Goldsmith* (London: Bradbury & Evans, 1848), 500–502 and James Prior, *The Life of Oliver Goldsmith* (2 vols.; London: Murray, 1837), II 208–9. She moved in the circles of Sir Joshua Reynolds (who painted her portrait; David Mannings, *Sir Joshua Reynolds: A Complete Catalogue of his Paintings* [2 vols.; New Haven/London: Yale University Press, 2000], I 263–64) and of Samuel Johnson and could have met Lennox through either.

Walter Harte (1709–74; ODNB XXV 600–601) received his M.A. from St. Mary Hall, Oxford in 1731. On or before publishing his first volume of poetry in 1727, Harte became close friends with Alexander Pope, and later he wrote an "Essay on Satire" and an "Essay on Reason" praising and imitating the "Essay on Man," while Pope in turn praised him. Harte's *History of the Life of Gustavus Adolphus, King of Sweden* (1759) was mocked for its stylistic awkwardness or foppery. Nevertheless, he was known for his erudition. At the recommendation of Sir George Lyttelton and because of his good reputation, Harte became tutor and traveling companion to Philip Stanhope, the illegitimate son of Philip Dormer Stanhope, fourth Earl of Chesterfield, from 1745 to 1749. In 1750, Chesterfield showed his gratitude by using his influence to make Harte prebend of Windsor at a salary of £450 p.a. In 1751, he became vicar of St. Austell and St. Blaizey in Cornwall. Because of bad health, he retired to Bath in 1763.

Through his connection with Chesterfield, Harte would have had the influence Lennox mentions (#32). The two probably knew each other through Samuel Johnson, who "much commended [Harte] as a scholar, and a man of the most companionable talents he had ever known" (BLJ II 120).

John Hawkesworth (c.1715–73; ODNB XXV 903–5) is called an "Eighteenth-Century Man of Letters" in the subtitle of his recent biography. From obscure origins, Hawkesworth succeeded Samuel Johnson in writing about Parliamentary debates for the *Gentleman's Magazine* in 1744 and cooperated with him in the publication of the essay journal *The Adventurer*. In 1756, Hawkesworth became the official literary editor of the *Gentleman's Magazine*, a position he held until he died in 1773. Hawkesworth adapted the works of others for Garrick's stage and wrote an oriental tale, *Almoran and Hamet* (1761), himself. Shortly before his death, he edited the controversial *Account of the Voyages Undertaken* [. . .] *for Making Discoveries in the Southern Hemisphere* (1773) and became a director of the East India Company.

The only book devoted entirely to Hawkesworth is John Lawrence Abbott's *John Hawkesworth: Eighteenth-Century Man of Letters* (Madison: University of Wisconsin Press, 1982). Hawkesworth would have met Lennox through Johnson. In addition, he probably wrote two reviews of *The Sister*—for the *Gentleman's Magazine* and for the *Monthly Review* (see #45).

William Hunter (1718–83; ODNB XXVIII 922–26) was an obstetrician, teacher, and writer who was educated in Glasgow, where he received his medical degree in 1750. Hunter moved to London in 1756, where he lectured on topics such as surgery and anatomy throughout his life and introduced the practice of students dissecting cadavers in Britain. He also tried to remove obstetrics from the hands of midwives and establish it as a regular branch of medicine. As the foremost specialist in his field, Hunter became physician extraordinary to Queen Charlotte in 1762. He became professor of anatomy when the Royal Academy was founded in 1768.

Hunter knew at least two friends of Lennox's: Johnson and Garrick. In an undated letter, Garrick asks Hunter to attend to his wife in a way that implies that two are fairly familiar. The connection to Johnson is even closer—it seems that at least at one point, Johnson was in the habit of referring patients to Hunter. There is a letter of June 1, 1778 from the painter Allan Ramsay (1713–84, who at some point painted a portrait of the obstetrician) which introduces a new patient to Hunter with the words,

> Dr Johnson, with his usual humanity interests himself for a young artist who lies ill of some distemper which requires the advice of a skillful anatomist, and has induced me to conspire with him in desiring that you would be so good as to call upon the young man when you happen to go to that part of the town where he lodges, which is at N°.3, Hedge Lane, Hay Market,—his name is Lowe. Being well acquainted with your benevolent disposition, I will make no apology for this request. (Royal College of Surgeons of England, Hunter-Baillie Papers I 73)

The Lowe mentioned here is Mauritius Lowe (1746–93), who received a gold medal for the historical painting "Time Discovering Truth" from the Royal Academy in 1769. Lowe "enjoyed the friendship and protection of Dr. Samuel Johnson, who left him a small legacy" (ODNB XXXIV 572) and who was the godfather to his son and one of his daughters, but he died in poverty. Back in 1778, Johnson seconds Ramsay's letter with one of his own on June 2, 1778, where he specifies that "Mr. Lowe [. . .] has a disorder which [is] very dangerous" and explains that "Mr. Ramsay did not well know what was desired" (Redford III 117–18).

But there is more to the connection between Johnson and Hunter: Both were appointed to the Royal Academy at the same time in 1768, Hunter as professor of anatomy and Johnson as professor of ancient literature. Only two months before Lennox's letter, there was a literary connection between Johnson and Hunter in that the former had asked the latter to present his latest publication *Journey to the Hebrides* to the King. On December 29, 1774, Johnson wrote to Hunter that he was "very much obliged by your willingness to present my book to his Majesty" (Redford II 164). Perhaps, knowing Hunter to be interested in literature and with wide connections in London society, Johnson suggested to Lennox that she approach him. On Hunter, see also *William Hunter and the Eighteenth-Century Medical World,* ed. W.F. Bynum and Roy Porter (Cambridge: Cambridge University Press, 1985) and *'My Highest Pleasures' William Hunter's Art Collection,* ed. Peter Black (London: The Hunterian, University of Glasgow, 2007).

Richard Johnson (1753–1807) in this correspondence is most likely the "East India servant and collector of oriental art and manuscripts" (ODNB XXX 297). This Johnson had a successful career in India—where he might have met Robert and Frances Chambers (see #A13)—before returning to England in 1790. He can be connected to the RLF in two ways. First, his father Alexander was one of the founders of the RLF and a vice-president at least until 1796 (cf. *Literary Fund: An Account of the Institution of the Society for the Establishment of a Literary Fund* [London: Nichols, 1796], 27), so it is possible he would have approached Richard for participation. Secondly, the annual report for 1795 (*Literary Fund: An Account of the Institution of the Society for the Establishment of a Literary Fund* [London: Nichols, 1795]) lists a "Richard Johnson, Esq. M.P." as a subscriber (37), while the 1796 report (see above) only has him as "Richard Johnson, Esq." (31). Taking into account a time lag between events and printing the reports, this fits with Richard Johnson's biography, who was a Member of Parliament for Milborne Port from 1791–94 (cf. R.G. Thorne, *The House of Commons 1790–1820,* 5 vols. [London: Secker & Warburg, 1986], IV 311–12). Lennox would have known Johnson "by name" because of his connection with the RLF, and perhaps through a connection with the Chambers.

There is also a remote possibility that the Richard Johnson in this correspondence is the nephew of Sir Joshua Reynolds, the son of his sister Elizabeth, who married William Johnson. This Richard Johnson was born around 1760 and might have met Lennox through his uncle, though he does not seem to have played an important part in Sir Joshua's life.

Samuel Johnson (1709–84; ODNB XXX 310–23) was arguably the greatest literary figure of his age, the second half of the eighteenth century that is sometimes called "The Age of Johnson." Born in Lichfield in the English midlands, he famously set out for London in 1737 with David Garrick (see #17). In the following years, Johnson wrote works such as *London* and *Life of Savage,* but he made his big mark in 1755 with the publication of his *Dictionary.* Throughout his career, Johnson founded or contributed to a series of periodicals—including *The Rambler, The Adventurer, The Idler,* and *The Literary Magazine*—that helped define the period's literary landscape. He was also influential through several literary clubs where members met and socialized, and through his interaction with female authors and intellectuals such as Frances Burney, Elizabeth Carter, Elizabeth Montagu, Hester Thrale, Hannah More, and of course Lennox. By 1762, Johnson was famous enough to warrant a royal pension of £300 per annum. Late in his life (1779–81), he published the *Lives of the Poets,* which played a major part in the formation of the English literary canon.

Many conjectures are possible about how Lennox first met Johnson. One possibility is Lennox's husband: The printer for Johnson's *Dictionary,* which was contracted in 1746, was William Strahan; Alexander Lennox was or had been an employee of Strahan's. However, the two had several other mutual acquaintances in the literary marketplace as well, such as Strahan himself, Edward Cave (see #1), Samuel Paterson (the publisher of Lennox's 1747 *Poems*), David Garrick (for whom Lennox acted in 1748), or Thomas Birch (see #33). In any case, the first meeting might have occurred as early as 1746, and had definitely happened by 1750. Furthermore, there are two anecdotes about the first meeting. For one thing, Frances Burney claimed that Lennox "among others, waited on Dr. Johnson, upon her commencing writer" (III/1 104–5), presumably to solicit his patronage. For another, an anonymous article in the *Lady's Monthly Museum* of June 1813 wrote:

> It was soon after the publication of the former work (The Female Quixote) that she was introduced to Dr. Johnson as a young lady of considerable genius; but nothing could exceed the astonishment of Mrs. Lennox at the odd manner in which she was received. The doctor took her on his knee, as if a mere child; after which he carried her in his arms, to shew her his library; and as if resolved to be uniform in his conduct, sent his servant to a pastry-cook, to purchase some cakes for the young lady. Mrs. Lennox found herself greatly embarrassed, but a respect for his character stifled even the idea of resentment, and she preserved an intimacy with him until near the period of his decease. (XIV 301)

The time of the first meeting identified here is clearly mistaken, since Johnson had already celebrated Lennox's *HS* with her. Johnson apparently had (young) women sitting on his knee regularly, for instance Thomas Percy's daughter (BLJ II 238) and a young woman from Staffordshire (BLJ 120). In one case, a married woman, "a lively pretty little woman, good-humouredly sat down upon Dr. Johnson's knee, and, being encouraged by some of the company, put her hands round his neck, and kissed him.—'Do it again, (said he,) and let us see who will tire first.'—He kept her on his knee some time, while he and she drank tea" (BLJ V 261).

The most distinguished biographies of Johnson include James Clifford, *Young Sam Johnson* (New York: McGraw-Hill, 1955), John Wain, *Samuel Johnson* (New York: Viking, 1974), and Walter Jackson Bate, *Samuel Johnson* (New York: Harcourt Brace Jovanovich, 1977). More recent biographical and encyclopedic works are David Nokes, *Samuel Johnson: A Life* (New York: Holt, 2010), Christopher Hibbert, *Samuel Johnson: A Personal History* (Houndsmill, Basingstoke: Palgrave Macmillan, 2009), Peter Martin's *Samuel Johnson: A Biography* (Cambridge, MA: Harvard University Press, 2008), and Pat Rogers's *The Samuel Johnson Encyclopedia* (Westport, CT: Greenwood Press, 1996). The most in-depth work on the author in the 1750s is *Dictionary Johnson: Samuel Johnson's Middle Years* by James Clifford (London: Heinemann, 1979). In *Dr. Johnson's Women* (London/New York: Hambledon, 2000), Norma Clarke focuses on Johnson's relationships with women. Another significant recent publication is the first comprehensive edition of *The Letters of Samuel Johnson* by Bruce Redford (5 vols.; Princeton: Princeton University Press, 1992–94).

Mary Jones (1707–78; ODNB XXX 583–84) was a poet and, at her death, postmistress of Oxford. She lived almost her entire life with her brother Oliver Jones, chanter and senior chaplain of Christ Church Oxford. For that reason, Johnson called her the "Chantress" (BLJ I 323 n.4). Jones was known for making friends in the nobility, including in Queen Caroline's household. Her greatest poetical achievement was the *Miscellanies in Prose and Verse* (Oxford: Dodsley, 1750), which was published by subscription with a 32-page list of subscribers. Jones's "poetry is well crafted and witty, her subjects typically epitaphs, mild moral counsel, and light satire" (ODNB XXX 583). Her poem "The Lass of the Hill" was frequently reprinted in anthologies throughout the eighteenth century.

Jones might have known Lennox through Johnson—this is certainly what the text of her letter indicates (#19). Alternately, Jones "was particularly friendly with the family of General Jasper Clayton, in whose regiment (Clayton's, or 14th Foot, now part of the Prince of Wales's Own Regiment of Yorkshire) Lennox's father, Captain James Ramsay, has spent most of his military career" (Isles 42 n.65).

Walker King (1755–1827) took his B.A. from Corpus Christi College at Oxford in 1771 and became private secretary of Charles Watson Wentworth, 2nd Marquess of Rockingham, shortly before the latter's death on July 1, 1782 (*The Correspondence of Edmund Burke*, 10 vols., ed. Thomas Copeland et al. [Chicago: The University of Chicago Press, 1958–68], II 525). Subsequently, King put Rockingham's papers in order with Edmund Burke, whose protégé he then became. King obtained a D.D. from Oxford in 1788 and worked as private secretary to Lord Portland. He also had his own career in the church, holding prebendaries in Canterbury, Peterborough, Westminster, and Exeter. At Rochester, he worked his way through the hierarchy, was consecrated Bishop on February 12, 1809, and became Archdeacon shortly before his death. Later in life, King edited many of Burke's works as well as his correspondence.

Vicesimus Knox (1752–1821; ODNB XXXII 46–50) was probably most famous as the author of the didactic *Essays Moral and Literary* (1778). These three volumes included a scathing indictment of novel reading (criticizing even Richardson, Fielding, Smollett, and Sterne) and circulating libraries and went through at least fourteen editions in the eighteenth century. Knox selected what he considered good literature in his *Elegant Extracts* of prose (1783) and poetry (1789) and wrote several other philosophical and theological works. *Liberal Education* (1781) was a pedagogical manifesto for teachers and parents—Knox followed his father as the headmaster of the Tonbridge (or Tunbridge) School with great success (and was in turn followed by his own son). He was also a preacher who promoted philanthropy and opposed the war against France.

Bennet Langton (1737–1801; ODNB XXXII 510–11) was the scion of an old Lincolnshire family and might have met Johnson as early as 1754 with his father Bennet Langton, Sr., who knew the writer. Johnson admired Langton for his classical learning, and the younger man became professor of ancient literature at the Royal Academy in 1788, succeeding Johnson. Throughout his life, Langton was involved with the militia, and he corresponded with literary and political figures in London including Boswell, Garrick, Hawkins, Reynolds, Edmund Burke, William Blackstone, Edward Young, and Thomas Warton. Langton's friend Topham Beauclerk "entrusted the guardianship of his children" (Rogers 222) to him, and perhaps Johnson similarly entrusted Lennox to his care after his own death. Langton and Hawkins both often visited Johnson during his final illness, sometimes together (Bertram Davis, *A Proof of Eminence: The Life of Sir John Hawkins* [Bloomington and London: Indiana University Press, 1973], 327f.).

The best biographical sketch of Langton can be found in *The Correspondence of James Boswell with Certain Members of the Club,* edited by Charles Fifer (London: Heinemann, 1976: lii–lxxv). Because of the mutual connection through Johnson, Langton and Lennox might have met much earlier, and they obviously knew each other in 1769 (Small 37) But most evidence of their acquaintance dates to after Johnson's death in 1784: #86, which mentions seeing Lennox at Langton's, is clearly written after Johnson's death, and Frances Chambers's letter in the RLF file (#A13 below) is dated 1802. In addition, Isles reports that "the MS Journal of BL's son George records that Lennox dined with BL and himself on 22 February 1798" (421). According to Fifer, Lennox was "apparently a good friend of the family" (lxii), and Langton reported visits to her in August or September 1796.

Alexander Lennox (d.1787/88?) was a Scot who married Lennox in 1747. At that time, he was working for the printer William Strahan, and Lennox apparently felt financially dependent on him. He was wealthy enough to loan Johnson money more than once. However, in the 1750s and 1760s he seems to have been both unemployed and frequently sick. He apparently used that time to assist Lennox in her career development, helping to compile the index for *Sully*, being involved in publication, and securing the services of Giuseppe Baretti to teach Lennox Italian. At the same time, though, he ran up debt and was afraid of his creditors. Lennox asked Johnson to procure Alexander a job, and, between 1760 and 1765, succeeded in getting the Duke of Newcastle to get him a position as a Deputy King's Waiter in the Customs Office, a job he held for about twenty years (Isles 59 n.121, 425–26 n.210). At least through the 1760s, the Lennox's were living together—they had two children, Harriet Holles and George Louis—and there is at least one reference to his "good character" (#39). Later, Alexander and Lennox drifted (and lived) apart, and she came to call him "the most ungrateful of men" (#74). She claimed that he had hindered their son from getting a position and had driven him to despair. He for his part saw Lennox's works as his property (which was legally correct) and made at least one contract concerning her books (#38). While he was interested in the money he could make from his wife's books, he does not seem to have been particularly involved in the process, leaving legal proceedings to Lennox. There is a good chance that Alexander served as a model for the indigent husband Mr. Neville in Lennox's novel *Euphemia*.

Most of what we know about Alexander Lennox comes from his wife's letters—so we have to be careful in assessing his character. In addition, there is some job information as well as scattered references in the letters of friends such as Johnson.

Andrew Millar (1706–68; ODNB XXXVIII 184–85) was perhaps the foremost bookseller of fiction around the middle of the eighteenth century and was involved in the publication of the works of Samuel Richardson, Henry Fielding, and James Thompson. He also traded in non-fiction such as Johnson's *Dictionary*, Hume's *History of England*, and Robertson's *History of Scotland* (see #34). Millar was known for his cordial relationships with his authors, for instance paying Fielding the then enormous (for fiction) sum of £600 for the copyright of *Tom Jones*—and adding another £100 to that when the book proved a huge success—contributing money towards a monument for Thompson in Westminster Abbey, and making Richardson one of the executors of his will. He was also innovative in his marketing and publishing endeavors, trying to create demand by claiming that the presses of his printers Strahan and Richardson were working overtime, circulating books for free in order to summon up readers' interest, and publishing editions of individual author's complete works. Toward the end of his life Millar was involved in legal disputes over copyright, winning a case to retain the copyright for Thompson's work and dying before the seminal decision of 1774. His success is generally attributed to his selection of good books and to his business acumen in selling them.

At least for the first part of her career, Millar was Lennox's main publisher. The two were probably introduced by Richardson, who suggested that Millar publish *FQ*. The correspondence between Richardson, Johnson, Orrery, and Lennox shows that the publication of that novel was not always easy because some of Millar's associates recommended major changes in the novel, and letters #20 and #21 demonstrate that Millar and Lennox had disputes about payment. Nevertheless, throughout most of the 1750s Millar and Lennox worked together closely, publishing her 1752 *Proposals* (#14), *SI, Philander, Henrietta,* and three more translations.

Apart from the ODNB entry, the best biographical source on Millar is Carol Hall, "Andrew Millar," in Bracken/Silver 184–90.

James Murray (1727–99), a wealthy Scottish landowner, was MP for the Scottish constituencies Wigtownshire 1762–68 and Kirkcudbright Stewartry 1768–74. In Parliament, Murray did not make a great figure (he never spoke) but consistently voted with the faction supporting Newcastle and Rockingham, who "secured [him] the salary of the receiver-general of the land tax in Scotland" (Namier/Brooke 185). Thus, he was opposed to the Earl of Bute's faction. Murray's wife Lady Catherine, née Stewart, was the sister of Lady Gower (see #42). Lennox might have known Murray since they were both members of the Newcastle/Rockingham faction. In addition, there was a connection through Boswell, who wrote about the Murrays in 1762: "He is a most amiable man, has very good sense, great knowledge of the World and easy politeness of manners. His Lady is very beautiful and, what is much more, very agreeable, being posest of the most engaging Affability. [...] They present a pleasing picture of matrimonial felicity. They seem like a Couple who have been married but a year and are indeed Evergreens in love" (*Private Papers* I 73–74). In the 1780s and 1790s, Murray owned the Lennox estate in

Scotland that Alexander Lennox claimed to be heir to, but no correspondence between Murray and the Lennoxes exists from that period.

Sir William Musgrave (1735–1800) was a "barrister, antiquarian, biographer, bibliophile, and outstanding public servant [. . .] Among his many appointments (such as Treasurer of the Middle Temple, Commissioner for auditing Public Accounts, Vice-President of the Royal Society, and Trustee of the British Museum) was a Commissionership of the Customs, in which capacity he was most likely to have come in contact with CL's husband" (Isles 56 n.113). He owned copies of Lennox's *FQ, Henrietta, The Sister,* and *OCM*—the two novels in illustrated editions, which were not published until the 1780s (Isles 57 n.114).

Lady Henrietta (Harriet) Godolphin, Duchess of Newcastle (d.1776—not to be confused with the poet Margaret Cavendish, Duchess of Newcastle [1623?–73]), was the wife of Thomas Pelham-Holles, Duke of Newcastle (1693–1768), one of the most influential politicians of the British eighteenth century. Their marriage, though arranged in difficult negotiations, was apparently "uncommonly and genuinely happy" (Browning 35). Browning lists as the Duchess's hobbies "her modest talents for painting, music, and sewing" (36), to which can be added patronizing literature. She also apparently enjoyed electioneering (ibid.). The Duchess of Newcastle was frequently sick and by the 1760s regularly experienced severe headaches and gout.

What little information there is on the Duchess comes from Browning's biography of her husband. She probably met Lennox as early as the late 1740s or the early 1750s, when Lennox was trying to establish herself as a writer.

Sir Joshua Reynolds (1723–92; ODNB XLVI 551–65) was the most important portraitist and history painter of the British eighteenth century. He began drawing as a child and was apprenticed to the artist Thomas Hudson in 1740. Around 1744, he started painting portraits for money. From 1749–52, he traveled in Italy and France with his patron Augustus Keppel. He studied images of antiquity in Rome and subsequently imitated them in his own pictures. On his return to London, Reynolds resumed painting portraits again. In 1753, he charged 48 guineas for a portrait, in 1759 100, and in 1764 150—and painted about 100 per year. By this time, he had established himself as the most prominent portraitist in London. In 1768, Reynolds co-founded the Royal Academy and immediately became its president. For fifteen years, he gave presentations at the Royal Academy, which were later collected as the *Discourses*. These *Discourses* constituted a significant contribution to British aesthetics and address topics such as artistic style, the relationship of Ancients and Moderns, and the importance of models. Reynolds also showed his paintings in the exhibitions of the Royal Academy from 1769 to 1790. During this period, he painted not just individuals who commissioned portraits, but also military heroes of the time as well as (particularly female) members of the *demi-monde*, helping to establish a cult of celebrity. By this time—he had been knighted in 1769—Reynolds was patronized by almost every single one of Britain's leading political and literary figures. In the early 1780s, he traveled to the Netherlands and used the art he saw there for inspiration. In 1784, Reynolds became painter-in-ordinary to the king, officially confirming his status and importance. Towards the end of the decade, his eyesight declined (he had been partially deaf at least since his tour to Italy), in effect ending his professional activities. Reynolds died at his home in London in 1792.

Reynolds surrounded himself with people from all walks of life not just as patrons and subjects, but as friends. His sister Frances, an artist and author in her own right, lived with him as a housekeeper for about twenty-five years (see #56). With Johnson, Reynolds had "the closest and warmest friendship [. . .] that he ever enjoyed" (McIntyre 97) from their meeting in 1756 until Johnson's death in 1784. Lennox almost certainly met Reynolds through Johnson and also became friends with Frances, with whom she might have lived later in her life (see #73).

The two most recent biographies of Sir Joshua Reynolds are Ian McIntyre, *Joshua Reynolds: The Life and Times of the First President of the Royal Academy* (London: Allen Lane, 2003) and Richard Wendorf, *Sir Joshua Reynolds: The Painter in Society* (London: National Portrait Gallery, 1996). His letters are collected in *The Letters of Sir Joshua Reynolds*, ed. John Ingamells and John Edgcumbe (New Haven: Published for the Paul Mellon Centre for Studies in British Art, 2000), and a *catalogue raisonné* of his paintings is *Sir Joshua Reynolds: A Complete Catalogue of his Paintings* (2 vols.; New Haven/London: Yale University Press, 2000) by David Mannings. A recent exhibition titled "Sir Joshua Reynolds: The Creation of Celebrity" was accompanied by a catalog of the same name by Martin Postle (London: Tate/Abrams, 2005).

Samuel Richardson (1689–1761; ODNB XLVI 845–54), one of the most important figures in eighteenth-century literature, was active around the middle of the century. As the author of *Pamela* (1740), *Clarissa* (1751), and *Sir Charles Grandison* (1753–54), Richardson contributed to the redefinition of the genre of the novel and the creation of the eighteenth-century literary marketplace. At the same time, he was an important printer, producing works such as the *Universal History*, the *Gardeners Dictionary*, and Sir George

Lyttelton's *Dialogues of the Dead*. For much of his career, Richardson's most profitable printing enterprise was the *Journals of the House of Commons*.

Frances Burney wrote that Lennox met Richardson through Johnson: According to Burney's diaries, Johnson claimed that "at her [Lennox's] request, he [Johnson] carried her to *Richardson*" (Burney III/1 105). Johnson continues, explaining that

> when we came to the House, she desired *me* to leave her, 'for, says she, I am un-der great restraint in your presence; but if you leave me *alone* with Richardson, I'll give you a very good account of him:' however, I fear poor Charlotte was disappointed, for she gave me no account at all! (III/1 105)

As the present letters show, Richardson printed *FQ*, but was also Lennox's literary mentor. Isaac Disraeli reports that Lennox was "a regular visitor at Richardson's house" and that she told him "she could scarcely recollect one visit which was not taxed by our author reading one of his voluminous let-ters, or two or three, if his auditor was quiet and friendly" (*Curiosities of Literature*, 3 vols., a new edition ed. Benjamin Disraeli [London: Warne, 1866], II 64).

The foremost work on Richardson's life is still the monumental *Samuel Richardson: A Biography* by T.C. Duncan Eaves and Ben D. Kimpel (Oxford: Clarendon Press, 1971). The best book-history investigation of his first novel is *Pamela in the Marketplace* by Tom Keymer and Peter Sabor (Cambridge: Cambridge University Press, 2005). The most comprehensive edition of Richardson's letters is still Anna Letitia Barbauld's *The Correspondence of Samuel Richardson* (6 vols.; London: Phillips, 1804). In spite—or perhaps because—of Eaves and Kimpel's astounding complete list of the author's correspondence (620–704), there is no contemporary edition except John Carroll's *Selected Letters of Samuel Richardson* (Oxford: Clarendon Press, 1964). Cambridge University Press is currently working on a new edition of the complete letters. In *The Work(s) of Samuel Richardson* (Newark: University of Delaware Press, 1997), Stephanie Fysh looks at Richardson's literary works in the context of his career as a printer.

William Robertson (1721–93; ODNB XLVII 272–79) was a prominent member of the Scottish Enlightenment as a historian, academic, and minister (in the Church of Scotland). He studied history, philosophy, and divinity at the University of Edinburgh from 1735, but never completed a degree. Robertson was ordained in the rural parish of Gladsmuir in 1744, but soon made his mark on a wider stage at the General Assembly of the Church of Scotland. There, he joined the moderate faction in questions such as patronage. In 1758, Robertson was called to ministry in Edinburgh, where he spent time with other Scottish Enlightenment thinkers such as Hume, Lord Kames, Adam Smith, and Allan Ramsay. The following year, he published his seminal *History of Scotland,* which placed Scotland in the mainstream of British history and was therefore well received by his countrymen. Robertson was made chaplain-in-ordinary to the influential Earl of Bute in 1761, and in 1762 he was elected president of the University of Edinburgh. During his tenure there, he "concentrated [. . .] on improving the university library, developing a museum, and making faculty appointments that would strengthen the university's teaching of science and medicine" (ODNB XLVII 275). In addition, he tried to improve the physical facilities of the university and build new buildings. Subsequently, he published two important works of history: *The History of the Reign of Charles V* (1769) and *The History of America* (1777). After 1778, he was frequently sick, and to a large extent he retired after 1784. At the same time, he gained recognition all across Europe with honorary degrees and other accolades. He also continued his work with revisions of his three histories in 1787/88 and *An Historical Disquisition Concerning the Knowledge which the Ancients Had of India* (1791). His histories are not academic in the contemporary sense, but noteworthy for their rhetorical and narrative power.

The most recent works on Robertson are Stewart J. Brown (ed.), *William Robertson and the Expansion of Empire* (Cambridge: Cambridge University Press, 1997) and John V. Howard, *The Celebrated Doctor Robertson* (Edinburgh: Edinburgh University Library, 1993). One possible connection between Lennox and Robertson would have been through her husband's Scottish connections, but even then the familiarity of tone is slightly mystifying.

Gregory Sharpe (1713–71; ODNB L 49–50) was a clergyman and author who was ordained in Bristol in 1737 and became a priest in Westminster in 1739. He was named prebendary of Yetminster secunda in Salisbury Cathedral in 1757 and vicar of Purton, Wiltshire in 1761—both positions he held until his death. Sharpe was also chaplain to George III 1762–71. At the time of his death, he was fellow and director of the Society of Antiquaries. He published his sermons and essays on religion, classical subjects, and language. Some of his writing was published in the *Monthly Review.* His main connection to Lennox is that he translated Aristophanes's *The Frogs* for her *Brumoy.*

Saunders Welch (1710–84) was a magistrate and occasional author. He was High Constable of Holborn under Henry Fielding about 1744–55. At Fielding's recommendation, Welch was appointed Justice of the Peace for Westminster in 1755, a post he held until his retirement in 1776. Welch authored two pamphlets: *Observations on the Office of Constable* (1754, rev. ed. as *An Essay on the Office of Constable* 1758) and *A Proposal to Render Effectual a Plan, to Remove the Nuisance of Common Prostitutes from the Streets of the Metropolis* (1758). According to E.L. McAdam in "Dr. Johnson and Saunders Welch's *Proposals*" (*Review of English Studies*, n.s. 4.16 [October 1953]: 337–45, also the best source for biographical information), large parts of the latter piece were written by Samuel Johnson. Welch was involved in the founding of the Magdalen Hospital for repentant prostitutes (Wheatley II 454) and had offices in Litchfield Street 1763–67 (*The London Encyclopedia*, ed. Ben Weinreb and Christopher Hibbert, fully revised and updated edition [London: Papermac, 1993], 474–75). He probably met Lennox since they were both friends of Johnson.

At some time, Welch's daughters Mary and Anne lived with Lennox, the former as a pupil. According to Lætitia-Matilda Hawkins, the situation in Lennox's household was deplorable, but Anne made the best of it: "When residing with her sister in the house of Mrs. Lennox, notwithstanding the want of all order and method, all decorum of appearance, and regularity of proceeding, she endeavoured to extract from the mind of her hostess what was good, and smiled at the rest" (*Memoirs* I 70–71). Hawkins clearly does not approve of Lennox, calling her "a lady of too eccentric a genius to render any service to a young person of less than moderate intellect" (ibid., I 54).

Thomas Winstanley in this correspondence is not the historian of the same name, but—according to Isles—Thomas Winstanley (c.1716–89), "Rector of the church of St. Dunstan-in-the-East, London, and a prebendary of Peterborough" (179 n.164). Winstanley's church on Idol Lane (Rocque 13Cb) was close to the Custom House on Lower Thames Street (Rocque 13Cb), where Alexander Lennox worked in the 1770s, and to Tower Hill Street (Rocque 13Ca/b), where Lennox lived at least from 1773–75. The three probably met during that time, and Lennox might have taken Winstanley as a spiritual advisor.

NOTES

1. This is probably the Richmond Theatre built in 1730 by Thomas Chapman, which survived until 1767.

2. In spite of the glowing review, this is the only known reference to Miss Clough. Garrick apparently did *not* hire her for Drury Lane after all.

3. At this time, Lennox was still using her maiden name even though she might have been married; cf. Small 7.

4. On the Barrys, see #52.

Appendix III

List of Charlotte Lennox's Addresses

#4	Plow Court, Fetter Lane	[November 21, 1751]
#15	over against the King's Bakers in Berry Street St James's	March 6, 1753
#23	at M[r]. Cooper's in Gerrard Street Soho	April 30, 1756
#27	at Mr Cooper's in Gerard Street Soho	March 10, [1757]
#30	at M[rs]. Wilks's in Hubbards buildings Kensington	April 23, 1758
#33	at M[r]. Austin's Engraver in great George Street Hanover Square	March 16, 1759
#36	at Kensington	May 29, [1759]
#37	at the Mineral Water Ware-house in Bury Street St. James's	October 6, 1760
#38	the first House on the right Hand on Camberwell Green with a Basket	July 7, 1761
#41	Somerset-house	October 25, 1768
#43	Somerset House	[*ante* February 12, 1769]
#44	Somerset House	[February 12, 1769]
#47	Great Tower Hill the corner of Muscovey Court	May 20, 1773
#48	at N° 6 Great Tower Hill	October 16, 1773
#55	Great Tower Hill	February 18, [1775]
#58	Great Tower Hill	November 14, 1775
#61	Great Tower Hill	August 30, [1776]
#63	N° 7 Nottingham Street near Marybon Church	June 16, 1777

#64	N° 7 Nottingham Street near Marybon Church	June 17, [1777]
#68	Westminster	January 25, [1782]
#69	to William Armitage Esqr Parson's Yard, Kensington	May 7, 1782
#71	at Mr Annis's on the Terrace Kensington No 2 Crown Street, Westminster	May 10, 1784 [c. 1785–92][1]
#74	at M^{rs}. Reynolds in Queen Square West^r	January 30, 1793
#76	at N° 17 in Dartmouth Street West	February 5, 1793
#77	Dartmouth Street	February 17, [1793]
#79	N° 6 Great Tufton Street West	[May 7, 1793]
#83	Ranelagh Walk Chelsea	April 26, 1794

Ill. 5. Calling Card of Charlotte Lennox, [c.1785-92] (Courtesy of Houghton Library, Harvard University, MS Hyde 10 [419])

Nottingham Street   George Street   Gerrard Street   Somerset House   Plow Court

Ranelagh   Berry   Queen   Tufton   Crown   Camberwell
Walk   Street   Street   Street   Street   Green

Ranelagh   Dartmouth
Street   Street

Ill. 6. Charlotte Lennox's Addresses Superimposed on Section of Carington Bowles's *Bowles Reduced New Pocket Plan of the Cities of London and Westminster* (1791) (© The British Library Board, Maps * 3480.[67.])

(Great) Tower
Hill Street

Ill. 6. *(Continued)*

NOTE

1. This is an address preserved only on Lennox's calling card (see Ill. 5) in the Hyde Collection at Harvard's Houghton Library (MS Hyde 10 [419]). The tentative date is based on the assumption that Lennox must have moved to Westminster after living in Kensington, but lived at No 2 Crown Street before she moved to Queen Square, Dartmouth Street, or Tufton Street.

Index

About the Author

Norbert Schürer is an associate professor in the English department at California State University, Long Beach (CSULB). His teaching and research focus on eighteenth-century British and postcolonial literature. More specifically, he works on women's writing, book history, and Anglo-Indian literature. Schürer recently published an edition (with a scholarly introduction and extensive appendices) of Charlotte Lennox's novel *Sophia* (Broadview 2008) and is the author of *Salman Rushdie's* Midnight's Children: *A Reader's Guide* (Continuum 2004). He has published articles in *Papers of the Bibliographical Society of America* (on the bookseller Thomas Lowndes), *Eighteenth-Century Life* (on the fall of the Bastille in British newspapers), and *Eighteenth-Century Studies* (on representations of *sati*). With Tim Keirn (CSULB, History), he edited the anthology *British Encounters with India, 1750–1830* (Palgrave 2011). Schürer holds a *Staatsexamen* from the Freie Universität Berlin and a Ph.D. from the Graduate Program in Literature at Duke University. Before joining the faculty at CSULB, he taught at Wake Forest University in Winston-Salem, NC, and at Xavier University of Louisiana in New Orleans, LA. Recent awards include a Leverhulme Visiting Fellowship to the University of Winchester, a fellowship at the Institute of Advanced Studies at Jawaharlal Nehru University in Delhi, and a travel award from the Bibliographical Society of America.

www.ingramcontent.com/pod-product-compliance
Lightning Source LLC
Chambersburg PA
CBHW020648110726
47901CB00001B/89